Harry Wells - S.B.T.S. - $7.\frac{45}{xx}$ - Fall '81

THE CHRISTIAN RELIGION
IN
ITS DOCTRINAL EXPRESSION

THE CHRISTIAN RELIGION

IN ITS DOCTRINAL EXPRESSION

By

EDGAR YOUNG MULLINS, D. D., LL. D.

President and Professor of Theology in
The Southern Baptist Theological Seminary
Louisville, Ky.

Author of

"Why is Christianity True?" "The Axioms of Religion," "Freedom
and Authority in Religion," "The Life in Christ," "Commentary
on Ephesians and Colossians," "Baptist Beliefs," etc.

JUDSON PRESS
VALLEY FORGE

International Standard Book No. 0-8170-0042-9

JUDSON PRESS   PRINTED IN U.S.A.

PREFACE

SEVERAL reasons have led the writer to prepare the present work on theology. He has been a teacher of the subject during the past eighteen years. His own method and standpoint in dealing with truth have, as a natural consequence, taken definite form. Theology is like any other science in the fact that if it is alive, it grows. This does not mean that it goes beyond Christ and the New Testament. It means, rather, that these are provocative of endless growth. The object of religion does not grow, but the subject never attains a final and static stage in the present life. Truth does not change, but we apprehend truth with increasing clearness.

Down to the middle of the nineteenth century, after Luther's age, theology was engaged chiefly with the issues growing out of the Reformation. The method of theology was that derived from a past age. Theologies were comprehensive, more or less philosophical and abstract treatises. There was a very commendable desire to systematize the truths of Christianity. But too often the biblical method and aim were sacrificed in the interest of a " school " of theology or a philosophical principle. For example, Arminianism overlooked certain essential truths about God in its strong championship of human freedom. As against it, Calvinism ran to extremes in some of its conclusions in its very earnest desire to safeguard the truth of God's sovereignty. We are learning to discard both names and to adhere more closely than either to the Scriptures, while retaining the truth in both systems.

During the nineteenth century the whole world of human thought underwent a remarkable revolution. In physical science a new method and ideal arose. In the social and economic sphere a new sociology and political economy took shape. In psychology a new method of study created an entirely new literature. In philosophy all the issues were restated in new forms, and new schools of thought arose. It was inevitable that these changes in human thought should introduce new issues and new crises in theology. Many looked upon the changes with fear and trembling lest the foundations be destroyed. Schleiermacher, at the beginning of the century, had already anticipated the need for a change in the method of dealing with religious truth. The remarkable system of Ritschl was a logical outcome of the impact of the new ways of looking at things upon the older ways of theology. As a system it had fatal weaknesses, and is now a waning force. But it is a notable landmark, indicating a particular crisis in the history of theology.

We are at length coming to see all things in a new perspective. Several things are entirely clear. One is that none of the ultimate facts of man's spiritual life has been destroyed by any development in recent times. Methods have changed. New issues have arisen. Old issues have assumed new forms. New statements of truth are required. But Christ remains the same "yesterday, to-day, and forever." The gospel remains. The best historical and critical methods of Bible study have given us clearer views of Christ and doctrine. We appreciate better than we ever did God's great wisdom and love in revealing himself gradually to mankind. This is made clear to us in the Scriptures of the Old and New Testaments. We have better methods of employing the Scriptures in proof of doctrines. We have learned to recognize that religion is a form of knowledge; that the spiritual universe is the greatest of all realities; that Christ is to-day the spiritual Creator in an ongoing civilization. Along with this we have learned that our religion is capable of clear and scientific exposition, and that new and stronger proofs of its truth and finality are possible. The gospel of Christ, not in an attenuated form, so reduced as to be scarcely recognizable, but with all its vital elements intact, is at home in the modern world and has nothing to fear from any form of sound learning. The author trusts that in some measure these truths may be made clear in the following pages.

Preface

It has been felt that the ends of clearness and readableness could be best attained by the use of language as untechnical and simple as possible. Some phases of theology are inherently difficult. But for the most part the author believes the reader will not find the book difficult to understand.

Primarily, the book has been written for use as a manual in the classroom. But the general reader has also been kept in mind. Care has been taken to avoid too many divisions and subdivisions. Overanalysis does not make a very attractive-looking page nor add to the interest of the reader. The analytical table of contents will help those who wish a brief summary of any particular section of the discussion.

It is impossible for the author to indicate, even in a general way, his indebtedness to other writers. Innumerable books on all phases of the subject have been read or consulted. Biblical Theologies, Systematic Theologies, Theologies of Christian Experience, Psychologies, Philosophies of Religion, and books on Comparative Religion and in other departments, have been placed under tribute. Occasionally these have been referred to in a footnote. But it has been impossible to do so in all instances. The author desires to express his appreciation of valuable suggestions based on a careful reading of the manuscript from a former student who is professor of theology in the Southwestern Baptist Theological Seminary at Forth Worth, Texas—Rev. W. T. Conner, D. D.

E. Y. M.

CONTENTS

Contents

Contents

Contents

[xiv]

Contents

Contents

Contents

[xvii]

Contents

Contents

Contents

[xxi]

Contents

Contents

[xxiii]

Contents

THE CHRISTIAN RELIGION

IN ITS DOCTRINAL EXPRESSION

CHAPTER I

RELIGION AND THEOLOGY

I. TWOFOLD AIM

THE aim of this treatise is twofold: first, to set forth the contents of the Christian religion; and, secondly, to set forth the doctrines of the religion which arise out of it and which are necessary to explain its meaning.

The aim implies a necessary connection between religion and theology. Theology has often been defined as the science which treats of God. This definition is based on the derivation of the word from the Greek words meaning God (*Theos*) and reason (*logos*). But Christian theology is something more than the science which treats of God. It also includes in its field of investigation man's relations to God. The reason for this wider definition of Christian theology becomes clear when we consider the nature of Christianity. The Christian religion is not a theory or speculation about God. It is more than deductions from objective facts concerning his nature and attributes. These are not altogether excluded from Christian theology, but they are not its foundations nor the chief elements of its content. Primarily religion is man's relations to the divine Being. It involves fellowship and obedience on man's part, and self-revelation on God's part. It is a form of experience and of life. It

The Christian Religion in Its Doctrinal Expression

is an order of facts. Theology is the systematic and scientific explanation of this order of facts. Sometimes the term theology is used in a narrower sense, meaning the doctrine of God as distinguished from the doctrine of man, or the doctrine of sin, or the doctrine of salvation, or other particular doctrines. This, however, is not in conflict with what has just been said as to the general use of the word. It has come to mean the whole range of doctrines regarding God in his relations to man.

This meaning appears in the use of the term in the various departments of theology. When we speak of the theology of the Old Testament we mean the systematic exposition of the truths about God and his revelations to man arising out of the rife and experience of God's people in the Old Testament history. New Testament theology means the corresponding truths given in the life and religion of the actors and writers of the New Testament. The Pauline or Johannine theology means the truths found in the writings of Paul or John. In general, biblical theology is the scientific exposition of the theology of the Bible unmixed with speculative or other elements drawn from physical nature or the human reason. But in every instance mentioned, theology covers all the relations between God and man. It is not limited to the doctrine of the divine nature or attributes. Systematic theology is the orderly and harmonious presentation of the truths of theology with a view to unity and completeness. Reason may supply certain elements in such presentation which would be inappropriate in a rigidly biblical method of treatment. Historical theology traces the stages in the development of doctrines through the Christian centuries, with a view to showing their inner connections from age to age.

Another method of dealing with the doctrines of the Christian religion is that which gives prominence to Christian experience. It is the method adopted in this work.

In principle the experiential way of dealing with Christian doctrine has been employed in every vital and living system which has been produced since New Testament times. But in most cases it has been implicit rather than explicit. Christian experience has been tacitly assumed. It is the principle which animates all the biblical writers of both the Old and New Testaments. It is the source of power in the writings of an Augustine, a Clement, a Schleiermacher. All theology must be vitalized by experience before it can become a real force for the regeneration of men.

But when we speak of making experience explicit in expounding the doctrines of Christianity, we are by no means adopting that as the sole criterion of truth. He would be a very unwise man who should attempt to deduce all Christian doctrine from his own subjective experience. As we shall soon see, Christianity is a historical religion. Jesus Christ is its sole founder and supreme authority as the revealer of God. The Scriptures are our only source of authoritative information about Christ and his earthly career. These are fundamental to any correct understanding of our religion.

When, therefore, we speak of making Christian experience explicit as a principle in theological statement, we are simply seeking to understand Christianity first of all as a religion. We certainly cannot know the meaning of the religion until we know what the religion is. There are ways of handling Christian doctrine which lead away from the truth. A theologian may adopt some abstract logical or philosophical principle and construct a system having but slight connection with the New Testament. To avoid this error the best recourse is the religion of the New Testament itself.

It will be noted, then, that the clear recognition in doctrinal discussion of the experience of Christians does not render theology less biblical, or less systematic, or less historical. The Bible is the greatest of all books of religious experience. The theology of its great writers is all, in a sense, the expression of their experience under the guidance of God's Holy Spirit. Paul's conversion was a formative influence in all his doctrinal teachings.

Again, our treatment is none the less systematic because it is experiential. We may be more cautious in drawing logical and philosophic inferences from doctrines revealed and known in experience. But this does not at all hinder a systematic arrangement and exposition of doctrine.

So also while the limits of space and method of treatment forbid any general review of the history of doctrine, the entire treatment of theology here represented implies the historical background and the whole course of doctrinal development through the Christian centuries.

We may now sum up in a general way the factors which must be taken into account if we are to understand the Christian religion and the doctrinal teachings which arise out of it.

First of all, we must recognize Jesus Christ as the historical revelation of God to men. What he is in himself, and what he means for our faith, are truths which must await development at a later stage of this book. But Christianity is bound up indissolubly with the facts of the historical Jesus.

Secondly, we must assign to their proper place the Scriptures of the New Testament as the indispensable source of our knowledge of the historical Jesus and his work for our salvation.

In the third place, we must recognize the place and work of the Holy Spirit in the hearts of men. He continues the work of Christ. It is through him that we are led to accept Christ. It is in and through him that the meaning of the Christian facts is brought home to us.

Fourthly, we must seek to define and understand the spiritual experiences of Christians as subject to the operation of God's Spirit revealing Christ to them. The history of doctrine will aid in this, but we must make also a direct study of experience itself.

Now it is in the combination and union of all these factors, and not in any one or two of them taken by themselves, that we find what we seek when we undertake a systematic study of the Christian religion and its theology. We may specify some of the advantages of this method of study in the following statements:

1. It enables us to avoid a false intellectualism in theology. It keeps theology properly anchored to facts and their meaning. It requires little discernment to see that systematic theologies

which are chiefly concerned with the logical or philosophical relations between truths in a unified order, may easily overlook vital interests of the spiritual life. The Scriptures rarely present truth in this way. They never present it apart from the vital needs of the soul. The sense of proportion in the emphasis upon truth may be easily lost in our admiration for the harmony and beauty of a systematic arrangement. A single doctrine or conception, such as the sovereignty of God, or election, or human freedom, may be given a dominating position and all other truths modified to make them conform. Theological controversy may lead to one-sided systems. Thus Calvinism and Arminianism have sometimes taken on extreme forms and have led to unfortunate results. Other issues, more common in modern times, produce the same reactions to extreme forms of statement.

Now when the interests of life and experience are made explicit, many errors of this kind are avoided. So also a restraint is felt thus which prevents too great license in speculative and metaphysical deductions from biblical truth. We cannot have theology without metaphysics, but our metaphysics should arise out of the data supplied by the Scriptures and understood through our living experience of God in Christ.

2. The method also affords the necessary fact basis for the scientific presentation of the truths of Christian theology. The finest thing in the modern scientific spirit is its demand for facts and its painstaking and conscientious interpretation of facts. The desire to know reality as it is in itself and not as we wish it to be, combined with the patient effort to express exactly its meaning, is of the essence of the scientific spirit. Now this motive and aim are most welcome to those who would study the Christian religion and who would express its meaning in a system of theology.

It is clear, upon reflection, that all the factors named are essential to such a thoroughgoing study of the Christian religion. If we study the historical Jesus apart from the other factors mentioned, we never get beyond a problem of history. If we devote ourselves solely to the study of the Scriptures by means of the most approved critical and scientific methods, we never rise above the issues involved in literary and historical criticism, or at best in questions of exegesis. In neither case do we rise to the level of religion itself. Again, if we grow weary of historical and exegetical study and devote ourselves to the work of the Holy Spirit in our hearts, to the exclusion of the other factors, we do indeed come to the study of religion. But under these conditions it is not and cannot be the Christian religion in its fulness and power. We cannot dispense with Christ, and we are indissolubly bound to the Scriptures in any attempt to understand that religious experience we call Christian.

Two fundamental questions arise at the outset in any adequate study of the Christian religion. One relates to Jesus Christ. Who is Jesus, and what is he to men? The other relates to our experience of God's redeeming power in the soul. What is the relation of Jesus Christ to that experience? Those questions inevitably lead back to the question of the New Testament, the historical source of our information about Christ. They also lead back to the work of God's Spirit in our hearts. Hence we conclude that all four of the factors named are essential to a scientific study of the Christian religion.

In the light of these statements we see how defective are some efforts which are called scientific, to express the meaning of Christianity. Numerous attempts have been made to set forth "the essence of Christianity." It is not our purpose here to dwell upon these at length. But usually they are efforts to extract from the Gospel records some small remainder of what is held to be the religion of the New Testament by Christians generally, and cast away the other elements as worthless. Of course it is always open to any one to raise the question whether the original gospel has been perverted. But too often efforts of this kind fail to take account of all the elements in the problem. Christianity cannot be reduced to a simple problem of historical criticism. The facts involved have a much wider range. Again, Christianity cannot be construed under the guidance of some previously formed world-view or philosophy of the universe. We

[6]

must begin with the facts in their totality and reckon with them. This is simply another way of saying that we must adopt the scientific method of dealing with the question.

3. Again, the method gives the best apologetic foundation for a system of theology. The term apologetics is perhaps not the most appropriate one for designating the scientific defense of the Christian religion against attack. But it has come into general use for this purpose and is well enough understood. Apologetics is, of course, a distinct department of theology, and calls for discussion of some problems which cannot be treated in systematic theology. And yet the latter requires a sound apologetic foundation in order to maintain itself among other sciences. The method adopted in this work affords the strongest apologetic foundation for theology because it emphasizes the facts of history and of experience. A comparison with some of the older apologetic defenses will show this. We name a few of these:

(1) The proof of God's existence from the phenomena of the universe has long been a favorite method. It possesses, no doubt, elements of great strength. But along with these there are elements of weakness. Logical deduction from physical phenomena lends itself to many theories of the universe. Each of them claims to be most in accord with the facts. There results always an unstable equilibrium of theories. None of them satisfies fully. Immanuel Kant held that we cannot know what is behind phenomena. We can only know reality in its manifestations. And so long as we are limited to deductive reasoning from data objective to the mind itself there is much truth in his view. That which arises is a high degree of probability rather than knowledge in the strict sense, when we reason deductively to prove God's existence. But for the Christian who recognizes the reality and meaning of his experience of God in Christ a new kind of knowledge of God arises. The "proofs" are transferred from the world without to the world within. Thus direct knowledge of God arises.

(2) Again, the proof of Christianity from miracles has always been questioned by many of the devotees of physical science

Christians have rightly replied that the objections were not well founded. But here again the proof resides in the realm of a remote history. Debate continues indefinitely because preference or preconception determines the view adopted. It is most probable that Christians themselves are not convinced entirely by the logical demonstration based on the reliability of the New Testament witnesses. Unconsciously they have been influenced by their own experience of a supernatural power working in them and redeeming them. It is easy to believe the New Testament miracles if the same power is known as a personal and vital experience. If then we make clear and explicit what that experience is, and combine it with the witness of the well-supported historical records, we have a much more powerful argument from miracles.

(3) The deity of Christ has been employed as a means of establishing the truth of Christianity. A powerful argument is constructed from the witness of Jesus to himself, from the impression he made on others, from his resurrection, from his place and power in Christian history, and in other ways. But when to these considerations we add the facts as to Christ's redeeming power in men, we have greatly increased the strength of the appeal to his divinity.

The above will suffice to show the nature of the apologetic foundation which is laid for theology when the redemptive experience of God in Christ is made explicit and clear as an essential factor in the interpretation of Christianity. This does not by any means imply that we are henceforth done with history or logical proofs, or any of the ordinary processes by which the mind works out its conclusions. It only implies that from the center of a well-founded history, as interpreted in the light of a divinely inwrought experience, we may properly estimate the value of all the proofs. The Christian religion as a power in the soul, redeeming and transforming it, is its own best evidence.

4. The method adopted has a further advantage in that it enables us to show the reality, the autonomy, and freedom of the Christian religion. These are great demands which the

modern world makes upon religion. A scientific age has given rise to a passionate demand for the real in the study of all subjects. Make-believes and shams of all kinds are subject to the most rigid scrutiny and criticism. Nothing can long remain secure which cannot endure the fierce heat and light of ruthless investigation. The religion of Christ welcomes this. It is the glory of Christ that he made the spiritual universe real to men. He brought God home to their souls. Those who know God in Christ find in him the supreme reality.

The religion of Christ is autonomous. This means that it has its resources in itself. The Christian has the guidance of God's Spirit when in humility he seeks it. He acquires a relation to and knowledge of the Bible which is for him most convincing and conclusive. He has the witness in himself. His faith performs for him a service, secures for him a power, brings to him a blessedness and a peace which he finds in no other way. The conflict between flesh and spirit, between the visible and invisible, between the temporal and eternal order, is reconciled and overcome in Christ. He does not value other forms of human activity less than he did before, but rather more. But he sees that religion is the supreme value of life, the supreme function of the soul. In it all else, art, science, education, philosophy, are transformed into new forms of development and of ministry. But he also sees that they all find their completion and fulfilment in religion itself.

The religion of Christ is free. It is not subject to the rule of any form of human culture alien to itself. It is in conflict with no legitimate activity of man. Each great department of life has its special method, its great underlying principle. Physical science works with the principle of causality. Philosophy employs that of rationality. Religion deals with personality. God and man in relations of mutual love and service are the great realities with which it deals. There is no conflict between any of these, as we shall see. It arises only when one of these spheres undertakes to rule the other.

As autonomous and free, and as dealing with the greatest of

all realities, the Christian religion in every age of the world comes to redeem men. They accept it under the conditions of their own age, confronted by their own difficulties and problems. Hence arises the need for restating its doctrines in terms of the living experience of each generation. Human creeds are valuable as such expressions. But they do not serve all the ends of doctrine. We must ever return to the Scriptures for new inspiration. We must ever ask anew the questions as to Christ and his relations to the needs of each generation. He does not change. His religion is the same in all ages. But our difficulties and problems are shaped anew by the forms of life which ever change about us. Hence we must revitalize our faith by deepening our communion with God and witnessing to his power in us.

5. The experiential method of dealing with Christian truth helps in defining the nature of the authority of the Bible. The Bible, against tradition and against the authority of the papal system, was one of the watchwords of the Reformation. Protestantism has from the beginning made the Bible the authoritative source of the knowledge of the gospel of Christ. Opponents have urged objections to the biblical authority on various grounds. It has been objected that the Bible is not infallible and hence cannot be an authority. The existence of textual errors, scientific, or historical deviations from exact truth, discrepancies of various kinds, proves that the Bible cannot be accepted as an infallible guide in religion, so it was argued. Christian apologists used to expend great energy and pains in answering all of these charges. Finally they came to see that the objector demanded more than faith required. We are not bound to prove in a way which compels assent that the Bible is the supreme authority for Christian faith. Such proof would not produce faith at all. It could only produce intellectual assent. The Christian's acceptance of the Bible arises in another way. It comes to him in " demonstration of the Spirit and of power." It is the life in him which answers to the life the Scriptures reveal which convinces him. So that the Bible is not for him an authority on all subjects, but in religion it is final and authoritative. At this stage the objector

took a further step and urged that no authority which is external to the soul can be accepted. Truth must be assimilated and understood, not imposed by authority of any kind, whether pope or church or Bible. The Christian then framed his reply on the basis of his own inner experience. He urged that the very essence of the redemption he knows in Christ is inwardly assimilated truth and actual knowledge of the great spiritual realities. He proceeded to define and expound the truth thus inwardly known and assimilated. But then the objector gave the argument another turn entirely. He charged that the alleged knowledge of the Christian was merely inward and subjective. It was lacking in objective reality, and hence was unreliable. Of course these objections contradict each other. We shall see them recurring in other connections in the following pages.

Now the Christian rises above and overcomes both forms of the objection by insisting that it is in the union and combination of the objective source and the subjective experience that certainty and assurance are found. He is no less interested in objective reality than his opponent. He is no less interested in inward assimilation of truth. But he finds both in the religion of Christ. He finds Jesus Christ to be for him the supreme revelation of God's redeeming grace. He finds the Scriptures the authoritative source of his knowledge of that revelation. And then he finds in his own soul that working of God's grace which enables him to know Christ and to understand the Scriptures. Thus the objective and subjective elements find a unity and harmony which is entirely satisfying.

Now if the opposite method is pursued and either the Bible or experience is taken alone, no such finality is possible. If the Bible is considered in an intellectual way merely, apart from the experience of God's redeeming grace in Christ, then again we have a recurrence of the old debate on grounds of history and criticism. Theories are then framed according to mental prepossessions, and unity of view is impossible. Again, if experience is taken apart from the history, the old charge of subjectivism at once recurs. Hence for the Christian there is no finally convincing and satisfying view except in the combination of the two elements. For the opponent of the Christian view this also makes the strongest appeal. There is an inward reality which corresponds to objective facts of history. God's approach to man in and through Christ finds its reaction in man's response. Faith completes the union, and the life of God flows into the life of man and transforms it.

II. MODERN WAYS OF REGARDING RELIGIOUS EXPERIENCE

In order to prepare the way for our treatment of the Christian religion and its theology, we consider some of the modern ways of dealing with the facts of religion and especially those of the Christian religion.

1. We consider first the view of Comte and the position of the Positive Philosophy. Comte held that religion is a form of superstition. Man is impressed by the powers and mysteries of nature. On account of his ignorance of natural laws he imagines a God or gods to account for them. This is the period of the childhood of the race. But gradually the reason works over the problems of existence. Metaphysical theories for explaining the universe arise, and man imagines he has found truth. But these metaphysical speculations are nothing more than the return of the old gods which were previously believed in. They are the shadows of the gods which are cast as the gods pass away. Finally men learn the truth. There are no gods. Metaphysics is an illusion. No truth comes through speculation. The only truth is that which arises out of the facts of matter, force, and motion. The most advanced races will therefore drop both religion and metaphysics out of consideration and devote themselves to the study of physical science. Of course under this view all forms of religious experience are regarded as purely emotional and subjective. There is no valid objective ground for them which can be found.

There is no need to reply to this theory at length here. All that follows in this volume is the Christian reply. But briefly the following may be said. The view does not explain religion; it merely explains it away. Religion is a universal fact. It calls for careful consideration which the theory does not give. The view is contrary to the nature of man as a spiritual being. Physical facts and laws do not satisfy the soul. Man craves the infinite. The craving is a part of his spiritual constitution. The theory ignores also the nature of personality and its significance. Man is himself as real as nature. What does personality mean in the interpretation of the universe? Comte gives no adequate reply. The view ignores history and experience. Men do not and cannot dispense with religion. The theory thus ignores half the facts known to us in the interest of the other half. It builds a philosophy on one aspect of being, the physical. It is abstract and unsatisfying in the highest degree.

2. Another view closely related to the above regards religion as a useful device or function which men have adopted to aid them in their struggle for existence. Religious psychology shows how fundamental faith in some form is for men generally. It is useful. They invent a God or gods to answer their needs. There is real value in religion. It makes men strong to endure and to struggle for victory. But the gods they believe in have no objective reality. Religion then is simply a " value " which men " conserve." But the time may come when these values will give place to higher values. Reason will take the place of faith. The religious value will thus be gathered up in a rational value. Thus religion will pass because men can do without it.

It will be seen that this view is just a slightly improved form of the view of Comte. All the objections to the latter hold against it. It is false in its estimate of man, of religion, and of the facts of history and experience. It attempts to show that the only valid satisfactions of the soul are those of the pure reason. Psychology shows clearly that man is a being with other needs and satisfactions. There is no such thing as pure reason, or reason apart from feeling and will and conscience. Man's nature has more than one dimension. God has set eternity in the heart. We are restless till we rest in God.

3. A third view is that of Mysticism. There is a real object for the soul in its outreaching for the infinite. We come in contact with it in our religious yearnings and strivings. But this is all we can say about it beyond the fact that the feelings are stirred by our contact with it. We cannot say it is a personal being. Personality implies limitation, it is urged. Thought cannot frame a definition of God because the infinite One rises above thought. It is enough if we can find it and rest in it.

Some adopt this view to avoid a clash with science or other forms of human thought. By avoiding assertions it avoids controversy. Others adopt it because for them religion is exclusively a matter of feeling. Thought does not enter into it. The view has had advocates throughout history. But it cannot answer all the ends of religion. It severs religion from ethics and the practical life of man because it gives no definite view of God and his requirements. It tends to inaction because it finds no purpose or plan of God to be carried out by men. The vagueness and indefiniteness of its conception of God impresses upon it a pantheistic stamp. It cannot avoid the evils of pantheism. In the end all pantheistic systems cancel the significance of ethics, of truth, of personality, of immortality, and of the eternal kingdom of God. Mysticism in this form cannot escape those evils. Mysticism in the sense of communion with the infinite is an essential element in Christian experience. But Christianity asserts at many points where mysticism denies.

4. A fourth view estimates the forms of Christian experience as judgments of value. It is based on a theory of knowledge which denies that we can know things in themselves. We know phenomena. We do not know what is behind phenomena. We know Christ in salvation. He has for us the value of God. But we do not know what he is in his essential nature. So also other forms of religious experience are estimates or judgments of value regarding God and the spiritual universe. The view asserts that we do not need to know things save as they relate to us. Their worth to us is the only interest we have in them.

The view is valuable in its emphasis upon experience. In

religion it is our personal interest and our personal relation to God which give vitality and power. Religion is not a speculation or theory about God. It is the experience of God. It is God known to us through communion and fellowship. Ritschl, who developed the idea of the value-judgment in religion, helped to emphasize the need of reality and power in the Christian life. But he went too far in his denials.

Here again the denials were intended as a means of avoiding conflict with physical science. It was an effort to escape from the old controversies about the person of Christ, the personality of God and related subjects. But the effort did not succeed. The old issue returned. The human mind will not rest content in negations about ultimate realities. The view failed to do justice to the Christian conception of revelation. It did not recognize the divine side of the religious relationship in a degree which Christianity requires. In religion God speaks as well as man. Jesus Christ is God's revelation to us in word and in deed. What Christ works in us is the best evidence of what he is in himself.

5. A watchword which has become common in modern times is based on the underestimate of doctrinal teaching and insists upon " religion without theology." " Give us the facts," it insists, " never mind about theories." As we may have flowers without botanies, so we may have religion without theology. And so with some there is an effort to avoid theological statements except in the smallest possible degree. Sometimes this is a protest against a mere barren orthodoxy of belief and against the passion for fruitless theological controversy. As such it is sometimes justified. But it often arises from the motive we have mentioned, the desire to avoid conflict with other forms of thought.

Now there are a number of strong reasons why it is impossible to dispense with theology and at the same time keep our religion. It is not denied that in the earliest stages of religious experience there may be little reflection upon it and a bare minimum of doctrinal belief. Some Christians seem never to advance beyond the childhood of faith in their reflective thought about religion. But for all advanced Christian experience there must be doctrinal beliefs to express its meaning. The necessity for theology arises from the following considerations:

(1) First, theology is necessary as a means of expressing the meaning of religion because of the nature of man. If man were feeling alone, we might dispense with doctrinal teaching. But our nature includes reason as well as feeling. It is impossible to draw a sharp line between the emotional, or moral, or volitional part of our nature on the one side, and our reason on the other. We are constituted with a knowing capacity, and it must be satisfied along with the other elements.

(2) The nature of all human experience shows the same truth. It is only by an abstract process of thought that we can separate the " fact " of religion from the " theory." The word " theory " is simply another word for " meaning." The so-called theory of religion is simply its meaning. And for an intelligent, thoughtful being, nothing can become a fact for the consciousness apart from some meaning connected with the fact. It is not a fact for consciousness except as a greater or less degree of meaning attends it. In a state of infancy or unconsciousness, facts may exist which have no meaning for us. But the further we are removed from these two states, the greater the necessity for meaning in all the facts of our conscious lives. Religion especially, which goes deepest into our consciousness, awakens a craving for the meaning. The doctrines of theology are the answer to that craving.

(3) Theology is necessary, therefore, if we would define our religion. We are not obliged to exhaust the meaning of religion in our definitions of it. The objects and experiences involved are beyond our capacity for knowing in some of their aspects. But we may apprehend what we cannot comprehend. We may know in part if we may not know altogether.

(4) Theology is necessary in order to defend religion against attack. The Christian may decide that he will abandon thought about religion. He will simply enjoy it. But very soon the

antichristian thinker advances a theory of the world which would completely set aside the Christian religion. This has been true throughout history. The effort to ignore the meaning of religion expressed in the form of doctrine is always rudely disturbed by some new assault upon the faith. At once the necessity arises for clear doctrinal statements to meet objections. We must define religion in order to defend it.

(5) Again, theology is necessary to religion in order to propagate it. Christianity is a missionary religion. It is aggressive and conquering in motive and aim. But no possible success can attend the propagation of a Christianity without doctrine. Experience breeds truth. Then truth is employed to produce experience. Experience then imparts a new appreciation of truth. But always if we would successfully propagate the Christian religion, we must have a Christian theology.

6. Again, the study of religion and theology is sometimes merged in the study of their history. Historical theology is held up by way of contrast with systematic or dogmatic theology. The history of religion and the history of doctrine are sufficient for our needs, it is held.

In regard to this method and point of view we may admit at once the very great value of the historical study of any great subject. The tendency to go back to beginnings and discover origins and causes is a very valuable one. To trace the variations and reactions of any movement through history is necessary to a comprehensive understanding. So long, therefore, as the historical study of theology is valued for its true worth, it is to be strongly commended. Such study, however, becomes a serious error when it is made a substitute for something else having a different motive and end. The objective and detached study of the history of religion or the history of theology is valuable from the point of view of critical research. The scholar and investigator who is this and nothing more finds it a field of fascinating interest. But if the scholar and investigator is also a Christian man, with a profound interest in religion and its spread over the earth, the historical study of theology is invariably qualified by a new motive and interest. For him scientific research is a means to a higher end. He wishes to discover the truth contained in the history that it may be employed as a means of advancing the kingdom of God. Otherwise the study of history is like watching the changing combinations of color in a kaleidoscope, or the variations in the appearance of an evening cloud. For the earnest Christian man, and especially for the preacher of the gospel, the merely objective study of theology as a historical movement apart from the deeper interest in truth itself, may become a hindrance rather than a help to efficiency. It is a fundamental fact of psychology made clear by all Christian history, that efficiency in propagating Christianity is based on intense conviction of the truths it contains. The preacher and teacher of the gospel cannot remain neutral to its content of truth and at the same time retain power in his efforts to lead others to accept it. This does not mean willingness to believe what is false. He passionately desires truth because of its supreme value for man's religious life.

III. CHRISTIAN EXPERIENCE AND REVELATION

We have already observed, and there will be frequent occasion to recur to the fact in the pages which follow, that the Christian religion has to do with two great groups of facts: the facts of experience and the facts of the historical revelation of God through Christ. The place of the Scriptures we consider at a later stage of the discussion. Here it is important to consider the general relations between these two groups of facts. What do we mean by Christian experience? The answer to this question will lead to the idea of the Christian revelation. The two are closely related. Neither can be fully understood apart from the other.

By the Christian experience we mean the totality of the experience which becomes ours through our fellowship with God in Christ. Reference is not made simply to conversion, much less to any particular type of conversion. The Christian experience, of course, includes its beginning. But it also includes all that follows. Regeneration and its results are all included. Christian experience includes also all that properly belongs to the experience in the community of Christians. It includes the life of all Christians, of the past as well as of the present. It is not the experience of any individual alone, or any particular type. It does include certain essential elements of experience, but these appear in endless variations among Christian men. Again, the Christian experience bears a definite relation to events outside the Christian's personal spiritual life. It is definitely related, in other words, to the providence of God. It is an experience which can grasp intelligently its place and meaning in a life lived under conditions of time and space and in human society. Finally, it is an experience which is capable of being defined in relation to all other forms of human experience and of human culture. While the experience of redemption through Jesus Christ is unique and exceptional among the earthly experiences of men, it is not unrelated to the others. Indeed, it is in part because it can be so clearly defined in relation to the natural life of man and to his various ideals and struggles, that for the Christian it brings such assurance and power. In its relations to science, to art, to ethics, to philosophy, and to the whole range of human interests and pursuits, the Christian experience is capable of clear and convincing exposition. It is the unifying bond of all human experience. All things become new under the light which shines from the heart of the Christian experience itself. All this will appear in various ways in the pages which follow.

Here once more we meet the ever-recurring objection that the experience of the Christian is subjective, the imaginings of his own heart rather than a great reality. The objection assumes that a subjective experience cannot be true; that God cannot make himself known to the Christian. No such assumption is justifiable. It is a question of fact, not of unfounded assumption. And as we have previously stated, the question of fact is not merely a question of our subjective experience. It is also a question of the historic revelation of God in Christ.

The Christian Religion in Its Doctrinal Expression

Theology has often considered the question of the " antecedent probability " of a revelation to mankind. Various arguments were advanced to establish such a probability. But the question and answer gain in clearness if it is asked whether religion is ever to be completed, or is to remain always a one-sided affair. Religion is communion between God and man. It is a reciprocal relationship. Does God ever speak? Is he forever dumb? Is religion merely a soliloquy on man's part?

Now the Christian revelation is God's answer to these questions. He has spoken to men in his Son. He is still speaking to them. There are three phases of that revelation which we must recognize if it is to become effective for our salvation. These will all receive more extended treatment subsequently. But meantime they need to be presented in outline.

1. The historic revelation in Jesus Christ. In that revelation we have the great central fact of the Christian religion outside of our consciousness entirely. He came to earth committed to a definite vocation. His consciousness clearly reflected the sense of divine approval at every stage of his ministry. He announced to men that he came to reveal God and to lead sinful men to God. He died and rose again. His death was an atonement for human sin. The gift of the Holy Spirit was his means for continuing his redemptive activity.

2. The result of the inworking of Christ in human souls was deliverance from sin and guilt and moral and spiritual transformation. A new movement in human history came as a result of his inworking spiritually in the hearts of men.

3. There were definite spiritual conditions to which men were required to conform in order to know the divine redeeming grace and power. Repentance and faith sum up the spiritual attitude involved. Thus the revelation of God in Christ possesses all the elements which are required to establish its truth. It is known as objective fact. It is then known in its results in subjective experience. It is known in the latter sense through clearly defined and well-understood spiritual conditions. These conditions are definitely related to objective facts. It is protected against

mere subjectivism by its objective ground in history. It is protected against the uncertainties of merely critical and literary processes by its results in our own experience. Professor Haering sums up the work of Jesus in the following language: [1] " Jesus is the personal self-revelation of God . . . of the God who in his kingdom unites sinners with himself and with each other in the eternal fellowship of his love, judging sin, pardoning guilt, renewing the will, vanquishing death. Jesus is the personal self-revelation of this God, since he evokes such trust as the actively real presence of the invisible God in the actual world, in which there is otherwise no real assured confidence in this God. He is the ground of faith, *i. e.,* of trust. This is the truth to which the faith of the New Testament testifies in the most varied forms. What is most important, it records the impression which Jesus himself produced, and which he always contrives to produce, as the ages pass."

The point which calls for emphasis here is that the basis on which the Christian doctrine of revelation rests is a basis of fact in all its aspects. History and experience combine to establish it upon irrefutable grounds. It is not necessary at this stage to consider the various means adopted to set aside this revelation and its fundamental significance for men. Broadly speaking, all these efforts have resorted to untenable methods of dealing with the question. So long as strictly critical and strictly scientific principles are allowed to control, the outcome is as we have indicated. It is only when *a priori* presuppositions or illegitimate assumptions are adopted that it is possible to arrive at any other result. It may be urged, for example, that all the elements of the Gospel records, except those which leave a simply human Jesus, are to be rejected. But this cannot be done on critical grounds. For criticism warrants no such conclusion. Or it may be urged that the early disciples were influenced by the ethnic religions about them to introduce many false elements into the Gospels. But this, as a mere supposition, does not convince. And labored efforts to connect the New

[1] T. Haering, " The Christian Faith," Vol. I, pp. 208, 209.

Testament with such influences have failed up to the present. Or again, objectors may insist upon the "Christ principle" as distinguished from Jesus the personal revelation of the eternal God. But this also is the result of a purely arbitrary handling of the Gospel material, based on a particular type of philosophic opinion. Once more in the interest of a general theory of evolutionism as the key to the meaning of the world, it may be insisted that no individual man can ever possess absolute and final significance for the human race. But here again it is a philosophic presupposition which yields the conclusion, not regard for the facts themselves. In a word, every other view except that which recognizes in Jesus God's revelation to men for their salvation, leaves out some part of the facts. They omit essential elements of the history, such as Christ's own claims, or the effects he produced upon his disciples, or the work he has wrought in and through men in the past and present. Philosophical speculation may set aside Christ, but science and criticism fail to do so.

IV. The Need for a Personal Self-revelation of God

We have then, in the Christian religion, a self-revelation of God in the domain of human history. Along with this the revelation is made real and vital for men in the realm of personal experience. If now we ask the question, why the self-revelation of God took this form, and keep in mind the needs and requirements of religion itself, a satisfactory answer is not far to seek.

1. In the first place, a human personality is the only adequate medium for the self-revelation of a personal God. Only personality can fully reveal and express the meaning of personality. Of course there are many intimations and suggestions of personality to be found in the physical universe. But those are not sufficient in themselves to express all the wealth of meaning in the nature of the infinite personal God. The moral qualities of God especially call for a personal, moral life in order that they may be clearly and fully expressed. The lower stages of nature, as we shall afterward show, give rise to the expectation of a personal

being as the crown of nature. And if God is to make himself fully known to men who, in the exercise of their freedom, came under the dominion of sin, it is most natural to expect that he would disclose himself to such personal beings in the form of a personal life.

2. Again, the personal and historical revelation of God was necessary to complete and establish firmly the inward revelation through his Spirit. In other words, it was necessary to save religion from the uncertainties and perils of subjectivism. So long as religion was without an objective ground, it was always exposed to the danger that it would fail to attain the stability and definiteness required by the religious life itself. Man must really know God if the idea and power of God are to bear their highest moral fruits in human life.

3. A third reason for such a self-revelation of God is that the deed of love and of righteousness is a far more powerful revelation of these qualities in God than the simple declaration of them could ever be. The Scriptures declare that God is love. They show also that he is righteousness. It is clear, therefore, that if God is such a being in his essential nature, a mere declaration of the fact would not constitute a real demonstration of it. To become love and righteousness in action would be the only adequate revelation of the fact of love and righteousness in God's essential nature. The incarnation and atonement of God in Christ thus become the only adequate means for a self-disclosure on his part which would do justice to the claim.

4. In the fourth place, such a revelation was required in order to the production of the necessary results in the moral and spiritual nature of man. This point becomes clear when we consider the insufficiency of any other form of revelation for the end in view. Miracles and outward wonders alone would not meet the need. They were employed for a time in order to awaken in men a sense of God's presence. But they were always employed for moral and personal ends. In themselves, however, they were never an adequate means of creating in men the full religious response to God. A man might indeed be convinced of

God's presence and activity in an intellectual way by wonders and signs, and remain untouched in the depths of his moral nature. But this is not the chief end of the gospel. That end is not understood until we perceive that in his self-revelation in Christ God's intention was to produce the " response of moral qualities in man to moral qualities in God." His end was to produce sons of God worthy in all respects of their Father in heaven. To accomplish this he gave his own Son, who revealed the inner nature of God as righteous love and became the medium through whom the power of God could reach personal beings and reproduce the same qualities in them. Thus the idea and the ideal of religion was fulfilled; God spoke to man, and man spoke to God; the divine love awakened human love. For the first time man understood clearly and fully the moral nature of God.

V. THEOLOGY AND TRUTH

Another matter which needs consideration in this introductory chapter is the relation of theology to truth. In presenting a connected system of theological doctrines, as we have seen, the aim is to set forth the meaning of religion. Christian theology is simply the interpretation of the Christian religion. But in this pursuit are we dealing with truth? Is theology in any proper sense a science? Enough has been said on the preceding pages to indicate very clearly the direction our answer will take. We declare without hesitation that in the Christian religion and in the theology which expresses its meaning, we are dealing with a form of real knowledge. In another connection we shall give a definition of knowledge and develop the contents of knowledge in Christian experience. Here it is sufficient to indicate in general terms the reasons for holding that Christian theology is a form of knowledge.

1. The Scriptures, with great uniformity, represent religion as a form of real knowledge. Jesus declared that " this is life eternal, that they should know thee, the only true God, and him whom thou didst send, even Jesus Christ " (John 17 : 3). In

fact, it is a fundamental teaching in all the Gospels and Epistles that in the experience men have of the grace of God in Christ, there is real knowledge and real truth. This will appear in many ways as we proceed.

2. Again, in Christian experience, we are dealing with the greatest of all realities, the spiritual universe, even with God himself. Religion is not an idea simply. It is not a philosophy primarily. It is a living experience of a very definite kind. In this respect it is like every other sphere of experience. It can be reduced to intelligible and systematic expression for the intellect. Hence it is properly a field in which a scientific expression of meaning is possible.

3. As a science, theology is closely related to many other fields of scientific research. All the social sciences differ from exact science in certain respects; but they are none the less sciences on that account. In them we do not find truth which can be set forth in the same exact formulæ as with those which are found in the realm of physical research. But this is due not to the absence of reality and of truth about it. It is due rather to the nature of the reality with which we deal. Truth in religion owes its scientific character not to its mathematical quality, but to its use as a means of systematically expressing the meaning of the uniformities which prevail in the religious realm.

4. The denial that truth and knowledge are found in religion is based upon a narrow and untenable conception of knowledge. Physical science has tended to narrow the idea of truth to propositions which can be proved in exact mathematical terms. But this narrowing of the conception is due to a confusion of truth itself with a particular form for expressing it. There are many ways of expressing the meaning of reality. The claim to truth cannot be based upon any one way to the exclusion of others. The test of the claim to truth is the test as to the reality with which it deals, at least this is the primary and fundamental test. Spiritual realities will not yield the same formulæ for expressing their meaning as those found in the sphere of physics. But they are none the less real and may find interpretation in terms of truth.

[25]

The Christian Religion in Its Doctrinal Expression

5. The truth of the Christian religion takes the form which religion requires, and makes the broadest and strongest appeal to our love of truth. As to the form, religion does not need nor require mathematical demonstration. Such demonstration does not and cannot produce faith. It cannot serve as a test for the reality of the contents of faith. Indeed, if it were substituted for faith, it would destroy its chief element of value. It follows, therefore, that such demonstration cannot destroy faith.

The kind of truth which is required by and found in the life of the religious man, is that which defines the relations of free moral beings to God and to each other. The relations of persons, not of physical forces, are in question. Not physical but free causation is in action in this sphere. The truths which express the relations of God to man are as comprehensive as life itself. Growth, development, progressive attainment of the moral and spiritual ideal, are the conditions which determine the forms of statement for the truths of religion.

Again, the appeal of the truths of religion is of the strongest kind. It is an intellectual appeal in the narrower sense of the word. The reason is satisfied because the truths of the Christian religion may be presented in a coherent system which has unity and self-consistency. The moral nature is satisfied because the result is the triumph of the moral nature over sin and self and the world. All the higher personal life is satisfied because in the Christian experience human personality comes to its own. Self-realization, a consciousness of having found the meaning of life and destiny, is bound up in the Christian experience. In all these and other ways truth comes home to the nature of man in Christian experience.

VI. Concluding Topics of Preliminary Survey

We have been giving a preliminary survey and discussion of certain fundamental principles which will reappear from time to time in the pages which follow. They will be treated in the connections which arise in the course of the systematic development of the truths of the Christian religion. There are several other topics which call for brief consideration before we close our preliminary survey. They are as follows: The Sources of Christian Theology; the Material and Formal Principles of Theology; the Order and Arrangement of Doctrines; and the Qualifications for the Study of Theology.

1. First, as to the sources of theology, our statement has been anticipated in our previous exposition. The source of Christian theology is the Christian religion. By the Christian religion we mean all the factors which enter into that religion, historical, literary, and spiritual. Fundamentally and most important of all, Jesus Christ, his life and teaching and atoning death and resurrection, is the source of the Christian religion. The Holy Spirit as the gift of Christ to men, the leader and guide in the inspired record of Christ's life and work, the ever-present guide to Christians in all ages, is necessary to us if we are to understand Christ and his religion. The Scriptures of the Old and of the New Testament are indispensable to Christian theology because they are a product, and at the same time a source of the Christian religion. Through them alone do we understand the great causes which operated to produce the Christian religion and make it a power on earth. Our own experience of the redeeming grace of God in Christ is necessary to a full understanding of Christian theology. Apart from that religious experience, theology is an intellectual movement, but lacks the vital elements required by the very nature of the Christian religion. Experience would ever go astray without the ever-present corrective influence of the Scriptures, and the authority of the Scriptures would never become for us a vital and transforming reality apart from the working of God's redeeming grace in us.

The above are the primary sources of the knowledge of the Christian religion which is expressed in Christian theology. Theology does not reject such truth as comes through nature, through history and psychology, or from any other source. But it plants itself firmly on the Christian facts and develops its doc-trinal views in the first instance from these facts.

[27]

2. The meaning of theology has often been expressed in terms of its material and its formal principles. By material principle is meant its vital and essential content; by formal principle is meant the form or medium through which the meaning is apprehended. We may say then that as here presented, the material principle of theology is man's fellowship with God as mediated through Jesus Christ. The formal principle is the Scriptures spiritually interpreted. Other ways of expressing these principles have been adopted. Justification by faith was regarded as the material principle of the Reformation. This of course touches the heart of the spiritual life and the essential content of Christianity. But as a statement of its inward meaning it is not distinctive enough. It is an Old Testament principle gathered up into the New Testament religion. But it does not specifically recognize Jesus Christ as the chief agent in the New Testament revelation. Christ's personal relations to our faith is a necessary element in any statement designed to express the central meaning of the gospel. The same objection holds to the kingdom of God as a means of expressing that central meaning. It lacks the specific reference to Jesus Christ. But when we speak of fellowship with God as mediated through Christ, we express the vital truth contained in both the other statements. Justification by faith is a justification conditioned on faith in him. The kingdom of God is a kingdom in which he is King. Fellowship with God as mediated through Jesus Christ is a phrase comprehensive enough to cover all the essential elements. It implies justification by faith. It implies and necessitates the reign of God in his eternal kingdom. It carries the thought of a progressive moral attainment, in which the Christian character is gradually transformed into the image of Christ. It involves the social aspects of the gospel according to which the relations of Christians to each other are determined by the common fellowship they have with Christ.

The formal principle of Christian theology is the Scriptures spiritually interpreted. This has particular reference to the New Testament. But the Old Testament is not excluded. It is

[28]

the preliminary revelation. The expression "spiritually interpreted" is employed to distinguish the method of a living theology from that of a merely critical or exegetical study of the Scriptures. If theology in the correct use of the term is an interpretation of the divine life in the soul, we are bound to express the relations between the life and the theology in defining the method of arriving at the truth. The pipe which conveys the water from the reservoir cannot be understood unless we keep in mind its relation to the water which it conveys. Biblical study and interpretation have often been a mere empty pipe with no relation to the true uses in the life of the soul.

3. Our next topic is the order and arrangement of doctrine. Sometimes theologies proceed upon the assumption that natural properly precedes revealed theology in a doctrinal treatise. Usually the arguments for God's existence drawn from man and nature are set forth in the first division. But the plan involves a double method of dealing with the material of theology which may be confusing. These arguments, while possessing great force, do not yield a strictly Christian conception of God. And they may leave the impression that the Christian belief in God is based on them as its chief foundation. Our own plan is to defer consideration of these proofs until the proof from the inner life of the Christian has been set forth. This is, for the Christian himself, the most convincing and satisfactory of proofs. And a great part of the force of the proofs from man and nature, even when they are given at the outset, is derived from the facts of Christian experience which are tacitly assumed. We prefer, therefore, to unify the doctrinal system by bringing all the elements of doctrine into relation with the central reality, the redemptive grace of God as manifested first in Jesus Christ himself, and secondly as manifested in the souls of believers.

Again, some treatises of theology in recent times have left the doctrine of the Trinity to be treated at the end of the doctrinal system. This is done upon the supposition that the truth regarding the Trinity lies out on the borderland of knowledge. It is a sort of remnant left over after the main things have been set forth. This method, however, overlooks the vital relations of the Trinity to experience itself. God is revealed as Father, Son, and Spirit very early in the regenerate life, as will appear. The practical uses and value of the doctrine of the Trinity are very great. It is true that we need to practise due reserve in the effort to give metaphysical definitions of the Trinity, just as the New Testament does. But the doctrine itself needs to be recognized, if not at the beginning, at least comparatively early in the doctrinal development. The order adopted in our treatment, then, differs from that of the older method in placing the consideration of the general proofs of God's existence after the exposition of the fundamental truths of Christian experience It differs from the sequence of doctrine as found in some mor recent treatises in placing the discussion of the doctrine of Go and of the Trinity earlier. This conforms to the requirement of experience and its relation to doctrine.

The point at which the doctrine of the Scripture is expounded accords with its nature as a spiritual authority as distinguished from one that is merely legal or ecclesiastical. The New Testament Scriptures were produced to set forth the meaning of the revelation through Christ and the salvation which he brings. Its authority is not due to decrees of early church councils. Its power and fundamental importance for Christians are not based upon external authority. They are due to its divine and self-evidencing content. It is for us the Book of Life, since it discloses to us the sources of our spiritual life and the great historical and divine causes which produced it. On this account it is best understood by those in whom the life itself has become a reality. It will be noted also that in the use of the Scriptures to establish the truth of doctrines the method of biblical theology is pursued. Where space does not forbid we trace the Scripture teaching in its historical unfolding. This is not always possible or necessary. But it is usually done in the treatment of the more fundamental doctrines. It has an advantage over the selection of proof-texts at random from the earlier and later stages of the Old and New Testament revelation. It serves to indicate the divinely guided process by which God made known the truth to his people.

We have devoted an extended section to the relations between Christian and other forms of knowledge. The aim in view is to make clear and distinct for the student the reality of the knowledge which accompanies our salvation in Christ, its independence and value for man's religious life, and its harmony with all other forms of human knowledge. We consider this aim as vitally important for Christian theology. There has been almost endless confusion in the minds of men at this point. There is a constant tendency to stifle man's religious life, or reduce it to a bare minimum of emotion, or of ethics, in the interest of some alien principle which, in its proper application, requires no such reduction. The provinces of the great kingdom of the human spirit ought to live side by side in peace. It is only when one province rises in revolt and seeks to reign supreme that confusion and strife arise. One of the chief advantages of considering doctrine as expressing the meaning of the divine life in the soul, is that it enables us to make clear for the intellect the place of religious truth in the great universe of truth. And in doing this we avoid any real conflict with science or other forms of human culture. We discover thus also how all other intellectual pursuits really end in the fundamental necessity for religion in order to provide for the full development of man's spiritual life.

The following is a brief preview of the order in which the material of this treatise is presented:

In Chapter II we give a definition of knowledge, with special reference to religion, and indicate the sources of our religious knowledge. This leads directly to Jesus Christ, the supreme revelation of God to men.

In Chapter III we present a preliminary study of Christian experience itself. Certain objections are pointed out, and the nature of the Christian knowledge and the Christian certainty is indicated. This leads naturally to the consideration of Christian in relation to other forms of knowledge. Chapter IV is devoted to this subject.

[31]

The Christian Religion in Its Doctrinal Expression

In Chapter V the record of the Christian revelation, as given in the Scriptures, is presented; and in Chapter VI the Person of Jesus Christ, who is himself the revelation of which the Scriptures are the record.

In Chapter VII we consider the question of the deity of Jesus Christ, and consider various phases of the modern discussion of his Person. This is followed in Chapter VIII by a consideration of the doctrine of the Holy Spirit, which, along with the doctrine of Christ's Person, occupies a central place in the Christian system.

In Chapter IX we consider the doctrine of God. This order is adopted because it is only after the Christian knows God in redemptive experience through Christ that he is in a position to understand God the Father whom Jesus Christ revealed.

In the three succeeding chapters, X, XI, and XII, the doctrines of Creation, Providence, and Sin are presented. In Chapter XIII the saving work of Christ is presented, and in Chapter XIV the doctrine of Election, or God's initiative in salvation; in Chapter XV, the Beginnings, and in Chapter XVI, the Continuance of the Christian Life, and in Chapter XVII, the doctrine of Last Things. It will be noted that throughout the volume the fundamental aim has been maintained, *viz.,* to present Christian doctrine as the necessary outcome and expression of the Christian religion. The experiential element in Christian knowledge and Christian certainty has been recognized at all points.

4. There are many qualities of mind which may be mentioned as assisting one who becomes a student of theology. But all these qualities are dependent upon one fundamental attitude of the mind and heart. The highest qualification for the study of theology is the religious attitude. In religion a man approaches God in a certain way. Through his communion with God certain experiences arise. Particularly is this true of the Christian religion. If one is to understand Christian theology, therefore, it is essential that the attitude required by the Christian religion be maintained. Theology is the interpretation of the religion, as we have seen. The interpretation is impossible apart from the reality itself. We conclude, then, that religion is the fundamental

qualification for the study of theology. In the light of this general truth we may note the qualifications which come from scholarship and general culture, from particular intellectual attainments, and from moral and spiritual qualities.

(1) All forms of scholarship and general culture aid in theological study when they are employed in the interest of man's religious life. Theology is, like philosophy, a very comprehensive study. There is scarcely any branch of learning which may not be made tributary to it. Especially is this true of every form of scholarship pertaining to the Bible, such as knowledge of the original languages, skill in exegesis and other departments of biblical science. So also is a knowledge of general science and philosophy valuable to the student of theology. The difficulty and the danger in using all the general results of scholarly research in the study of theology is that some other interest or ideal will displace that which is peculiar to Christian theology, the religious interest and ideal. The religious life must be seen in its totality of manifestation and in its true inner meaning and value. If a student's chief interest is something else besides religion, there is danger that religion be smothered or crucified. Much of the so-called "objective and disinterested" study of religion and theology is of this kind. In bringing scientific methods to the study of religion and theology, the first thing to remember is that religion is necessarily personal and subjective to the student who hopes to penetrate to its true inward meaning. Otherwise we never get below the surface of religion, and never obtain the true material for the construction of theology.

(2) So also intellectual endowments of all kinds are valuable in the study of theology. The ability to think clearly and patiently, the desire for accuracy and thoroughness, the desire for unity and coherency of view, are very admirable qualities in the theologian. Especially is the quality which is usually called intuition helpful in this realm. The word simply means mental and spiritual insight, the feeling for truth based on broad intellectual sympathies. It is thus distinguished from the logical process of deducing conclusions from premises. No man can ever

hope to attain great proficiency in theology who is unwilling or incapable in the matter of patient and sustained effort. But the rewards of such effort are abundant and of the highest value.

(3) The moral and spiritual qualities are the most fundamental in theological study. We name some of these. A sense of dependence upon God and the guidance of his Spirit is necessary. The more the student penetrates into the great mysteries of religion, the more he is impressed with this sense of need for divine help in understanding them and expressing their meaning. Docility or tractableness, coupled with humility and openness of mind, is a fundamental requirement. The desire to know the truth and a submissive will go with the true theologian. Obedience is indeed in a true sense an " organ of knowledge," although, of course, not the sole organ. Pride of opinion must be laid aside if one is to come into living fellowship with God in Christ. Jesus upon one occasion thanked God that he had hid the truths of the gospel from the " wise and understanding " and revealed them " unto babes " (Matt. 11 : 25). This great truth is slowly coming to recognition in modern psychology and theories of knowledge. There are great realms of reality, great tides of life and power which flow into man from God upon condition of a docile and receptive attitude on man's part. In other words, faith is the bond of union between man and God, which brings not only new life and new power, but new knowledge. Theology is the systematic expression and arrangement of that knowledge.

CHAPTER II

THE KNOWLEDGE OF GOD

THE question which stands out at the very beginning of a treatise on theology is the following: Can we know God? If we answer this in the affirmative we are confronted with the further question: How do we know God? This latter leads in turn to the further question: How is knowledge related to faith? And finally, all these questions having been satisfactorily answered, we need to define the relations between religious and other forms of knowledge.

I. Definition of Knowledge and of Religion

The following definition gives briefly the essential elements of knowledge:

1. That which is self-evident in the nature of reason: mathematical axioms illustrate this, such as that a straight line is the shortest distance between two points.

2. That which is immediately given in experience, as the manifestations of nature in a thunder-storm to a man passing through it.

3. That which is cogently inferred from the given, as that lightning struck a tree, inferred from the condition of the shattered trunk.

It will be noted that in this definition there is an internal factor of knowledge, the reason itself. There is also an external factor, something which may, and often does, come from without, but which is immediately given in our experience. There is also a process of inference which includes both the internal factor, reason, and the external factor, the object or objects given immediately to us in experience.

[35]

The above definition of knowledge is of great importance for theology for the following reasons: First, it makes clear the point that in religion and in theology, which is the systematic and orderly explanation of religion, we have to do with real knowledge. In the second place, it keeps knowledge properly based in a sound psychology. The definition recognizes the nature of reason itself, as contributing to our knowledge, and does not leave us passive recipients merely of impressions from without. Man's reason gives its impress to all the contents of knowledge, as a dipper gives shape to the water it takes up from a stream. The definition also emphasizes experience itself, the life processes by which we come into contact with the world about us. And finally, it is a definition which recognizes the presence in the knowing process of all the faculties and powers of man. Man is not abstract reason, or abstract will, or abstract feeling. He is all these in combination. No one of these ever acts by itself. This conception of knowledge is of great importance for theology. It is a point of vital contact and agreement between modern scientific psychology and the Bible, as we shall see.

We proceed next to define religion. This will prepare the way for a statement of how the knowledge of God arises, and how theology becomes necessary as the orderly and systematic expression of the meaning of religion. There are many ways of defining religion. Some adopt the lowest types of religion, such as fetishism, or animism, and claim that the various religions are simply developments of these. Others begin at the other end, and adopt some highly intellectual or philosophic principle as containing the essence of all religion. Advocates of certain forms of idealism adopt the latter method. Religion thus becomes a process of the intellect in its reactions upon the world about us. There are various other methods adopted for defining religion.

The best method, however, is not to take that which is lowest, nor yet, in an abstract way, that which is highest, if we would get a general definition of religion. The best method is to set forth the essential elements which belong to the idea of religion itself, and which are found to exist actually among religious men.

The Knowledge of God

This will naturally lead to the consideration of the Christian religion, which is the ideal and completion of all lower and imperfect approximations of religion.

In the most general terms, then, we define religion (1) as the recognition of a power not ourselves, and an effort to establish harmonious relations with it. (2) The object in religion is personal, superhuman spirits, or a supreme personal spirit. (3) The adjustment with these superhuman powers is in personal terms and on the basis of personal relationships. This personal adjustment has in it at least the following elements: (a) Revelation on the part of the God or gods worshiped, and (b) trust and worship on the part of man. (4) Religion also includes, as essential to the personal adjustment, an exercise of the feelings, the will, and the intellect. The feelings come into action because there is a sense of dependence and need. The will is involved because there is an act of submission and conformity to the will of the object of worship. The intellect is active because there arises a knowledge of the object of worship as the result of the religious adjustment. (5) We add that the aim of religion is redemption. Redemption is distinctively a Christian word. But there is a lower and elementary sense in which the idea exists in all religions. Men seek to form alliances with the supreme powers to secure deliverance in war, or to avoid dangers of various kinds. The idea of redemption is completely transformed in the Christian religion.

It will be noted that the definition just given is designed to set forth the contents of religious belief as it is found among the nations generally. They are the common elements held in a more or less crude and indefinite way wherever there is religious activity among men. It is to be noted also that the definition does not enter upon the question of the degree of truth, or falsity, of the forms of religion to which it applies. The aim in it is simply to express the meaning of religion in a comprehensive way. In order to make the definition inclusive of the Christian religion, we need only to emphasize the central place of Jesus Christ as the revealer and mediator of God to men along with those elements which arise out of the life redeemed in and through Christ.

II. Sources of Religious Knowledge

There are a number of sources of religious knowledge. Most of them are insufficient for man's religious needs unless combined with the Christian revelation. We consider briefly a few of these.

1. One of the sources of the knowledge of God is the facts of nature and of man. In the past men have usually begun treatises on theology by undertaking to prove the existence of God by logical inference from nature and man. There are the arguments from causation, from order and arrangement, from design, from the moral order, from the necessities of reason itself, and others. We shall have occasion to notice these at a later stage. They are valuable in their place, and are by no means to be rejected. But they are not primary and fundamental for Christian theology. Their value will appear as subordinate to another source of knowledge about God.

The unsatisfactory nature of the arguments based on logical inference from man and nature appears in the following considerations. *a.* They never lead to the Christian view of God. Through them we derive some idea of God's power, wisdom, purpose, and other qualities of the divine Being. But they fail to give us a satisfactory view of God's moral character and of his attitude toward man, especially of his grace and forgiving love. *b.* Again, the knowledge concerning God derived from the logical process alone, is never really made the basis of the doctrinal systems of Christian theologians. Even when they make such proofs of God's existence primary in their treatment of the question how we know God, they depart from it in the doctrinal system which follows. *c.* Again, proofs of this character do not produce the kind of certainty required in the religious life. We shall of course have to indicate the kind of certainty required in the religious life. For the present we simply remark that it is a certainty which results from the actual contact of the soul with the religious

Object. It is a certainty based on a knowledge of reality, and not simply on the cogency of a logical inference. *d.* Proofs based on logical deduction from the facts of nature are deficient in another respect. Psychology, in its best modern forms, shows clearly that our knowledge is built up out of our life experiences rather than through the activity of the abstract reason. We live and struggle and suffer; we are defeated, or we win victories; we pursue aims and are disappointed; we make discoveries and suffer losses. In this way we gradually discover truth. The truth we acquire becomes thus a treasury made up of the "small change," as it were, of human discovery in the struggle for life and in our life adjustments. Nothing could be farther removed from the facts than to suppose that truth arises chiefly through the reasonings of wise men who have isolated themselves from the struggles of life itself. *e.* Finally, the logical proofs of God's existence by themselves are unsatisfactory because, with those who have had the Christian experience, the logical deductions are always colored by the experience. This is inevitable and necessary from the nature of man. He cannot detach his reasoning processes from his own nature.

2. A second method for arriving at the knowledge of God which is much followed by moderns is to study the facts of the religious consciousness. The psychology of religion has thus become a distinct branch of inquiry. It has already yielded large results, and will in the future no doubt become more productive. Here we have an important point of contact between theology and the other sciences. Theology observes the facts of man's religious life, traces its laws, and sets forth the results in a formal way. It is the method pursued in the physical sciences, except that in theology and the psychology of religion we do not arrive at mathematically exact laws. We do obtain knowledge based on data, on real experiences. Our knowledge in religion thus obtains a fact basis.

But the psychology of religion is insufficient for the purposes of Christian theology unless it rises to the distinctively Christian point of view. The question arises whether or not the experiences of the religious consciousness are merely subjective. Is the Object of Christian faith real? Now the Christian religion is a historical religion, and as such it rises above the mere subjective play of the forces of consciousness. It becomes a cause operative in and upon man's religious consciousness, yet remaining objective to that consciousness. It has introduced into the world a set of religious forces which work in a very definite way. It is necessary to reckon with Christianity on this basis if we are to understand it.

3. A third source of religious knowledge is the study of comparative religion. The universal religious life of mankind is an interesting and significant fact. Christianity claims to present in perfect form all the valid elements of religion found in any other system. All it asks is candid recognition of the facts which are peculiar and exceptional in itself in addition to those common to all religions. The superiority of Christianity thus is easily made to appear.

4. A fourth source of religious knowledge is the decisions of ecclesiastical courts and councils as expressed in creeds and articles of faith. Now as to creeds issued under ecclesiastical authority, they are not and can never be original sources of religious knowledge. For all except those who frame them, they are second-hand knowledge, echoes rather than original voices. They are sometimes of great value. They declare the doctrinal beliefs of the age or people who put them forth. But religious knowledge does not arise primarily by subscription to creeds. It comes rather through the presence of God in the soul. Men learn of God through the experience of God. One of the favorite maxims of the schoolmen of the Middle Ages was, "I believe in order that I may know." There is an element of truth in the saying. But it may be very misleading. If it means by belief the mere acceptance of an article of a creed on the basis of the *implicit faith* required by the Catholic Church, it is far from true. If to believe, however, means to accept Christ in the saving sense of the New Testament, then the saying is deeply true. To know Christ by faith is to know God.

[40]

5. We name the Bible as another source of the knowledge of God. The Bible is indeed our supreme and authoritative literary source of the revelation of God which leads to salvation. But salvation is not conditioned upon our belief in, or acceptance of, a book. The knowledge of God of which we now speak is not derived from merely reading the pages of the Bible, or from the most rigidly scientific interpretation of its teachings. God's revelation of himself to us comes through his direct action upon our spirits. He comes to us in redeeming grace. There is a spiritual transaction within us. We are regenerated by his power, and lifted to a new moral and spiritual level. It is then that we acquire a new appreciation of the Bible. God thus becomes our supreme authority, and the Bible is recognized as the authoritative record of his supreme revelation.

6. It is now time to ask and answer the question, What is our supreme source of the knowledge of God which gives rise to the doctrines of the Christian religion? The answer is the revelation of God in and through Jesus Christ. In order to develop fully this fundamental thought we shall need to consider the following topics: (1) Christ as a historic person; (2) Christ as a superhistoric person acting upon history. In later chapters we shall discuss the character and attributes of the God whom Christ reveals, the nature of the experience which he mediates to us, and the various other topics arising out of the religious experience and requirements of theology.

(1) The first topic is Jesus Christ as a historic person. It is needless to consider the question of fact as to the existence in New Testament times of the being known as Jesus Christ. This has never been questioned with sufficient seriousness to justify our devoting space to it here. A summary of his earthly career and its significance is called for by the relation which he bears to Christian theology.

The essential points in the New Testament representation are the following:

a. The Virgin Birth. Matthew and Luke both record the story of his birth of the Virgin Mary The authenticity of these records has been questioned. But the arguments against them are inconclusive. Certainly the superhuman origin of Christ as thus recorded is in complete harmony with the great features of the life which followed.

We cannot consider in detail the issue as to the virgin birth. Very strong reasons have led Christians of all ages to retain it as an article of faith. The testimony of ancient manuscripts is practically unanimous in favor of the accounts in Matthew and Luke. Ancient versions are equally at one in the evidence they afford. The witness of early Christian writers is also practically unanimous in favor of the accounts. The Ebionites and some of the Gnostics opposed the virgin birth. But there were reasons for this. The former were anti-Pauline and the latter denied the true humanity of Christ. Throughout Christian history the virgin birth has been an accepted article of faith. It is, as is well known, a part of the Apostles' Creed.

Some of the objections urged against it are the following: (a) It is not in the Gospel of Mark or of John. Paul does not refer to the virgin birth, nor does any other New Testament writer. The reply is that Mark's purpose did not require him to deal with the infancy of Jesus. He begins with the public ministry. John's Gospel deals with the preincarnate Christ in the Prologue, but his account harmonizes best with the idea of the virgin birth. So also in Paul there is no express reference to the virgin birth. But his doctrine in no way contradicts it. His lofty teaching as to the preincarnate Christ also harmonizes with it. (b) Some objectors hold that the Old Testament and Jewish beliefs are the source of the birth stories; while others urge that they are derived from Gentile sources. These mutually contradict each other. One group says the virgin birth idea could not have had a Jewish, the other that it could not possibly have had a Gentile origin. But neither theory has shown a clear connection between the alleged source and the accounts as we have them. They are surmises rather than scientifically valid conclusions from facts. (c) It is urged also that in any case belief in the virgin birth is not necessary to faith. If it is meant it is not necessary to saving faith, it is true in the sense that many who trust Christ do not consciously accept or reject it. But this is apart from the main question. The main point here is that we cannot determine beforehand what is or is not necessary to the gospel. If the virgin birth took place we may be sure that it was necessary. God does not do the unnecessary thing in achieving his purposes. The virgin birth is the best explanation of Christ's supernatural person. It best explains his sinlessness. It best explains his headship of the new spiritual race of men. It accords best with his calling as divine Revealer and Redeemer of men.

b. We note next his sinlessness. Jesus Christ claimed to be without sin.

He challenged men to convict him of sin. (John 8 : 46.) He assumed an attitude of superiority to sinners in that he actually pronounced forgiveness of sins in his dealings with them. (Matt. 9 : 2.) He announced that his blood was to be shed for the remission of sins. (Matt. 26 : 28.)

c. Christ the revealer of God to men. He claimed to sustain a unique relationship to God the Father, whose Son he was, and whom he came to reveal. (John 1 : 18.)

We name the following elements in Christ's revelation of God: First, he *brings God near in a human life.* Christ's revelation of God was not primarily the communication of truths about God. It was rather the embodiment in a human life of the reality of the divine life. The truths arose out of the facts about God. Again, Jesus reveals God *as a Person.* In nature and history there are dim revelations of God. He appeared as Law, as Force, as Life, as Purpose, as moral Principle, and in other ways. But these are partial and fragmentary revelations, as we shall find. The stages in the revelation of God could reach their climax only in the highest medium known to us, personality. All the lower forms of the revelation are thus unified in the personality of God as revealed in Christ. God then was present in the personal life of Jesus of Nazareth. The law was " given," but grace and truth " came " (John 1 : 17). Again, the revelation in and through Jesus Christ teaches us what *God is in his character.*

Natural theology may give us certain simple truths about God. It does not give satisfactory knowledge of his moral qualities. We may briefly sum up these qualities in the phrase *righteous love*. This leads to the further statement that the revelation of God in Christ gives knowledge of the *attitude of God toward men*. He is a God of grace. He is intensely interested in the lives of men. He watches over them and cares for them. He bestows good gifts upon all men. He made men for himself. He constituted them for sonship in his eternal kingdom. In the highest, deepest, and richest manifestation of his nature he is infinite Father. As Father he has an eternal purpose of good toward men.

d. We consider next Christ as Redeemer of men. Redemption is an essential element in the revelation of God in Christ. A few brief statements will sum up in broad outline the redemptive activity of Christ. First, in him *God draws near to men* for their salvation. Not only does God draw near in Christ; Christ also embodies the power of God for the salvation of men. He came to seek and to save that which was lost. (Matt. 18 : 11; Luke 15 : 4.) His " mighty works " were the evidence of the divine power working in him. (Matt. 11 : 20; 13 : 54; Luke 9 : 43.)

Again, the redeeming activity of Christ had as an essential part of it his sufferings and death. The New Testament ascribes unique value and efficacy to the atoning sufferings of Christ. This is not only true of the Epistles, but also of the Gospels. (Matt. 20 : 28; 26 : 28.) The doctrine of the atonement will be developed at a later stage. Here we mention it as essential to Christ's redemptive work.

Finally, the resurrection of Christ, his ascension to the right hand of the Father, and his intercession for us, are the necessary crown and culmination of his redeeming activity.

(2) We are brought thus to the second general statement regarding God's revelation in Christ, *viz.,* that Christ is more than a historic person. He is superhistoric. He acts upon history from without. The personal self-revelation of God in Christ did not end with the death of Jesus. This statement brings us to the very heart of the meaning of Christianity. Did Jesus Christ

continue to act in a causal and direct way upon the course of Christian history? Does he now so act? The answer to these questions will go far toward determining the answer to other fundamental questions as to the meaning of the incarnation and atonement. We do not hesitate to answer both questions in the affirmative.

The facts of the earthly life must be combined with Christ's creative activity afterward if we are to estimate properly his real significance for the religious life of man. Christ was not only a teacher sent from God, he was also spiritual creator.

The following considerations establish the truth of these statements:

a. We note first the explicit statements of Jesus himself as to his continued activity after death. These are clear and sufficient. He declared that he would build his church and that the gates of Hades should not prevail against it. (Matt. 16 : 18.) He commissioned the disciples to evangelize the world, with the promise of his continued presence with them. (Matt. 28 : 20; Mark 16 : 20.) He promised the Holy Spirit through whom he would speak to them. (John 14 : 16, 17; Acts 1 : 5.) He predicted his own return in glory to judge the world. (Matt. 25 : 31-46.) *b.* In accordance with these predictions we have the Pentecostal outpouring of the Holy Spirit, the witnessing of the apostles to Christ's agency therein, and all the subsequent history of the book of Acts. *c.* The uniform testimony of the Epistles confirms these passages of the Gospels and the history in Acts. Everywhere Jesus is regarded as the spiritual power acting upon men through the Holy Spirit. *d.* We have also the career and writings of the apostle Paul. Paul describes the origin of his spiritual career as the moment when it pleased God to reveal his Son in him. (Gal. 1 : 16.) Christ is everywhere the center of his gospel and the efficient cause operating through him. One of the most convincing proofs of Christ's resurrection is the fifteenth chapter of First Corinthians. Some have attempted to explain Christianity through Paul. But this only removes the difficulty in appearance. How can we account for Paul? Whence did he derive the creative energy which has revolutionized the civilization of the West? Besides, the view is at variance with Paul himself, who was passionately devoted to Christ as his own Redeemer and as the Saviour of the world.

e. We mention the fact also that our earliest Christian literature sustains the view we advocate. Paul wrote the Epistles to the Romans, the Galatians, and the two Corinthian Epistles before any of our Gospels were composed. These are our first interpretations of the meaning of Christianity. They all assign to Jesus Christ the place and function of spiritual creator.

f. Observe further the place of the resurrection in early Christianity. The Christian movement began as a world-conquering movement with the resurrection of Jesus. There is no material divergence of view on this point among exegetes or historians. Belief in the resurrection is conceded with practical unanimity to have been the prime conviction behind the Christian movement. The fact on which the belief rested is the only sufficient explanation of that movement.

g. The place of Christ as spiritual creator is confirmed by the origin of the Synoptic Gospels. These arose as a result of the spiritual life in Christ. These records were composed after the four great Epistles of Paul. They did not cause, but were caused by, the Christian movement.

Two documents are at present regarded by criticism as containing our oldest records of the life of Christ. One of these is the Gospel of Mark; the other, a common source behind Matthew and Luke, from which both drew part of their material. But in both these sources all the essential features of the life of Jesus reappear as we have them in our present Matthew and Luke. All the supernatural and transcendent elements of his person and ministry remain.

Thus literary and historical criticism has failed completely to eliminate the supernatural Jesus from the New Testament. The outcome of critical research, therefore, is without result for the antichristian view. It is seen more clearly than ever before that there is agreement in essentials in all the New Testament representations of the place of Jesus Christ in our spiritual life. Nowhere do we find contradictions which affect the truth of the gospel. It is beyond belief that if Paul had changed the commonly accepted view as to the person of Christ, we should find no question raised by any of his contemporaries. There is no hint of a controversy in the New Testament over the modern issue between a simply human, naturalistic, and a supernatural Christ.

This issue, however, has taken on a new form. It is now a difference of philosophical theories or world-views. Opponents of Christianity start with a world-view which denies the supernatural. They proceed on this assumption to explain the supernatural elements in the gospel by ascribing them to the imagination of the early disciples, to the prevalence of myths which were incorporated in the records, or to a tendency to read unwarranted meanings into plain facts.

Conclusion

Our conclusion from the above brief survey of the sources of our knowledge of God may now be stated. It is as follows: Jesus Christ is the supreme source of religious knowledge for men. In God's revelation of himself to men through Jesus Christ, there are two chief elements. One of these is historical. The other is experiential. Both are essential to Christianity. In the life and words and deeds of Jesus of Nazareth we have the historical elements of God's self-revelation. But to these must be added the superhistoric work of Christ, who continued to act upon men through the Holy Spirit, after his ascension.

This leads to the idea of the record of the revelation of God to men in the Scriptures. The Old Testament is the record of the preliminary revelation. The New Testament is the completion of the record. Through these New Testament Scriptures we maintain connection with the historical facts on which Christianity rests. These are our sufficient and authoritative source of knowledge for the great deed of the redeeming God who entered humanity to save through Jesus Christ our Lord.

But the truth of the historic deeds and of the record of the deeds does not become ours in the full sense of the saving knowledge of God until we have the experience of God in our own souls. "This is life eternal, that they should know thee, the only true God, and him whom thou didst send, even Jesus Christ" (John 17 : 3). The knowledge of God becomes ours then in a threefold way: First, from the original source, Jesus Christ; secondly, through the authoritative record, the New Testament; and thirdly, through the experience of God's grace in Christ, wrought in us by the Holy Spirit. We can only understand Christ and the Bible through the experience of God's saving grace. As possessors of life we trace the stream of our life back to its source.

What we have just said does not imply that no importance is to be attached to the knowledge of God which may come to us from the study of nature, from comparative religion, from the psychology of religion, from creeds issued by ecclesiastical authority, and from other similar sources. The point of emphasis here is that these are secondary sources of religious knowledge, not primary. The revelation of God in Christ is primary. We arrive at a knowledge of that revelation through the Scriptures. We pass to our study of the facts and their record through our living experience of God's redeeming grace in Christ. Our first task then is a preliminary study of the experience itself.

CHAPTER III

PRELIMINARY STUDY OF CHRISTIAN EXPERIENCE

I. Six Assumptions

THE assumptions of the argument from Christian experience are to be noted here. There are six of these. They may be very briefly stated.

First, it is assumed that the world external to man is real. There are objects apart from man himself, apart from human consciousness, which act upon that consciousness. The world is not illusion, or the mere subjective creation of consciousness. It is objectively real.

Secondly, it is assumed that we live in a universe. Things are in some real sense a unity. Nature is not a chaos without meaning. The world is not a hopeless riddle.

Thirdly, that in this universe the parts cohere, or match each other, in both the physical and the spiritual realm. We are not to suppose that all is orderly and replete with meaning in the realm of natural law, while truth and reality are beyond us in the realm of spirit. On the contrary, the spiritual world is also a realm of truth and order.

Fourthly, we assume that our faculties and powers when normally related to objective reality are reliable. When we observe, and feel, and think, and exert our wills in the struggles of life, we may be sure that we are led thus into the possession of real truth about the objects with which we deal. There are no valid grounds for discrediting, but rather every reason for trusting our powers.

Fifthly, it is assumed that we discover truth in the processes of life, in the quest for and fulfilment of our needs. The discovery of truth is not an abstract process of the intellect merely. It is not simply the result of an academic quest. The reason is

D   [49]

of course necessary in the discovery of truth. But so is the will, and so are the feelings. Man's whole nature is involved.

We assume, in the sixth place, the fact of human personality. That personality is endowed with remarkable powers and capacities. It can act upon, and be acted upon, by natural objects. The human self knows itself as distinct from and capable of interaction with other human selves. These are among the facts which are given to us, not theories to be proved.

The above assumptions are among the simplest and most fundamental postulates of all human thought. They are not peculiar to the reasoning of the Christian theologian. They underlie all science and all philosophy. They are essential to all knowledge. Without them the very idea of truth itself would be impossible or meaningless. Knowledge arises for the Christian, therefore, on the same principles as for all other men. The difference is that in the exercise of faith in Christ as the revealer of God, and redeemer, he relates himself to a new object, a new realm of reality, in a living and transforming way which others do not know.

We can understand the nature of Christian experience only as we keep in mind the fact that it is a transaction between the divine and human persons. The key to the correct understanding of the matter is the idea of personality. It has to do with man, not as intellect, or feeling, or will, or conscience simply, but with man in the totality of his spiritual nature. The Christian experience thus completes the ideal of religion, since it is not only man submitting himself to God, but also God communicating himself to man.

II. The Analysis of Christian Experience

The initiative comes from the divine side. The message reaches us through human agencies for the most part. Its chief import is that God was in Christ reconciling the world to himself. (2 Cor. 5 : 19.) Salvation from sin and its consequences is the burden of the gospel call. Men are invited and commanded to turn from their sins, and to trust and obey God, who has come near to them in Jesus Christ. It thus appears that Jesus Christ is central and vital in the gospel message. It loses its meaning apart from him.

1. The point of contact of the gospel message in men is the consciousness of sin. There are other subordinate elements of the sin-consciousness, such as the feeling of helplessness and dependence, and the sense of need. These are attended in varying degrees by a sense of ill-desert and of guilt. In many instances it takes the form of self-condemnation and of utter despair. In the language of psychology this state of mind is sometimes described as an " inner contradiction," " a sense of wrongness with us as we naturally stand," and " the divided self," and in other ways.

The gospel intensifies the consciousness of sin. In the unregenerate there are various degrees of its manifestation. Sometimes it does not exist as sin-consciousness at all, but rather in some of the less central forms, as the sense of dependence, or a yearning for higher things. In every instance, however, the effect of the gospel appeal, when the natural consciousness is awakened, is a deepening of the sense of sin and guilt. The creative action of the Holy Spirit in applying the gospel message is seen in the fact that the sinner enters a new moral universe with new moral powers as he passes from the stage of conviction to that of regeneration.

2. The sinner's response to the gospel message is an act of moral freedom. God graciously approaches men with the offer of salvation through Christ. But the divine forces which operate through the gospel are adjusted and adapted to evoke a free moral response on man's part. Coercion here, as elsewhere in the moral realm, would destroy the highest element in man's nature.

The human response to the gospel appeal consists, in the earlier stages, of two acts: first, in a turning away from sin, and secondly, in an act of trust in Jesus Christ as atoning Redeemer. Repentance, or the turning away from sin, is a necessary part of the transaction between God and man, since a renewal of fellowship is impossible so long as the sin which had previously destroyed the fellowship remains. Faith, or trust in God as revealed in the atoning Christ, is also essential, because the union with God which brings a renewal of the spiritual nature is impossible otherwise.

3. The divine activity in Christian experience is correlative with the human. There are four aspects of that activity to be mentioned. The first is forgiveness. The assurance of forgiveness becomes a spiritual necessity so soon as sin is conceived as a breach of fellowship with a divine person. If sin is regarded as an infirmity or mistake merely, or as ignorance, or a stage in man's growth simply, forgiveness would not be one of the imperatives of religious experience. A pantheistic world-view goes with these lower conceptions of sin. The Christian revelation exalts personality in God and man. Hence forgiveness becomes an absolute necessity if the consciousness of redemption is to be made effective for man.

Closely related to forgiveness is justification. Justification is God's act, declaring the guilty free from the penalty of sin, and it is grounded in the atoning work of Christ. Thus God justifies the ungodly and provides for him a new standing. Forgiveness and justification are related in the closest manner. In the New Testament justification is the act of God which declares the new relation. Forgiveness establishes that relation. In it man is accepted and restored to God's favor.

Regeneration is the result of the direct action of the Holy Spirit upon man's spirit. In it the penitent believer receives a new nature. There is a radical change in the aim and purpose of life, the advent of a new set of motives, and a moral and spiritual renewal of the will. In Scripture the change of nature is described as the " new birth " or the " new creation."

Adoption is God's act, accepting the regenerate person as his own child. In it the Holy Spirit imparts the filial consciousness whereby we cry, " Abba, Father." Our sonship thus is a relation of nature, since we have been born again, and also a relation constituted by divine appointment, since it is God's gracious act.

Preliminary Study of Christian Experience

The consciousness of our sonship and God's Fatherhood is the climax of the Christian consciousness. In it is folded every possibility of moral transformation for the individual and for society. In this filial consciousness indeed all experience and all life are transfigured for the Christian and all lower experiences are fulfilled in their higher forms. We know obedience in lower forms, but filial obedience is our supreme emancipation. We know sin in our social relations, but the sense of sin against the heavenly Father becomes the most poignant of all griefs and sorrows. We know shame in our human relations; but in this relation shame becomes self-abasement, by the side of which all other shame seems mild. We have known hope, even religious hope, based on reasoned doctrines of philosophies, perhaps. But filial hope, based on the experiential knowledge of God the Father is the climax and glorification of all hope. Love we have personally known, but this filial affection is even for us on the human side a " love divine, all other loves excelling." Our filial consciousness thus becomes the dominant consciousness of all life, and the transforming fulfilment of every element of our being.

Conversion is man's outward act which corresponds to the spiritual transaction just described in outline. The inward turning of the will from sin to righteousness has its proper outward expression in daily conduct. What we call Christian experience, therefore, is not merely what is ordinarily known as the conversion experience. The conversion experience is the initial stage in a lifelong process. Moreover, it concentrates in itself all the elements which operate afterward. It is the Christian life in germ. But we must avoid thinking of Christian experience merely in terms of the conversion experience, which is but a fragment of the whole.

The preceding analysis of Christian experience has been purposely made very brief. It constitutes the groundwork of the doctrinal system which follows in this treatise. It is also vital to the discussion of the question before us at present, viz., How may we know God?

There are certain characteristics of the Christian experience

[53]

which must be considered as a means of showing how it yields a knowledge of God, and prepares the way for a general conclusion on the subject.

III. The Synthetic Unity of Christian Experience

The first characteristic to be noted is the unitary nature of the experience. By this is meant the inner connectedness, the mutual dependence, and the moral and spiritual completeness of the elements of Christian experience.

It is obvious at once, in the light of Christian experience, that the divine and the human personalities are alike in their moral and spiritual endowments and capacities. Since God made man in his own image, he may communicate a knowledge of himself to man; and since man bears the divine image, he has capacity for God.

Out of this human capacity for God arises the possibility of the new birth. In regeneration God imparts his own nature to man, renews in him the image which has been marred by sin.

Out of man's capacity for God arises also the necessity for a free moral choice on man's part in order to restoration of the divine and gracious activity within. It is clear that forgiveness could not be bestowed upon the impenitent by God. Forgiveness pronounced upon the unforgiving would be lacking in all that is essential in forgiveness. It would be an arbitrary declaration merely, not a vital fact of the spiritual life. Hence repentance becomes an absolute essential in the moral and spiritual transaction between God and man.

The necessity for justification appears in the same connection. The forgiven man craves to know his permanent status before God. Justification is God's answer to his awakened conscience. He is repeatedly forgiven, but he remains justified. Christian justification is thus not a legal element retained in a spiritual religion. It is a divine act which abolishes the legal motive in obedience, and prepares the way thus for the operation of the filial motive. Just as regeneration imparts the new nature out of which the filial life arises, so justification constitutes a new status wherein the filial motive has free play.

From the above it is seen that while the analysis of Christian experience into its separate elements is necessary and valuable, it is equally essential that we keep in mind the synthetic unity of those elements. Most of the objections to the Christian doctrines arise from the abstract method of handling the material. An example or two will make this point clear. It is argued that the atoning work of Christ, if a real satisfaction for our sins, logically releases us from the obligation to righteousness. "Let us sin that grace may abound." But enlightened Christian experience never falls into an error so superficial. It knows that the grace which wrought through the atoning work of Christ, wrought also within the soul the deepest impulse to righteousness. It sees clearly that it is only by attempting to separate these inseparable things that the false conclusion is reached. Only an abstract method, a false logic, which attempts to separate the parts of an experience which is one and indivisible, can result in such an error.

In like manner repentance may be mistaken for mere reformation, and faith for blind belief, when taken apart from their place in the organic unity of Christian experience. Repentance is "toward God." It is an element in a personal transaction which awakens the will and emotions. The whole nature is stirred to the depths in this personal return to God in obedience. So faith is vital union with God through Christ, and not the acceptance merely of propositions about God or Christ.

Again, it is objected that justification gives a fictitious or *fiat* righteousness. But vital Christian experience knows that the end and result of justification is not the establishment but the abolition of a fictitious legal righteousness, and the foundation for the most vital filial love and obedience. Justification does not establish a legal relation between God and man, but rather abolishes the legal relation. In each of these cases, and in many others, the objector takes some element of Christian experience out of its connection in the living whole and arrives at some unwarranted result. We can only understand the parts of Christian experience in the light of the whole. One of the conclusions which already thrusts itself upon us from the preceding is that in Christian experience we are dealing with a distinct order of facts, a system of moral and spiritual forces, whose laws may be traced and systematically set forth. But we are also warned against the danger of a purely analytic and abstract method of dealing with facts and forces whose true meaning can be found only in the life processes in which they operate. Doctrine must keep in vital touch with religious experience. But religious experience inevitably yields itself to doctrinal expression if it be of a high order. In Christian experience we deal with a group of spiritual causes which produce their proper effects in human consciousness and in man's moral and spiritual activities. To interpret this system of spiritual causes and effects is to set forth the doctrines of the Christian religion. But here again we remind ourselves that the objective facts of God's historic revelation in Christ, and the record of those facts in the New Testament under the guidance of God's Spirit, constitute the basis of all we know of God in experience.

IV. Psychological Aspects of Christian Experience

It is not necessary that we enter minutely into the details of the psychology of Christian experience. These will appear in many forms in the course of the doctrinal discussions which follow. Here it is only necessary to indicate a few of the more general and fundamental facts of psychology which are related directly to Christian experience.

A fundamental conception of psychology is that of the " self " and its development. The infant does not distinguish itself from its surroundings. Sensation gradually instils this truth. When the babe burns its finger in the flame of the candle, it may be an epochal event in the development of its self-consciousness. The gradual process results in the distinction between the self and the world, the " me " and the " not me."

Preliminary Study of Christian Experience

The self as acted upon by the world is discriminated further into the material me, the social me, and the spiritual me. The material me has as its center the body. Its chief interests are the things which affect the body. The social me is the self as it is affected by other persons. The spiritual me is the self in its higher interests as distinguished from the lower.

The development of the self is attended by internal struggle and conflict in many forms. The various selves clash with each other. In order to win social preferment the material self must be sacrificed. And sometimes the good opinion of our fellows must be surrendered for a higher good. It is here that the study of the natural consciousness leads to the discovery of the deep religious implications which are involved in its activities.

We note one path by which the natural consciousness awakens religious expectations. In the efforts of the social and spiritual self we seek the approval of those about us. We idealize our own social self and also the companion or friend whose approval we seek. Ultimately the ideal judge of our conduct takes, in our thinking, the form of God. The desire for God is awakened in our social nature in the highest ranges of its desires. We fear the condemnation and desire the approval of the Supreme Judge. Says Professor James: [1] "This judge is God, the absolute mind, the 'Great Companion.' We hear in these days of scientific enlightenment a great deal of discussion about the efficacy of prayer, and many reasons are given us why we should not pray, whilst others are given us why we should. But in all this very little is said of the reason why we *do* pray, which is simply that we cannot help praying. It seems probable that in spite of all that 'science' may do to the contrary, men will continue to pray to the end of time, unless their mental natures change in a manner which nothing we know should lead us to expect. The impulse to pray is a necessary consequence of the fact that whilst the innermost of the empirical selves of a man is a Self of the *social* sort, it can yet find its only adequate *socius* in an ideal world."

It would seem, then, that in the unfolding of the natural con-

[1] "Psychology," p. 192.

sciousness there are four stages which may be clearly distinguished: (1) The conception of the self; (2) the conception of the world; (3) the conception of other selves; (4) the conception of the highest self, God.

Now the analysis of Christian experience which has preceded shows how this outreaching and upward striving of the natural religious consciousness is met and answered in the gospel of Christ. The sense of sin and dependence which arises in the struggle takes a new form and finds a new satisfaction in Christian experience. So also the Supreme Judge and Great Companion discloses himself to us, not as an idea merely for the reason to grasp, but as a Reality which we experience in our inmost being.

This leads to the statement that Christian experience arises as the result of the response of our entire nature to the gospel call. Christian experience is primarily an adjustment of personal relations between God and man. The disturbed relationship is chiefly in the moral realm. The disturbing factor is sin. The restoration of man is fundamentally a moral and spiritual restoration. But this necessarily involves the will, the feelings, and the intellect. It involves the will, because the submission of the human to the divine will is of the essence of the readjustment of relations. It involves the emotions, because a transaction which is so far-reaching and profound inevitably stirs men to their depths. It involves the reason, because there is an irrepressible desire to define and understand a process so revolutionary in its outcome.

The question has been raised whether or not God works the religious change in man through operations in the region of the subconscious mind. There are strong considerations in favor of the view. Among them are the mysteriousness and sometimes the suddenness of the change. The process is one which the subject himself cannot always fully trace. It must be admitted, indeed, that there is an inexplicable element in regeneration. " The wind bloweth where it listeth, and thou hearest the sound thereof, but knowest not whence it cometh, and whither it goeth. So is every one that is born of the Spirit " (John 3 : 8). In all probability the Spirit acts upon us in ways unknown to us in the subconscious region of our spirits.

On the other hand, however, the essential facts of regeneration and conversion present themselves in the center of consciousness. There is reciprocal action between God and man. This reciprocity and mutuality are necessary to the completeness of the divine operation. The response of our wills, the conscious acceptance of Christ as Saviour and Lord, are the human response to the divine approach without which the moral change could not take place. If the operations of God were confined to the subconscious region, it would resemble the action of a physical force. It would be without the essential marks of free moral action. The subject of God's regenerating activity may not, at the time, fully grasp or define the significance of the moral change. The analyzing activity of the intellect will come into play afterward upon the facts, but notwithstanding this, the change itself will be effected within the framework of consciousness.

The study of the psychology of religion reveals many varieties of Christian experience. Thus types of conversion are distinguished, in which particular phases of the soul's reactions come into prominence. There are emotional conversions, in which the feelings predominate; intellectual conversions, in which the reason plays a leading rôle. In others the will and a new course of action stand out most distinctly. There are child conversions, and those of adults, with varying manifestations. There are some which result from a gradual and slow educational process. In others the crisis arises suddenly and the decision follows quickly. In some, again, the transition is only known in its after effects. The subject is not conscious of it at the time. In recent years much emphasis has been given to the value of the period of adolescence for the conversion of boys and girls.

In reference to these types of experience several statements may be made. The first is that they simply recognize the varying types of human personality. He would be a very poor physician of souls who tried to force all varieties of human religious

[59]

experience in the same mold. Experiences will vary so long as people vary. Spiritual diagnosis requires skill in reading symptoms and breadth in interpreting them and in prescribing.

Again, the gospel is adapted to every type of man and woman. It appeals to no particular cast of mind, no particular temperament or nationality. Its aim is to readjust the most fundamental relations of all types and temperaments, the relationship between the soul and God.

We must add, however, that with all the types and varieties in Christian experience, there are certain universal and indispensable elements. One is the turning away from self and sin. Another is trust in God for forgiveness. Another is the direct action of God's grace in the soul, creating it anew in Christ. Becoming a Christian is more than the evolution of the natural man. It is a rising to a new moral and spiritual level through God's grace. Adolescence is no doubt an important period for parents and teachers and spiritual leaders to recognize. But in itself it has no religious significance. It may, under evil influences, mark a decline in the soul's life. It is a great opportunity for good or evil.

V. The Natural and the Regenerate Consciousness

It is important to discriminate carefully between the natural and the regenerate consciousness. Converted men who have an intelligent grasp of the nature of the change which has taken place in them, are immovably confident of the divine factors in conversion. Unconverted men are often equally immovable in their rejection of the Christian explanation. The Scriptures explain this controversy very simply. It is the conflict between the natural and the regenerate consciousness. "The natural man receiveth not the things of the Spirit of God" (1 Cor. 2 : 14). "But he that is spiritual judgeth all things" (1 Cor. 2 : 15).

It is too much to expect that any exposition of the relations between the natural and regenerate consciousness will prove fully satisfactory to unconverted men. But something may be done to make clear the reasons for the inevitable failure of the natural man to appreciate the regenerative character of Christian experience.

The Christian passes from the experience of the natural to that of the regenerate state. Looking back upon the spiritual change in himself, he gives an account of it which meets fully the requirements of the situation. The account contains the following elements:

1. The struggle and failure of the natural self. Any ordinary psychology presents the facts. They have been indicated in a preceding section of this work. A study of religious phenomena in any department of comparative religion confirms the conclusions of ordinary psychology. In brief, it is the natural self striving for self-realization and being defeated. The material self, the social self, and the spiritual self bound together in the unity of a personal life, are yet unable to find harmonious adjustment. The moral, intellectual, and emotional ideals come short of realization.

2. The gospel call to repentance and faith. Christ is presented to the soul. A new sense of sin is awakened through the power of the Holy Spirit within. At length the will is surrendered to God in Christ.

3. The incoming of a new power from without into the heart and life. It is known to be a new spiritual power from without because it is preceded by a sense of helplessness and dependence. The consciousness of moral and spiritual weakness is an essential element of the experience itself. Schleiermacher did not give an adequate account of religion when he defined it as the feeling of absolute dependence. But he sounded therein a true note. The Christian redemption is in explicit terms redemption from a state of moral need and helplessness. It is the combination cf this consciousness of need, with the consciousness of moral re-enforcement and power that imparts immovable conviction to the regenerate man. The regenerate moral and spiritual consciousness thus transcends the natural moral and spiritual consciousness in a form which makes doubt as to the reality of the transforming power impossible. The regenerate consciousness thus confirms the verdict of the natural in its struggle and failure. The

struggle of the natural self for self-realization finds the solution of the problem and the end of the struggle in the discovery of the true self in the regenerate life. There appears thus to be not an unintelligible relation or inexplicable breach between the natural and regenerate consciousness, but rather a close and intimate connection.

4. Three new elements in the regenerate consciousness may be noted. Human personality contains at least three essential elements—will, intellect, and emotions. We may therefore contrast: *a*. the natural and regenerate will-consciousness; *b*. the natural and regenerate intellectual consciousness; *c*. the natural and regenerate emotional consciousness.

a. The natural and regenerate will-consciousness. Freedom of the will, broadly defined, is self-determination. The power of contrary choice is one form of the manifestation of this self-determining power. But it is not the highest or truest freedom of the will if a man is self-determined wholly or predominantly to evil. In being so determined he misses the end and goal of his being. True freedom is self-determination to the morally and spiritually good.

Now the natural will-consciousness is a consciousness of failure in the region of the will. The highest moral goal always remains remote, unattained. The regenerate will, on the contrary, is armed with an entirely new power for moral achievement, and while the final victory is deferred, there is the inward assurance of a renewal which guarantees a successful outcome. The natural will first finds itself in the regenerate life.

b. The natural and regenerate intellectual consciousness. The highest knowledge is the knowledge of God. The natural consciousness often arrives at the idea of God either by deductions from natural phenomena, or the idea of God which is regarded as necessary to human thought. But at best the result of the efforts of the natural consciousness is a bare theism. Whether grounded in deductions from nature or from human personality, it remains an objective theoretical conception.

In the regenerate consciousness, on the other hand, the idea or conception of God gives place to the fact and reality of God in a living experience. God now gives himself to us. He is a datum, a fact of life, not to be explained away, but to be reckoned with. The intellectual search for God now gives place to the discovery of God and immediate knowledge of him. Thus in Christian experience the highest form of knowledge is attained, and man realizes in the highest degree the intellectual ideal toward which he had been struggling.

c. The natural and regenerate emotional consciousness. In the natural state man seeks to realize an emotional ideal. He desires inward peace and blessedness and a well-grounded hope. He seeks also an ideal of love in motive and object. But here again in his natural striving he fails of complete attainment. He works out, intellectually perhaps, certain grounds on which he bases the expectation of peace and blessedness in the future. He may attain to a conception of a reasoned immortality. So also he may cherish an intellectual ideal of love. But in the midst of all he fails to attain to fellowship with the Great Companion, the Divine Friend, the Supreme Judge of life and conduct. But in the Christian redemption through Christ, the inward peace and blessedness and the ideal of love become living realities. Man comes to a state of rest in his emotional life. The springs of tranquillity are opened within his spirit. He rests in God. Out of his fellowship with God there arises a new moral impulse to love which makes the regenerate man the servant of his fellow men.

VI. THE TRANSITION FROM THE NATURAL TO THE REGENERATE STATE

The transition from the natural to the regenerate state is to be noted in the next place. We have been contrasting the natural and regenerate consciousness. How is the transition from the one to the other made? In the analysis of Christian experience it appeared that conviction for sin, repentance, and faith are the terms descriptive of the human conditions of the transition. In

other words, it is the renunciation of the natural self in order
to the realization of the true self. But it is the renunciation of
the natural self only as sinful and in abnormal relations with
God. Jesus Christ has become at once the sin-bearer and the
moral goal for men. All that is potential in the natural man is
released, and he is put in the way of complete self-realization
by faith in Christ. This is what Jesus means by the saying:
" He that findeth his life shall lose it; and he that loseth his life
for my sake shall find it " (Matt. 10 : 39).

It must be kept in mind that the transition from the natural
to the regenerate state is not by means of forces resident in
the natural man, and by an evolution of those forces. The change
is of the nature of a new spiritual creation by divine power.
This is not to say that it is always cataclysmic and sudden. It
often comes gradually and quietly. The chief point is the entrance
into the consciousness of new divine spiritual power.

There arises thus a new regenerate personality. The regenerate
consciousness is that of a new moral and spiritual personal life
with very definite and clear connection with the preceding natural
life. Paul expresses it thus: " I have been crucified with Christ;
and it is no longer I that live, but Christ liveth in me " (Gal. 2 :
20). The new " I " in Paul bore a very definite and conscious
relation to the old " I." The transition from the one to the
other was through a new relation to Jesus Christ. Paul had
ceased to be a separate and isolated individual and had risen to
the estate of a moral and spiritual person. His personality was
incomplete apart from fellowship with God, and he entered into
that fellowship through faith in Christ, the Revealer of God.

VII. OBJECTIONS CONSIDERED

The preceding description of the natural in its relation to the
regenerate consciousness will aid us in understanding certain objections.

1. First, there is an intellectual objection. The natural reason
approaches the facts of the spiritual life and concludes that the

explanations of the regenerate life of the Christian are wholly irrational. Nothing is easier than to show the logical fallacy and inconsistency of the Christian explanations on the assumptions of the natural consciousness. The difference, however, is not a difference between the natural and regenerate reason as reason. The reasoning processes are unchanged by conversion. It is a difference of data on which the reasoning powers are exerted. The contents of consciousness are radically different in the two cases. The Christian makes no claim to superior reason. But he knows he is in possession of new moral and spiritual realities. His nature is sustained by new forces. Hence he is inevitably led to conclusions which the natural man fails to appreciate.

It follows from the preceding that practically all the objections of the natural man to the Christian account of religious experience are due to an effort to reduce the factors of that experience to the natural plane. There are no resources in the natural life to produce the Christian results. The prime condition for understanding the regenerate life is to know the forces which operate in it.

2. There are also moral objections. The unconverted man opposes the Christian requirement of renunciation, of humility, of faith, and repentance. He denies that he has any such sense of helplessness and sin as has been described. On the other hand, he feels a deep antagonism to the moral and spiritual conditions involved in Christian experience.

Now to the Christian man there is nothing strange in this. He has passed through this phase of experience also. Indeed, it is his previous sense of self-sufficiency, and his previous antagonism to the condition of Christian experience which constitute an essential element in his present certainty. Because he has transcended that earlier stage of the natural consciousness he has come into the fulness and freedom of self-realization in the divine life. In the light of the present fulness and freedom and power of his personal spiritual life he knows how fragmentary and inadequate was that earlier stage. The regenerate man has thus converted into an element of certainty the precise elements

E

[65]

in the natural state which led him at first to reject the Christian call.

Thus it appears that the three elements which hindered the natural man at first become elements of the knowledge and certainty which come with Christian experience. The sense of weakness and dependence, the doubts of the Christian explanation, and the antagonism to the Christian moral conditions, all become elements of the certainty which ensues upon conversion. All of them are transcended and overcome in the new spiritual life. They have all been eliminated as disturbing factors of the mind and heart and gathered up into the new victorious life as the background of a new certainty in Christ.

The controversy thus resolves itself into a question of how we may know the divine life, whether by submission, docility, humility, and self-renunciation, or otherwise. For the Christian there is the sense of the fulfilment of all the ideals and longings of his being in the experience he has of God in Christ. He has passed out of death into life. He has been created anew in Christ Jesus unto good works. He has found himself in a manner so complete and satisfying that to doubt the forces which operate in him would be to doubt himself.

The attitude of the regenerate man to the natural man, then, is not one of vaunted superiority in intellectual power. It is simply the claim that the natural man may attain to moral heights, may find an intellectual and spiritual satisfaction, may come to a self-realization, by compliance with the Christian requirements, which he cannot attain otherwise. This is at once a higher view of the capacity and possibilities of the natural man than he himself admits. The prime condition of this self-realization is the self-renouncing humility of spirit which is analogous to that which the scientific man practises in his efforts to discover the secrets of nature. Here of course it is not nature, but the revelation of God in Christ to which the approach is made, and from which the response comes. Ultimately, therefore, the issue is over the question of how we may know God. The Christian answer is that to know him we must be converted and become as a little child. (Matt. 18 : 3.) We are led thus to our next topic, which is the knowledge of God which arises through experience and the Christian certainty which attends it.

VIII. How Knowledge Arises in Christian Experience

We call to mind here the necessary presupposition of all knowledge. It is that we live in a coherent universe. If there are truths, they must correspond to facts and realities. The truths are parallel to the facts. A coherent system of truths arises out of a coherent system of facts. And of course this implies that we are so constituted that our mental nature corresponds to the world about us and above us. Our intellect must be congruous with the objects we know, else there could be no knowledge. All this is true in the sphere of religion, as in other spheres.

The knowledge which comes to us through Christian experience arises out of the realities which are given to us in experience. Our knowledge is not merely " information about " these realities, but " acquaintance with " them. They are given to us. And yet our own minds are not in a merely passive state. The mind itself is active. Indeed the whole of man's spiritual nature is aroused in the redeeming grace of God in Christ. The Christian is rationalistic in his conception of knowledge because the reason comes into play. He is emotionalistic because his feelings enter into the transaction. He is moralistic and voluntaristic because his conscience and will are involved. Above all, he is personalistic in his conception of knowledge because what he knows is the result of the reaction of his total nature upon God as revealed in Christ. It is the result of the interaction of persons.

The elementary Christian experience becomes definite knowledge by the same kind of processes which operate when other forms of experience are converted into formal knowledge. The infant mind slowly organizes the data of the earliest experience into a coherent world. By discrimination various objects are singled out from the mass. The pieces of furniture in the house, the parts of the house, objects in the surrounding region, are distinguished from each other, and slowly the mind builds up its universe. So also in the inner world of Christian experience. By means of discrimination and association, by means of intuition, and memory, and inference, and all the resources of the soul for dealing with the spiritual realities of religion, the Christian builds up the knowledge of his spiritual universe. There is an analytic process by which the elements of experience are separated from each other, and a synthetic process by which they are recombined with each other and with new forms of knowledge as these arise in experience. In all these processes the Christian is guided by the Scriptures. The revelation of God in Christ is the foundation which supports him in all his mental and spiritual activities. But the processes of the mind continue just the same.

The Christian doctrinal system thus arises out of the facts of Christian experience. It is not implied, however, that the data of experience are sufficient apart from the New Testament. It is in and through his experience that the Christian acquires a vital relation to the New Testament which enables him to understand it. This point will be discussed in a succeeding section. Here we are chiefly concerned with the knowledge contained in the experience itself.

IX. ELEMENTS OF KNOWLEDGE IN CHRISTIAN EXPERIENCE

The Christian experience yields a number of elements of knowledge which may be set forth as follows:

1. First of all, we know therein a power from without which has begun to act and continues to act within us. It is known as a power not previously in our consciousness. It sought us and found us. It is thus completely discriminated from our previous subjective states.

2. Secondly, it is known to us as a spiritual power. We are familiar with the action of physical forces. We know this power now acting upon us to be entirely different from any form of physical power. We also easily discriminate it from the social forces which operate about us. The new power within possesses

qualities entirely distinct from these. This does not overlook the social influences which usually mediate the redemptive power to us. The gospel is preached to us; Christian lives illustrate it; the power of Christ finds a medium in the church and other Christian agencies. All this is recognized. But the power which we know in redemption is as distinct from that which resides in these media by themselves, as it is from our natural power.

3. In the third place, we know this new power operating within us as redemptive. Through it has come the blessing of forgiveness and justification, and along with these the sense of reconciliation with God and sonship to him. But especially do we know this new power within as recreative of our moral nature. The moral center of gravity of our being has been completely changed. A new spiritual energy has created the soul anew in Christ Jesus. We have been redeemed from the guilt and power of sin.

4. In the fourth place, we know the new power within us as personal. This may be made clear by considering several essential phases of the experience itself. In it our own personality is created anew. There arises a new " I " in contrast with the old " I." There is of course continuity between the old and the new through memory and other elements of consciousness. But in motive and aim, in the direction and purpose of the life, in the moral energy which supports it, in the consciousness of power for moral achievement, there has taken place a complete revolution. Remnants of the old " I " remain, and antagonize the new. But this very contrast and inward struggle between the old and the new, the deadly clash between what we once were and what we now are, is an element in the guaranty to us that regeneration has taken place in us. Thus we come to ourselves in the Christian redemption. We win our own true personality and discover that for which we were naturally constituted, but which we were unable to attain in our natural state.

Now a most clear and distinct element in our regenerate consciousness is the recognition of Another, of a Presence which is dealing personally with us. We become in the highest degree conscious of our own freedom through our interaction with the divine and spiritual Person whom we know in experience. Our own free response to the approach of divine love, and the response of that love to us, belong to the very inward nature of the experience itself. Our fellowship with the regenerating power is a fellowship in personal terms. The sense of sin and reconciliation, the acts of trust and obedience, of prayer and praise, and all other elements in the experience involve personality in the religious object.

That this is true is clear from the effort to express the meaning of the experience in other than personal terms. If it is assumed that the power we know is below the personal level, most of the significance of the Christian experience is lost. If the reality we know, the religious object, be devoid of intelligence, self-consciousness, and will, then we can only conceive of it as an attenuated form of physical force. It is without the attributes of spirit, and all fellowship in personal terms is illusion. Sin and righteousness, faith and hope and love are without meaning. Pantheistic reabsorption in the All is then the only possible outcome of our personal life.

If it be asserted that the religious reality or object is above the personal plane and that it retains the qualities which we recognize as belonging to personality, there is no serious objection. It is but another way of saying that God the infinite is greater than man the finite. The interests of the Christian experience are conserved when we recognize the fact that the attributes of personality necessarily belong to the object worshiped by the Christian.

In what has just been said let it be clearly understood that we are not engaged merely in a process of reasoning by which we deduce the idea of God's personality from some general principle. It is rather a process of observation and explanation. It is a matter of fact beyond all gainsaying, that the regenerate life of the Christian is carried on with the religious object in personal terms. We only assume what is necessary to all truth in all spheres, indeed to the very conception of truth, *viz.*, that the universe is a coherent system, and that the parts of being correspond with each other. The effort to explain the reality known in experience by the Christian, therefore, in impersonal or non-personal terms is sheer arbitrariness, unwarranted by the facts. It is an effort to impose upon facts criteria of explanation wholly apart from the facts themselves. The only interest the Christian has in the matter is that the facts be permitted to speak for themselves.

5. In the fifth place, we know the religious object in our Christion experience as triune. We come thus to the transcendent objects of faith. Our knowledge of them, however, is due to the fact that they are immanent objects of knowledge as well as transcendent. We know them as being within and without consciousness at the same time. We have to do in Christian experience with the infinite, personal God. It was our moral relations with him which gave rise to our earliest religious experience and interest. The gospel came to us, and we found God revealed in Christ. Thus God became an object for our contemplation. As objective to us we found what God is in his relations to man through the revelation in Christ. But we also needed to know what God is as subject. We needed an interior view of God, a union with him in personal fellowship. This blessing we obtained through the operation of the Holy Spirit within us. Thus we know God as Father, Son, and Holy Spirit. It was through the atoning work of the incarnated Christ that we found and experienced the forgiving love of God, and it was through the operation of the Holy Spirit that we became united with God in holy love.

There are objections, of course, which are urged against this Trinitarian interpretation of Christian experience. These we shall take account of when we come to treat the doctrines of Christ's person and the Holy Spirit. Here we are simply analyzing the experience itself. There is no possibility of gainsaying the facts. All the great creeds of Christendom express the consensus of Christians in Trinitarian forms of statement. Sometimes perhaps they overshoot the mark by attempting to express more than the Scriptures or experience may warrant. We are of course not bound to subscribe to this or that particular formulation of the doctrine of the Trinity. But our own Christian experience and the clear teaching of the New Testament require a doctrine of the Trinity. Otherwise faith will remain inarticulate and vague and never acquire the strength necessary for self-defense, or the clearness required for scientific statement.

We add one point in anticipation of the later discussion of the questions connected with the Trinity. It is this: Most objections to the Christian doctrine of the Trinity start from a false premise. They begin with some presupposition as to how the ultimate reality must be constituted, and end by a denial that it can be constituted as the Christian doctrine requires. They indulge in metaphysics of a most radical character, to determine beforehand what God must be in himself. The strength of the Christian reply is that it constructs its Trinitarian doctrine on a fact basis. Metaphysical questions are involved, indeed, but the Christian makes the metaphysics wait on the facts and not the facts on abstract metaphysics.

X. The Christian Knowledge and the Christian Certainty

It is in order next to indicate the nature of the certainty which the Christian knowledge yields. In a sense knowledge is certainty, and certainty is knowledge. But there are varieties of knowledge and degrees of certainty. Hence the importance of defining more precisely the kind of certainty which the Christian experience brings.

1. On the negative side several things are clear. In the first place, the certainty of the Christian is not that of mathematical proof. The exact terms of mathematics do not apply in the realm of free personal action. Nor is the Christian certainty that of mere logical or philosophical inference from objective facts. The mind may acquire a high degree of confidence in a given proposition because it seems in general to accord with the rational demands of his nature. The Christian certainty includes this element beyond a doubt. But it is important to observe that it is far more than this. Nor, again, is it simply the certainty

of a moral ideal. Moral ideals arise out of man's moral constitution and he often holds them as grounded in the nature of the ultimate reality, with profound conviction. Christian certainty includes this element also, but far more. Again, the Christian certainty is not merely the certainty which belongs to religious values. The highest religious values are involved, but in Christian experience they are verified in ways unknown in connection with ordinary religious values. The need and value of religion and its function in human struggle may be recognized apart from the system of forces which operate in Christian experience. " The will to believe " is a universal human right. Life itself vindicates the act of religious belief wherever and whenever it is sincerely exercised. But even belief, when exercised exclusively as an act of the will, is not the same as Christian trust. A value therefore apart from the religious object does not answer the needs of religion.

2. We note next positively that the Christian certainty is a certainty of facts of consciousness. That which we know most indubitably are the facts of inner experience. Descartes began his philosophic reasonings with the fundamental statement, universally valid, *Cogito, ergo sum,* " I think, therefore I am." The fact of thought is a primary or first truth. In the realm of Christian experience the same principle applies. There is of course the biblical revelation which is vital and fundamental, as we shall soon show. Meantime it is important to recognize that Christian certainty has a fact basis in life itself.

We spoke of the insufficiency of mere ideals as the measure of the Christian certainty. We now remark that it is the presence of a power in the Christian, enabling him to realize gradually and progressively the meaning of those ideals. " All things are possible to him that believeth " (Mark 9 : 23). It is then a new causal agency at work in the Christian which imparts the certainty. He is conscious of a new meaning in the old ideals. They have been created anew in Christ. But he is also conscious of power to realize them as he never could have done before. The form of the causal power working in the Christian is clearly distinguished by him from physical causation. The cause he knows in experience is personal and spiritual. It involves a great and universal principle of life as we know it on the human plane, the principle of free causation.

3. The question of degrees of certainty may arise at this point. We know the immanent objects of our religious life. But do we know the transcendent objects? We are conscious of inward peace, forgiveness, and moral renewal. But are we certain in an equal degree that Jesus Christ as the Revealer of God and the Holy Spirit as the Regenerator are the objective causes at work in us? The full answer to this question we defer to a later section of the discussion. This much may be said now: The Christian knows beyond a peradventure that the change in him was in terms of Christ and the Holy Spirit. He called to Christ, and Christ answered, and the Holy Spirit renewed him in the image of Christ. His spiritual nature in all its parts now answers to the moral likeness of Christ, not perfectly of course, but in principle. If then the Christian knows that a new power from without has entered his spiritual life, creating him anew and readjusting his relations to God; and if that readjustment was consciously a readjustment through Jesus Christ and the inworking Spirit of God; and if the result is the restoration in him of the image of God and the fulfilment in the Christian of the inmost and deepest demands of his nature, there cannot be for him a question of the causal agency of Christ and the Holy Spirit. Having attained to self-realization in the deepest impulses and ideals of his nature through a deliberate and free act of choice and trust, he can no more doubt the efficient causes which have recreated him in his moral and spiritual nature, than he can doubt his own personality. In short, his certainty is part and parcel of the organic unity of a system of spiritual causes and effects which are indissolubly bound together. The effects and the causes are so bound together that neither can be understood without the other. In accordance with the fundamental principles of all knowledge, the Christian simply recognizes the link of connection between the causes and the effects. This is not to assert

that the connection is equally clear to all regenerate men. Experience can only become clear and articulate by means of conscious thought and definition. But when thought becomes active with the evangelical Christian experience, it inevitably leads to the result we have indicated.

XI. OBJECTIONS TO THE CHRISTIAN CERTAINTY

We note next a few objections to the Christian knowledge and certainty arising therefrom.

1. First, it is objected that it is not a form of certainty which compels assent. In reply we say that compulsion is out of consideration in the religious and moral sphere. The idea of an assent-compelling certainty implies a wholly indifferent or hostile attitude of mind on the part of the man whose assent is sought. Such a mental attitude can never result in religious certainty, since the religious life is a joint activity of God and man. Free moral activity on man's part, that is to say, a free moral choice, is of the very essence of religion in the Christian sense.

Again, assent-compelling demonstration is usually of the mathematical kind. Christian certainty would lose all its distinctive and high qualities if it could produce certainty of the mathematical order. It is a general law that the higher you rise in the scale of being, from the mechanical to the biological, and from the biological to the personal and moral, the less able you are to state your knowledge in exact mathematical formulæ. Such statements would destroy the moral and spiritual qualities of being and level them with the mathematical. Suppose, for example, it were possible to express what we call freedom as we express the law of rotation of a planet on its axis as so many miles per second; or suppose we could express what we think of as God's action upon us, as an exact formula like the law of gravitation. At once the idea of freedom and the idea of God would lose every element which makes them valuable and attractive to us. Indeed, the ideas of God and freedom would thus be destroyed. We do not want mathematical certainty in religion. It would destroy it as religion. It is not deficiency of truth and reality in man's religious relations to God which forbids their expression in mathematical terms. It is rather the abounding fulness of truth and reality in them which forbids such expression.

2. A second objection is that the standard of knowledge and certainty contained in the Christian experience is narrow. The objection is based on a misunderstanding of the nature of Christian experience. In reality that experience involves the highest moral and spiritual conception of God the world has ever known. That conception includes all the valid lower and partial conceptions of God. The experience involves also every phase of religious fellowship between man and God. It is distinguished in fact by its comprehensiveness rather than by its exclusiveness. It is an error to confine Christian experience to this or that particular type of emotional experience. Psychologists of religion, as we have seen, analyze the conversion experience and the life which follows into various types. In some the emotional elements prevail; in others, the ethical or practical; in yet others, the intellectual. In some instances there is an overwhelming sense of sin and guilt. In others there is the quiet act of obedience which inaugurates the new life in Christ. In some there is the joyous realization of God's fatherhood which dominates the experience. Sometimes the religious change is cataclysmic and sudden. At other times it is quiet, the result of gradual processes of education in the truths of the gospel. No variation of the experience due to individual temperament, to previous training, to environment and social influences, is excluded. All the varying types of experience thus find their place in the comprehensive Christian experience. The essential facts are: a. The revelation of God in Christ; b. the abnormal and sinful state of the natural man in his relations to God; c. the action of the Holy Spirit in regenerating the heart and creating normal relations between man and God. There is no possible form of genuine religious experience which may not be included in the true Christian experience. This will appear more clearly when we speak of the relation of Christian experience to the psychology of religion.

3. Another objection is that the criterion or standard of truth we urge is subjective. The reply here also is that the objector has not grasped the full truth of the matter. The norm or standard of truth involved in Christian experience is by no means, merely subjective. It is first of all grounded in the revelation of God in Christ. The Bible brings us the knowledge of that revelation. The Christian truth then is first objective and historical. Then it is subjective and experiential. We recognize and assert strongly that a merely subjective faith is unstable, uncertain, and unsatisfactory. The history of human thought about religion proves this.

Now the strength of the Christian position is that it provides for both the objective and subjective elements of religion. Some modern men object vigorously to external authorities of all kinds. They are exceedingly narrow and provincial in their outlook in taking up this position. But on another side of their view they are correct. They insist that truth must be assimilated by us, if it is to be effective for us. The criticism of the Christian position has run at one time thus: Your historical biblical revelation is not to be considered because you seek to impose it as an external authority. At another time the criticism has run thus: Your evangelical experience is not to be taken seriously because it is merely subjective.

To this we reply, first, that these objections contradict each other. One objector insists that objective standards and authorities do not suffice. The truth must be inwardly assimilated. The soul must say Amen to it. To this the Christian agrees. The other objector insists upon objective reality, something outside of experience to which it must conform. To this also the Christian agrees. But the Christian here has a great advantage. The objectors do not agree with each other. Their theories of truth clash. The Christian combines the two principles. He recognizes the relative truth in each of them. But he also insists that either of them by itself is a half-truth. It is in the combination of the two that the two hemispheres become the rounded sphere of truth. In experience we know truth is inward and vital. We assimilate it. But in Christ and the New Testament we know it as objective. Truth is a great world outside the soul. The soul enters it and finds the meaning of that world. In this respect the Christian religion is like physical science. We know because we enter in and discover and report our discoveries. These discoveries are open to all who will enter.

We shall soon discuss the objective revelation in Christ. It is the causal agency at work in the world which has produced the social and religious revolution which we describe as Christian. Meantime the purpose is to show that the Christian experience as subjective imparts a reality and a power to the Christian religion in the convictions of men which nothing can destroy. The experience of salvation through Christ is indeed just that inner assimilation of the truth which is so insisted upon by objectors to authority. It is the truth becoming real and vital for the individual, not merely truth imposed upon or prescribed to him, and yet it is first of all objective truth in the divine revelation in Christ and recorded in the New Testament.

The criticism of Christian experience as subjective takes another form which needs to be briefly noticed. Some apparent conversions turn out to be no conversions at all. Hence a theory is framed to the effect that all so-called conversions are due to emotional excitement and superficial psychic experiences. The reply is that the New Testament long ago discriminated between these counterfeit conversions and the genuine. In the parable of the Sower and in various passages in the Gospels and Epistles we have clear recognition of this type of so-called conversion by way of contrast with the genuine. (See Matt. 13 : 9-23; John 6 : 66; 2 Peter 2 : 22.) The marks of the regenerate life are wanting in them. The moral transformation, the stability and progress, required by and found in the genuine conversions, are not present in the lives of those who have known simply an emotional change.

4. A fourth objection is that the knowledge of God derived from Christian experience rests on an anthropomorphic basis. It is the same objection, applied in a different way, which has

long been urged against the arguments for God's existence. The chief point in it is that man conceives of God as a magnified image of himself. Man has will, intelligence, purpose, personality. He projects these into the universe about him, and imagines he has found God.

The reply may begin by assuming for the moment that the ultimate reality is a power merely which we know as a regenerating power in experience. But as soon as we analyze the contents of the experience we find that every element in it requires personality in the object. The experience itself knows no impersonal object. If that reality speaks to us at all, it must speak in personal terms and relations. The Christian then interprets the ultimate reality as personal because he knows it only as personal. He does not therefore merely project his own personality into the universe about him. He explores the universe rather, and finds personality. The outcome thus agrees with the assumption of all knowledge, *viz.*, that the world without is congruous with the world within, that the universe is congruous with human reason.

Religion and physical science proceed upon exactly the same principle here. The scientist finds within himself a craving for truth, and seeks the truth in nature. The laws of nature are discovered and formulated. These are the guaranty to him that nature is rational as he is rational. In the work of an orchestra, the hearers must be in tune with the players else the instruments make mere noises rather than grand harmonies. Intelligence speaks to intelligence. So science finds reason in every part of nature in response to the craving for truth.

Now religion carries out this principle more fully. Man finds in himself a craving for will since he needs a power greater than himself; he finds in himself a craving for love and righteousness beyond any that he possesses. He also craves to know ultimate truth. Then by enlisting his will, his intellect, his emotions, his moral nature, he finds all of these in response to his craving. The personal God comes to him and speaks to him, and a life of fellowship with God follows.

The Christian Religion in Its Doctrinal Expression

It is clear from the preceding that the religious knowledge of God is not one whit more anthropomorphic than the scientific knowledge of nature. In each realm there is a congruity between man's nature and the realities around him in the physical and spiritual universe. Science in its craving for truth evokes a response of nature. Art in its craving for beauty evokes a like response. The moral faculty in us, in its craving for the good, calls forth a response in terms of good. Religion, in its craving for God and redemption, evokes its appropriate response. God answers. In the religious experience of the Christian all the powers of the soul come into action, and man finds the universe answering to him in all his cravings. These are summed up in the supreme revelation of God in Christ.

5. A fifth objection is that it is unfair for Christians to impose upon non-Christians a form of proof which is personal and subjective instead of one that is universal and demonstrative. The Christian reply is that the proof is open to any and all who will submit to the conditions; that humility and faith and obedience are organs of knowledge as truly as the discursive reason; that the evidence is such that it can easily become universal since it is within the reach of the humblest intellect as well as the highest; that it is thoroughly convincing to all who are willing to widen the spiritual foundations of knowledge and thus escape from the provincialism of adherence to the rational principle alone.

The Christian replies further that religious certainty is in the nature of the case religiously conditioned. The principle is familiar in many departments of life that certain forms of confidence, certain elements of knowledge, can only be acquired in particular ways. Indeed, this is true in every sphere where knowledge is highly developed. The sailor's confidence of eye and hand are only acquired by the life at sea; the Indian can track a foe by signs invisible to others; the art critic must be trained to artistic insight if he is ever to acquire certainty and authority. The expert scientist alone can conduct successful scientific demonstrations. Mathematical certainty is limited to

[80]

the mathematically skilful. So religious certainty comes only in the religious way. As scientific, and mathematical, and artistic certainty is conditioned by the peculiar requirements of the sphere in which it exists, so religious certainty is religiously conditioned. The charge of unfairness therefore breaks down.

CHAPTER IV

CHRISTIAN AND OTHER FORMS OF KNOWLEDGE

𝕴T has been shown that our knowledge of God in Christian experience is conditioned in a religious way. This is necessarily true since religious knowledge in the strict sense arises only out of the religious life. There are, however, certain questions which require attention at this point, growing out of the conclusions already reached. One is: How is the knowledge derived from Christian experience related to other forms of knowledge? Is there conflict or harmony between them? Can the truths which arise out of Christian experience be unified or correlated with other forms of human knowledge? These questions must now receive attention. It will appear that the knowledge derived from Christian experience is not only not opposed to other forms of human knowledge, but is capable of being interpreted in close and vital correlation with them.

There are several general statements to be made first. They are mainly a summing up of what has been said already in various connections on the preceding pages, as follows: The same general principles of knowledge apply in the sphere of Christian experience as in other spheres of knowledge. Among these are the following: There is a harmony between our knowing powers and the world about us. The truth as to the world about us arises as a result of our reactions upon it rather than as the result of abstract thought. General world-views or theories of reality should be constructed out of the data of experience. There is no essential difference in the application of logic in the religious sphere from its application elsewhere. Thus it follows that whatever differences there are in dealing with the data of religious experience, they arise not from a difference in the principles of knowledge, but from the distinctiveness of the data of religion. The Christian life is a distinct sphere of human experience. Religion is a form of human activity calling for treatment in accordance with its own nature.

It may be objected that the claim of a divine revelation forbids our applying the above general principles of all knowledge to the Christian religion. The objection, however, is not well grounded. It is true that God speaks to us in the Christian revelation, just as nature speaks to us in physical science. The source of our knowledge is objective to us in both spheres. But in both alike our own self-activity is a part of the knowing process. We apprehend, and by slow stages comprehend what is revealed. Revelations become our discoveries. The general principles of knowledge therefore apply in both spheres.

There are several departments of knowledge to be considered more specifically.

I. PHYSICAL SCIENCE

The word science is not very clearly fixed in meaning in modern thought. As a consequence many misunderstandings arise. Physical science deals with the facts of physical nature; the social and moral sciences, with the data of human society in its varied forms; religious science, with the facts of the religious life. In all sciences the aim is to discover and formulate, in a manner as exact as the field of investigation admits, the laws which express the meaning of the forces which operate therein.

a. There are certain points of agreement between the methods of physical science and theological science. In both, facts and only facts are taken into account. In both the realities observed are only partially known. In both systematic explanation is sought.

b. There are also points of contrast. The realities known are not the same. In physical science it is the world of matter; in religion, the world of spirit. The modes of knowing are not the same. In physical science sensation supplies the data; in religion, inward experiences of fellowship with God. The relation of cause and effect is not the same in the two spheres. In physical science continuity, or the transformation of energy, is the form in which the causal relation is set forth. In Christian experience the causal relation is expressed in terms of the interaction of persons. Not physical, but free causation is the form of statement which must be employed in religion. The formulations of the results are not the same. In physical science mathematical laws express the meaning. In the social sciences, and in the sciences connected with religion, general principles, or teachings, or doctrines expressive of personal relations, are alone adequate.

c. The supreme excellence of exact science which states in mathematical formulæ the laws of matter, force, and motion, becomes its chief defect in dealing with the data of the higher spheres. In the realm of the organic and living mathematical statements of law are impossible as in mechanical nature. In the realm of personality, of freedom, and of the spirit the ordinary methods of physical science cannot be employed. It follows from the method of physical science and from the data with which it deals that it is bound to leave the facts of the spiritual world to moral and religious science. The questions as to God, the soul, and immortality do not enter directly into the problems of physical science at all. Its methods do not apply. It can neither prove nor disprove in this sphere. Other standards of judgment and criteria of truth must be employed. It is of fundamental importance that this distinctiveness of sphere and method be recognized. Only thus can we avoid a great variety of false or misleading issues or alleged " contradictions " between science and religion.

The Alleged Disinterestedness of Science

Sometimes science is contrasted with religion by the assertion that it is interested in truth as truth, while religion is always absorbed in a personal interest and need. It is then concluded that science yields results which are more reliable than religion. It is supposed that if interest and need are absent, truth is more easily discovered. Prof. Theodore Haering, in his treatise

on " The Christian Faith," [1] speaking of science and religion in
their search for truth, says that both have " in common an
intense interest in truth in the simple sense of the word. But,"
he continues, " how they differ in their anxiety for the truth!
The purer science is, the nearer it attains to its ideal, the more
entirely does it separate what it seeks to know from the value
that this has for the knowing subject. It sinks itself so completely in the object that it forgets the subject. This is not
to say that the human mind is capable of doing anything value-
less for itself; but the value of knowledge depends upon its
comprehending the object to be known as completely, as exactly,
and as little influenced by any outside consideration as is at all
possible. The religious man, on the other hand, seeks to know
the truth of God, because his own life depends thereon; he has
the greatest conceivable personal interest in the truth of the world
of his faith. He has as little intention of deceiving himself as the
scientific investigator—in this respect truth has precisely the
same significance for both—but he is anxious not to deceive himself regarding the object because of the importance of the object
for the subject, while the man of science is anxious for the sake
of the object, is concerned about its nature, apart altogether from
its importance for the subject."

Now as a broad general statement the above may be justified
as defining the difference between science and religion. But
Professor Haering declares here, and shows in many ways, that
the religious man is as much interested in finding the truth as
the scientific worker.

He overstates the contrast at certain points, and seems to assume a motive in the scientific man more likely to lead to the
truth. His statement needs modifying somewhat. The following statements may be added:

1. It is not correct to assume that the absence of " interest "
is the best condition for finding the truth. Recent discussions
of theories of knowledge show that interest is a necessary condition for its discovery. Our struggle for life in all its forms,

[1] Vol. I, p. 61.

our reactions upon the world in the pursuit of our vital needs, are our chief sources of knowledge. The man of science is not detached from " interest," in a realm of " pure thought." There is no such thing as pure thought, that is, thought detached from feeling and desire. The true scientist is passionately and enthusiastically devoted to the ideal of truth because for him such devotion is the chief value of the life of research. As his passion and enthusiasm wane, he is likely to be a decreasing value for scientific progress. He has a very great personal interest in his life pursuit.

2. Again, the apparent interest of the scientific man in objective truth for its own sake is due to the nature of the material of his investigations. Physical nature is objective to man. His reactions upon it are through the senses. In religion man knows an inward reality, a spiritual presence; this may seem less real, and conclusions about it less reliable than those about matter, force, and motion. It is also true that the religious need and interest is the deepest of all human interests. It enlists the human soul as nothing else enlists it.

3. We may not say then that the scientific man and the religious man differ in that the former cares supremely for truth for its own sake, while the latter is thinking chiefly about himself and is willing to be deceived. The student of nature and the student of religion, if we take both in their highest forms, are fundamentally alike in their passionate devotion to reality and truth. Both alike hate falsehoods and make-believes. Both desire to know all the truth which is discoverable. For both the prime condition of discovery is whole-hearted devotion to the objects of study.

II. The Psychology of Religion

The study of the Christian consciousness in regeneration and conversion is related in important ways to general psychology and the psychology of religion. These may now be considered.

1. Psychology vindicates the spiritual view of man. The

parallelism between brain states and mind states is a common-place truth in all recent psychology. But no evidence has been produced which indicates that mental activity is an instance of the physical conservation of energy. Brain states are not convertible into mind states, nor mind states into brain states. Any general theory of the universe must reckon with this fact. If materialism could demonstrate that mind is a product of matter, of course our whole view would be radically changed. But no such demonstration has been found. The Christian view maintains the spiritual nature of God and man. Nothing in physics or psychology has been discovered to modify this view in any essential particular.

2. The psychology of religion emphasizes the varieties of religious experience. The normal religious experience is that in which all the spiritual elements of our nature combine in due proportion. The intellect, the emotions, the moral nature, and the will enter into all genuine Christian experience. But in some the intellect predominates, in others the feelings, and in others the will. Thus innumerable varieties and types of conversion arise. This should prepare us for making due allowance for variations of experience, and at the same time safeguard us against drawing hasty general conclusions from a narrow range of facts.

There are many abnormal types of religious experience which cannot be considered in detail. They are properly classed under the head of "the pathology of religion." In some cases they are genuine examples of religious experience, marked by certain excesses of extreme tendencies. In others they are due to other than religious causes. Extreme forms of mysticism, of ecstasy, and of vision in which the will and the reason are reduced to the vanishing-point, are instances of the former. These are due to the predominance of feelings over the other elements of the religious nature.

At the other extreme is an overdone intellectual type of religion. In this religion is reduced to the idea of a "value" which man seeks. In its extreme form it denies the objective reality of a personal God corresponding to the "value." In the course of human history as man advances this "value" will be "transvaluated" into some other than a religious value, and religion will disappear. This implies the strangulation or gradual starvation of the religious nature of man. Hence we class this conception with the pathological types of religion. It is entirely abnormal and at variance with all that the science of comparative religion and the psychology of religion teach as to normal religious life.

3. The psychology of religion shows the prevalence of law in the subjective religious life of man. A very few illustrations of this point may be given here. Religion has been connected vitally with what is known in psychology as the subconscious mind. It is declared that the divine influences reach us through the subconscious in our nature. This is undoubtedly true in some sense because religion affects our whole nature. But we have very little knowledge of the modes of the divine action upon us. What we do know includes at least two points: First, that a power outside and apart from ourselves produces the results in us, and secondly, that when the divine power becomes effective for our moral transformation, it acts in our consciousness. Our own choices or acts of will are an essential factor in the regenerate life.

Another instance of the reign of law in religious experience is the connection between religious interest and adolescence in boys and girls. A physical, coupled with an intellectual, change takes place during the period from eleven to fifteen years in girls, and from twelve to seventeen in boys. It is a period fraught with great possibilities of good or evil. A great number of conversions occur during this period. We have already had occasion to speak of adolescence and its significance for the religious life. A truth already expressed may be repeated for emphasis. It is an error to hold that the change is in itself religious. A widening horizon of life, the releasing of latent powers, the rise to a new level of natural experience, are accompanied by a new capacity for moral and religious truth. The wise teacher and pastor will avail themselves of the opportunity this affords. But they will not mistake a physical and mental change for divine renewal. There are also clearly defined differences between juvenile and adult types of conversion. These involve differences in the point of contact and the form of appeal, which will be adapted to the various stages.

4. The psychology of religion suggests the working of a divine energy in conversion. Sometimes the fact of the presence of law and order in religious experience has led men to infer purely natural causes for all the effects produced. But, on the contrary, the presence of orderly and uniform modes of activity is suggestive quite as strongly of a divine agency. God is a God of order, not of confusion.

There are three possible attitudes which the student of religious psychology may take with reference to the presence of a divine factor in religious experience. *a.* First, he may confine his view simply to the " stream of consciousness," without inquiring into causes. If his interest is purely psychological this will usually be his line of approach. He will neither affirm nor deny the divine action in conversion. *b.* Secondly, he may be constrained, even as a psychologist, to recognize a superhuman power in man's religious life without attempting to define it further. An increasing number of the profounder students of the subject have reached this conclusion. Prof. William James, at the conclusion of his notable work, " The Varieties of Religious Experience," admits a miraculous element in conversion. He denies, however, that we are able to define more accurately the nature of the divine power. He calls any conclusion on this point an " overbelief."

c. In the third place, the student of the psychology of religion may frankly and boldly investigate the cause or energy which produces the regenerate life. The Christian psychologist is acquainted with the system of Christian influences and forces. He knows the nature of Christianity as a historic religion. He knows the claims of Jesus Christ. He knows how the moral and spiritual change was produced in himself. To him the Holy Spirit is a definite reality. It is impossible, therefore, even if it were desirable, for him to detach himself from these factors in his knowledge. He is bound to consider causes and effects together.

For the Christian psychologist the presence of the divine Agent in regeneration is indubitable because the change itself could have been effected in no other way. He has become a new creature. He was once a self-centered individual; he is now a God-centered person. He has not only been given power to achieve what he previously sought; he now seeks totally new and higher objects. He has not only found, but has also been found by, the great Reality of the soul's life. He knows the antecedents of his own consciousness, the elements of his own nature, and he knows that these were devoid of regenerating power. Moreover, he knows the biblical explanation of his new life. It is God in Christ acting upon his spirit through the immanent Spirit of God.

All the above accords with the general principles of knowledge. We know objects because our mental constitution belongs to a coherent system of things. Nature is found to be rational in response to the cravings of rational mind. Science is grounded in this correspondence or unity between man and nature. So also the Christian psychologist finds a religious object in response to the cravings of a religious nature. It follows that a denial of the religious object would be fatal in two respects. First, it would undermine all knowledge. This is true because the principles on which we assert the possibility of any knowledge on any subject are practically identical with those of religious knowledge. Secondly, it would undermine all religion. It is vain to talk of religion as merely a subjective play of the imagination, or a useful function merely in the struggle for life. Religion must be seen to rest on solid foundations of fact or else men will have none of it. The love of reality and of truth is too deeply imbedded in our nature to permit us to rest content with any explanation of religion which makes it merely a " psychological " or " functional " activity without a God to whom we may really pray, and with whom we may really have fellowship.

III. The Relation of Christian Experience to Ethics

Christian experience in its beginning, continuance, and end is ethical to the core. Ethics defines the relations of men and their obligations to each other in a social order. Christianity proclaims its goal as the highest of all social orders, the kingdom of God. A divine society wherein God and men are associated in loving fellowship; where the will of God is done by men; where love is the expression of their relations with, and conduct toward, each other; and where God graciously manifests himself in the fulness of his grace to men: this is the New Testament teaching as to the kingdom of God. The ethical ideal attains thus its highest expression.

Now the experience of the Christian in regeneration and conversion, and in the spiritual life which follows, bears a vital relation to ethics at the following points:

1. It incorporates the ethical ideal in the religious experience at the outset. The initial act of the sinner in becoming a Christian is repentance. It is of course repentance toward God. But it is with reference to all wrong conduct toward men. Every form of sin toward our fellow men is rebuked in the gospel call to repentance. Nothing is more impressive in the New Testament than the merciless exposure and condemnation of unethical conduct. Yet this is coupled with God's gracious invitation and offer of pardon. Christianity is a religion in which a readjustment of relations with God involves of necessity a readjustment of relations with men. The Christian redemption is an ethical redemption.

2. Christian experience solves the problem with which theoretical ethics has long struggled. What is the ultimate ground of ethics? Some form of utilitarianism has usually been the answer apart from Christian teaching. The natural reason, seeking to explain the moral ideal, has often asserted that it arose as the result of experience in social relations. Men found that they prospered better when acting under moral sanctions than when not doing so. The modern evolutionary doctrine of development

and survival in the struggle for life has aided in producing the view. Ethics thus came to be regarded simply as a useful provision for aiding man in attaining his objects.

There is of course no need to deny the relative truth or half-truth contained in this view. But it is seen with increasing clearness that some form of belief in God is the necessary ground for any stable form of ethical theory. It is here that Christian experience renders a great service to ethical theory by converting it into reality. The moral ideal is found in Christian experience not only to be an essential part of the experience; but it is also made possible of realization through the direct action of God upon the heart. Thus the moral ideal is bound up indissolubly with religion.

3. Christian experience leads to a new and higher ethical ideal. The deepening and heightening of moral principles in Christ's teachings are their most striking features. Nothing so radical or drastic has ever been expressed elsewhere. The Sermon on the Mount is the outstanding example of this teaching. It has often been pronounced visionary and wholly unattainable by man in his present state. But for the Christian the ethics of Jesus become practicable. This is because the ethical teachings do not stand alone. They are part of a system which includes also regenerating grace. The new " I " of the regenerate man knows himself as a new moral creation. He knows he has not attained the Christian moral ideal. But he knows himself as the subject of the working of a moral energy which has put him in the way of its gradual attainment. The lofty ethical teachings of Jesus do not cause the Christian to despair, because he knows that the demands are accompanied by a power putting him in the way of realizing them.

4. Christian experience reveals a new and effective method in religion and ethics. The central idea in Christianity is the cross, and what it signifies. Self-realization through self-renunciation; dying in order that we may live; being crucified that we may rise to a new life in Christ; losing the life that we may find it: these are some of the ways in which that idea is expressed.

[92]

The modern psychological study of religion has discovered this as the supreme law of the religious life. It is thus expressed by one of the most gifted and discerning of modern students of the psychology of religion, who was not in the technical sense a Christian believer:[2] " The phenomenon is that of new ranges of life succeeding on our most despairing moments. There are resources in us that naturalism with its literal and legal virtues never recks of, possibilities that take our breath away, of another kind of happiness and power, based on giving up our own will and letting something higher work for us, and these seem to show a world wider than either physics or philistine ethics can imagine. Here is a world in which all is well, in *spite* of certain forms of death, indeed *because* of certain forms of death—death of hope, death of struggle, death of responsibility, of fear and worry, competency and desert, death of everything that paganism, naturalism, and legalism pin their faith on—and tie their trust to." Again, the same writer says:[3] " In spite of rationalism's disdain for the particular, the personal, and the unwholesome, the drift of all the evidence we have seems to me to sweep us very strongly toward the belief in some form of superhuman life with which we may, unknown to ourselves, be coconscious."

Thus the modern scientific psychologist expresses the law of the spiritual life so amply and clearly taught by Jesus and Paul. We find ourselves; we cease to be isolated individuals, self-centered, and self-sufficient, and become religious and social persons, vitally united with God and man in a new spiritual life. The ethical consciousness becomes the other side of the religious consciousness, and self-realization becomes simply the task of finding our place and work in the eternal kingdom of God. We thus find that the unregenerate ethical life with its struggles and failures comes to realization and fulfilment in the regenerate life in Christ. It comes to pass, then, that the former unregenerate moral consciousness becomes an important factor in our Christian certainty. This is because of the contrast between the old and the new

[2] William James: " A Pluralistic Universe," pp. 305, 306.
[3] *Ibid.*, p. 309.

moral consciousness. It is also because the new regenerate consciousness of power to overcome sin and gradually attain the moral ideal is the fulfilment of the old struggle on the natural level.

IV. CHRISTIAN EXPERIENCE AND COMPARATIVE RELIGION

In recent times a great deal of study has been bestowed upon the subject of comparative religion. A great mass of data has been accumulated. Sometimes it seems like attempting to find one's way through a pathless jungle, when an effort is made to interpret the data. And yet real progress has been made. The science of comparative religion sheds a real light upon the value of Christianity. The treatment of the subject here can only include certain general conclusions which relate to the topic before us.

Among the results of the scientific study of religion are the following: *a*. Religion is a universal phenomenon of human life. Paul was impressed that the Athenians were very religious. Modern students are impressed with the universal religious tendency of men. Alleged exceptions to the rule usually turn out to be no exceptions at all. *b*. The many forms of religious belief and practice found among the peoples of the earth represent different stages of advancement in religion. *c*. None of the many forms of religion, apart from Christianity, presents us with the ideal or perfect religion. They may be regarded as stages in man's progress toward the perfect religion. Indeed in a real sense they prepare the way for and foretoken the coming of the perfect religion. *d*. They are, therefore, not to be regarded as wholly false, but rather as unfinished and inadequate. They represent man's quest for God while blinded by ignorance and sin. They served a highly important place in man's religious life preparatory to the coming of the perfect religion, somewhat as Judaism prepared the way for Christ. They fail, however, to provide the spiritual and moral redemption which is the chief boon of the Christian religion to needy men. *e*. In the fifth place, Christianity brings to man the realities which answer to the longings and values discovered in the study of comparative religion. The Christian religion brings more than this. It creates new longings, and suggests new values, and along with them supplies the realities needed for their salvation. At present, however, the point of emphasis is that Christianity is the fulfilment and realization of all the permanent values of other religions.

It is not necessary to the argument here to discuss the much disputed point as to the origin of religious belief. The Old Testament represents the primitive religion as monotheistic. Dorner thinks that later forms of lower religion are perversions of this original form, while those who insist on the evolutionary hypothesis claim that the lowest was also the earliest. There are many traces of higher forms of religion as we go back toward the earlier history of some of the leading nations. The object in view at present is to point out the tentative and imperfect character of all other forms of religion, and along with this to show that Christianity gathers up into a higher unity all the valid religious elements contained in them.

We can best accomplish this object by showing how religions take their character from the object of worship. Variations in the conception of God are attended by variations in the conception of man's nature and the nature of worship. Or to state the same truth in another form, we may say that the perfecting of the idea of God is accompanied by a perfecting of the idea of religion. Now looking at the religions of the world as a whole, we may represent the progress of religious ideas under the following general plan:

1. The gods of the various religions tend more and more to become personal. Some scholars question whether or not in certain of the lower animistic forms of religion, the god, or fetish, or object of worship, is regarded by the worshiper as a person. It may simply be looked upon as vital, or living, and as having power without possessing personality. It is beyond all question, however, that at a very early stage the god begins to be regarded as a personal being. Some derive this from ancestor-worship, others from the phenomena of dreams in which it is

thought the soul leaves the body, others from the tendency among men to attribute their own human qualities to objects around them possessing power. In the Western races there appear elaborate polytheistic systems of gods, like those of the Greeks described by Homer and Hesiod. These are in the main simply magnified men, with the infirmities and limitations of other men. Polytheism is grounded in a pantheistic conception of the world. This is an element of great weakness because men are thus prevented from rising to the idea of a God who is transcendent over the world. The polytheistic gods always remain dependent. They never attain to the dignity of the absolute God.

In India there was early a reaction against polytheism. Thoughtful men renounced the many gods and conceived the universe as a vast system of appearances. Instead of many gods, or one God, they assumed a universal substance of which man and nature are passing manifestations. These are destined to be reabsorbed into the universal substance as waves subside and coalesce again with the sea.

In both India and Greece, however, there came reactions against these general views: in Greece, from polytheism to an abstract philosophy and an impersonal universe; in India, from the abstract philosophy back to polytheism. As Dorner says, heathen thought moved in a circle, unable to emancipate itself.

The chief difficulty in these great religious systems was that of properly conceiving God's relations to the world. In the one case he is thought of as a personal being or beings, but always under limitations which are unworthy of the divine. In the other he ceases to be personal and becomes a universal substance, which really reduces him to the level of the physical.

In Judaism a new thought of God arises. God is conceived of as both personal and absolute. He is not confused or confounded with the world, nor is he subordinate to it. He is creator and sustainer of all things. Israel thus escaped the peril of pantheism in both its forms. It escaped polytheism by making Jehovah the only God; and it escaped the abstract pantheism of Hindu thought by making the world dependent on the personal God.

The Old Testament exhibits growth and development in Israel's conception. The revelation in the earlier stages of the history emphasizes the attributes of power; in the later, the attributes of character. In the earlier stages Jehovah's relations to Israel are dwelt upon; in the later prophets his dominion over the universe is clearly set forth.

2. The gods of the various religions exhibit a tendency to become increasingly ethical. In the lowest religions it is difficult often to find any connection between religion and ethics. But in some of the higher ethnic faiths the connection becomes very clear. In Judaism it is most pronounced. The religion of Israel is ethical monotheism. The supreme moral sanction is the fear or the love of Jehovah. Now this ethical ideal for the people arises out of the ethical quality in Jehovah; " Ye shall be holy, for I am holy."

In this way man himself acquires, in Judaism, a new dignity. So long as God was thought of as power merely, his omnipotence dwarfed man. But when God is thought of as moral character it is seen that man may imitate him. It is then seen that God and man belong to the same class of beings. Man is made in God's image. In the New Testament the crown is placed upon the revelation of God's moral attributes, as we shall see. But in the Old Testament God is revealed as righteous love.

3. A third tendency in the phenomena presented by comparative religion is the gradual advance in the idea of revelation. Some form of revelation appears in nearly all religions. The gods speak to men in dreams, or through oracles of various kinds. There are earlier and later stages of revelation in the Old Testament. Here, however, the prophet is the chief medium of God's self-revelation to men. The prophets spoke through the Spirit of God in them. Sometimes they declare themselves to be constrained to speak by the indwelling Spirit, against their own wills. (Jer. 20 : 9.) The prophetic message is varied from age to age. Yet there are permanent elements that are never absent. Among these are the following: God is one; he is jealous of the loyalty and love of his people; he is holy; he has a plan for mankind; he will

G

in the future work mightily for the redemption of men. His revelation is a historical process. It is seen in the life of the people as well as the words of the prophets. It is gradual revelation of his plan and purpose for mankind, exhibited in the first instance in the life of Israel.

4. A fourth point is the increasing recognition of the purposiveness of God and his providential control of the world. In the lower faiths there are household gods, tribal and national gods. In Judaism God discloses himself not only as the one God of all nations, but as the one God of all time. There are three elements of Old Testament teaching especially which make this clear: *a*. There is the element of typology. Certain persons or institutions are typical of future events or persons in the plan of God. History is thought of as if it were a vital organism. As all parts of the future tree are in the planted seed, so the future kingdom of God is bound up in every stage of the ongoing kingdom. The type thus becomes the imperfect expression of the meaning of the antitype. The latter of course we find in the New Testament revelation. *b*. There is also the Messianic element, which is very pronounced in the Old Testament at certain stages of the history. The king and the kingdom, the prophet and other forms of representation are employed to express the idea of a coming Messiah or deliverer. *c*. There is the idea of a future judgment. Eschatology is very imperfectly developed in the Old Testament, but it is present in a number of forms. It reaches its climax, of course, in the New Testament. Men sometimes speak as if religion ought to dispense with eschatology. The hope of reward and the fear of punishment are regarded by some as low motives. But eschatology is a necessary element in the completion of the idea of God. God as the absolute, who controls the future, was a necessary stage in the perfecting of the idea of the divine being. Religious psychology also confirms the value of eschatology in religion. We are so made that we cannot escape the influence of fear and hope. Our belief in immortality and our moral dignity as persons impel us irresistibly to considerations of the ultimate consequences of present conduct.

5. Again, there is a gradual advance in the idea of redemption. Deliverance from enemies, from disease and pestilence, and from the powers of nature, are a few of the forms of redemption found in the less developed religions of the world. Everywhere the idea is that the god or gods act in behalf of men. They are believed to be real helpers in our human struggles. There is a gradual transition to the ideal of redemption from sin. In the Old Testament the ethical ideal is accompanied all along the course of its development with a deepening and intensifying of the sense of sin and guilt. Other forms of deliverance gradually become subordinate to redemption in this higher sense, moral and spiritual deliverance. The Old Testament revelation in its later stages distinctly recognizes the supreme place of moral and spiritual redemption in God's plan. This is seen in the new interpretation of God's purpose through Israel after the national life is destroyed. (Isa. 42 : 1-9; 60 : 1-14.) It is seen also in the later predictions of the new covenant which should be inward and moral in its provisions. (Jer. 31 : 31; Heb. 8 : 8.) It is clearly seen in the later longing for and expectation of the gift of the Holy Spirit with new creative power for regenerating man and establishing a new order. (Joel 2 : 28; Acts 2 : 17.) The same ideal of moral and spiritual redemption appears very clearly in the later Messianic predictions, wherein the work of the Messiah is described in terms of the highest moral and spiritual purification. (Isa. 61 : 1; 42 : 1-9; Matt. 12 : 18.)

6. The ideas of atonement and reconciliation gradually assume higher forms and reach their climax in the Christian teaching. There is much obscurity as to the meaning of many sacrificial offerings found in the religions of mankind. Even in the Old Testament the meaning is not always entirely clear. There is, however, in the later sacrifices clear recognition of the principle of substitution. Respect for the divine righteousness must be concerned in all reconciliations between God and man. This also finds its adequate explanation and expression in Christianity.

7. The immanence and transcendence of God attain their perfect expression in the Christian religion. Heathen faiths tended

constantly to pantheism. Everything seemed to be equally divine. Judaism escaped this danger through its ethical monotheism, which holds that God is the moral and spiritual absolute Person, on whom all things depend, and from whom all things proceed. The doctrine of creation was a natural reflection of this view of God. God is not identical with the world. He made it, and it is dependent on him. The doctrine of creation was a necessary element in the completion of the idea of God. We can only conceive of God as the perfect moral and spiritual Person by thinking of him as the Creator of the universe. Otherwise he becomes entangled in it, and there is great difficulty in avoiding low estimates of the divine character.

There is, however, a danger in the other direction. God may be thought of as above the world and apart from it and beyond the reach of man. The Old Testament in a remarkable way overcame this danger by its teaching as to the Spirit of God. The Spirit of God is God immanent in nature and in man. This prepared the way for the perfecting of the idea of God, and therewith the perfecting of the idea of religion.

It is now in order to indicate in a brief summary how Christianity perfects all the preceding elements in religion. It will thus appear that comparative religion presents us the religious values or needs to which Christianity brings the corresponding realities.

a. Jesus Christ is the revealer of God as a person. " He that hath seen me hath seen the Father " (John 14 : 9), was one of his own sayings. " No man hath seen God at any time; the only begotten Son, who is in the bosom of the Father, he hath declared him " (John 1 : 18). Jesus brought to perfection the idea of God as ethical. He revealed him to us as righteous love. In his supreme relation to us God is Father, everlasting in his desire to bless. He is infinite in all his perfections, but condescends to our low estate in order that he may lift us to his own.

b. Jesus Christ completes the idea of revelation. Inorganic nature, organic nature, sentient and animal nature, are gradual stages in God's revelation to man. But in none of these was there an adequate revelation of God. In addition to the revelation in nature there was the dim revelation of God in the various religions of the world. In the words of Tennyson, mankind seemed

> to hear a Heavenly Friend,
> And thro' thick veils to apprehend
> A labor working to an end.

But here again revelation came short of the goal. In these faiths we see man seeking God. When Christ came, God came seeking man. In these lower revelations there is created an expectation of the supreme revelation in Christ. The religious relationship could not be perfected until God spoke to man. The Old Testament is a new stage in the religious life of the world. Now God founds his kingdom. All the conditions are gradually produced for the coming of the Messianic Son of God and Redeemer of man. God speaks in Christ the supreme authoritative word, and the idea of revelation is completed. It has attained its highest possible development.

c. The revelation of a divine purpose and providential government of the world culminates in the great thought of God's universal moral kingdom. This is the key to history and its goal. The typical, Messianic, and eschatological elements attain their full expression in the ideal of God's universal kingdom.

d. Again, the redemptive idea culminates in Christ. The blood of bulls and goats could not take away sin. The redemptive righteousness of God comes to full expression in the atoning death of Christ. This is presented in the New Testament, not as sometimes urged, as if it were merely a device or contrivance of the divine ingenuity, with a view to letting the guilty go free. It is the provision of infinite wisdom and love, and while it meets the ends of divine righteousness, at the same time it is an energy which operates to produce holy character in men. It is not a merely legal or judicial transaction. It is a moral and spiritual reconciliation.

e. Again, in the New Testament doctrine of the Holy Spirit we have the completion of the idea of God. Through the Spirit God is revealed as immanent in the world. Thus is avoided the danger of conceiving God as apart from the world. Through the operation of the Holy Spirit also religion becomes inward, moral, and personal. Through the Holy Spirit man's spirit is created anew in Christ Jesus. Through the Spirit religion becomes fellowship between God and man. Through the Spirit revelation becomes a personal transaction of God in the soul. Through the Spirit the sense of sonship to God the Father is imparted to man. Through the Spirit the truths of the revelation of God in Christ become for the believer an articulate system of truths expressing the meaning of the facts of his new life. Through the Holy Spirit religion becomes power for realizing the moral and spiritual ideal in the individual life and in the social order. The Spirit creates the spiritual community or church, and the church leavens society, and the kingdom of God gradually comes on earth.

f. Attention is here called to the important fact that the Trinitarian view as to God develops side by side with the perfecting of the idea of religion and the completing of the religious relationship between God and man. God reveals himself *to* us through Christ; he reveals himself *in* us through the Holy Spirit.

We began the present section by undertaking to show the relation of Christian experience to the phenomena of religion generally. In the end we find that religion finds its consummation and completion only as it becomes experiential. The grace of God in Christ applied to the heart of the believer through the Holy Spirit in an ethically transforming life " under the eye and in the strength " of the Eternal Father, becomes the crown and goal of man's religious life.

Conclusions from the Study of Comparative Religion

Certain conclusions thrust themselves upon us as a result of the preceding survey of the religious life of men. First, the higher elements in all the others are found in superior form in the Christian religion. Secondly, all the others lack something which the Christian religion supplies. Thirdly, the argument for the truth of Christianity gains great strength from the fact that it is the goal and crown of the other religions. It is foolish to argue against Christianity because it contains all the fine elements of the ethnic faiths, as if it were derived from them. Its greatness appears in part, in the fact that it presents in synthetic unity all the elements of true religion. Fourthly, apart from Christianity, there are only three courses conceivable in the future religious life of mankind. Men may go backward to the faith below the Christian level; or they may reject all the distinctive elements of religion and attempt to substitute something else in its place; or there may arise a religion superior to Christianity. The first course is not at all probable. Mankind are not likely to accept Buddhism or Mohammedanism instead of Christianity; and if not these, certainly none of the other ethnic religions. The second is also unlikely. Some moderns who approach religion from the purely rationalistic standpoint fail to understand it, and devise theories of " values " which may be pursued to the neglect of the distinctively religious values. But men are " incorrigibly " religious in their instincts. Comparative religion shows this. No merely scientific or intellectual values can ever supply the place of religion in man's life. As to the third course, it is always open to any one to predict the rise of a religion superior to Christianity. But no one can now intimate wherein such superiority may or can consist. Besides this, Christianity leaves no religious value or craving unsatisfied for any who know it in an experiential way. For them it is sufficient, and final, and, in the legitimate sense of the word, absolute. There is no occasion for hesitation in asserting, therefore, that Christianity is the final religion.

V. CHRISTIAN EXPERIENCE IN RELATION TO PHILOSOPHY

The history of the word philosophy shows that it has undergone many changes of meaning. As used by most modern writers and as employed here it means the explanation of experience, of truth, and of reality, regarded as a whole. The aim of philosophy is to discover the underlying principle or principles of the universe. Its further aim is to express the meaning of the universe in a world-view which combines all the parts of being into a coherent unity. There are several points of emphasis in the above definition of philosophy. The first is that philosophy arises out of human experience. This is the great and significant gain of modern as compared with ancient philosophies. Men formerly adopted some *a priori* or abstract principle, and from it deduced the meaning of the universe. Now they ask, first of all, What are the facts of life and experience? Then they inquire into the ultimate meaning of the facts. Thus all modern philosophy which challenges attention has an empirical or experiential foundation. It has sometimes been felt that this fact renders philosophy hostile to religion. On the contrary, it is in the highest degree favorable if we are to regard religion itself as founded on facts. Human experience in general, on which philosophy is founded, is very closely related to religious experience and the realities disclosed in it.

A second point of emphasis is truth. One of the most crucial and fundamental questions in philosophy is that regarding truth, what it is, and how it arises. Here again there is the closest possible connection with experience. We know truth in and through human experience. All the special sciences have their modes of approach and methods of discovering truth. Physical science is especially concerned with the mechanical system of causation as seen in physical nature. Biology deals with the series of living forms and the laws of their development. Psychology traces the laws of mental action. So with all the sciences. The study of the data actually given in the various departments, our concrete human reactions upon the realities with which we deal, gives rise to the truths discovered in all the sciences. Philosophy seeks to combine all departments of truth into a universal and coherent system of truth.

A third point of emphasis is reality. Philosophy seeks to go beyond the real as given in phenomena. It asks, What is ultimate reality? The various systems of philosophy arise out of the attempt to answer this question. But it is of the utmost importance to remember that we can only know what ultimate reality is by observing reality as we know it in experience. Of course we cannot thus know the supreme reality in a perfect manner. But our knowledge of the ultimately real must, for philosophy, be grounded in the actual realities of life itself.

A fourth point of emphasis is unity and comprehensiveness. Philosophy seeks a complete explanation of all things, so far as this is humanly possible. It would discover, as it were, a cord long enough and strong enough to tie up all the facts and realities of existence in a single bundle. The passion and romance of modern philosophy have grown out of the anxious search for such a comprehensive principle of being. The ideal and demand for unity are irrepressible in the minds of thinking men. We yearn for a key which will unlock all the mysteries. We are discontented until we find it.

The four points just presented supply a framework for indicating where and how many systems of modern philosophy come short and will serve as a warning to us in the effort to relate philosophy to Christian experience.

As based on experience, any philosophy will fail which does not recognize human experience as a whole. All men, even philosophers and theologians, are fragments of humanity. It is not at all easy to do full justice to all human experience. In an age of specialism many men lose the capacity to sympathize with other forms of life and experience. The great soul with the great horizon, and the corresponding wisdom, is rare. As a consequence of this, philosophers tend to become the result of individual and personal reactions upon the world. A great modern writer has said that philosophic systems are largely esthetic productions, matters of taste and preference rather than convincing world-views. There is truth enough in the statement to put every one on guard. A man's predispositions and preferences, due to early or later training, inevitably influence him in the formation of his world-view. But it is obvious that the true and final philosophy must be derived, not from merely individual experience, but from human experience as a whole, or some form of that experience which is comprehensive of all other forms.

Again, philosophies often fail because they do not do justice to the idea of truth. Philosophy is often described as an attempt to give a rational interpretation of the universe. The logical faculty is thus emphasized. The reason is made supreme. The feelings, the will, and the moral nature of man are ignored, or regarded as irrelevant in the search of " pure reason " for ultimate truth. The fatal objection to this is that the existence of a " pure reason " is an unfounded assumption. Man knows nothing of a reason detached from feeling and will. Abstract rationality is a very poor guide to truth. The logical faculty may operate with unerring precision in dealing with myths and fancies, as well as with facts. We must first obtain the material for thought from life's experiences before logic can advance a single step toward truth. All recent psychology confirms this statement. The day of abstract philosophies, built up out of the truths derived from a so-called " pure reason," is past. The system of truth is built up out of the processes of life. Philosophy must reckon with this fact.

Again, error arises in philosophy when the philosopher adopts a narrow view of reality. Broadly speaking, there are two spheres of reality as known to us, the physical and the spiritual. Both matter and mind are given to us in experience. They are the data, the material, on which thought must work. They are not so much problems for thought as they are the materials of thought. They are objects to be explained, but not objects to be explained away. It has often occurred in the history of philosophy that thinkers have assumed the reality of some one element of being and the unreality of the others. Entire systems have been built up in this way. It is of course quite proper to search for a unifying principle, but it must really unify, not ignore or annul any of the real factors of life and being.

Again, philosophies, or world-views, are often defective in the failure to find a comprehensive principle of explanation. Philosophy seeks some phase or aspect of being, some type-phenomenon, which is a key to the meaning of the whole. Now it is clear at once that there is a wide range of choice in this matter. One thinker may be most impressed with the uniformity of natural law, and conclude that the key to the meaning of all things is to be found in matter, force, and motion. Another may be impressed particularly with the processes of human thought, and conclude that all forms of being are forms of thought. Another is most impressed with will, and by means of the will-principle he constructs his philosophy. Yet another is most deeply moved by the fact and the idea of personality, and on it he founds his philosophy. Thus arise the various philosophies. They are many, and to a certain extent they increase from generation to generation. The three or four to which we have just referred are among the most typical of current philosophies, *viz.,* materialism, idealism, and personalism. The point of emphasis here is that to be final, a philosophy must be truly comprehensive of the various elements of the realities we know in experience. Otherwise it is certain to be a transient mode of thought.

Once more, a philosophy may come short in its effort to unify the elements of being. The monistic principle has had great emphasis in modern systems. But many of the monistic explanations fail at certain crucial points. As a result, contradictory systems have arisen. Men have adopted a dualistic, or pluralistic theory on the assumption that it is not possible to find a really monistic bond among the varied forms of reality.

Now it is clear that the search for unity is an irrepressible instinct of the human mind. It seems to be organic in our mental constitution. Hence it is inevitable in the philosophic movement. But one of the greatest needs to-day is sanity and wisdom in the use of the principle. Monistic explanations which do not explain, unifying bonds which do not unify, are dangerous instruments of thought. And while these are certain to arise as working principles, hypotheses for verification, it is the part of the highest wisdom to recognize them as such until some principle is proved to be the true and final one.

VI. MODERN WORLD-VIEWS

We may now examine briefly a few of the philosophic systems which specially claim attention from theology.

1. We begin with Agnosticism, which denies the possibility of knowledge of ultimate reality. In its modern form agnosticism is founded on Kant's distinction between phenomena and noumena, or appearances and the thing-in-itself. The view is that we may observe and know appearances, but not the realities behind them. The latter are entirely hidden from our view. It is not denied that there are such realities, but only that they are beyond our faculties and powers. The agnostic attitude is adopted sometimes in the interest of religion itself, and sometimes in the interest of natural science, which is held to be the sole realm of genuine knowledge. But in both respects it is an untenable and dangerous attitude of mind.

The objections to agnosticism, briefly stated, are the following:

First, there is no ground for assuming that ultimate reality is unrelated to our finite knowing powers. In all our reasonings, we take it for granted that there is a correspondence or agreement between our knowing and the objects known. The real test is in what we actually know, not in some theory of what we can or cannot know.

Secondly, agnosticism asserts much in its assertions as to our inability to know and our objects of knowledge. To assert that there is an unknowable which cannot be known is self-contradictory. To know that it exists is important knowledge, and to know that we cannot know it implies almost infinite knowledge about our own minds as well as of its objects.

Thirdly, agnosticism contradicts itself in its view of our capacity to know and our limitations of knowledge. Its conclusion as to ultimate reality is itself an item of knowledge for the agnostic. But the assertion of our incapacity to know it at once suggests a doubt also as to the reliability of this item of knowledge. Thus the corner-stone of all knowledge is destroyed along with the superstructure in the agnostic view of the world.

Fourthly, agnosticism builds on a narrow view of human knowledge. Huxley gave the word currency in recent times, and he limited knowledge and proof to mathematical formulæ and the laws of nature. This limitation is now a very generally discredited view of knowledge. The moral and spiritual worlds also contain objects of knowledge. These must be taken into account. Our theory of knowledge must conform to the facts. Agnosticism ignores some of the facts.

Fifthly, agnosticism is destructive of our moral and spiritual values. To assert man's incapacity to know God is to take away the most powerful moral and spiritual incentive.

Finally, agnosticism is built upon a partial and abstract theory of the world of experience. We do not know nature and her laws, as apart from and independent of our own minds. All the facts of man's mental, moral, and spiritual life must be included in any theory of knowledge which will hold in philosophy. It is a mere abstraction therefore to take the physical world by itself and leave out of account the world of spirit. In other words, we know many forms of mental activity which do not belong to the world of phenomena at all. Yet they are quite as real, indeed they are the most real of all forms of reality known to us. The facts require, therefore, that we shall include in our theory of knowledge, not only appearances, things seen and heard and felt, but also the invisible things of the mind and spirit.

2. Materialism takes matter to be the key to the ultimate meaning of the universe. Given matter, force, and motion, as these are found in nature, and you can explain all else, according to materialism. Mind states are the product of brain states. Materialism makes use of the law of the conservation, or transformation, of energy to make good its claim. All mental or physical phenomena, all the moral and spiritual activities of man are simply aspects of the transformation of force. The objections to materialism are most conclusive.

(1) The foundation on which materialism rests is much too narrow in view of the facts of nature and the world of human experience. The law of the transformation of energy is limited

in its application. It does not explain life. The living does not arise from the non-living. At least, science has not shown that it does. Mind states have nothing in common with brain states. These never pass into each other. There is a close parallelism between them, indeed, but a great gulf separates them.

(2) Mind and will have qualities rising above the physical. Man can make himself an object of thought. There is nothing like this power found in matter. The human will is a true cause. It can originate movements. Matter is always an effect. It originates nothing. Man's power of choice, his freedom, his power of attention, are all traits which lift him high above the world of matter. Human personality transcends physical nature. Man's moral and religious life are entirely above all that we discover in the realm of the merely physical. Man employs matter for his ends. Nature becomes his instrument. Thus man's superiority to nature appears.

(3) The evidence of purpose or plan in nature is strong and clear. We can understand this if we refer it to a personal Spirit who controls, but it is wholly beyond us if the world is nothing but matter, force, and motion. Materialism ignores all morality and religion. It is helpless wherever it attempts to explain them. Yet these are facts, the most significant facts of all man's human experience.

Our conclusion is that materialism does not explain mind, will, and spirit. It only explains them away. It cancels one set of facts in order to exalt another set. It does not take experience as it is given to us. It rather makes experience over again into its own image and likeness. It is an abstract system. It seeks to unify the facts of being, but ignores the higher facts of being. It is to be rejected, therefore, without hesitation.

3. Idealism takes thought itself as the principle of explanation. Thus it is in its fundamental meaning the opposite of materialism. There are many varieties of idealism. We deal here with its essential elements only.

Idealism begins with the assertion that the only world we know is a thought-world. This does not mean that our individual personal thoughts are the only realities. That form of subjective idealism need not detain us. Idealism asserts rather that the real objective world of things is known to us only in thoughts about them. They are presented to us, and we think them, their colors, shapes, sounds, all their qualities and attributes. Apart from our thoughts about these objects they have for us no existence. Things then are essentially thoughts. But since there are undoubtedly things beyond our consciousness which have never entered our thoughts, there must be another and higher consciousness for which they exist. Unless things exist for some consciousness somewhere, we cannot conceive of them as existing at all. If things are anywhere and at any time unrelated to thought, they cease to have any meaning. They become wholly unknowable, which is equivalent to saying they are non-existent.

Idealism generalizes the above view into a philosophy of the nature of being as a whole. Not matter, but thought is the cornerstone of our whole human experience. This basal fact is the key to the meaning of the world. The world is a universal consciousness. God is the great thinker. He is realizing himself in us and in nature by thinking us. We are parts of him. Our imperfect thoughts, our hunger for more knowledge, are just the infinite mind expressing itself in our finite minds. The world is thus unified by the conception that thoughts and things are one, and that all finite thinkers are aspects or phases of the thought of the infinite thinker. Idealism is thus a monistic system. Fundamentally living is reduced to one element.

(1) We note briefly how far it is tenable and how far untenable. Idealism is right in asserting that all things are constituted in and for thought. We cannot escape this conviction if we reflect upon the matter at all. Idealism is correct also in the denial of the independent reality of matter. The only matter we know, or can know, is matter as related to thought, dependent upon thought. Thus idealism is correct also in passing from outward things into consciousness to find the true meaning of ultimate reality. Idealism pursues a correct method in building its world-view on the facts of our experience.

(2) On the other hand, however, it must be said that idealism does not fully explain the differences between thoughts and things. Things have extension; thought has not. Again, it is to a certain extent abstract in separating thought from the other elements of consciousness. Will and emotion, moral and spiritual impulses, are found there as well as thought. Again, idealism makes finite beings parts of the infinite in ways that are hard to understand. If we as thinkers are merely organs of the infinite thinker, it is not easy to see how he, the infinite, can be omniscient in himself and commit the many errors and sins which abound in the finite phases of himself. There is also a strong tendency in idealism to cancel human freedom and personality. A monistic view of the universe which makes the thought process supreme finds it exceedingly difficult to care for the interests of the will and the moral and spiritual in man. Idealism is a great improvement on materialism, and in some of its later forms gives more attention to the interests named. But in its abstract form it may lead to results which are little if any better than those of materialism and fatalism.

4. Personalism is another type of modern philosophic thought. It is a decided improvement on abstract idealism. It sees clearly that life is more than thoughts, more than presentations and ideas. Personalism emphasizes the synthetic unity of consciousness. It recognizes all the factors of consciousness, including the will and feelings as well as the intellect. It emphasizes man's growth in knowledge and experience. It takes man in the totality of his relations, to nature, to other persons in human society, and to God. It recognizes the common experiences of men and the law of reason by which they understand each other and their own experiences.[4]

From these fundamental facts, recognized and admitted by all thinkers of all schools, personalism builds up its general worldview. Its conclusions are that the ultimate reality is a Person; that we as the creation of his hands are true persons; that we are endowed with freedom; that the divine Person is working

'Cf. Bowne, " Personalism," pp. 20, 21.

out a purpose in human society; and that the goal of history is a perfect society of men and women in fellowship with God.

In reference to physical nature, personalism agrees with idealism in the view that nature in all its parts is constituted in and for thought; that time and space are forms of thought under which we apprehend the world rather than independent realities. It holds further that the infinite Person, God, contains all finite existence in himself. The finite is related to the infinite and is in actual communication with it and not separated from it by an impassable gulf. Personalism maintains that the key to the meaning of physical nature is the divine purpose which runs through it; that the crown and goal of nature is its highest outcome, man himself; that we must understand the beginning in the light of the outcome and not attempt to cancel the higher elements in the outcome. This is done when we assume some single primary element of being like matter, force, or motion, or even abstract thought, and then resolve all the higher elements back into this.

The considerations advanced to support this view are many and cogent. First of all, personalism is a philosophy erected on a broad foundation of fact and experience. One method of philosophy is to abstract matter from thought and draw the conclusion of materialism. Another is to abstract thought itself from its context in our human personal life and draw the conclusion of abstract idealism. Personalism avoids both abstractions. It takes reality as it finds it. Man is subject. He thinks. The world is object for man's thoughts. Reality as we know it, then, includes the subject-object relation. But the object is not a bare thinker. He is an acting person with will, plan, purpose, and a goal of endeavor. Personalism thus recognizes all that the conception of personality implies and employs it as the "type-phenomenon" to explain the world.

Secondly, personalism is strong in its explanation of first and final causes. The idea of causation is a very difficult one. We cannot dwell upon it here except to point out one or two pertinent facts. Physical science knows no first cause. All the natural causes are, first of all, effects of previous causes. There is thus only an infinite regress of causes, all of which are on the physical level. *A* causes *b,* and *b* causes *c,* and *c* causes *d,* and so on indefinitely. No first cause, that is, no real cause, is ever found by this method. Now personalism asserts that the human will is, in a relative sense at least, a first cause. From it we derive our first and fundamental conception of causation. The will is not the result of the transformation of force. It is a cause on a higher level. Personalism thus reaches the idea of the divine will on an experiential basis. The will of God is the moving and efficient cause of all things working toward a divine end.

In the third place, personalism is strong in its account of human knowledge. Recognizing that men communicate with each other, that the thoughts of one mind may be known by other minds, it finds no difficulty in the further thought that God can make known to us the contents of his mind. Recognizing also that all objective things are constituted in and for thought, it is not difficult to make the transition to the idea that the world about us is God speaking to us. As language requires for its understanding intelligence in the speaker and hearer, so the created world as a language intelligible to us implies intelligence in the power which produces and maintains it. Our intelligence is thus the response to the divine intelligence and marks the universe as a coherent and harmonious whole. We do not live in chaos, but in a world where the part answers to the whole and the whole can communicate itself to the part.

Fourthly, personalism also gives an account of freedom which places it high among philosophic world-views. As the world is the result of God's action, the self-impartation of the divine Being to his creation, so man is, in a higher sense, God imparting himself to his creature. It is but one step from this to the doctrine of man's freedom. God is the most free of all beings and in making man in his own image he makes man free. It belongs to the very essence of the divine image in man that he should be free. Thus personalism escapes the pantheistic result which follows the denial of personality in God. If God is merely an impersonal substance identical with the totality of being, then man cannot be a free person. He is then only a transient, a passing phase of the eternal substance.

Fifthly, personalism is strong in interpretation of the meaning of physical nature. There are here the following points to be noted: (1) Nature, being constituted in and for thought, is a part of God's self-revelation to man; (2) since the only nature we know is the nature we find in our human experience (nature related to personality), we are bound to take nature in its relation to the infinite Person as its deepest meaning; (3) since man is the crown of nature we must assume that he is its end and goal; (4) and since man employs nature in a thousand ways for his ends, we must conclude that personality is superior to the physical and more completely fulfils the divine ends; and (5) in interpreting nature as a system of laws, and as under the operation of causation in the physical sense, we are not warranted in taking it as if it existed independently of all personal relationships. Our view of nature must include the most immediate and insistent of all the facts we know about it, namely, its relation to personal beings. This will prevent the dangerous tendency so often observed, to permit physical nature to impose its laws on the higher personal world. We may not, in Tennyson's words, in another connection, " set the feet above the brain and swear the brain is in the feet."

Sixthly, personalism has much to commend in its account of God's relations to the universe. (1) It insists upon the unity of nature, man, and God. It interprets the universe as spirit. Time and space are forms of our apprehension of the objective world. This, however, is not the pantheistic unity which identifies God and nature and makes matter coeternal with God. The world is God's creation. It is the sphere in which he is fulfilling his purposes. The monistic principle of personalism simply means that there is no irreconcilable dualism as between God and nature. It refuses to make nature coeval with God, but insists that it came forth from God, and is yet subject to his guiding hand. (2) Personalism insists upon the immanence of God in the world. But here again it is not the pantheistic immanence which asserts that reality is a two-sided impersonal substance, one of which is thought and the other extension. Personalism is strongly opposed to pantheism at this point. But personalism asserts strongly God's presence in the natural order, his action within it and his movement through it toward his goal. (3) Personalism emphasizes the transcendence of God as well as his immanence. But here again it is not a transcendence in the old deistic sense. The world is not a machine which God made and then abandoned to itself. God is, indeed, above the world, but not apart from it. His transcendence means his superiority to the created universe. It means that the world does not exhaust God. God is more than all created things. (4) Personalism insists also upon God's presence in human history. As personality is the most significant, the highest factor of being known to us, personalism takes the view, well supported by its premises, that the development and perfecting of a society of persons is the chief end of history, the divine goal in the ongoing of the world.

It is in connection with God's presence in history that we find some of the clearest and strongest of all the supports of personalism. Every department of human endeavor at once becomes radiant with divine light when we consider them from this point of view. They all converge upon the one central truth of personality as the key to the meaning of the world. We look briefly at the chief departments of human activity.

a. First, consider physical science. Man's achievements in this department and his thirst for ever greater knowledge are the tokens of the divine presence in man working toward the goal of a universal kingdom of truth. Then too, the response of creation to man's efforts, the secrets which it yields up to his search, are sure tokens that it was constituted for the truth-seeker, that behind it is the great Being who is infinite truth. Man's insatiable desire for greater and greater knowledge of nature, and nature's response to his quest are both powerful witnesses to God's existence, yea, rather to his presence everywhere in his creation. The scientific consciousness thus has implicit in it the consciousness of God. It is the consciousness of the finite knower seeking satisfaction in the knowledge of the infinite.

b. Consider next morality. Since the days of Immanuel Kant, the presence in man of a moral imperative has been a commonplace in philosophic thought. What does the presence of that imperative signify? It signifies that the supreme moral ideal is inwrought in the very fabric of man's being. The existence of a supreme moral standard is not something we infer from something else. It is rather something we find existing in the very texture of reality itself, in man's moral nature. In the last analysis the ground and source of that moral standard can only be found in God himself, the infinite Person. A pantheistic worldground has no moral significance. The distinction between right and wrong is meaningless apart from the fact of a supreme moral person. Man's failure to attain the moral ideal, his struggle and slow progress toward it in his individual and social life, are not opposed to, but in harmony with, the idea of the supremely good Being who is the fountain of all good. Man's quest for the moral ideal, his gradual approach to liberty, justice, and love in the social order, particularly his discontent with all actual attainments, can only be explained as the expression of his relations with the infinite, the eternal goodness. Personalism thus supplies a key for the explanation of moral phenomena which can scarcely be found in any system denying the cardinal position of personality in the universe. The moral is but another name for the personal.

c. Consider also briefly man's esthetic and artistic activities. The love of the beautiful is implanted in us when we come into the world. But here again man's motto is, " I count not myself to have attained." The genius paints a great picture, carves a great statue, writes a great poem, produces a great musical composition, or erects an architectural masterpiece. There is a momentary contentment with his handiwork. He may even feel that this is the end and goal. Nothing more splendid seems possible. But it is a transient emotion. There soon rises in him a sense of higher possibilities, and once more he seizes brush or chisel and produces other masterpieces. Thus man's masterpieces become steps of the endless stairway leading up toward the infinite ideal of the beautiful. And this again is a witness to the fact that the nature of man reflects God's image.

d. We arrive at the same conclusion when we trace the history of philosophy. The craving for a rational interpretation of the universe is insatiable in man. From one point of view the history of philosophy is a discouraging study. System succeeds system in ceaseless procession. Old systems return in modified forms. New systems arise. Every system embodies some principle of explanation adequate from its own point of view. The conflict is really a conflict of premises rather than of argument or conclusions. But the supremely interesting thing about the whole philosophic movement is man's unquenchable thirst for new attempts to solve the world riddle. But for this and what is implied in it, the unstable equilibrium of philosophy would seem to present a hopeless outlook. But man was made for truth, and we must also hold that truth awaits man's discovery. The quest for truth is not hopeless. Now we can only account for this thirst of man for a knowledge of the whole, this intellectual torment which will not let him rest, by the view that it is the reflection in him of the nature God gave him. It is the eternal seeking expression in and through man, and guiding him to his true heritage in the realm of universal truth. The bearing of personalism on this is obvious. If there is a realm of universal truth, if reality is constituted in a particular way open to the investigation and discovery of personal beings, it can only be because a supreme personal Being gave its constitution to the real world. The distinction between truth and error is meaningless apart from the idea of personality. A truth is truth only for some one. It cannot be truth merely suspended in midair. Error can only be error because it is a departure from facts as those facts have been constituted in truth. Pantheism here again also cancels the conception of truth. Personalism alone can maintain it.

e. Psychology and the psychology of religion bear witness to the same consciousness of the infinite in the finite consciousness of man. We need only recall here what was said in another place. Man's social consciousness, his desire to realize himself in a society of persons, awakens in him a craving for the society of the perfect, the ideal, and supreme Person. This explains the human instinct of prayer. The primary question about prayer is not whether God does or can answer prayer. It is rather the question why men actually pray. Of course the prayer instinct is marred by sin, blinded by ignorance and superstition often, sometimes almost entirely absent from certain types of men. Yet when we take a wide view of the psychology of religion the impulse to pray is practically universal among men. Here again we encounter the ineradicable conviction in man of the reality of the infinite Person from whom we came and on whom we depend.

f. Comparative religion bears witness to the same truth. The personal view of the universe supplies the key to all the phenomena of the general religious life of mankind. If God is an infinite person, and finite man is made in his image and likeness holy and loving, we can rationally account for the irrepressible human longing for God. The disturbed relations between God and man can be explained by the sin principle in man. And Christianity enters the scene of human struggle to find God, and announces God's self-revelation in Christ and response to the human need.

An Impersonal Universe

We need only consider briefly the opposing view in order to receive a fresh and powerful impression of the general truth of the personal interpretation of the world. Suppose the universe is impersonal. Then every edifice of human culture and of higher civilization falls in ruins. We note three of these. First, the whole fabric of human thought collapses. This is because the distinction between truth and error ceases to have any meaning. Error can be accounted for as the mistake of a free intelligent person missing the way in his search for truth. But unless there is an infinite Person who establishes standards and criteria of truth, there is no such thing as error. Every thought of every thinker is then but the manifestation of an impersonal substance or reality through the human consciousness. It is not then the error of a self-determined free being, but thought predetermined in precisely the same way as physical results are predetermined by physical causes.

It follows, secondly, that all moral attainment ceases to have meaning or value. Right means conformity to the moral constitution of the universe. Wrong means departure from it. But if the world-ground is impersonal, nothing can be wrong or right in the moral sense. Men are then no more than plants or flowers or beasts who follow their natural instincts. To resist those instincts is not only futile, but foolish. They are of the very texture of our nature and thus of the nature of the universe. It is thus utterly vain to seek an ethical basis for life on any other than a personal view of the world.

In the third place, man's religious life becomes empty of all meaning on the impersonal view. Religion then becomes a mere functional make-believe. Men imagine gods because gods are useful in the struggle for existence, not because they exist and respond to man's needs. The ordinary intellect has little difficulty in perceiving that such a view is the doom of religion. Intelligent men despise make-believes and shams of all sort. Religion would be very short-lived should this view prevail. But it cannot prevail because it clashes sharply with the whole religious history of mankind. It is an abstract theory built out of elements of religion taken apart from their context in man's religious life. The reality of the religious object is essential to the religious idea.

General Conclusion as to Christian Experience and Other Forms of Knowledge

We have now reviewed at some length the relation of Christian experience to various other forms of knowledge. The aim has been to show the unity of knowledge and the harmony of the Christian view of the world with the most advanced forms of modern culture. It is now in order to sum up the results of this discussion in a brief general statement.

Broadly speaking, we may say that the Christian experience of redemption through Christ is the true goal of all human experience and the key to its meaning. We are redeemed from sin into fellowship with the eternal God through Christ. We thus know God actually by living contact with him. Christian experience thus brings the question of God's existence out of the speculative realm down into the sphere of the most vital realities of life. It thus becomes the capstone in the structure of human endeavor for the higher realities of the spirit. It is the distinct answer to the scientific craving for universal truth. It is the end of the quest of the soul in search of the supreme fellowship as psychology exhibits it. It definitely supplies all that man's religious life seeks, and brings religion itself to realization. It is the answer to man's philosophic inquiries as to the meaning of the world. But it is an answer not in terms of logical deduction or abstract reasoning. It is rather an answer in terms of life and power. Christian experience is the dynamic required for the realization of man's moral ideals. Thus it becomes the fundamental condition for the full realization of his own personal nature. Thus also it is the supreme constructive principle for the realization of the ideal society, the kingdom of God.

We conclude then that all human experience implies what we mean by religious experience. Psychology discloses man's desire for the supreme Companion. Science as a method and ideal exhibits man's sense of the unity of the parts of being and the human thirst for complete knowledge. Ethics implies man's sense of the morally perfect, the supremely good. Philosophy is the ceaseless quest for ultimate explanation. Every form of religion exhibits man's quest for victory and blessedness in fellowship with some object of worship. Christianity is the response of God to these human cravings in the crowning revelation of himself through Jesus Christ.

The Christian Religion in Its Doctrinal Expression

VII. PERSONALISM AND CHRISTIAN THEISM

It has been customary hitherto in books of theology to discuss at length formal arguments in proof of God's existence. We have adopted another method made familiar by modern science. That method is to seek the general view which seems to be required by the facts. We have sought to indicate how personalism explains the facts of nature and those which relate to man. We have purposely omitted reference to difficulties and objections in order that we might exhibit the view in all its strength. It is in order now to notice two or three points by way of addition and qualification.

The first thing to be observed is the relation of personalism to the biblical teachings as to God. The biblical representations of God are non-speculative. They do not deal with questions of ontology, of essence and being. The Scriptures are not philosophic in their dealing with the facts of religion. Christian theism, however, as taught in the New Testament, is in the chief essentials the same as personalism as we have expounded it. The Christian theistic view is that God is the infinite Spirit, personal, holy, loving, purposive, immanent in the world, and transcendent. Personalism is in exact agreement with the New Testament in these respects. The point at which personalism goes beyond the Christian theistic view is its monistic tendency. Personalism seeks to explain matter from the point of view of a spiritual world-ground. It comes nearer to success in this respect than any other form of modern philosophic thought. But it does not remove all the difficulties, and until it does this it need not be regarded as having reached its final form. But personalism is unlike the monistic systems generally in certain fundamental particulars, as follows: *a.* It insists upon the reality of human personality. It combats the pantheistic tendency to make man a transient phase of the impersonal and eternal substance. *b.* It insists upon the personality of God. It is on this basis that it explains man's personality. *c.* It insists upon human freedom. *d.* It insists on purpose as the controlling factor in nature and history. *e.* It insists on freedom and immortality. *f.* It insists upon man's capacity for God and the possibility of fellowship between the infinite and finite persons.

It thus appears that personalism conserves the Christian values while it goes beyond the Christian teaching at certain points. The Christian interest has nothing to lose in welcoming every effort of man's intellect to explain the ultimate meaning of the world. As men increase in knowledge and wisdom and widen their experience, they gradually approach the Christian view of the world. Personalism is one of the finest flowers of philosophic thought to-day. And it is interesting to observe its close affinity with our Christian conception of God.

It may be well in closing this section to point out briefly how Christian theism is related to philosophic world-views generally. The former holds, on the most solid grounds, that God is one, personal, spiritual, righteous, loving, purposive, and redemptive. This is the religious conviction as to God. Philosophy seeks to explain the nature of being as a whole, the relations of mind and matter, God's relations to the physical universe, and deals indeed with all the ultimate problems of thought. With many of these religion is only indirectly concerned. There is therefore no necessary conflict between the interests of thought in these ultimate forms and the interests of religion. Religion should not attempt to curb the intellect, nor should the intellect attempt to force world-views upon the religious man which are subversive of religion itself. In the last resort the two interests are identical. Man's activity in each sphere is the necessary complement to his activity in the other. But pending his attainment of the ultimate goal of thought, and the complete unity of all the elements of life, we must stand for the principle of freedom both for the religious and for the intellectual life of man. This point may be made clear by reminding ourselves that our experience of God in Christ may be interpreted for the ends of the religious life, in which case it becomes a system of theology; or it may be interpreted for the ends of the general world-view, in which case it becomes a system of metaphysics. Theology inevitably and invariably runs back to methaphysics. But there are problems in metaphysics whose solution is not essential to religion or theology.

THE PROOFS OF GOD'S EXISTENCE

We have not developed in the preceding pages the arguments for God's existence known in theology as the cosmological, teleological, anthropological, ontological, and moral proofs. As a matter of fact, every one of them has been involved directly or indirectly in what has been written as to the personal view of the universe. In their ordinary forms these arguments do not make so strong an appeal as formerly on account of the prevalence of the exact methods of physical science. As has been stated previously, they are less convincing to the Christian believer than the knowledge of God derived from the revelation in Christ. But when combined with the testimony of Christian experience the older proofs contain great force. We consider them briefly.

1. We begin with the cosmological argument. This infers the existence of God from the necessity of a cause adequate to account for the universe. Every effect must have an adequate cause. The universe is an effect. God is the only adequate cause. The familiar objection is that this only proves a finite cause since the universe is not infinite. But the scientific objection is that it is not a cause discovered or given, but merely inferred. Science explains by means of the principle of continuity or the transformation of energy. You do not find any real explanation until you find the identity between the consequence and its antecedent. Moreover, in inferring God from matter you leap across the chasm which separates matter and spirit. The idea of God, then, the scientist urges, explains nothing at all, or it explains everything equally. This is a method of explanation which has no scientific value whatever. This illustration will serve for the other forms of proof. The older ways of stating them have for many lost much of their force, not because they are without force, but because they do not conform to modern methods and criteria for estimating truth.

[124]

Christian and Other Forms of Knowledge

The truth in the cosmological argument is best seen by considering the idea of causation. The older form of the argument failed to grasp this idea properly, and the objection to it is based on the same defect. We must distinguish between physical and free causation. In the former we are thinking of the transformation of energy. In the latter we think of the free acts of the will. The question is as to which of these is to be given the fundamental position. The Christian theist asserts that all our conception of force, even in its physical manifestations, are derived ultimately from experience of the power of our own free acts through the will. Man is a part of the universe, indeed the highest of its finite parts known to us. In looking for the first cause we are justified only if we take the highest form of cause known to us as the type of cause which explains the universe as a whole. So far Christian theism is warranted in going. Idealism and personalism go a step further, and resolve all physical forms of causation into forms of free causation. This is an interesting philosophic explanation, but not necessary to Christian theism. In a way it confirms the conclusion of the latter while not supplying its chief ground.

The cosmological argument, however, is greatly reenforced by the testimony of man's religious consciousness, his sense of dependence. This sense of personal dependence on a higher Power brings home to the heart the conviction which the reason deduced from a contingent and dependent universe. If we extend the cosmological argument and make it include the last-named phase, we may trace the process of the reason in arriving at the idea of God, in the following steps:

(1) Science discovers a series of causes which never reach above the physical level. Causes and effects in nature present an endless regress. *A* is produced by *b,* and *b* by *c,* and so on to the end, if there were any end. The series is like a row of bricks falling one against the other. But the mind cannot permanently rest in explanation in this form. The reason inevitably demands and seeks an originating cause which is not partly effect as well as cause. What started the row of bricks to falling?

(2) In searching for this originating cause the human will supplies the best clue for our guidance. It is not the product of physical continuity, it is free, and in a true sense it is an originating finite cause. From the will then as a datum, a fact given, we rise to the thought of an infinite will which originates and sustains the universe. Thus a link of connection is found between the world without and the world within.

(3) At this point another form of human experience comes to reenforce the reason. It is the sense of dependence found in the universal religious consciousness. Schleiermacher declared this sense of dependence to be of the essence of religion. It is not now a dependent universe without, but a dependent personal life within. The idea of contingency and dependence being thus enlarged, the inference to an infinite First Cause is greatly strengthened.

(4) Another step is taken in the Christian experience of redemption through Christ. In it logical deduction finds new material for its processes. Man's sense of dependence is met by the personal redeeming God of love. The First Cause now becomes a personal and purposive and loving power in the soul. The craving of the reason is satisfied in a new way. But all the other higher cravings of man are satisfied as well. Man finds himself in his ethical nature, in his desire for power over sin, in his sense of need for reconciliation with God, in his triumph over the discords and contradictions of life. In a word, he finds the end of the endless regress of causes. He finds God and mental rest and spiritual blessedness and peace.

2. The teleological argument, based on the presence of evidence of design in the world, may be treated in a similar way. The older form of the argument selected individual instances of the adaptation of means to end, or of function to use, and inferred a divine intention. The argument is very impressive, even in its older form. On the lowest mechanical plane there are many indications of the adaptation of means to end. The fitness of the planet to be a dwelling-place for man depends upon marvelous combinations of material forces. These involve the relations of the earth

to the sun, giving rise to seasons, to suitable temperature, and to meteorological conditions, and many other adaptations we need not name here. There are also impressive evidences in the organic world. The human eye and hand, the wing of a bird, the fin of a fish, and a thousand other forms of adaptation of organ to the preservation of life indicate the force of this proof of God's existence from the indications of purposive adaptation of means to end in the universe.

Modern evolution, however, seemed at first to destroy this argument. All these adaptations, evolution insisted, are the result of slow growth in the struggle for life, and not of design on the part of the Creator. But this hypothesis was not a real answer to the design argument. For the only result was to widen the range of the proof and make it cover the whole history of the universe and to embrace every detail and not merely occasional striking parts of being. If the universe is so organized that order, beauty, and adaptation of means to end emerge step by step all the way, then the argument is greatly strengthened. Nature begins with the inorganic, and rises to the vital, and then to the sentient, and then to the rational, moral, and personal, reaching its climax in man. Thus the whole vast sweep of cosmic history is an enlargement of the argument from design. One phase of this argument applies to the development of the idea of God. All growth is due to the adaptation of internal to external relations. The organism corresponds to the environment. Now the failure of either organism or environment results in death. The idea of God or of gods is universal among men. It has undergone change and development. The Scriptures exhibit belief in one supreme God, who has revealed himself to men. But that which has kept alive the idea of God has been the reality of God himself. Men are constituted for God, and apart from him they are without peace. We may thus conceive of man's spirit as a spiritual organism, and God as its necessary environment. The adaptation of this organism to this environment, and of environment to organism, is one of the most impressive of all the arguments from design.

[127]

The Christian Religion in Its Doctrinal Expression

There are two well-known objections to the argument from design. One is that it does not prove a Creator of the world, but only an architect, a builder, who used previously existing materials. In reply we first refer to the cosmological proof which deals especially with the original causal relation of God to the world. But it is to be replied further that the objection overlooks the need for preexisting material which was itself adapted to the end in view. The atom, or molecule, or whatever was the ultimate form of matter, must have had particular qualities which the alleged builder employed in the building. The bricks must have possessed durability and other qualities required for a structure which could endure. It follows from this that the objection does not eliminate the need for an original Creator, since the alleged preexisting material could only have originated as a part of a larger plan. All must have been designed. In other words, no beginning can be imagined which did not contain potentially all that was evolved from it. Thus we come again upon the endless row of bricks and the endless regress of causes in searching for the beginning of design. And once again we conclude that a personal and purposive Being created the world.

Another objection to the design argument is that it does not prove an infinite, but only a very great intelligence, since the universe is not infinite. This, however, is not a very serious objection. The mind has little difficulty in ascribing infinite power and wisdom to a Being who could produce so vast a system as our universe. Besides, the objection proceeds on the absurd assumption that an infinite Being would have to create another infinite in order to prove his infinitude. So to become an infinite cause God would have to produce a second God who was his equal.

We may now restate the design argument in somewhat different terms, although inclusive of the valid elements in former statements. Fundamentally our question is whether the universe as a whole, including man and nature, gives evidence of intelligence and purpose. Or did it originate by chance? The answer to these questions includes far more than particular instances of

[128]

adaptation. There are a number of powerful considerations pointing to the presence of design in the universe.

(1) The gradualness of nature's methods is not opposed to, but rather favors design. It was often urged by opponents of design that if you only allow time enough you can explain everything by natural causes without the need of design. For example, nature unaided can produce an eye by infinitesimal changes covering great periods of time. She could not do this by a sudden leap forward. God is not needed in a world that moves forward by slow degrees. This reasoning confounded cause with method. It taxes credulity to the limit to suppose that there was no thought of an eye originally if any eye results from the ongoing of the world. The necessity for design and purpose is deepened and intensified thus, not eliminated. The various forms of the evolutionary theory are now contesting the question as to the genetic relationships between organic forms. The mutation theory of progress by sudden leaps now holds the center of the stage. But the evidence of design is not in any sense weakened, but rather increased, on the hypothesis of long periods of growth.

(2) The presence of design is made clear by the answer of intelligence in nature to intelligence in man. Every science dealing with natural law assumes the intelligibility of the world about us. It is the fact that nature thus responds to our intelligence which convinces us that intelligence was here before us. The footprints of a personal God are everywhere before us in nature. As the lump of wet clay which you hold in your hand carries the impression of the lines of your palm, so the universe is stamped with the intelligence of the Maker. The idealistic philosophy insists that reason is the very warp and woof of all being. At all events there is no spot or aspect of nature which does not bear the stamp of intelligence.

(3) The design argument is greatly strengthened by the progressive series of organic forms leading up to man, who is the crown and goal of nature. Orderly progress, covering vast periods, and moving with undeviating steps toward the goal, is exceedingly impressive. The true continuity of the world thus

I

appears to be the continuity of a vast purpose inclusive of all the parts. A superintending intelligence which knew the end from the beginning is the only possible explanation. The lower continuity of physical nature which can be best understood as orderly progress toward a prearranged goal, is best understood as secondary and subordinate to the higher personal end which appears in man. All of nature thus becomes a vast system of design.

(4) Here again we return to the teaching of Christ and the Christian experience. In his providential dealings with his child, God continually gives proof of his superintending intelligence and power. And so in man's own personal life is to be found a supplementary proof for the design argument. Especially does the goal of a perfected moral character in a perfected moral kingdom, which we see in its earthly beginnings, enhance the value of the proof from design.

3. The anthropological proof of God's existence, which infers from man's spiritual constitution a cause adequate to the production of the effect, is changed in form, but loses nothing in force. The more recent statement of it simply takes man as the highest type of being, and from his personality and spirituality erects a world-view which provides for an infinite personal spirit. It is the same in method with all modern opposing theories, but very much stronger in its appeal. Every modern philosophy, as we have seen, finds some representative " type-phenomenon " in the world as we know it, and constructs its philosophy on this foundation. Now to take man himself as the " type-phenomenon " is by far the best selection. It is superior to materialism, because materialism takes the lowest form of existence to explain the highest. It is superior to abstract idealism because the latter takes thought apart from personality. It is superior to all other general world-views in that it employs the highest form of reality known to us to explain all other forms.

4. We note briefly the ontological argument for God's existence. This proceeds as follows: Man has in his mind a conception of the perfect being. A perfect being cannot be dependent,

but must be self-existent. Now since God is the perfect being and existence an attribute of perfection, God must exist. This is essentially the argument, although it is not so simply stated by Anselm and Descartes and others. It is curious how many people have misunderstood this form of argument for God's existence. It is simply a combination of the idea of perfection and that of necessary existence, and then an inference that a being corresponding to this conception must exist. It is really a definition of God, not a proof that he exists.

And yet approached in another and less formal manner, human experience has something to say in confirmation of what is intended in the ontological argument.

(1) The restatement of the ontological argument takes the form of an inference from the unity of the human reason with the universe of reality around us. Nature may be compared to a book which we read. Our capacity for reading it implies that there is agreement between our mental constitution and the constitution of nature. And this agreement implies further that nature originates in a source which is itself constituted in essentially the same way. The author of the book, the book itself, and the reader of the book are united in a common bond of intelligence. The conclusion is drawn that the reason which we find in ourselves is part of a universe grounded in reason. And since reason is joined to will and personality in us, we infer will and personality also in God.

The same idea may be expressed as follows: We think of all material objects in terms of time and space, of cause and effect, of number and quantity, of substance and quality. Our minds are so made that we cannot think otherwise. These relations and others express the fundamental laws of thought. Our mental life would come to an end, our minds would cease to be minds, if this power should fail us. Now in nature we find objects existing in these relations. They are in time and space, they follow each other, as cause and effect, they are presented to us in these various relationships in the world around us. And thus by a necessity of thought we are driven to the inference of an underlying unity. A supreme intelligence is the only clue to the bond of unity between man and nature.

(2) Observe the nature of the argument. I do not infer that God exists simply because I have in my mind a conception of a perfect being to whom belongs the quality of self-existence. I infer that he exists because I find the whole of being known to me constituted in and for intelligence. Man and nature answer to each other in their rational constitution. Nothing exists which is unrelated to reason. The thought expressed on the pages of the book, the capacity of the reader to understand the thought, and the author of the book are all bound together by a common bond. In each of them the other two are implicated.

(3) The force of the argument will become clearer if we express it in the form of our intuitions of truth. An intuition is a self-evident truth. It arises upon presentation to our minds of the data to which it relates. There are a number of these which illustrate what is meant. They arise as a result of our interaction with nature and society, and in our religious life. The intuition of cause and effect is an invariable form of human experience. Only a highly speculative process of reasoning can shake our belief in it, and even then not for long at a time. We have also the moral intuition of right and wrong. Moral standards vary, but the intuition remains. Again, we have the intuition of dependence and independence. The two are indissolubly joined together. The one cannot be conceived apart from the other. So also is the intuition of the finite and the infinite. The thought of one implies the thought of the other.

(4) Now if we stop at this point we have strong cumulative proof of God's existence. When we unify these intuitions in our thought, we cannot escape the conclusion that a being exists who unites in himself all the supreme qualities implied in these intuitions. He is the supreme cause, the ultimate moral standard, the perfectly independent and underived being, the infinite and perfect God. But we cannot consistently refrain from going a step farther. We have also the religious intuition. We seek help and fellowship from higher powers. This is distinct from the

intuitions of the reason we have just named. It arises in the depths of our being, from a deep sense of need. All the other intuitions in some degree enter into it, but it is more than all the others. And here again in the revelation of God in Christ and in the redemption he brings, we find our true goal. The intuitive and spontaneous processes of the soul are met by the great reality itself. Thus man finds self-fulfilment in all the parts of his rational, moral, emotional, and spiritual nature. He now perceives that the very make and pattern of his soul carried the idea and the evidence of God's existence.

5. We consider finally the moral argument for God's existence. Here all modern thinking runs back to Kant. And it is in connection with his view and that of his followers we can best set forth with clearness our own. Kant's theory of knowledge lay at the foundation. We can only know phenomena, not the realities behind the phenomena. God is not a phenomenon. He is, if he exists, a spiritual being. Hence he is not for us an object of knowledge. But conscience is a reality in man. The sense of right and wrong, of freedom, of obligation to avoid the wrong and do the right, is a part of our very being. A God of eternal right, who seeks to produce moral character in us and an eternal moral kingdom, is thus a postulate of the " practical reason." We do not prove God's existence, but we need God and infer that he exists.

(1) By this reasoning we advance beyond the conclusion of any argument from physical nature. In these we may deduce a God of intelligence, of skill, and of boundless power. But in the moral argument from man's practical needs we deduce a God who is moral and personal. With this thought we return to nature and see that it also has a moral end. We descend from man as moral and personal to the material universe and annex it as a province, as it were, of a universal moral kingdom.

(2) There is great force in this argument. But Christianity has enabled us to state it with much greater force than it contains in Kant and in the Ritschlians who build on this theory of knowledge. Our experience of redemption through Christ brings

knowledge of the reality behind phenomena. It brings direct knowledge of God. We deduce God from our moral constitution. But we meet God in our redeemed life. Moreover, the new life which we have in Christ makes possible the attainment of the moral ideal as never before. This knowledge of God and this power of attainment are not only inferences from objective data; they are also realities of our own spiritual life.

(3) If it be objected that the claim to direct knowledge of God contravenes Kant's theory of knowledge, the Christian replies that theories of knowledge cannot alter facts. They must conform to facts as they are found. Facts can be made to conform to theories of knowledge only when the latter are adequate to the end in view. But facts must come first, not theories about them. The objector must first disprove the facts, not seek to impose a theory of knowledge which fails to explain them.

General Conclusion

1. In concluding this section we may add that all the older proofs of God's existence based on inference from the world about us, are greatly reenforced by the proofs derived from Christian experience. The same ideas are reproduced out of a different group of facts. Man's religious life of fellowship with God in Christ is an orderly system of facts, of forces, and of experiences. The observation of these facts and forces yields an explanation, or explanations, which are even more convincing to the reason than any conclusion derived from the physical universe. We know a cause producing a given set of results in our soul's life. We know it as coming from without us, and yet producing its effects in us. This answers to the cosmological argument. Again, this cause operating in us works ever toward a moral end, our transformation into Christ's image. The process of the gradual transformation is a matter of daily consciousness in our experience. This answers to the teleological argument. Again, man's need of a God who is infinite to satisfy the needs of his personal life, along with his discovery of such a God in

Christ, gathers up the essential element of the anthropological argument. In this case, however, it is not an inference from man to a cause capable of producing men. It is rather man finding in his own nature and need a reflection of God's image in himself. When he comes to a knowledge of God in Christ, it is direct knowledge of God entering his human personality in redemptive power. So also the ontological proof has its analogue in man's religious craving for God, his intuition of the infinite and Holy One upon whom he depends and for whom he was made. God is thus seen to be not only a necessity for reason, but also for the self-realization of man in redemption and blessedness.

2. There can be no higher proofs of God's existence than these we have given, because they exhaust all spheres of reality which are known to us, the world without and the world within man, and God himself. We infer God from nature. We infer God from man's nature as moral and spiritual and personal. But above all, we know God within us as a living redemptive reality. In the first and second instances we deal with logical inference. In the third we deal with a vital fact.

3. It is always possible for the objector to bring the charge of subjectivism against any proof of God's existence. Man finds what he looks for because he wants to find it, not because it is there. It has been expressed thus: If many grains of wheat are thrown promiscuously on a table, you can, by picking out some grains and leaving others, produce any pattern or spell any word you desire. You can make the grains spell God or atheism. So you can manipulate the facts of nature and experience. But this objection is more formidable in appearance than in reality. It overlooks the other truth. You can just as easily manipulate the grains of wheat so as to spoil what is already there. The man who refuses to see is quite as subjective as the man who claims to see. The Christian has had both forms of experience. Once he was blind, now he sees. This is a form of certainty unknown to the objector. The charge of subjectivism may be brought by any objector to any conclusion in any sphere. All the data which we handle in our reasonings must pass through the human mold.

Our intellect impresses its forms upon all facts, just as a dipper shapes the water it takes out of the bucket. But all truth becomes truth only on the supposition that our reason gives us reliable information. The fact that reason is satisfied and a religious need is met surely cannot be justly held to discredit it. It is rather the strongest of proofs that it is true. And when a form of experience like the Christian's, which belongs to a great order of experience running through nearly two thousand years, and embracing millions of other Christians, and which can be scientifically analyzed and explained—when such an experience is under consideration the charge of subjectivism loses all its force. If the experience were merely individual and exceptional there would be some point in the objection. But not otherwise.

CHAPTER V

REVELATION

NO topic dealt with in theology calls for more careful attention to facts as contrasted with theories than revelation. The subject has often been beclouded by the introduction of needless problems. Abstract and *a priori* considerations have often ruled the minds of thinkers here. Attention to the facts of man's common religious life, and particularly to those presented in the Christian revelation, will lead to the conclusions which are called for by a system of Christian doctrine.

There are several facts fundamental to clearness of view which may be named at this point. The first is that the very conception of religion contains at its heart the idea of revelation. No definition of religion which omits the idea can stand in the light of the facts. If the worshiper speaks to God, and God is forever silent to the worshiper, we have only one side of religion. Religion then becomes a meaningless make-believe. The second fact is that the general religious life of mankind, with scarcely any exception, exhibits belief in revelation as essential to religion. The apparent exceptions are instances like Brahmanism and Buddhism, which are speculative systems of thought rather than religions. They are philosophies which mark the insufficiency of the ethnic religions. They never have succeeded as philosophies. Always the religious impulse reasserts itself and the gods swarm back into consciousness. The third fact is the unique and unparalleled revelation which God has made in and through Jesus Christ. With the revelation in Christ is to be taken the revelation of God to Israel. The remarkable record of this revelation is presented to us in the Scriptures of the Old and New Testaments. The above considerations show how the doctrine of revelation arises out of the facts of experience and of history.

The chief problem is to interpret the facts. In the Scriptures we find an interpretation of the facts. In brief, it is that God revealed himself to Israel in the life and history of the people, and that prophetic men have left us a record of the revelation, and that God spoke supremely in and through Jesus Christ and the apostles.

There can be no question that the biblical writers regarded the revelations which came to them as supernatural. It is equally clear that the revelation was mediated to them for the most part through their experience and needs. God was present with his people. He dwelt in them. He guided and cared for them, and slowly made himself known to them.

I. Opposing Views

Before developing the idea of a supernatural revelation further we may note here a few of the opposing views, based on certain philosophic assumptions and world-views.

1. The agnostic does not assert or deny the reality of God, but he does deny that God can communicate with us. The absolute and infinite is too far removed from man to make himself known to him. Of course we agree at once that we cannot know God perfectly. But we deny strongly the radical theory of knowledge which asserts man's total incapacity for knowing God and God's total incapacity for revealing himself to man. As we have seen, man is constituted for God in every part of his being. In his psychic, moral, scientific, philosophic, and religious life, he seeks and progressively attains the truth. Agnosticism denies all meaning to these facts. For him the world is not coherent, not a unitary system. It is awry. The parts of being are out of relation to each other. There is no food for man's soul-hunger. All of this shows that the agnostic denial of the possibility of revelation is grounded in an unscientific theory of knowledge. In principle it is subversive of all thought in all spheres.

2. The pantheistic denial of the possibility of a supernatural revelation is destructive of the true religious life in another way.

It cancels the distinct reality of God as a personal being. It makes of man simply a part of the infinite substance. He is as divine as any other part of being. This view often expresses itself in the form of an exaggerated doctrine of the divine immanence. God is in all things and through all things, and, according to this view, we need not think of him as also above all things. The reply is that if God only speaks through the natural and human development of events, then he is absorbed and exhausted as it were in his own universe.

The doctrine of the divine immanence, which teaches that God is equally present everywhere, leaves no room for anything distinctive in revelation. Everything is divine revelation on this view. And this amounts virtually to the statement that nothing is divine revelation. God never can distinguish himself to our consciousness from his finite creation if we try to explain his action by means of an exclusive doctrine of the divine immanence. The immanence of God is a great and important truth. The Scriptures everywhere recognize it. But the transcendence of God is equally important. God's transcendence is involved in his personality. Personality in man is the chief element in his constitution as bearing the image of God. Man's personality is developed on the natural level through interaction with matter and human society. On the spiritual level it is developed through interaction with God. The unfolding of man's personal religious life then marks his distinction from God at every point. This distinction is a fundamental condition of all the religious life of man. Religion means man in fellowship with God in personal terms. This implies both the immanence and transcendence of God.

3. Another view which opposes a supernatural revelation takes the form of what is commonly known as natural religion. Its position is that the world about us, along with the human reason and conscience, sufficiently reveals God to us. There is therefore no need of a supernatural revelation. God's existence we infer from the works of nature. Human freedom we know as being conscious of moral obligation. Immortality we infer from our own spirituality and the necessity of a future life to adjust the

wrongs and inequalities of the present life. Thus reasons natural religion.

There are various objections to the view. The first is that it is a creed based on philosophic inferences rather than a religion. A man might hold all the above items of belief and not be a religious man at all. Religion is experience of fellowship with God, not logical deductions from a particular set of objective facts. The view is defective also in that it does not contain enough knowledge of God to supply human need. Particularly does it come short in its failure to show the redemptive love and purpose of God. It is also glaringly deficient in its suggestions as to the moral and spiritual power needed for the victorious religious life. It has no suggestion for a renewal of man's nature and the implanting of a love for holiness. The view of natural religion is radically objectionable because it leaves God himself forever silent. His works indeed reveal something of God, the elementary truths of religion. In this natural religion is right. But according to it God never becomes active for man's enlightenment or salvation. Reason discovers what it can. But God speaks no direct word to the most earnest seeker for truth. The view is essentially deistic. God made the universe and left it running. In a general way he upholds it. He may, as it were, keep it " spinning round his finger," but he never touches it.

These three types of objection to the idea of a supernatural revelation will sufficiently indicate the prevailing views. None of them can make good its claim. The whole subject must be carried over from the realm of speculation and *a priori* reasoning into that of living experience. The Christian doctrine of revelation rests on a fact basis. It is not an abstract theory, but an explanation of certain events in the spiritual history of the race. The record of these events is found in the Christian Scriptures.

II. CONTENTS OF REVELATION

Christian revelation may be defined as containing the following elements:

Revelation

1. It is primarily a revelation of God himself rather than of truths about God. This is a cardinal fact. Revelation is in the first instance God making himself known. Truths there are of course. Doctrines inevitably shape themselves as the revelation proceeds. But the primal fact is God entering human experience, and man becoming conscious of his presence and power.

2. On the human side revelation is primarily a spiritual transaction rather than mere illumination of the intellect. Revelation is an event in the soul, an act of man's whole nature in response to God's self-disclosure. Thus revelation is primarily salvation. God makes himself known by saving acts to the individual or to the redeemed society. It is easy to see how far removed this is from the bare communication of truth to the mind. There were indeed instances of the latter recorded in the Old Testament. But the uniform law was revelation through the redeeming activity of God.

There is a great principle of religious psychology involved in this point. No bare truth about God can be a revelation of God in the Christian sense. Revelation is " acquaintance with " and not mere " knowledge about " God. Even the revelation in and through Jesus Christ would never have been complete without the group of redeemed men to whom it was made. What Christ was as the Revealer of God could only be known through his redeeming power in the disciples. And the world at large could never have known that revelation unless the first group of disciples had left a record of their own experiences. The revelation included necessarily therefore the objective self-disclosure of God in the historical Jesus Christ; the subjective experience of the redeeming power of Jesus in the regenerated society; and the permanent record of that power and that redemption given us in the New Testament. The gospel thus became the possession of the world at large and became an actual transforming power organic in the human race.

3. Again, revelation was rooted in the life and needs of the people. We should not think of it as a foreign thing grafted on Israel. It was not unrelated to their life and needs, but sprang

directly therefrom. The message through the prophets and apostles met an actual situation. It did not spring out of the natural life of the people as its producing cause. It was rather the coming of God into their life to meet an urgent need.

4. Revelation on God's part evoked an active response on man's part. This is a matter of vital importance. It is frequently forgotten in discussions of the subject. Here, as elsewhere in the religious life, man must conform to the universal law expressed by the apostle Paul: We work out what God works in us.

There is nothing in the Bible to warrant the Roman Catholic notion of implicit faith; that is, the unintelligent acceptance on sheer authority of the dogma of an ecclesiastical superior. There is nothing in Scripture to warrant the idea of mechanically dictated truth to a merely passive intellect. Men sometimes think of revelation as if the mind of the prophet were as a blank sheet of paper on which the Holy Spirit inscribed God's message. On the contrary, the human faculties were, as a rule, intensely alive and active. The truth disclosed was molded in the forms required by the personality, training, and circumstances of the human organ of revelation.

Here again we have a principle of great significance. God's revelation is designed to awaken and develop human personality. Never is it intended to crush or weaken it. Observe the care with which Jesus revealed himself to the early disciples. " Who do men say that I am?" was his question at one stage of his public ministry. When Peter replied correctly Jesus pronounced him blessed. Jesus meant that men should discover him. The revelation was not complete until they responded actively. His parables were framed expressly to awaken thought about him. In a sense then God's revelations can only become revelations when they become our discoveries.

III. THE RECORD OF REVELATION

We have in the Scriptures of the Old and New Testaments the record of God's revelation of himself to his people. There are two ways of approaching the question of the authoritativeness of the Scriptures. One puts much emphasis on the processes, the other upon the results, of inspiration. The former seeks to enter the realm of religious psychology and to show how God's Spirit imparted the light necessary for the inspiration of the biblical writers. The latter is more practical and dwells rather upon the outcome of the process in the Bible as we have it.

1. The psychological method seeks to distinguish between revelation, illumination, and inspiration. Revelation is the supernatural communication of truth to the human messenger. Illumination is the spiritual insight imparted by God's Spirit, enabling the human mind to grasp the meaning of the truth. Inspiration is the divine guidance and control of the messenger in delivering or recording the message. These distinctions, when properly understood, are justified. The revelation in and through Christ was given before the illumination required for its understanding in the minds of the early disciples. Again, illumination is bestowed by the Holy Spirit upon all obedient children of God. Spiritual insight, without revelation and inspiration in the strict sense, is the common possession of believers. It would be a mistake, however, to hold these distinctions in too radical a manner. They are useful for thought. But the elements separated in thought are not always separate in fact. Revelation is usually accompanied by illumination. Inspiration also is most frequently attended by revelation and illumination.

2. As a result of the psychological method certain theories of inspiration have arisen. In brief outline they are as follows: The naturalistic theory of inspiration holds that as God dwells in all men, all are inspired. The degree of inspiration depends upon their natural capacity, mental and spiritual. It is obvious that this is not the biblical doctrine of inspiration. Another theory is that inspiration is illumination rather than infallible guidance into truth. It thus leaves room for many and varying degrees of truth and of error in the outcome. Another is called the plenary verbal theory of inspiration. It holds that every word of Scripture was selected by the Holy Spirit and

dictated to the writer. One form of the theory of plenary inspiration is called the theory of dynamical inspiration. This maintains that the thought rather than the language was inspired, and that men were enabled to declare truth unmixed with error, but permitted to convey their ideas in forms of their own selection.

a. With regard to these theories it may be remarked that none of them is an exhaustive or adequate expression of the teaching of Scripture. Most of them no doubt contain elements of truth, but they attempt the impossible. It is not within our power to analyze fully the process by which God's Spirit operates upon the human mind in providing for us a record of his redemptive dealings with men. There was great variety in the circumstances of the biblical writers, and great diversity in their gifts and capacities and in the forms employed for setting forth the truths revealed. In some cases inspiration led to the selection merely of historical material, as in the historical books of the Old Testament. In others the facts were given and inspiration led to their interpretation. In the case of Luke, as he informs us, careful research was necessary. Inspiration did not exempt him from the ordinary task of the diligent historian.

b. Most of the psychological theories of inspiration start from a false premise. They begin by asking how God could have given to us a reliable guide for our religious life, and they proceed to answer the question by a theory which seems to meet the end in view. They proceed thus: If the Bible is God's word to us, then it must have been given in such and such a manner. The true method, on the contrary, is to study the Bible inductively in order to learn what its claims are and what success it has had in meeting those claims, in the experience of Christians of the past and present. This is the experiential and practical method of approaching the doctrine of inspiration. It is much more concerned with the result than it is with the process of inspiration. What is the Bible, and what place does it hold in our religious life to-day? How does it meet the religious needs of men? This is the practical question. The Bible itself contains the best answer.

[144]

IV. DISTINGUISHING MARKS OF THE BIBLICAL REVELATION

In harmony with what has just been said we proceed next to name some of the leading characteristics of the Scriptures. These are given as a general survey of the contents of the Bible itself.

1. The biblical revelation is historical and experiential. This means that individuals in Israel and the people of Israel lived in conscious relations with Jehovah. It means also that Jehovah made himself known to them in their individual and national history. Nothing stands out in clearer light as to the writers of the Old Testament than their consciousness of God. This appears in many passages. Many of the psalms are little more than fervid narrations of God's dealings with Israel. (See Deut. 26 : 16; 28 : 1; Ps. 107 : 1ff.; 44 : 1ff.; 105 : 1ff.) The prophets lived in the divine presence. The consciousness of God with them was a part of their own self-consciousness. It was their uniform claim that Jehovah spoke in and through them. (See Jer. 1 : 4; Ezek. 2 : 1; Hosea 1 : 1; Micah 1 : 1; Hag. 1 : 1.) The same fact appears in the New Testament, but under changed conditions. Jesus declares the truth about God, and those who receive the revelation record it in our New Testament books. The promise to them is that they shall be guided into truth by the Holy Spirit. (John 16 : 13.)

2. The biblical revelation is regenerative and morally transforming. In the early stages of the revelation the ethical qualities of the people do not shine with the same radiance as in the later. But it is clear that one chief object of the revelation is moral transformation. To think of the sheer communication of supernatural truth as the most important object or result of revelation is to misconceive it. There is a growth from immature forms of morality in the early parts of the Old Testament to a perfected morality in the New Testament which presents a striking contrast between the outward and inward, the temporary and permanent, the special and the universal, the provisional and the final. The Sermon on the Mount alone is abundant proof of this statement. (Matt. 5 to 7.)

The Christian Religion in Its Doctrinal Expression

3. The biblical revelation is genetic. This means that the parts are vitally related to each other. The revelation proceeds like the unfolding of an inner life principle: We do not find the prophets warring with each other in sentiment and aim. Each takes up the thread of teaching at the point where his predecessors left it off. They build on each other. This is the fundamental law of all progress. The traditionalist worships the ancient forms and will have no change. The radical is so intolerant of the old that he would destroy it. The prophets and apostles avoided both errors. The continuity of the teaching of the Bible is one of its most marked qualities.

4. Another outstanding characteristic of the revelation of the Bible is that it is gradual and progressive. The recognition of this fact is one of the most important results of the modern critical study of the Bible. It is an easy task to show that every leading idea of the biblical revelation undergoes change in the sense of growth and expansion in the course of the history. The conception of Jehovah himself is first presented with emphasis on the attribute of power. He is thought of chiefly in his relations with Israel. Slowly the idea is transformed into the splendid conception of Isaiah in which Jehovah is portrayed as infinite in all his attributes, and yet full of condescension, grace, and love. In the New Testament we have the crowning revelation of God as the infinite Father who sends his Son to redeem the world.

The principle of a gradual and progressive revelation sheds light on several problems which may be mentioned here.

a. It supplies the key for the interpretation of certain psalms and other Old Testament passages in which God seems to be represented as a vindictive being, rejoicing in his power to inflict suffering even upon the innocent along with the guilty. (See Ps. 137 : 9; 109 : 5-20.) The Old Testament law of divorce is not the same as that of the New Testament. Certain offenses which civilization no longer visits with penalties so severe were punishable in Israel by death. Now all these facts can be understood if we think of the Bible as the record of God's self-disclosure to a people incapable of more rapid development.

[146]

It is impossible to reconcile them with any theory of inspiration which regards all parts of the Bible as equally absolute and final. Jesus expressly rejected the view. A large part of Paul's writings are opposed to it. The book of Hebrews is an elaborate and formal argument to show that the Old Testament revelation was preparatory rather than final.

All this is but illustrative of the divine pedagogy in the training of a race. There was no moral and spiritual method of forcing the process of growth. It required free action on man's part. Men must *learn* obedience. Often it required severe discipline to teach it. But until they could grasp the truth it was vain to proclaim it. And so Jehovah gently led his people and bore with their infirmities and moral blindness until he could lead them out into a larger moral and spiritual life.

b. The gradualness of revelation sheds light on the question of delay in the great revelation in Christ. In the New Testament Paul often employs the phrase " the fulness of times " in relation to the coming of Christ into the world. There was a ripening of the divine purpose. But there was also a maturing of human receptiveness for Christ. If Christ had come at the beginning of the revelation, the moral and spiritual preparation necessary on the part of the people would have been wanting. No doubt he came as soon as the incarnation could prove effective for the end in view. The idea of epochs and dispensations in God's dealing with men is based on a profound law of man's spiritual development. It has to be kept in mind by all who would understand the revelation in Christ.

c. The gradualness of revelation sheds light on the principle of development, in so far as that principle is applicable to the Scriptures. Many moderns have sought to apply to the Old Testament history a theory of natural development which eliminates entirely the need for any supernatural presence or power of God. As we have seen, there is beyond question a principle of growth and development in revelation. Indeed, there is no body of religious literature on earth which compares with the Scriptures in steady progress from lower to higher forms. But this is not evidence against, but rather in favor of the divine guidance. It is an impressive mark of divine wisdom. Here were writers of varied gifts, separated by long intervals of time, surrounded often by unbelief and deadly hostility, speaking out their messages often at fearful cost in pain and suffering. Sometimes they spoke under protest, as in the case of Jeremiah, and yet urged on by an inward voice they could not resist. The result is a body of literature covering a period of a thousand years, possessing a marvelous unity along with a marvelous progress.

We may indicate the underlying principle of progress by the following statements: at each stage there was a communication of life and truth needed for that stage; the revelation contained in itself the principle for development to the next higher stage; the advanced stage in turn conserved the principle of the preceding stage and contained the germ which should expand into the next higher; the lines of development all converged toward fulfilment in Jesus Christ, the crowning revelation.

It is unnecessary to trace here the various lines of development in the progressive revelation. It is sufficient to point out that it is ethical, containing a deepening appreciation of the higher moral ideals; that along with this there is a marked development of the consciousness of sin and guilt; that this deepening sin-consciousness is attended by a growth in the sense of need for atonement; that the need for atonement is coupled in a marvelous manner with an enriched conception of God's grace; that the conception of God himself is slowly rounded out into that of a Being whose purposes include all mankind; that the course of the history slowly converges upon the One who in his Person and work is to transform the temporal kingdom into a spiritual and universal one for the redemption of mankind. These facts are "writ large" on the pages of Scripture.

One point needs to be added as to the gradualness of revelation. By this it is not meant that revelation was continuous and uninterrupted throughout the Old Testament period. There were great deliverances and deeds of Jehovah at special periods and great crises of Israel's history. The deliverance from Egyptian bondage and the great events which followed was one of these. To this period the people ever looked back with gratitude. In the period of the Exile there was a great revival of the prophetic inspiration and power. The miracles of Jesus, and especially his resurrection, were the most notable of all God's great acts of deliverance. The special deed and the special redemptive message were outstanding features of a revelation which, regarded in its whole course and extent, was also progressive and gradual. Both aspects of the truth should be held in mind.

5. Closely connected with the idea of this gradual and progressive revelation is that it is also unitary and purposive. All that we have just said as to the gradualness indicates as well the unity and purposiveness of God's revelation. It is only necessary to add a few points to bring the latter into greater clearness. There are at least five things which serve this end. First, the purpose of God is seen in his selection of one nation from among many. Through that nation he reaches all nations with his saving truth. Secondly, his purpose appears in the geographical position of Israel, the very center of the inhabited world of that age. Thus, like leaven in a lump, the life of Israel could slowly transform the rest of the world. Thirdly, his purpose appears in the divine guidance which led to the permanent record in writing of God's dealings with his chosen people. None of the prophets knew the place their words would hold in the literature of the race. Fourthly, God's purpose is seen in the supreme rôle which his recorded revelation has played in the actual history of the world. We note in the fifth place that the same purposive action of God is seen in the providential steps which led to the formation of the canon of Scripture. This arose not as an expression of ecclesiastical authority; it was the result of a vital inner process of selection. The divinity of the contents of the Scripture books, not church decrees, led to their incorporation in one body of literature.

6. The biblical revelation is congruous with man's general intellectual and religious life. The Bible, correctly understood, interferes in no way with man's search for truth in the realm

of science, philosophy, and other departments of intellectual effort. The Bible is not a book of science nor of philosophy. It is a book of religion. It only asks that science and philosophy recognize the facts of man's religious life for which it stands.

The biblical revelation does not require us to hold that no truths about God were known to the nations other than Israel. Many of the fundamental ideas of the Bible are seen in imperfect or distorted form in the general religious life of mankind. This does not discredit, but confirms the truth of the biblical revelation. These religious ideas were God's means of preparing men for the revelation in Christ. Men were enfeebled and blinded by sin. Yet the religious impulse never died in them. They sought God. The various systems are the result of their seeking. The special revelation in Christ is God's clear answer to them.

7. The biblical revelation is supernatural. The Old Testament prophets constantly claimed divine authority for their words. This reference of their messages to God or God's Spirit is so uniform, so unvarying, that it has all the impressiveness of a phenomenon and a law. (Num. 11 : 23; 20 : 24; Isa. 55 : 11; 66 : 2; Jer. 1 : 12; 4 : 27; 23 : 28-30; Matt. 24 : 35; John 5 : 24; 2 Tim. 3 : 16.)

How shall we account for it? Were these men self-deceived? Were they afflicted with diseased minds? It is impossible to believe this in the light of their lofty and sane moral teachings and of their commanding position in the world to-day.

If men object that such revelations are psychologically impossible, we may reply by pointing to the influence of our human mind and will upon other minds and wills. Mysterious? Yes. But nothing is more mysterious than the action of our own wills. The prophets knew as we know what came from without to them. Their whole personal and religious life was developed in reaction upon God and his will, revealed in and to them. Their own self-consciousness was the proof of their God-consciousness. Their own wills and God's will interacted without confusion of the one with the other, without absorption of their will in God's, or loss of their individuality in the infinite substance. Certainly these are the conclusions thrust upon us as we read what these men say to us in their written words. We cannot analyze or define accurately all the processes. The details elude us. But the great outstanding fact is beyond dispute if we are to credit what these men tell us about their own experiences.

Jesus Christ clearly recognized the unique and permanent value of the revelation of God through the Old Testament writings. (Matt. 21 : 42; 22 : 29; Mark 14 : 49; Luke 24 : 27; John 5 : 39.) They spoke of him. With Jesus it was a commonplace thought that the Old Testament was God's self-revelation.

The apostles also claimed divine guidance for their messages. They were the witnesses to the facts of the life of Jesus. They were the interpreters of Christ to us. Jesus promised the Holy Spirit to them for future guidance.

The apostle Paul is especially clear in his statements regarding the influence of God's Spirit in his work. (1 Cor. 2 : 4, 5, 10-16.) In one notable passage he states generally the doctrine of inspiration: " Every Scripture inspired of God is also profitable for teaching, for reproof, for correction, for instruction in righteousness; that the man of God may be complete, furnished completely unto every good work " (2 Tim. 3 : 16).

However we may translate these words, the great outstanding fact remains that the apostle regarded the Scriptures as derived from men who were guided by the Holy Spirit of God.

A general opposition to everything supernatural on the part of many of course forbids the idea of anything supernatural or special in the biblical revelation. For the present it need only be replied that the facts as we know them do not warrant an impersonal conception of being as a whole; that personality is the supreme fact; and that personality cannot be confined within the chain of physical law; and that if the universe is ultimately personal, and if God is a God of grace and love, there can be no possible objection on theoretical grounds to the idea of a supernatural revelation.

8. The biblical revelation is sufficient, certain, and authoritative for all religious ends. This means that the Bible meets all the

requirements of the religious life of man as the inspired literary record of the self-revelation of God.

Here we note one or two errors which are to be avoided. First, we must not imagine that the biblical revelation removes the necessity for the direct action of God's Spirit upon men. Man's approach to God is direct. Spirit with Spirit can meet. It is the presence of God's Spirit in men that enables them to understand, appreciate, and use the Scriptures aright. The Bible is not statutory. It is not of the nature of a legal code. It is a book of life principles. To the regenerate man the most convincing of all the evidences of the divine origin of the Bible is the identity of his own spiritual life with that revealed in the Bible. The Christian finds a saving gospel there. The Bible is the collection of writings which explains to him the life he has found in Christ. He thus sustains a relation to the Bible which is independent of all theories pertaining to its literary structure.

Another error to be avoided is the application of false standards to the Scriptures. This mistake has often been made. Men have applied the scientific or philosophic test to the Bible and have rejected it because it does not at all points square with their own conclusions. This is the cardinal error of some modern men in their approach to the Bible. Modern scientific methods are of recent origin. If the biblical writers had been divinely taught the truths of modern science and had announced them prematurely, the result would have been to discredit rather than to commend their messages. Suppose, for example, that in the Nineteenth Psalm, which has much to say about the heavenly bodies, the writer had announced the modern scientific formulation of the law of gravitation: Bodies attract each other directly as the mass and inversely as the square of the distance. What would have been the result? The mere supposition shows how completely foreign to the biblical writers was this modern scientific point of view. What is the infallibility of the Bible? How is it to be tested? Dr. Marcus Dods says:[1] "The whole matter hinges here. What is the infallibility we claim for the Bible? Is it

[1] "The Bible: Its Origin and Nature," pp. 151, 152.

infallibility in grammar, in style, . . in science, or what? Its infallibility must be determined by its purpose. If you say that your watch is infallible, you mean, as a timepiece; not that it has a flawless case, not that it will tell you the day of the month, or predict to-morrow's weather. The navigator finds his chart infallible as a guide to lighthouses, and shallows, and sunken rocks, but useless to give him the time of day or to inform him of the products and races of the lands he is bound for. A guide may infallibly lead you over a difficult and not easily found pass, although he is ignorant of any language but his own and knows little that happens beyond his own mountains."

It is strange indeed how often the friends and foes of the Bible have created false issues about it. We must let the Bible tell its own story and not hold it to false standards and tests. It shows us God's presence among his people using men of varying capacities, who were guided in the selection of a great variety of means for conveying the truth; adapting the means to the end in view and the need to be supplied; employing always the language of common life; sometimes using forms of pictorial representation suitable for a child-race; at others rising to the lofty eloquence of Isaiah and the sublime conceptions of a God infinite in majesty, power, grace, and truth; the whole culminating in the matchless revelation of God in Christ. The Bible then is a book of religion, not of science. As such it has proved hitherto and will continue to prove in the future, man's sufficient and authoritative guide.

In conclusion, then, the Bible remains in its place of authority for Christians. It is a vital and living authority, and not a mechanical and ecclesiastical one. It is our authoritative source of information as to the historical revelation of God in Christ. It is regulative of Christian experience and Christian doctrine. It is the instrument of the Holy Spirit in his regenerative and sanctifying influences. As regulative and authoritative it saves us from subjectivism on the one hand and from a bare rationalism on the other. It holds us to the great saving deeds of God in Jesus Christ, the Redeemer and Lord. It is final for us in all the matters of our Christian faith and practice.

[153]

CHAPTER VI

THE SUPREME REVELATION: JESUS CHRIST

I. Christ the Key to Scripture

JESUS CHRIST is the key to the interpretation of Scripture. He is the keystone in this vast arch of spiritual truth. One of the most conspicuous features in the Old Testament literature is its Messianic element. In many and varied forms the rich contents of the Messianic hope are expressed. Interpreters may attempt too much in the process of tracing out details of prophecy and fulfilment. But the great salient fact remains. The prophets expected a Deliverer, a great Leader, a holy kingdom, a reign of a righteous King, God's presence among men, a world transformed under the power of God's chosen One.

It follows, then, that the Gospels are for us central in our approach to the Bible. The Old Testament in all its lines of development culminates in Jesus Christ. He is the great historical fact and corner-stone of Christianity. The Epistles of the New Testament are devoted to the task of interpreting him.

We come into very close relations with the first Christians when we consider the question who and what was Jesus of Nazareth. The modern regenerate man knows in himself the working of a power which calls for explanation. The New Testament Christians faced the same question. These men who saw and heard Jesus undertake to tell us in a conscious and deliberate way their own impressions of his power and of his person. Without any knowledge whatever of modern scientific methods these men adopt a strictly scientific spirit in their approach to the subject. There is no theory, no speculation, no abstract reasoning. They begin with the words and deeds of Jesus. They follow him through his life and the events which followed. They consider him in relation to the facts of their own redeemed and morally transformed life, and in relation to the Christian movement.

[154]

The Supreme Revelation: Jesus Christ

In this way arose the doctrine of the person of Jesus. There are at least three general stages which may be noted in the New Testament representations. First, that contained in the synoptic Gospels; secondly, that found in the Book of Acts; thirdly, that presented by Paul and John. The teachings of Hebrews, of James, and of the book of Revelation might be specified further as containing distinctive elements. But space forbids exhaustive treatment, and the latter books do not contain material which affects the general result. Hence they are not given separate treatment here. It will be necessary to limit ourselves to the more salient passages.

1. In the synoptic Gospels there are at least five facts which stand forth clearly in the accounts of Jesus: First, his complete humanity; secondly, his sense of Messianic calling; thirdly, his sinlessness; fourthly, his unique relation to God; and fifthly, as a consequence to the preceding, his unique relation to man, to nature, and to history.

(1) The humanity of Jesus is manifest in all the synoptic records. Luke declares that Jesus grew in wisdom and stature and in favor with God and man. (Luke 2 : 52.) He suffered from hunger (Matt. 4 : 2), weariness, and pain (Matt. 26 : 38), and finally death. He was tempted not only at the beginning (Matt. 4 : 1-11), but throughout his ministry. (Luke 22 : 28.) He prayed. (Matt. 14 : 23.) He declared himself ignorant of the " day and hour " concerning which disciples made inquiry. (Mark 13 : 32.) He had a human body and a human soul.

(2) His sense of Messianic calling is another outstanding fact in the synoptic account of Jesus. Criticism has expended much labor to prove that this sense of vocation was wanting in Jesus, but it is impossible to expunge it from the record without violence. The name " Christ " designates Jesus as Messiah or anointed of God. At his baptism the approving voice of God the Father must have deepened in him this conviction. (Matt. 3 : 17.) The temptation in the wilderness can only be explained on the basis of a deep-seated conviction of Messianic vocation on the part of Jesus. (Matt. 4 : 1ff.) The incident of the confession

of Peter at Cæsarea Philippi brings it into great prominence. (Mark 8 : 27-30.) Many incidents in the life of Christ point in the same direction, such as his message to John the Baptist in prison (Matt. 11 : 2ff.), his confession before the high priest (Matt. 26 : 64), and other incidents. There is not space to discuss the self-designation of Jesus as Son of Man. It was probably based on the passage in Daniel 7 : 13, and was intended by Jesus as a Messianic title pointing to his universal relations to men. It involved the idea of suffering and future glory which would come to Jesus in his Messianic vocation.

The reserve of Jesus in announcing his Messiahship in the early stages of his ministry was probably owing to the danger of abruptly thrusting the idea of his own spiritual kingdom upon a people looking for a kingdom of temporal power, and to the desire that the disciples might grow spiritually into an appreciation of him and his work. He desired that his revelation might become their discovery.

(3) The sinlessness of Jesus. The formal claim to sinlessness did not constitute a leading element in the teaching of Jesus. But it is clearly implied in all his words and actions. Alleged weaknesses and sins, such as his anger at the hypocrisy of the Pharisees, are virtues, not faults. One passage seems to imply a denial of sinlessness. In Mark 10 : 18 Jesus declares that " none is good save one, even God." But here Jesus is thinking of goodness in its absolute or eternal form as it exists in God. The goodness of Jesus was a human goodness achieved through temptation and struggle. He learned obedience. (Heb. 4 : 15; 5 : 8.) He was made perfect through sufferings. But his imperfection was not that of sin, but rather of an unfolding life. If this be not true, how can we explain the absence of confession of sin? Why is it that we search in vain for any trace of penitence in his recorded words and deeds? How can we explain his unclouded and unbroken fellowship with God?

In John's Gospel we have a saying which denies sinfulness: " Which of you convicteth me of sin? " (John 8 : 46.) In numerous other passages in the Epistles we find the same view expressed. (1 Peter 2 : 21; Phil. 2 : 7, 8; 1 John 3 : 5; Heb. 7 : 26.)

His baptism was not a confession of sin, but a self-dedication to righteousness and to his Messianic vocation.

(4) Jesus sustained a unique relation to God. Central in his consciousness was the relation to the Father. He never addresses God as " our Father." He frequently says, " My Father " (Matt. 7 : 21; 10 : 32; 12 : 50). He never refers to himself as " a son of God," but he often refers to himself as " the Son." The most notable passage is that in Matthew 11 : 27: " All things are delivered unto me of my Father; neither doth any know the Father, save the Son, and he to whomsoever the Son willeth to reveal him." [1] This passage is one of the most remarkable found anywhere in the Gospels. It declares that Jesus sustains to the Father an extraordinary relation; possesses unparalleled knowledge of the Father; and performs a unique function in revealing the Father. He correlates his own knowledge of God with God's knowledge of him. He claims to possess " all things " from the Father. His own consciousness dwells completely in the divine consciousness. The center of his own will coincides with the center of God's will. Doctor Denney remarks [2] on this passage: " The sentence as a whole tells us plainly that Jesus is both to God and man what no other can be." Dr. H. R. Mackintosh adds the following [3] as to the special sonship here defined: " Looking at both Jesus' own mind and at Christian experience, there is no reason why we should not use the word metaphysical to denote this special Sonship, not as though metaphysical stood in contrast with ethical, but to mark the circumstance that this Sonship is part of the ultimate realities of being."

(5) Jesus Christ sustains a unique relation to man, to nature, and to history. In the synoptic Gospels there is a remarkable unity in the portrait of Jesus as that portrait stands related

---

[1] Critical objections to this passage in its present form are not supported by any strong evidence. They are objections based on the assumption that the passage partakes too much of a Johannine character. But this is a departure from scientific criticism and the adoption of *a priori* considerations.

[2] " Jesus and the Gospel," p. 272.

[3] " The Doctrine of the Person of Jesus Christ," p. 28.

to man, nature, and history. We give here a bare summary merely. We have already noted his own sinlessness. We add here that he forgives sin in others and thus exercises a divine prerogative. (Mark 2 : 6, 7, 10-12.) His blood was shed for remission of sins. (Matt. 26 : 28) ; and he declared after his resurrection that repentance and remission of sins would be preached in his name. (Luke 24 : 47.) In his relations to Moses and the law, Jesus declares that he came to fulfil (*i. e.,* complete) the law. (Matt. 5 : 17.) He is greater than the temple (Matt. 12 : 6) ; he is Lord of the sabbath (Matt. 12 : 8) ; he is the King who founds and rules in the kingdom of heaven (Matt. 5 to 7; Luke 22 : 29, 30; 19 : 12.) Jesus controlled the forces of nature, as witness the stilling of the tempest and other miracles. Future events were under his control. In the twenty-fourth and twenty-fifth chapters of Matthew we have an extended prophecy of his future relations to mankind. He is to be the judge on the throne before whom all nations are to be gathered.

The preceding is by no means an exhaustive statement. It is rather a bare suggestion of the salient features. But they are sufficient to show how high above the level of ordinary men was this man. He assumes a central place in man's religious life. He is not only our religious example, but also our religious object. In the Son we find the Father. His resurrection and ascension complete the picture. His gift of the Holy Spirit is the true explanation of his continued presence and power among men.

2. In the book of Acts, the teachings as to the person of Christ mark an advance over those in the synoptic Gospels in some respects. This is due to the changed situation. Jesus has been raised from the dead and has ascended to the right hand of the Father. The outpouring of the Holy Spirit has followed. A new era in the experience of the disciples has dawned. New powers work in and through them.

One passage contains a brief summary of the teaching in Acts. They are the words of Peter, " God hath made him both Lord and Christ, this Jesus whom ye crucified " (Acts 2 : 36). Two points require emphasis. First, Jesus the crucified is the Christ, the anointed of God, the Messiah. It was he who was predicted in the Old Testament. It is he who is to be received by faith as the Redeemer sent from God. Secondly, this crucified Jesus, who is the Christ of God, is also Lord. From every possible point of view the work of Jesus as the anointed Lord is set forth in the early chapters of the book of Acts. His miracles are mentioned. (Acts 10 : 38.) His resurrection from the dead is the supreme disclosure of his Messianic dignity and Lordship. (Acts 2 : 32; 10 : 41.) His gift of the Holy Spirit is especially pointed out. (Acts 1 : 4, 5.) In his name alone is salvation to be found. (Acts 4 : 12.) He is to return and restore all things. (Acts 3 : 21.) He is to judge the world. (Acts 17 : 31.)

3. The teachings of Paul occupy an important place in the New Testament history as to Christ's person.

The Christology of Paul presents two important aspects. First, that which is the immediate expression of the experience of salvation through Christ, and secondly, the theological statements which interpret this experience.

Paul's conversion on the road to Damascus is the key to his theology. Jesus Christ there appeared to him in glory. There his pharisaic creed collapsed and fell in ruins. There the new life of faith began with Paul. No explanation of the marvelous revolution of this man's life other than that contained in his own simple narrative can adequately account for it.

The mystical or inward and experiential elements in Paul's life run through all his Epistles. A man becomes a new creature in Christ. (2 Cor. 5 : 17.) In him the Christian is created anew unto good works. (Eph. 2 : 10.) "In Christ" is Paul's comprehensive phrase employed in every possible connection to set forth the believer's relation to his Lord.

The Holy Spirit dwells in the believer, and in the church he is the bond of unity in Christ. Jesus Christ is the head of the body in vital union with it through the Holy Spirit. (Col. 1 : 18; Eph. 4 : 15.) A man who is in Christ is in the Spirit. He who has the Spirit of Christ alone belongs to Christ. (Rom. 8 : 9.)

Paul does not identify Christ and the Spirit. But he clearly defines the sphere of the Spirit's activity by means of the phrase " in Christ."

In the teachings of Paul there is not a great deal about the earthly life of Jesus. Yet this element is not lacking. The resurrection is especially emphasized. (Rom. 1 : 4.) Here the statement is not that Christ became, but was declared to be, the Son of God by the resurrection. The resurrection of Christ, along with the crucifixion, is the central fact in Paul's gospel. The resurrection is the guaranty of the resurrection of believers. The exalted Christ is Lord of the church, just as in Acts. (1 Cor. 15 : 4, 12, 13, 20-28.) Jesus is the new spiritual head of the human race, as Adam was the natural head. (Rom. 5 : 12; 1 Cor. 15 : 22.)

Paul's statements as to the deity of Christ are usually incidental to other teachings. But they are the more rather than less impressive on this account. His hearers raised no question on the point. It was the accepted view. What he says, however, is entirely clear and convincing as to how he regarded Christ. In Romans 9 : 5 the word " blessed " follows the word " God," which would not be the case if it were simply a doxology. Moreover, the word " is " would be out of place in a doxology. The translation as Doctor Sanday gives it is, " of whom is the Christ as concerning the flesh, who is over all, God blessed forever."

In Hebrews 1 : 8 we have a quotation from the Old Testament in which Christ is addressed as God. So by Paul in Titus 2 : 13 he is described as " our great God and Saviour Jesus Christ."

In Philippians 2 : 6 begins an extended passage describing Christ as preexisting in the form of God, as emptying himself and taking the form of a servant, and being exalted and given a name above every name.

A passage in Colossians, 1 : 15-17, expresses Christ's relations to the universe in very explicit language. The following is asserted: (a) Christ was the medium of creation: " through him were all things created." (b) He was before all things, although not as a creature; " He is the first-born of the whole creation."

(c) He is the bond of unity of all things: " In him all things consist," cohere, are held together. (d) He is the end and goal of creation; all things are " unto him."

In the benedictions of Paul's Epistles he uniformly combines the name of Christ with the name of the Father and the Spirit, clearly showing the dignity with which he invests him in his ordinary thought.

We pass by many other notable passages in Paul's writings to consider a few in those of John. In the prologue to the Gospel Jesus is described as the eternal Word who was in the beginning, *i. e.*, possessed an eternal existence; who was " with God," *i. e.*, distinct from God; who was the creator of all things: " All things were made through him "; who " was God "; who was the source of all life and all light to all created beings; who became incarnate and dwelt among us; and who gave to those who received him power (authority) to become sons of God.

Philo, the Jewish-Alexandrian philosopher, had developed a speculative doctrine of the logos or divine reason. Some have thought John borrowed his conception from Philo. Upon this point two things may be said. First, if John was influenced by the logos idea of philosophy, it was in harmony with the Christian movement generally. Not to combat or destroy, but to transform and purify the partial and inadequate ideas of men was the Christian method of dealing with these ideas. Secondly, a comparison of John's Logos with that of Philo presents a marked contrast. In Philo the idea is abstract, speculative, variable in meaning, and bound up with the intellectual attempt to explain the divine being. In John the idea is very definite, ethical, and inspired by the historic facts as to Jesus, and bound up with the redemptive aim of the gospel.

The whole of John's Gospel is an account of the manifestation of the divine Son of God, and the results of that manifestation among men. John is at once historian and interpreter. In a great variety of passages his teaching as to Christ appears. In 5 : 23 the Son receives equal honor with the Father. In 5 : 27-29 authority to judge man is given to the Son. In 6 : 62

L

the Son of man is described as ascending where he was before. In 16 : 28 he is said to have "come out" from the Father. In 17 : 5, in his intercessory prayer, Jesus prays to the Father that he may be glorified with the glory which he had with the Father before the world was made. In 20 : 28 Thomas addresses Jesus as "my Lord and my God."

The above is by no means an exhaustive setting forth of the New Testament doctrine of the Person of Christ. There is really an embarrassment of riches in the material. It has seemed better to select a limited number of typical and representative passages than to attempt an exhaustive array of citations. That the deity and preexistence of Christ are taught in the New Testament is one of the most assured results of modern scientific exegesis. Scholars who object to the supernatural of course reject the doctrine as untrue. But as a matter of exegesis there are few who question the conclusion we have reached.

We may now sum up briefly our review of the New Testament teachings.

(1) We are impressed, in the synoptic records, with the fact of the perfect humanity of Jesus. That humanity is seen in the life of his body with its limitations, its hunger and thirst, its need and dependence. It is seen in his mental growth in wisdom, along with his physical growth in stature. It is seen in the reality of the temptations he endured. These he overcame without sin, but they were none the less real. His humanity is seen further in his dependence on the Holy Spirit. It is seen finally in his gradual achievement of his life purpose and mission under the earthly conditions of time and space.

(2) In the synoptic Gospels we have also an account of the human Jesus which presents him as possessing attributes and functions which are wholly extraordinary. His relations to God and man are far above the level of ordinary men. He is in relation to God the supreme and authoritative revelation. In relation to man he is the religious object and medium of salvation.

(3) In the book of Acts we find the next stage in the development of the doctrine of Christ's Person. The new facts of the

resurrection and ascension, along with the outpouring of the Holy Spirit, called for a corresponding expression of Christ's significance for the individual believer and for the church. That expression we find in the declarations as to his crucified and risen life, his Messiahship and Lordship, his exaltation at God's right hand, his reign over his kingdom, and his expected return in glory. The interpretation of his person kept pace with his redeeming activity.

(4) In the writings of Paul and John we find the answer to the questions which inevitably arose out of the redemptive power of Christ in the experience of the first Christians. The mind could not rest in the assertion that Jesus was Lord and Saviour. Men were certain to ask what were the relations of this Lord and Saviour to God himself. In the words of Paul and John we find the following: *a.* There was an eternal relation between the Father and the Son. There was mutual knowledge and love, a mutual sharing in the divine life. *b.* The coming of Christ into the world cannot be explained in terms of ordinary evolution or natural causation. He did not arise out of time, but entered into time relations for a divine end. *c.* The coming of Christ into the world was more than the entrance of God into the life of an ordinary man. It was a coming of God into the world, not the rise of an extraordinary man into unique relations with God. In Jesus Christ, God himself has come near to men for their redemption. He lives and reigns in and through Jesus Christ and in him fulfils his eternal purpose of love. *d.* This relation of Christ to the fulfilment of God's eternal purpose among men arises out of an eternal relation between the Father and the Son, and is in harmony with the activity of the Son as the outgoing principle of the divine nature. In virtue of this relation the Son is the eternal medium of creation for the entire universe. *e.* As a consequence of the redemptive activity of the incarnate Son, a new interpretation of history is given. In this interpretation all lines of development converge upon and meet in Jesus Christ. Without him the course of the world cannot be understood. *f.* In his incarnate life he is sometimes

represented as being subordinate to the Father. This is due to the human conditions and the life of obedience. It does not detract from the reality of his deity.

II. JESUS CHRIST IN MODERN RELIGIOUS EXPERIENCE

The preceding view of Jesus in its main points has been central in the development of Christian life and doctrine. The great creeds of Christendom are conclusive on this point. Recent biblical scholarship is practically unanimous in its conclusion to the same effect. But the experience which modern regenerate men have of God in Christ is, for them, the most convincing evidence.

It is well to recall at this point how the doctrine of Christ's Person arose in the New Testament, and how it arises with us. For one thing we do not frame our teaching as the result of *a priori* reasoning or merely logical inference from objective facts. Again, while the knowledge of Christ is mediated to us through the New Testament, and while the New Testament is absolutely indispensable for that knowledge, our faith in Christ is not to be confounded with mere belief in a record of past events, however convincing in itself. It is rather a view which results from the redeeming activity of Christ in our experience. It is thus the revelation of God in and through Christ, completed and made effective for us by the redemption wrought for us and in us. Since Christ works now as he wrought then, our own experience becomes the Amen, as it were, of the New Testament experience. What we have, then, on the one hand is not the bare belief of a history of events which took place two thousand years ago; nor, on the other hand, mere trust in our own subjective experience apart from the historical records. It is the union of the two forms of knowledge which completes our view of Christ. Our construction of Christian doctrine rests on a fact basis entirely: first and primarily, the facts of the New Testament records, and secondly, our direct and immediate experience of Christ as redeeming Lord.

[164]

The Supreme Revelation: Jesus Christ

Affirmations as to Christ in Experience

The following statements are necessary to express what Christ is to the redeemed man. First, Christ is the revealer of God. In him we have not indeed a disclosure as to the " substance " of the divine nature. Ultimate realities of this kind are the material of philosophic speculation. But in Jesus is made known to us the ultimate reality of God as a moral and spiritual being. In him God appears as righteous love. In him God comes near for our salvation. In him the grace and power of God are manifested for our redemption. In him God takes the initiative in seeking us. We are found and awakened by the gospel. But our sin binds us. We know ourselves alienated in heart and life from God. We are unable to redeem ourselves. We belong to a kingdom of evil and are held captive. We need forgiveness and reconciliation. Through his atoning work Christ brings God near in forgiving grace. We need moral and spiritual transformation. Christ supplies the motives which lead to repentance and the new life. He also supplies through the indwelling Spirit the ideal for our inner life. " In Christ " is the phrase which expresses the total meaning of the new life. He is its source, its structural law, and its goal. We are, in other words, regenerated and spiritually reconstituted in Jesus Christ.

Secondly, through Christ we now become identified with the community of believers, the church. In it our social relations are reconstituted in Christ. The goal and end of his activity and of ours is the kingdom of God as it is summed up in the great petition of the prayer he taught his disciples. Our wills become identified with his.

Thirdly, we thus come to know Jesus Christ as Lord of the kingdom, who guides and rules in it, and assumes a relation to all secular history and to the powers of nature. It is impossible that he should remain as a merely detached and spiritual influence over men if his kingdom is a reality in the world. The kingdom of evil is everywhere in evidence. The New Testament Christians, as clearly seen in the book of Revelation, thought of Jesus as the Lord of all history gradually conquering the hostile powers.

In the fourth place, Christ is the key to doctrine. If we know objects by what they do, by their activities, we are bound to seek some satisfactory expression of the meaning of Jesus in all his various relations. He works in us in our salvation that which we recognize as a divine work. Hence we seek to know his relations to God through definitions of his person. He emancipates from sin. Hence out of experience arises a consciousness of sin in relation to him. Thus we are led to formulate a doctrine of man and his sin. We see in him the central movement of God's purpose toward mankind. In this way we are led to the doctrine of the eternal purpose or decrees of God. Christ's relations to the ongoing of the world bring us to the doctrine of Providence. His atoning work, which, along with his incarnation, constitutes the basis of his redeeming activity, leads to the general doctrine of salvation in its personal significance, its present ethical and social expression, and in its outcome in the future life. All these themes will be developed in the following pages. In the next chapter we discuss the deity of Jesus Christ. In the proofs therein presented we assume all the New Testament evidence of his deity we have set forth in the present chapter.

CHAPTER VII

THE DEITY OF JESUS CHRIST

I. A NECESSARY ARTICLE OF FAITH

FOR the Christian believer the deity of Christ is a necessary article of faith for the following reasons:

1. First, Jesus works in us a divine result. There is an urgent necessity in Christian experience which cannot be ignored. We must either formally repudiate Christ as Redeemer, or go on and construe him as Redeemer. If he is not divine he has become a tremendous burden to Christianity. We must either estimate him as no more than a great teacher or a great saint, or else we must recognize in him God manifest in the flesh. For the believer there can be no hesitation. In his redeeming work in the Christian Jesus has done the following things: He has made religion a free and autonomous activity of man's spirit in direct relations with God. He has created a world of spiritual realities for the redeemed man and holds him in stedfast communion with that world. He has revealed God as eternal Father, whose fundamental character is righteous love which ever seeks the lost. Jesus has also disclosed the inner being of God as a sphere in which that love is active in the relations between the eternal Father and the eternal Son.

2. This conviction that Christ is God, arising out of the redeeming activity of Christ, contains implicitly a group of great intuitions which lie at the heart of man's spiritual life. It contains the psychological intuition of the self and the not-self, since it knows Another in the inner life of the soul. It contains the ethical intuition of right and wrong because the Christian's choice of Christ is the supreme choice of duty as such. It contains the rational intuition in its twofold form as the perception of the distinction between truth and error, and of cause

and effect. Christ as the truth is for the believer distinguished from all forms of error in the religious life. He is distinctly and explicitly recognized as the cause producing the effects in the morally transformed life. The several forms of the religious intuition are also involved in the experience of redemption through Christ: such as our sense of dependence of the finite upon the infinite; and also our sense of unrest and inner conflict which finds relief and inner blessedness through the discovery of the soul's true object.

3. The Christian believer holds the deity of Christ for the further reason that his experience of God in Christ unifies and completes many lines of evidence. Logic and philosophy draw inferences from objective facts and arrive at rational belief in God. In our redemption in Christ we find God as a fact. The psychology of religion presents us the manifestations of the religious consciousness of man. But it leaves unsolved the problem of causes. Christ gives us the solution. Physical science deals with causation in the sense of continuity or the conservation of energy, and never rises above the chain of material forces. Our experience of redemption in Christ is an experience of free causation, in which through personal interaction Christ draws us to himself and becomes a transforming power within. The study of comparative religion introduces us to a great mass of interesting data, but leaves unsolved the problem of the unity, coherence, and finality of religion. Our experience in Christ brings all religious values to a focus and unifies the religious life and fulfils its highest ideals. The philosophy of religion seeks to apply the rational process to the phenomena of religion, but remains abstract and unstable until the thinker himself knows experientially the religious object. Our experience in Christ puts us in possession of the realities of the spiritual life and affords the material out of which the philosophy of religion may construct its world-view.

4. Our belief in the deity of Christ arises also from the fact that our redemption in him is not a merely individual experience. It is also social and historical. A new spiritual order

arose with the Christian movement. It has continued thro ,gh Christian history. The creeds of Christendom witness to the great fundamental facts. No one can understand Christian history without recognizing the centrality of Christ in the experience of the individual and of the church. Many errors and abuses have arisen. Many lapses from the lofty standards of Christ's kingdom have occurred. But the great central truth remains. Jesus Christ stands at the heart of the whole movement.

5. Through the historical connections of faith we are brought back to the New Testament itself. There it is abundantly clear that the risen Jesus is everywhere regarded as the Lord of the church and the redeemer of man. His resurrection from the dead was a great crisis and turning-point in his Messianic work. It marked a new stage in the development of the divine purpose of redemption in and through him. It was the gospel of the risen Jesus that transformed the early disciples. By the side of the resurrection we must place certain other great facts which come to us through the synoptic records of his life and work. One of these is the sinlessness of Jesus. Another is his Messianic consciousness. Yet another is his self-disclosure as the religious object and final judge and only mediator between God and man. And finally, his unique relations as Son with the eternal Father.

On any critical view whatever as to the sources of the synoptic Gospels which is tenable, the above facts stand forth in great clearness. Certain forms of modern religious philosophy, in an abstract and unhistorical and uncritical manner, seek to eliminate some of the above elements. But if the Gospels are permitted to speak at all, they speak the message as we have outlined it. The message is clear and unequivocal.

II. General Considerations

We may add to the above a number of general considerations which will aid us in understanding the place of Christ in our religious experience. It is inevitable that one who means so much for the religious life of man should sustain a number of

great relations also to God and the world. We mention some
of these.

1. The revelation of God in Christ makes known to us in most
impressive form the personality of God. God's self-disclosure
in the universe is progressive.

Interpret the world in terms of matter, and you get law. Interpret the world in terms of intellect, and you get thought. Interpret it in terms of power, and ultimately you get will. Interpret the world in terms of the conscience, and you get righteousness. Interpret it in terms of the heart, and you get love. Interpret the universe in terms of personality, and you get God.[1] All
this means that in our study of the aspects of being we are led
by slow stages to the various attributes and qualities of God.
But we need a particular manifestation of God in order to our
understanding of the unity of all the qualities in him. If men
were ever to know God as a Person, it was needful that he reveal
himself as personal. No other phase of being, nor all the phases
combined, could impart this knowledge except by inference.
Nature presents a progressive series, from inorganic to organic;
from organic to sentient; from sentient to self-conscious; and
from self-conscious to moral and personal. Man is the crown
and goal. Every art and every science, all philosophy and all
civilization, are man's obedience to the instinct planted in him
which reaches out for the perfect, the ideal, the final truth, beauty,
and goodness. And these have no final meaning save as embodied in an infinite person.

Now we have in Jesus Christ God's response to this upward
movement of the human spirit. The descent of God into human
life by the incarnation in Christ is not an abrupt and violent
disturbance of the order of nature. In a real sense it is the
logical outcome of the course of nature. Man, who is nature's
crown, is burdened with a sense of need for help from above;
he yearns for knowledge, for moral power, for blessedness and
peace. Jesus Christ is made unto him, in response to these needs,
wisdom, righteousness, sanctification, and redemption. The par-

[1] Cf. Twing, " History of Higher Education," p. 463.

tial aspects of personality below man and its imperfect form in man are thus brought to unity and complete realization in Christ. "In him," as Paul says, "dwelt" not a fragment or part, but "all the fulness of the Godhead bodily" (Col. 2 : 9).

2. Again, the revelation of God in Christ is the key to the higher continuity needed to explain the world. Continuity in the physical sense means the transformation of energy. Consequents in nature are explained solely in terms of antecedents. Materialism has sought to level the universe down so that all else save physical continuity is excluded. But this principle fails at many crucial points. It has not yet explained how life can arise from the non-living; or how consciousness and thought can arise from the material forms of existence; and still less how the moral and personal can so arise. Modern theistic and ideal. istic thought begins at the end of the progressive series instead of the beginning. It finds the true continuity in the non-material, non-spatial factors. Life, thought, will, purpose, love— these are the true key to the process. In these are to be found the true continuity. Jesus Christ, the revealer of God, declares himself to be the way, the truth, and the life, and in him the infinite Life, Thought, Will, Purpose, and Love, which are before and in and through all things, come near to us. So that Christian theology does not deny continuity, but seeks it in its higher and only adequate form, and finds it in Jesus Christ the revealer of God. What is explicit in him was implicit in all that came before. The end reveals the beginning, not the beginning the end.

3. Again, Jesus Christ reveals God by demonstrating what God is in himself by outward act. God is holy love. Without this he would not be God. A mere declaration to us that he is holy love would not and could not be a revelation of God as holy love. Love is incomplete save in act. Love is demonstrated only in the deed which corresponds to the emotion. The incarnation of God in Christ was the divine act which was necessary if God was to give us a revelation of himself which contained the essential elements of his being.

The Christian Religion in Its Doctrinal Expression

4. The revelation of God in Christ was necessary for the completion of the historical and objective factor in man's religious life. Man is body as well as spirit. He is a creature of sense as well as thought. His life in all its forms has an outward which corresponds with an inward. God's self-disclosure to man's spirit by inward energy was real, but inadequate. In the prophets of Israel we have it in unique power. In philosophic thought the Greeks were foremost among the nations of antiquity. But prophetic inspiration, and Greek thought alike, failed to attain finality. There was always a lack of permanency in the solution and an expectation and need for more knowledge. This result was due to the conditions of man's life as body and spirit, inward and outward. It is because he lives in the temporal and the eternal at one and the same time. It is his identity with and transcendence above the temporal life which create for man the need of an inward religion of the spirit and an outward embodiment of it. Jesus as the revelation of God brought the eternal into the temporal. He made the conception of God practically workable for man. He made of the God of faith a winning, gracious, yet holy and majestic being.

Man's free religious action was involved in this outward revelation in Christ. No doubt, as a matter of sheer power, God could have coerced the human mind into holding conceptions of himself which were true. He could have compelled a completion of the prophetic message in human thought. But this would have involved a continuous miracle. It would have tended to destroy freedom in man. An objective gospel, a historical Christ, presents, on the other hand, an objective revelation of God for man to interpret and understand, an object for man to choose or reject. This is directly opposed to the type of thought which asserts that the historical element is unnecessary in Christianity. Man's full development is dependent on the historical. This is based both on what Christianity is in itself and what man is in his physical and spiritual constitution. He is a citizen of time and of eternity. He lives in the world of outward events and the world of Spirit.

[172]

The Deity of Jesus Christ
The Deity of Jesus Christ

5. The revelation of God in Christ was the completion of the ideas of the world of man, of God, and of religion. (1) It was the completion of the idea of the world. Here we need only the data supplied by science as a basis for the statement. The world arises gradually from the mechanical and merely physical, through all gradations of life and feeling, to its apex in man. Assume now that through all God progressively imparts himself to his creation. In man we have the image of God, a finite likeness of God's moral and spiritual nature. Finite man, however, could not contain the " fulness of the Godhead." And this limitation was vastly intensified by human sin. If then the principle of self-impartation guided all the preceding history, does not the world, viewed as a whole, require the incarnation as its crowning stage? God dwelt in Christ. Self-impartation is now complete. The progressive series reaches its climax.

(2) This revelation completes also the idea of man. Humanity could not become perfect as a group of detached individuals. Man could not reflect the divine image in a non-social form of existence. Again, he could not realize the divine end as a merely natural man. He must become spiritual. The human race must become a moral and spiritual unity in order to the realization of God's purpose. Jesus Christ becomes the supreme head of the race and establishes it in fellowship with God. He called himself the " Son of man," not the son of Abraham. He was Son of man because he was Son of God. He was conscious of a relation to the race as a whole. The apostles dwelt upon the breaking down of the walls of partition between Jew and Gentile. He is the head and his redeemed society the members. In Christ humanity is to become an organism living in fellowship with God and in mutual love and service. Christ's revelation, then, is a revelation of humanity.

(3) The revelation of Christ completes the idea of God. We have already shown that it reveals God as a person and as holy love. It remains to be said that in Christ we find the union of the immanent and transcendent principles. God is immanent in all nature below Christ. But his immanence is progressive as

the forms of being are progressive. Nowhere do we find a stage capable of receiving the transcendent God until we reach Christ. Even here we are not to conceive God quantitatively as if he were an extended substance or physical magnitude. The entire process is ethical and personal. It is a spiritual, not a physical, reality we are to conceive. The self-communication of God as spiritual does not limit or impoverish him. It does not subtract from his Godhead. It rather enhances it and illustrates the resourcefulness of divine love and grace.

In this we are not to think of the incarnation as essential to the divine nature itself by an inner compulsion or necessity of any kind. It was a free act of God, an expression of his righteous love. It was the completion of the great and wonderful act of his love in laying the foundations of the universe. It was an act consistent with his gracious activity in all the preceding history of the universe.

(4) The revelation of God in Jesus completes for us the idea of religion. The relation of Jesus to God was the realization in time of the ideal fellowship between God and man. No element can be conceived which would in any way add to the perfect inner life of Jesus, in his communion with the Father. The consciousness of Jesus is the center from which all our reckonings must be made.

We add to this a twofold caution. First, we must not make the mistake of ignoring the sin-consciousness in man in our emphasis upon the perfect communion of Jesus with God. What we must do is to approach the sin-consciousness in man from the standpoint of the attitude of Jesus toward man's sin and his need. Secondly, we must not make the mistake of conceiving of the religious consciousness of Jesus as the exhaustive explanation of his person. As we shall see, Jesus is not only our religious example, our spiritual archetype; he is also our religious object. God himself comes near to us in Jesus. This brings us face to face with the doctrine of the Person of Jesus Christ and his significance for man's religious life.

As a summary of the preceding statements as to Christ's person, we may recapitulate as follows: There are relations in the Godhead. God is not a bare and isolated unity without relationships in his eternal life. His personality, like our own, is not complete by itself, but in relations of love. Fatherhood and Sonship are immanent and essential relations in the Godhead. Creation in its material, and in its spiritual-human phases, are expressions of the immanent qualities in the divine nature. The universe of matter, force, and motion is the groundwork, the platform, or arena for the production and manifestation of the sons of God. Man is nature's crown and bears the divine image. The moral freedom of man, which is the core and center of that image, was abused and sin entered. Christ the eternal Son came and wrought that he might bring many sons to glory. The outcome of the cosmic struggle shall be the filial manifestation, the redemption of men through Christ into the liberty of the glory of the sons of God. This is the goal of nature as well as of history and grace.

It thus appears that what God is in himself is learned not by philosophic speculations, but by his own deed of redeeming love. The central truth about nature and man is just an extension of the central truth about God. That truth is righteous love manifested in Fatherhood and Sonship. If we do not learn what God is by his acts in time and space, then God remains for us unknown. If righteous love be not essential in God before time, it could not become essential for him in time. In that case righteousness and love are relative terms. All that we see and know in the finite world of time and space is without real significance for the interpretation of God. In that case God retires into the impenetrable depths of his own being, and blank agnosticism remains. If, on the other hand, righteous love is the central fact of the Godhead as expressed in Fatherhood and Sonship we can in some measure understand the finite workings of God. His is a love so vast that it requires the immeasurable reaches of space and time for its adequate unfolding. It is so rich, so deep, and so high, that nothing short of sonship can express it. It is so precious and gives so much joy to God in its contemplation, that he pursues the task of training his sons with infinite patience through the slow ages. Since the whole process is grounded in his own essential nature, the bringing in of his eternal kingdom of free and redeemed spirits becomes God's supreme and absorbing task.

In view of these things it is clear why regenerate men who know Christ as their Redeemer cling to him as the final and sufficient revelation of God. He is for them the religious ultimate. They find all the values and ideals and satisfactions in him. Just as the ear knows music, as the eye knows light, and as the mind knows truth, so man in his whole spiritual nature knows God as revealed to him in Christ. For believers in Christ, there-fore, the attack upon his deity is equivalent to an attack upon the foundations of man's spiritual nature. It would be as easy to uproot the foundations of all knowledge and of all religion as to destroy their belief in his divine function and work. The question behind all our Christian experience is this: What is the ultimate nature of human experience? In what form does it find fulfilment? Is it feeling, or volition, or thought? Is it fellowship between man and God? Is it religion? Christian experience says the latter. Human experience comes to itself in Christian experience in the widest sense of a life of fellowship with God. Christ is final for that experience because he mediates that fellowship.

III. HUMAN AND DIVINE ELEMENTS IN CHRIST

As we have seen, Christ was truly and fully man, and he was really God. The effort to express the meaning of his person in terms of the human and divine has been an engrossing task of theology during the Christian centuries. It is doubtful whether we shall ever be able to formulate a definition altogether satisfactory. The New Testament does not attempt formally to do so. It simply gives the facts as they stood forth in Christ's life and work. At one time the human, at another the divine, aspect of his person is emphasized. But there is no evidence of disunion or contradiction manifested at any time. It is necessary, however, that an effort be made to harmonize the facts of the record for our own thinking.

First, we look briefly at the early attempts to state the doctrine of Christ's person.

The Ebionites (A. D. 107) held that Christ was merely a man. He did not possess a divine nature. As man he was in peculiar and special relations with God, and from his baptism onward enjoyed the unmeasured fulness of the presence and power of the Holy Spirit. Ebionism shared the intense monotheistic belief of the Jews, and on this account recoiled from attributing divine qualities to Christ.

The Docetæ (A. D. 70-170) denied the reality of Christ's human body. They embraced the philosophic view current among the Gnostics and Manicheans in the early Christian centuries, that matter is inherently evil. Their view of Christ was the result of an effort to reconcile the purity and glory of Christ's person with their philosophy. Thoroughly false as it is, the docetic view is one of the landmarks in the early history of doctrine, showing the exalted place Christ held in the estimation of men.

The Arians (A. D. 325) held that Christ was more than man, but less than God. He was the first and greatest of created beings. The Arians thought that the Sonship of Christ involved subordination and origin in time. The Logos united humanity to himself in the person of Christ. But the Logos was not a being equal with God, but derived and dependent. The Arians were condemned at the Council of Nicæa in A. D. 325, and the view has never had wide acceptance in the succeeding centuries.

The Appolinarians (A. D. 381) denied that Christ had a human mind or spirit. He possessed a soul or vital, animating principle of the body. The divine Logos took the place of the human mind or spirit. This involves a trichotomous view of human nature which is unwarranted, and it denies an essential element of human nature itself.

The Nestorians (A. D. 431) denied the union of the human and divine natures in Christ's person. There was simply a close

M   [177]

and intimate connection between the human Jesus and God. It was God and man thus morally related to each other, but not united in an incarnate life. It was an alliance between God and man rather than God becoming man.

The Eutychians (A. D. 451) held that the human and divine natures of Christ were mingled into one. The inevitable result of this was that the human was overpowered by the divine and absorbed into it. The Eutychians were known also as Monophysites, because they virtually denied the human nature of Christ and reduced the two natures to one.

The definition of Christ's person which has been most generally accepted was that of the Council at Chalcedon (A. D. 451). It holds that in Christ's person there are two natures. A complete human and a complete divine nature are united in the one person. The requirement has ever been that we must not " divide the person or confound the natures."

The last is the definition which most fully gathers up the statements of the New Testament. Yet there are present in the formula certain speculative elements to which objection has been and may be made. For example, the conception of two natures, a divine and a human, in one person is a difficult one. If the divine nature is complete, how did the self-emptying take place with the consequent limitations of the incarnate Son? If the human nature is complete, how could the divine consciousness become active in the incarnate life? If there was a human will and a divine will, how avoid the conclusion that there were two persons instead of one? If the human personality found itself in the divine so that the human nature did not develop an independent personality, how can we avoid the conclusion that it was a curtailed or partial rather than a complete human nature?

Later writers, as loyal to the New Testament teaching as the earlier, have attempted a different form of statement, with varying success. One thing seems clear: the two-nature conception has been made to dominate too completely in many efforts to define Christ's person. It has been almost impossible to hold the one-person conception in combination with that of the two-natures where the latter is taken as the fundamental fact. In the end it cannot be excluded. But it is the element lying behind the scene as it were. The divine nature and human nature, as ultimate essences, are difficult conceptions. If we begin with the one Person who unites in himself the divine and human elements, who is both God and man, we are much closer to the New Testament teaching generally, much closer to the facts as they are recorded in the Gospels, and much closer to our own religious experience and that of the New Testament Christians.

We should keep clearly in mind the aim in any effort to express in words the doctrine of Christ's person. It is to unify our impressions of Jesus as he stands forth in the New Testament and in Christian experience generally. This involves his preexistence, his deity, his sinlessness, his humanity with its humiliations and limitations of knowledge, his subordination, along with his equality with the Father.

There are several possible attitudes which men have taken to this great task. First, they have denied outright the possibility of unifying the various elements since these seem to be hopelessly discordant and incompatible. But this is to prejudge what God is in himself, and what man is, and their possible relations.

Secondly, men have accepted the deliverances of faith and renounced the effort to state more precisely the meaning of Christ's person. This attitude may serve the average Christian very well. But Christianity commits a fatal mistake if it renounces the task of thinking through its own great problems. For the Christian thinker the attitude is not only cowardly, it is also vain. The problem is thrust upon him by unbelief. He is bound sooner or later to face it.

Thirdly, men have adopted a narrowly exacting criterion of judgment or standard of truth, and have tested the Christian facts by this. Such a standard is that of causation in the physical sense as employed by science, or rationality as employed by the older philosophies. Both of these, proper for their own ends, become narrowly sectarian and provincial when forced upon religious phenomena as the sole criteria of explanation. There is involved a confusion of spheres. Religion deals with personal relations. In the religious sphere free causation rules, not physical. It is now widely recognized that the so-called "pure thought," or "rationality," of the older philosophies is an abstraction. Experience as a whole is the basis of truth and knowledge. Religious experience is the starting-point of religious knowledge. Of course the facts concerning which we obtain knowledge exist independently of us. But we acquire truth about these facts through experience.

The fourth attitude is to recognize the facts of Christian experience and the relation of Jesus Christ to the experience, and on this basis to seek constructively to define his person in the light of New Testament teaching. This is the correct attitude. There will of course come into view certain aspects of the truth which will remain obscure. At some points we shall have to confess our ignorance. But in the great essentials faith will not be disappointed. The facts will yield the necessary statements of truth.

IV. THE PREEXISTENCE OF THE DIVINE SON

We begin with the preexistence. 1. There can be no question as to the New Testament teaching on this point. It appears repeatedly in the writings of John, as in the Gospel, 1 : 1f. and 17 : 5. It is entirely clear in various passages in the Epistles of Paul, as in Philippians 2 : 5-11. Even in the synoptic Gospels it is clearly implied occasionally, as in Matthew 11 : 27. The synoptic teaching that Jesus is to judge the world, along with the exercise of other divine functions, calls for his preexistence. Only thus could his person be made to square with his work.

2. This is not merely ideal preexistence, as some have contended. There is no conclusive evidence that the Jews taught such an ideal preexistence of the Messiah. The New Testament and the contemporary Jewish literature both recognize an ideal preexistence with reference to other objects, the temple, Jerusalem, and other things. Instances of this kind are easily recognized. (Cf. Heb. 9 : 11, 24.) But when dealing with the

person of Christ the New Testament describes the preexistence in unmistakable terms. He existed in the " form of God." He counted divinity not a " thing to be grasped." " He became poor." Those and many other passages forbid us to interpret the preexistence as merely ideal.

3. The preexistence was necessary to explain the experience of the redeeming power of Christ on the part of the New Testament believers. He wrought in a creative manner in them. They began with the risen Christ who gave the Holy Spirit. They read the meaning of his person back from the end to the beginning. The full meaning was disclosed only when the development was complete.

Only thus can any unfolding life be fully understood. He was " marked out " to be the Son of God by the resurrection. He wrought in them a creative, divine, and redeeming work. Their conviction of his preexistence was in no sense a metaphysical speculation or a mere logical deduction. It was on the contrary, first of all, a religious necessity. They were seeking a foundation strong enough to bear the weight of the superstructure. The divine Christ could not have *become* divine. He must have *been* divine in the beginning. Otherwise their worship of him would have been idolatry.

4. His preexistent form was that of the divine Son. Here the disciples began with the historic and passed back from him to the eternal Christ. They knew the Son in his earthly life. Then they knew him as Redeemer and Lord. It was against their Jewish training and preconceptions to take the next step and attribute deity to the Son. But so great was Christ's power in them that they did not hesitate. They dared to conclude that there are relations in the Godhead. Eternal Fatherhood and eternal Sonship are central in God. With this they clung as tenaciously as ever to their monotheism. God is one, but he is not an isolated point, a barren monad, an infinite negation. In this way the religious experience of the New Testament saints enabled them to transcend the current philosophic speculations. The Logos conception was thus transfigured. It was no longer

an abstraction of the speculative reason. It was rather an eternal reality, rich in ethical content and spiritual power. Righteous love is the heart of things because it is central in God. Jesus, the divine Son, is the only interpreter of the eternal Father. (John 1 : 18.)

5. Thus the work of Christ is unified. His creative and redemptive work appears in a rounded view. Creation and redemption are parts of the one great purpose of God. In the creation of man a plane is reached whereon an incarnation is possible. God in Christ enters his world. He now becomes immanent in creation in a new and higher sense. Eternal Sonship was behind the first creative act. It is now disclosed as the basis of God's eternal purpose toward man.

V. THE DIVINE SELF-EMPTYING

1. We have already seen that the incarnation implied in some sense a divine self-emptying. The New Testament repeatedly states the fact. The classic passage is that in Philippians 2 : 5-11, where it is declared that Christ Jesus " emptied himself." He passed from a state of glory to a state of humiliation. This fact has a vital relation to every effort to express the meaning of Christ's person.

It is to be noted first that it is a *self*-emptying. There was no compulsion in the descent of Christ into human conditions. It was his own voluntary act. It was a divine self-limitation for a purpose. The Father sent the Son, it is true, but the Son freely came.

But is it possible for deity to limit itself? it may be asked. In reply it may be said that creation itself is an instance of self-limitation on God's part. Creation does not exhaust God. He has expended himself only partially therein. The stages of being show this. The crystal, the plant, the sentient animal, human beings with moral and spiritual endowments, are successive stages in the self-limitation and self-impartation of God. He reveals only so much of himself in chemistry, in biology, in astronomy, as these spheres make possible. All created spheres of being do not exhaust God. The capacity for self-limitation is a mark of the infinite perfection of God. It reveals him as a moral and spiritual and personal being who can conceive ends and devise means for carrying them into effect.

2. The incarnation was a divine self-emptying for redemptive ends, under the form of human personality. Deity in the distinctive sense could become incarnate in human form because human personality contains the essential elements of all personality, *viz.,* self-consciousness, intelligence, feelings, moral nature, will. Personality is the point at which creation in its ascent returns to God. Man bears the divine image. Personality thus becomes the medium through which a divine self-revelation is possible in the form of an incarnation.

3. Again, the self-emptying of God in Christ reveals the infinite mobility of divine love. The word grace is the New Testament word describing this divine act. God's immutability is not compromised in any way. It is, on the contrary, made prominent in the incarnation. God's immutability is his moral self-consistency. It is his eternal loyalty to himself. Incarnation is his act of sacrifice which was necessary to express his eternal desire to bless and to save. If the ends of love required an incarnation, and God were without capacity for incarnation, then love would have been impotent. God's arm would have been shortened that it could not save. The incarnation, then, is a mark of the infinite perfection of God. It expresses the immutability, the moral self-consistency of God because it was essential to the manifestation of the love essential in God.

4. The self-emptying of Christ the eternal Son carries with it great consequences for our own salvation and spiritual destiny. It enables us to see that Fatherhood and Sonship are essential in the Godhead, and that our own sonship is grounded in God's eternal life. Again, it enables us to see that God in Christ has entered the arena of time and space for our redemption. The whole foundation of Christianity is changed radically if we deny the deity of Christ. Unless divine love stooped and

[183]

came for our salvation, then we have another kind of religion entirely. Again, if we deny that Christ is God, we have no revelation of God which is central and essential. In that event Jesus becomes simply one among the many leaders of men, not their Saviour and Lord. His view of God is not God's word to us, but only the expression he gave of his finite human reaction upon ultimate reality. God remains hidden from us. The New Testament writers clearly perceived this and did not hesitate to assert that the incarnation was the result of a pretemporal divine act, a self-emptying, an act of sacrifice of the eternal Son.

5. The self-emptying of Christ was not a putting off absolutely of divine attributes. Some kenotic theories attempt a distinction between the relative and the essential attributes coupled with the view that the relative were laid aside while the essential were retained. Omnipotence, and omniscience, and omnipresence are the relative, while love and holiness are essential. Others have held that the divine actually became human and ceased to be divine. Both views are erroneous. The deity in all its parts remained. But it subsisted in the incarnation in human form. It was this fact which constituted the incarnation. We must keep in mind the fact that the life of Jesus Christ was continuous with the life of God. It was the outcome of a pretemporal act. Its end was the redemption of men. In a real sense the incarnation was an instance of the exercise of divine omnipotence and omniscience as well as of the divine love. It was infinite wisdom devising a way to achieve a holy end, and infinite power bringing it to pass. It indicates in a striking manner the infinite resourcefulness of divine love. It displays the infinite mobility of the divine immutability. It opens to us the infinite moral wealth and grace within the Godhead itself. In a word the incarnation, paradoxical as it may seem, is the embodiment in a supreme saving act, of the omnipotence and omniscience and the unchangeableness of the infinite God, in obedience to the supreme and central reality of his own being, his righteous love.

The self-emptying of Christ in the incarnation, then, meant the retention of divine qualities and powers, but under the restraints and limitations of a human life. There was a voluntary suspension of the full exercise of divine attributes in the incarnation. But potentially all divine resources were present. For the time and purpose of the incarnate life there was in part a self-reduced form of being. "He emptied himself." "He took the form of a servant."

6. We cannot fully grasp the process by which this self-emptying took place. The psychology of the incarnation is beyond us. But there are certain analogies which may help. Take the case of a mathematical genius, and think of him at the beginning and then at the end of his training. As a boy he has merely the elements of mathematical knowledge. Yet there is present a capacity for all knowledge. Years afterward he is master of all mathematical learning. What was implicit in him has become explicit. Now conceive of him as teaching a beginner. Again he empties his mind of the riches of acquired knowledge and becomes a beginner again. Yet the acquired knowledge, while out of consciousness, is at his command.

Again, consider the case of a musical genius. He is a great pianist, a master of his art. But for sufficient reasons one day he performs with gloves on his hands. You may detect certain qualities which identify the player, but his performance is an inadequate expression of his power because of the medium through which he plays. The powers are there, but not fully expressed.

Again, take the case of a father whose little son has been hurt in an accident and lies at the point of death. The father drops out of his consciousness entirely the knowledge of a great system of department stores of which he is owner. He now devotes himself night and day to the task of seeing that his child be saved from death. Money, time, comfort, all are surrendered for love's sake.

These are imperfect analogies, but they are suggestive. In the first we have the oblivion of the teacher for the sake of the pupil. In the last, the oblivion of affection in the interest of the beloved. In the second we have an instance of suspended power because of an inadequate medium for its exercise.

[185]

Now the above illustrations are characteristic of human nature as limited in intellectual range, and as functioning in thought through a brain. If deity becomes incarnate it can only be under such limitations. An incarnate life is an enfleshed life. It is not a divine coupled with a human life. This is the old Nestorian theory. It is not two consciousnesses and two wills, much less two personalities. It was not that Jesus did certain things in his divine, and others in his human nature, as if he were sometimes God and at other times man. In brief, there were not two consciousnesses, nor two wills, nor two personalities, but one consciousness, one will, and one personality. This one personality was divine-human. It was constituted by the indissoluble union of a divine and a human factor. These factors were not merely placed side by side, or in relations of fellowship. They were rather in relations of mutual interpenetration and vital union. All sense of dual consciousness and dual life is absent. We are not to think of the divine imparting its qualities to the human and *vice versa,* as if there were an interval between to be bridged over. We are to think rather of a personality constituted by the vital union of the two factors and qualified or conditioned by the action of both.

7. Finally, the self-emptying of Christ was the answer to the human search for God. These two are correlatives: man's upward striving and God's gracious descent. All religion marks man's ceaseless quest for God. The dim light that shines through nature, through conscience, and through the ethnic faiths, discloses God's impulse to reveal himself and to bless. Step by step the creation ascends toward God. In man it is not divine, but possesses capacity for God. It is made " a little lower than God." It is the matrix, the receptacle into which God can pour his fulness. In humanity the divine immanence rises to a new level. There is but one step to its completion. The incarnation is that step. Henceforth, through his redemptive work which is a new creation, Christ will raise men to the level of the divine in that they will become partakers of the divine nature.

From the preceding it is clear that the incarnation is not an abrupt or violent incursion into an orderly universe. It is rather the completion of the movement in creation and in God. Humanity, under the dominion of sin, yet felt its destiny and forever yearned for the eternal life. The outgoing movement of right-eous love in God from which creation sprang, now takes the new form of incarnation to meet the human need.

In Jesus Christ, God and humanity become one. Humanity finds itself ideally and forever in him. He expresses ideally and forever the inner core of God's heart and life. The blending in a vital union of the two forms of life in a simple indissoluble and enduring personal life is thus the self-fulfilment of both God and man.

VI. Stages in the Reascent of Christ

If we are to be true to the New Testament representations we must recognize clearly the human conditions of the earthly life of Christ. The fact of the incarnation means his entrance into those conditions. It was not mere contact at a single point. He "took hold" of our nature at all points. Rather he passed into and tabernacled in it, and we beheld his glory as of the only-begotten Son of God. This fact carries with it certain important truths. First, as a human life it was subject to the laws of growth. There is no proof in Scripture that the infinite divine consciousness was present in the early life of Jesus. "He grew in wisdom and in stature, and in favor with God and men" (Luke 2 : 52). At the age of twelve his temple experience was a turning-point in his spiritual consciousness; "Knew ye not that I must be in my Father's house?" His baptism was epochal for the growth of his consciousness. The voice from heaven confirmed and reassured him as to his calling and mission. "Thou art my beloved Son" (Luke 3 : 22). The temptation was a great moral crisis. The assaults of the tempter clarified his sense of his mission, and strengthened him in his power of resistance. At a later period his soul seems deeply stirred by the foreseen necessity of his death and resurrection. (Luke 12: 50.) On the cross he uttered the memorable words, "It is finished." A process had in some sense reached its end. Paul declares that the resurrection "marked out" Jesus to be the Son of God with power. The life after the resurrection was lived under wholly different conditions. It was during this period he delivered the Great Commission in which he declared, "All authority hath been given unto me, in heaven and on earth" (Matt. 28 : 18). His ascent to the right hand of God consummated his earthly career and marked the resumption of full divine activities.

Secondly, Christ's conformity to the law of growth was not an element of imperfection, but of human perfection. There is no stage at which an ideal or perfect human life can become static. When growth ceases, decline begins. The wide interval between the early and later stages of Jesus' life in the great elements of growth and development is the outstanding evidence of his perfection as man. A perfect life lived under the conditions of time and space must have succession, novelty of experience, accumulated wisdom, moral reserve, expanding horizon, and deepening of the spiritual consciousness. All these were present in the unfolding of the unique consciousness of Jesus. It is apparent, therefore, that if we witness in Jesus a real incarnation, we must accept the human conditions under which it took place.

Thirdly, it is to be noted that there were at least three factors in this unfolding life of Christ. There was an intellectual factor. His growth in wisdom is expressly declared. Also he asserts that in one respect at least he was ignorant as to the future, the day and hour of his return. (Matt. 24 : 36.) We must accept this statement at its face value. We must avoid assuming a double consciousness which destroys the unity of his person.

There was also a moral factor in his growth. He was tempted throughout his life, yet without sin. (Luke 22 : 28; Heb. 4 : 15.) He learned obedience through the things that he suffered. (Heb. 5 : 8.) He was made perfect through sufferings. We are not of course to conceive of his growth from the imperfection of sin or moral weakness to a state of sinlessness. His moral growth means that his life was morally conditioned. Character

The Deity of Jesus Christ

is an achievement under God's grace. He was sinless because he had moral power to conquer, not because he was irresistibly compelled to do right. The self-emptying meant the entrance of the eternal Word into the conditions of moral struggle, that is, into human conditions. All this is but saying that the human life was real, and that the incarnation was real. Both great realities are involved, the one equally with the other. A life without growth or moral struggle means an exclusively divine life, not an incarnation.

Another factor in the unfolding of Jesus' consciousness was the Messianic. He began his public career with the conviction of his Messianic calling. But that calling was to be progressively realized through his life experiences. Its full contents, therefore, came to him by degrees. He never for a moment wavered, nor was he hastened prematurely to the goal. But there is no evidence that all the details of the future lay before him like an open book from the first day of his public ministry. He moved step by step to the goal. The great issues he knew in advance. The details came in their proper order. Sometimes he expressed surprise. He marvels at the unbelief of men. (Matt. 8 : 10; Mark 6 : 6.)

His Messiahship, of course, rested upon his eternal relation to God as Son. Very early his sense of Sonship appears in the records. But here also there was unfolding to larger things. The babe could not have the consciousness of the mature man. We may not fathom the mystery of his consciousness at this point. We can only understand it in the light of the facts as recorded. Certainly there are moments when Christ is conscious of an eternal relation to God. (Matt. 11 : 27; John 17 : 4.)

Dorner has held that the incarnation was gradual, and that it was complete only at the end of Christ's earthly career. This, however, is not in accord with the facts as they are recorded. The incarnation was complete at all stages of the earthly life. But it was the completeness of a humanly conditioned mode of being. If we distinguish the two elements of his person we may assert with equal truth that the human factor was also

[189]

incomplete in the earlier stages. It was not a gradualness of incarnation, but rather the progressive unfolding of the consciousness of the incarnate. It was the unique and supreme personality of all time realizing itself through the successive experiences of an earthly conditioned life. The supreme moral and religious consciousness of man became indissolubly one with the eternal redemptive consciousness of God's Son.

Fourthly, the spiritual principle of the incarnation comes to clear expression in the cross. Life through death is the clue to its meaning. The grain of wheat must die if it is to live again in fulness and power. Christ was exalted because he had taken the form of a servant. God realizes himself in the essential meaning of his deity when he gives himself for his creatures. Thus the most intimate bond of union between God and man is the capacity for self-sacrificing love, common to both. The incarnation is the concrete expression of that capacity in God. The Christian life is man's response to God's act, and it embodies the same ethical ideal, the same law of self-realization, life through death. The doctrine of the incarnation, therefore, is no speculative abstraction. It is no merely rationalistic conclusion of metaphysics. It is rather the most intensely religious and experiential truth of Christianity. At its heart is contained the deepest truth as to the moral and spiritual nature of God and man. In other words, our capacity to humble ourselves, to serve, to sympathize, to come under the conditions which rule in the lives of others, to submit and obey in order to bless— this capacity, we say, is not a mark of our unlikeness to God, but of our kinship to him. And God's own capacity to stoop to human conditions, to seek out and redeem men, is not the lowest, but rather the most divine impulse of his nature.

VII. OBJECTIONS

A number of objections have been anticipated and answered in one form or another in the preceding exposition. A few others may now be noted.

1. First, it is objected that the doctrine of the incarnation compromises the unity of God. The ancient charge of ditheism or tritheism is always in evidence against the Christian view. Many seem to think the case is closed when the charge is made. More will be said in reply when the Trinity is considered. For the present one or two points may be noted. Christianity is monotheistic to the core. Let not this be forgotten. But Christianity derives its doctrine of God from the facts of history and of experience. It adheres not to a speculative, but to an experiential monotheism. God's word to us and in us, God's great deed of revelation and redemption, supply the basis. Theology brings no abstract theory of knowledge to the facts in an effort to coerce the facts into conformity with the theory. It accepts the facts and seeks to interpret them.

Again, the non-Trinitarian view is more difficult to maintain on rational grounds than the Trinitarian, as we shall see.

The revelation of God in Christ solves for us all the great spiritual mysteries as far as they may be solved for us men in this life. The other view is based on an abstract conception of unity which leaves God as an unrelated monad. Internal relations are not inconsistent with the idea of deity if they are so conceived as to enhance and enrich our view of the infinite wealth of God's grace and to conserve the unity of his action. Certainly the preexistence of Christ reveals eternal love as real in God, and supplies a ground in God's essential being for all the great ethical and spiritual realities of faith.

2. A second objection is that man as finite cannot reveal God as the infinite. Here, again, is involved a false view of the relations between finite and infinite. As has been remarked, the principle of deism was that the finite has not capacity for the infinite. Man cannot grasp God. But the principle of Christian theism is that the infinite has capacity for the finite. In other words, finite and infinite are not mutually exclusive terms. If so, then agnosticism would be true. God could not reach man because of his infinitude, and man could not reach God because of his finitude. The usual argument in all forms of theism,

whether Trinitarian or not, implies the possibility of an incarnation. We infer that God has will, intelligence, consciousness, from the possession of these qualities by men. That is, we argue God's personality from our own. There is no warrant for taking a leap into the unknown and inferring further that the divine personality is incapable of expression in human form. On the contrary, the possession of personality by both God and man implies that such expression is possible. Observe also that our own personality is the highest mode of finite being known to us. If God cannot express himself through it, there remains no medium whatever. We are at once driven to the unknowable and to the paralysis of all religion.

3. It is also objected that the mystery of the incarnation is too great for us to accept. It is sometimes declared to be "unthinkable." As to the latter expression, it may be replied that unthinkableness is relative to the thinker. One might almost claim that the Christian Trinity is simplicity itself compared with many modern views, for example, the various forms of Hegelianism and Neo-Hegelianism, pluralism, the view of Bergson, and others.

In fact, we accept many truths which are inexplicable to reason. One is the truth of man's freedom and God's sovereignty. Another is the possibility of prayer and God's eternal purpose. Another is the possibility of human initiative through the action of the will. Another is the truth that God is self-caused, an absolutely unique fact.

4. It is also objected that the doctrine of the incarnation is inconsistent with modern thought. We reply that the phrase "modern thought" is very elastic, and more or less vague. There is a threefold answer, however, to the general objection. Modern thought in its lower form has no right to speak on the subject at all. Modern thought in its higher form is too self-contradictory to speak with authority. Modern thought, when properly unified, speaks in favor of the Christian view.

Let us consider these points in order. By lower we mean that which deals with matter rather than spirit. (1) Modern thought in its lower form has no right to speak on the subject of the incarnation. The lower ranges of modern thought deal with physical phenomena, and explain in terms of continuity or physical causation. On all questions regarding the soul, immortality, God, and religion, it is silent. Its sphere is different. Confusion and conflict arise only when it attempts to intrude into the spiritual sphere and to impose its standards, its criteria of truth and reality, there.

(2) Modern thought in its higher forms is too self-contradictory to speak with authority. A few only of many examples are given from able and representative modern writers. Professor Royce holds that incarnation and atonement in principle is the real key to the meaning of the universe, but denies that the principle found expression in Jesus in an unique and exceptional sense. He waives the question as to Jesus and works solely with philosophic principles. Professor Eucken holds that regeneration through the union of man with God is necessary to self-realization on man's part. Only thus can he overcome the contradictions of life and find himself in the highest sense. But Professor Eucken rules out Jesus very positively as unnecessary to man's religious development.

Another group of idealists, or personalists, who are quite as able and modern as Eucken and Royce, hold that an incarnation, such as we have in Jesus Christ in the evangelical sense, is the necessary and only rational expression of the meaning of God. Idealism here takes on the personal form, and incarnation and atonement, life through death, becomes an act of God as incarnate through the Son. Eternal Fatherhood and eternal Sonship are essential to God, and all other forms of fatherhood and sonship are derived from this.

Again, Prof. William James holds that conversion is the result of a supernatural working of God in the soul. It is a miraculous act, not in the pantheistic sense according to which all is miracle in nature and man; but rather in the strict and proper sense of a direct action of God producing an exceptional result. But Professor James is an agnostic as to the cause of Christian experience. We cannot with assurance assert that it is Jesus

N

Christ. As against him, Ritschl holds that the one thing we do know certainly is that the knowledge and power of God is mediated to us through Jesus Christ. It would be easy to multiply examples, but it is unnecessary. Thinkers of many schools, all intensely modern in spirit and attitude, hold most diverse views as to the relation of Christ to God and to human salvation. Hence the vague charge that the Christian view is against modern thought is without adequate support. All depends upon the particular phase of modern thought the objector represents.

(3) The third reply is that when properly unified modern thought speaks a real message in favor of the Christian view. The following considerations are in point here. As stages in man's progressive understanding of the universe, the various types of opinion easily find place. Physical science discloses the arena, or platform, for the working out of a higher spiritual end. Idealism in its more abstract form is a logical outcome of man's intellectual effort to grasp the meaning of the world. He finds an immanent reason everywhere. But personal idealism is sure to arise, since we only know reason in ourselves in personal form. We never have it in abstraction. Personality involves freedom, and this carries us above physical causation to a new order of being. Here religion enters with all it implies as to fellowship between God and man. The phenomena of the religious life find their true key in Jesus Christ. He alone explains them all. Recent philosophy, in its theories of knowledge, confirms strongly the method of Jesus. We learn by doing. Truth is tested through the processes of life. The will, the emotions, the moral nature, enter into our apprehension of spiritual truth. This is the direction of modern thought in its conception of how we know things. Not speculation, not abstractions, not *a priori* deductions, but living experience, this is the modern and the Christian method as well. This is the method of Jesus. In him all lines of modern thought may be unified.

Again, modern thought in its higher representations builds on aspects of Christian truth. Royce employs the conception of incarnation and atonement. Eucken makes use of the doctrine of the new birth. James, in his "Varieties of Religious Experience," utilizes the idea of regeneration also, but adds the conception of the supernatural. All these thinkers work with the central Christian conception of the cross, dying to live. Ritschl goes farther and asserts the divine function of Jesus in it all, but has not the courage to assert all that the function involves as to Christ's nature. Blewett and Bowne combine all the lower elements into a self-consistent personalism, or Christian theism, which unifies the many elements of modern thought, thus approximating very closely an evangelical Christian result. Many modern Christian thinkers carry out the process completely. Thus it appears that modern thought at no vital point contradicts the Christian view.

VIII. RIVAL THEORIES

Modern theories which compete with that presented here are too numerous to review in detail. We select a few only as sufficiently representative of the various types.

1. The first is that of the humanitarian Christ. Jesus was in no sense God. He was divine only as all men are divine. He was the prince of saints, the consummate flower of the race up to his own time. He had fellowship with God as a religious man. We may imitate his faith. We may strive to be like him. But he is no divine Redeemer. Those who hold this view do not regard him as sinless, but recognize the exalted nature of his piety. His miracles are denied. All the sayings which make him man's religious object and the judge of the world are eliminated. The answer to this will be given in the reply to the next theory to be mentioned. What belongs to the reply there will be even more applicable here.

2. The second is the theory that Jesus was a man only, but as man he was filled with the divine presence. He was a miracle in the sense that he sustained a perfect and unwavering fellowship with God. His consciousness was a God-consciousness in this sense alone. He was thus God's revelation to us. He is the archetypal man. He is our Saviour in that he shows us the

way to God. This is the theory of Schleiermacher. It is widely
diffused in modern times, with variant features. Some who hold
it exalt him almost to a position equal with that of the Trinitarian
view, including resurrection from the dead and the future return
in glory to judge the world. Others leave the latter as open
questions, with a strong tendency to deny them or to relegate
them as without value for faith.

The reply to these theories have already been indicated in the
previous exposition. Here a brief summary will suffice.

(1) Christian experience speaks otherwise about Christ. We
cannot, if we would, elminate him therefrom. The factors of
our Christian consciousness all imply a present Christ. We know
him as Redeemer and Lord.

(2) Christian history agrees with our own experience. In it
is recorded the consensus of believers of all Christian time. The
creeds of Christendom, the hymns of the redeemed, the art of
the centuries, all bear witness to the deity of Jesus in man's experience of the Christian salvation. A divine place must be
attributed to Christ unless we are to repudiate all the evidence.

(3) The witness of the New Testament writers is everywhere against the view. There is no question as to Paul and
John. Both taught that Christ preexisted before the foundation of the world, and that he was eternal Son, God manifest in
the flesh.

The synoptic writers present the same kind of Messiah, although the development does not therein reach its climax. But
in the synoptics he is the miracle-worker; the religious object;
the Son who alone knows and reveals the Father; the future
judge of the world. The very words of Jesus as recorded in
the synoptics give us those conceptions of his person. Criticism
has left all the great sayings of Jesus intact. Some critics, on
a priori grounds, reject all as untrustworthy except a half dozen
or so sayings. A very few even deny the historicity of Jesus.

But scientific and legitimate criticism, which only rejects or
accepts on critical grounds, leaves the great supernatural Christ
as Christian faith has ever held him.

With reference to the first theory, it should be said that it can be maintained only by refusing to let the New Testament writers or Jesus testify as to his person. The current effort to reduce Christ to a merely human level is in the highest degree unscientific and uncritical in its attitude toward the witness of the New Testament. Contemporary tendencies, ideals, worldviews, are arbitrarily assumed to be the source of all the extraordinary statements about Jesus. Yet Jesus is retained as a religious man of the highest order and helpful in some sense to us. There is no sound critical basis for this view since the attempted reconstruction had already undermined the entire witness of Jesus and the New Testament. The humanitarian Jesus is the product of naturalism working in the religious sphere, and *a priori* rejection of the supernatural in advance. The whole question is prejudged, because the critic assumes as a fundamental basis of his theory a particular view of how the universe is made. He does not let the facts answer, but imposes his views on the facts.

As to the second theory, that of a supernatural yet human Christ, it is to be said that it asserts too little or too much. The assumptions which go with it are those which in many respects go with the first theory. Yet it asserts too much for that theory. Why a miraculous human Christ if we do not need a divine Saviour? The first theory is logical in rejecting all the supernatural on the basis of its assumptions. The second theory goes too far unless it will go farther. The first Christians, the later Christians, and modern Christians find a divine Christ through their religious experience. Their salvation is a divine deed. They construe its author as divine. The view is self-consistent. It is not surprising that the second view tends to drop back to the level of the first, or to go forward to the true view.

3. The third theory regards Christ as preexistent only in an ideal sense. He was the fulfilment in time of a divine ideal in God's mind in eternity, but not the incarnation of a preexistent divine person.

In reply, we note first that this view is without New Testament warrant. Formerly men strove to interpret Jesus, Paul, and John in this sense. But scientific exegesis no longer does so. A real personal preexistence is the New Testament teaching, however modern rationalism may attempt to set it aside. The New Testament indeed knows of ideal preexistence with reference to some things. But it is in marked contrast to this that Christ is regarded as personally preexistent. In Hebrews 9 : 23, the writer, in speaking of the vessels and services of the tabernacle, says: " It was necessary therefore that the copies of the things in the heavens should be cleansed with these." The Jewish mind was familiar with the thought of ideal preexistence in God's mind, and it could clearly express that idea. But it was also capable of expressing the thought of actual preexistence and has done so through Paul and John and others in many places in the New Testament.

The theory of ideal preexistence is usually based on the objection to the evangelical view of Jesus as too metaphysical. But ideal preexistence is quite as metaphysical as the opposing view. It seeks to penetrate as deeply into the being of God. It merely reaches another conclusion.

The fact is that the theory of ideal preexistence is closely akin to the metaphysical speculation of Philo, which is even older than the New Testament doctrine. The conception of Philo was that the Logos, or divine reason, is an eternal principle in the nature of God. It came into action in all God's creative work. Sometimes Philo seems to think of the Logos as an eternal person in the Godhead, but usually it is the principle of the eternal reason. The modern conception of ideal preexistence is very similar as a metaphysical speculation. But the New Testament teaching is quite different. The conception is that of a real person. The motive is moral and spiritual and practical, not metaphysical. Here a divine Redeemer is in question with power to save, not a problem of the speculative reason.

Again, this theory weakens our view of the ethical fulness of the divine nature, and leads to a relativism which compromises many great interests. Fatherhood and Sonship, if real in God, supply the eternal ground of the earthly relation. If love be real in God, then human love, and an eternal kingdom of love have their roots deep in the ultimate being of God. If, on the other hand, God be a monad, existing without internal relations, without any mutuality or reciprocity within, all ethical and social relations among men sink to a level far below that which we are accustomed to hold. If God is love, he must be so eternally. If God is our Father, then fatherhood must be original in him and not merely derived from its temporal form in man. If it be said that fatherhood and sonship and love are merely parables or symbols of what God is, and that they do not assure us of essential realities in God, the reply is that this is agnosticism. It is fundamental for Christian theism to hold that God expresses himself in the finite. God is not concealed, but revealed by the things he has made. Every pathway running through the marvelous creation of God leads up to the glory of his being: the pathway of power, of order, of beauty, of life, of thought, of will, of feeling, of personality, of freedom, of love, of fatherhood, of sonship—all lead up to the Eternal, who pours himself into his creation, and builds it into a kingdom radiant with all that is highest in himself.

4. A fourth theory is that of Prof. William Sanday. It is not a denial of the evangelical view, but rather an effort to explain how the incarnation took place. Doctor Sanday makes use of the subconscious in our mental nature as the key to the incarnation. Psychology has emphasized the fact that our mental life has two departments. One of these is consciousness; the other the realm of the subconscious. Consciousness is, as it were, the front room, and subconsciousness the back room of our psychic life. In the subconscious we carry the accumulations of memory and experience. These are called forth through the operation of the laws of association as our need requires. Many students of the psychology of religion have emphasized the teaching that in regeneration God acts upon us through the subconscious, producing therein the necessary change in our nature. Professor Sanday goes a step farther, and asserts that in be-

coming incarnate the divine entered Jesus in the subconscious part of his being, and that his person is to be defined from this point of view. The divine and human elements were fused into unity in this way.

What shall we say of this view? It contains an interesting suggestion, and no doubt an element of truth. But it is not an adequate explanation of the incarnation. Several statements may be made to show this.

(1) First, we may say that the subconscious is not superior to the conscious department of our mental life. It contains rather the results of previous conscious states. Or, at best, it is a potentiality in us. It is like the state of infancy or sleep. The most significant of our states are those of consciousness, in which we think and will and feel. It is when we reason or resolve or love that our nature shows itself in its higher meanings. It follows from this that in Christ the most important elements of his spiritual life were those of consciousness. His deity found expression in what he said and did.

(2) Again, the view is objectionable in that it involves an irreconcilable dualism in Christ's nature. If the human side of Christ's being found expression in his conscious states and the divine side in the subconscious, no real unity of the person can be asserted. The theory divides the person into higher and lower elements. The biblical teaching and the unity of human personality generally require unity in our conception of the person of Jesus. Instances of multiple personality, as shown in the researches of psychology, are not cases of normal personal life. They do indeed impress us with the complexity and mystery of all personal life, but they are not to be taken as typical of the highest forms of that life. They are pathological or abnormal types, and do not serve to explain in any way the highest of all forms of personal life, that of Jesus, the Son of God.

(3) A third objection is that the theory results in a form of agnosticism. It leaves the deity in Christ unknown if we conceive it as confined to the subconscious in Jesus. The very heart of the revelation of God in Christ is that the divine

declared itself in clear and explicit terms for our understanding. We read the words and study the deeds of the incarnate One, and in so doing we learn what the infinite and eternal God is in himself. But this is impossible if we think of God as confined in Jesus below consciousness.

(4) We add in conclusion that there is no doubt an element of truth in Doctor Sanday's suggestion. Human nature contains as a part of itself the subconscious side along with the conscious. Jesus as truly human possessed both. As the incarnate One, no doubt both were influenced by all the exceptional elements in his personality. There is no means of separating the two realms from each other in any radical way. They are constantly reacting upon each other. That which is now in consciousness soon passes into the subconscious. The contents of the latter are continually returning to consciousness through the processes of memory in the experiences of life.

5. The fifth theory is the Ritschlian. It takes the name from Albrecht Ritschl, and holds that Jesus has for us Christians the value of God. Through him we come to the knowledge of God. The divine power finds us in and through him. Our judgment of value regarding him, therefore, is that he is God. But a judgment of value is not a judgment of reality since we cannot know ultimate reality. We know phenomena only. To assert the deity of Christ on the basis of his divine action is an attempt to go beyond the proper sphere of our human knowledge.

In reply there are several things to be said. Some that are favorable. There is a real truth in the idea of the "value-judgment." Christ's worth to us is the necessary basis of our personal estimate of him. Again, what Christ does is a starting-point for our view of his person. Further, it is true that we can never compass all reality in our knowledge. We know in part.

On the other hand, it is entirely erroneous to assert that reality as it is in itself is concealed rather than revealed by its manifestations. The assertion that ultimate reality is unknowable is self-contradictory. It requires vast knowledge about it to make that assertion. Not many now attempt a theoretical or scientific justification of agnosticism based on the Kantian distinction between phenomenal and noumenal reality. Ritschlianism is based on that distinction in the vain effort to avoid metaphysics in theology. Men are simply driven by the make of their minds to ask as to the ultimate meaning of the world. But modern philosophy builds on facts, not abstractions.

In the light of this it is clear that Ritschl is wrong in asserting that Christ's function as Saviour does not reveal what he is in himself. We know what things are precisely by their functions. Effects are our means of knowing causes. Negation regarding Christ's person and assertions regarding his work may easily present a combination of ideas fatal to the Christian life. Human thought cannot be arrested in its search for truth. We are bound to ask and answer the question about Jesus as best we may and as far as the facts warrant. Ritschl gave great emphasis to the New Testament sources of Christianity, but it is quite evident from all the preceding discussion that his view as to the unknowableness of God in Christ can be derived from the New Testament only by a violent method of interpretation. Ritschl's emphasis on experience, apart from its denial of the mystical element, is quite in harmony with the gospel. Experience, the facts of life, the saving power of God as he comes to us in Christ, supply the foundation for the true view as to Christ's person. But Ritschl, in deference to the criteria and methods of physical science, was not bold enough to claim all that he had a right to claim as a Christian and thinker.

CHAPTER VIII

THE HOLY SPIRIT AND THE TRINITY

I. THE HOLY SPIRIT

THE biblical doctrine of the Spirit of God exhibits many marks of progress in the revelation from the earliest to the latest stages. The Hebrew word for spirit originally meant " breath." From this it came to mean " wind," and gradually it passed into the meaning " spirit." Originally the Spirit of God meant his energy or power in contrast with the weakness of the flesh. (Isa. 31 : 3.)

1. In the Old Testament the following are the leading points in the teaching as to the Spirit of God: (1) The Spirit of God was God in action accomplishing an end. The Spirit was sometimes distinguished from God in the Old Testament, but not in the later Trinitarian sense. (Gen. 1 : 2; 6 : 3; Ps. 51 : 11.) (2) The Spirit was the energizing power in the primeval chaos, bringing out beauty and order. (Gen. 1 : 2; Ps. 104 : 28-30; Job 26 : 3.) (3) Life is imparted to man through God's Spirit. (Gen. 2 : 7.) (4) Many powers were conferred on men through the Spirit, as on Samson and others. (Judg. 14 : 6; 11 : 29.) (5) Wisdom and skill were conferred by the Spirit, as in the case of Bezaleel. (Exod. 31 : 2-5; 35 : 31; 28 : 3.) (6) The Spirit endowed the prophets with wisdom and revealed divine truth to them. (Ezek. 2 : 2; 8 : 3; 11 : 1, 24.) In the earlier stages the prophetic gift took the form of enthusiasm or ecstasy. (1 Sam. 10.) Later the prophets were especially chosen as messengers to convey truth from Jehovah. (7) Moral and spiritual character is traced to the Holy Spirit also. The ethical quality of the Spirit's work becomes quite manifest. (Ps. 51 : 11; Isa. 63 : 10.) The expression " Holy " came to be applied as the special designation of the Spirit. (8) The Messiah is to be

[203]

anointed by the Holy Spirit for his work, and predictions of a future outpouring of the Spirit appear in the later Old Testament teachings. (Isa. 11 : 1-5; 42 : 1ff.; 61 : 1; so also; Isa. 44 : 3; 59 : 21; Joel 2 : 28-32.)

2. In the New Testament the work of the Spirit of God appears in great fulness.

(1) Observe his work in relation to Jesus. He is present at the birth of Jesus. He anoints him at his baptism. (Mark 1 : 10; Luke 3 : 22.) Through the Spirit Jesus endured temptation (Matt. 4 : 1); Jesus taught, and healed, and cast out demons through the Holy Spirit. (Luke 4 : 14-21; Matt. 12 : 18, 31; Mark 3 : 28, 29.) Jesus offers himself upon the cross by the "eternal Spirit." (Heb. 9 : 14.) He was raised from the dead according to the Spirit of Holiness. (Rom. 1 : 4.) It is he who baptizes with the Holy Spirit. (Matt. 3 : 11; Mark 1 : 8; Luke 3 : 16; John 20 : 22; Acts 1 : 5.)

(2) Pentecost is the fulfilment of the prophecies concerning the outpouring of the Spirit, and marks the turning-point in the activities of the first generation of Christians. This is the baptism of the Spirit referred to above. (Acts 2.)

(3) As the result of the pentecostal outpouring there were many charismatic gifts or enduements of power bestowed by the Holy Spirit upon early Christians, such as speaking with tongues, power to work miracles, and others.

(4) The Spirit of God convicts the world of sin, righteousness, and judgment. This was to be a special feature of his mission to the world. (John 16 : 9ff.)

(5) Chiefly, however, the work of the Spirit in regenerating sinners and in imparting power for holy living receives increasing emphasis. In the later New Testament writings especially the ethical results of the Spirit's action are made prominent. Paul's entire conception of the Christian life involves at every point the presence and fellowship of the Holy Spirit. Believers " walk in the Spirit." They are commanded to " grieve not the Spirit," to be " filled with the Spirit." Paul's own preaching was " in demonstration of the Spirit."

The Holy Spirit and the Trinity

(6) In the New Testament the attributes of personality are ascribed to the Holy Spirit, and the teachings on which the doctrine of the Trinity is founded come into clear expression. Jesus describes the Spirit as " another Comforter," whom he will send from the Father. Masculine pronouns are applied to the Spirit: " He shall teach you," " He shall bring to your remembrance," " He shall testify of me." The Spirit " comes," is " sent," " teaches," may be " grieved," or " resisted." All these expressions indicate the growing sense of the special and distinctive work of the Spirit and the personal qualities manifest in his action. Another group of passages especially emphasize the Trinitarian aspect of the teaching as to the Spirit of God. The commission commands baptism in the name of the Father, the Son, and the Holy Spirit. (Matt. 28 : 19.) In 2 Corinthians 13 : 14 Paul clearly distinguishes Father, Son, and Spirit. So also in 1 Corinthians 12 : 4-6 Paul mentions the three as sources of spiritual blessings for believers. (See Eph. 2 : 18; 3 : 2-5, 14, 17; 4 : 4-6; 5 : 18-20.)

3. From the preceding outline of Scripture teaching the following points are clear: (1) The teaching as to the Holy Spirit in the New Testament is the culmination of the Old Testament teaching on the subject; (2) in the New Testament the Holy Spirit is revealed as personal in his action upon men; (3) the Father, Son, and Holy Spirit are grouped together and regarded as belonging to the same class; (4) on the basis of these facts the Christian doctrine of the Trinity arises. The word Trinity does not occur anywhere in the Bible, but the thought expressed by the word is clearly taught therein.

II. The Trinity

1. Before proceeding to the chief question in regard to the Trinity, several preliminary statements are necessary. The first is that the Christian conception of the Trinity does not imperil the conception of the unity of God. The Old Testament gave us monotheism. New Testament writers, mostly Jews, give us the

Trinitarian teaching with no sense of conflict or inconsistency. The unity of God is clearly held in the New Testament. Sometimes the Trinitarian doctrine has been stated in theological works in a manner which makes it difficult to distinguish it from tritheism. This is a fundamental error, and should be carefully avoided.

In the second place, it is to be noted that when we employ the terms " person " and " personal " in connection with the Trinity, we do not mean precisely what we have in mind when we apply the terms to men. With men a person is a separate and distinct individual, having no essential connection with other individuals. In reference to the Trinity we mean by personalities inner distinctions in the Godhead. These distinctions, however, are qualified by the most intimate relations of unity. They express the meaning of a single divine life, not of three separate and externally related divine lives. There are not three Gods, but one. A divine person is not less than a human person, but more. The divine life is richer and more complete than the human.

In the third place, the Christian doctrine of the Trinity is not the result of an effort to solve an abstract metaphysical problem. It arises out of the revelation in and through Jesus Christ and out of our experience of the grace of God in him. That is to say, God has spoken to us in Christ, and our experience of God in Christ is accompanied by a need which the Trinitarian truth alone supplies. In the realm of experience, therefore, we find the solution of several pressing speculative problems.

2. Is the Trinity immanent or economic? The most fundamental question regarding the Trinity is whether the distinctions are to be thought of as inside the Godhead itself or as manifested simply in the outward activities of God. Some are content to adopt an agnostic attitude and deny the possibility of solving the problem. This is an untenable position. The Christian teacher must not expose himself to the charge of evasion. The human mind refuses to ignore ultimate questions. The agnostic attitude on this point is no more justifiable than on others. At the same time we may and should admit that knowledge here is

partial. All the questions of ultimate being remain and will remain partly in shadow until our capacities are enlarged. But we do have real knowledge. God's revelations do not conceal. Our discoveries all imply growing capacity for knowledge and an expanding realm of truth. The infinite is implicit in the finite.

Both Scripture and experience warrant the view that the distinctions in the Trinity are not merely economic. They are immanent. They are distinctions in the Godhead. The grounds for this statement are manifold.

(1) All the evidence for the deity and preexistence of Christ confirms the Trinitarian doctrine. By this it is not meant that the Trinitarian doctrine is a necessity for thought to those who accept the preexistence doctrine. It is only meant that by the teaching of preexistence we ascribe immanent distinctions to the Godhead. If God is eternally Father and Son, then provision is made for a further distinction of Father and Son and Spirit.

(2) The evidence for the personal action of the Spirit confirms the Trinitarian view. Beyond all question, the Spirit of God is revealed as distinct in some sense from God, both in the Old and in the New Testament. In the New he is clearly revealed as personal. Indeed, a mere " principle " could not mediate the inner life of the religious man. Personality and personal relations are essential to the very idea of religion. The Spirit of God, regarded as a mere principle or impersonal force in man's religious life, is a self-contradictory conception. Only a pantheistic view of the world, in which personality loses its meaning, is in harmony with it.

(3) The Christian doctrine of the Trinity aids man in his speculative endeavors. A standing problem of thought is the difficulty of relating the abstract and infinite being to the finite as conditioned. This is not the place to enter fully into the controversy. But a brief statement is in order. As soon as we attempt to abolish all distinctions in the Godhead, we come upon insoluble difficulties. A God without such distinctions has no relations either within or without. He is unlike and apart from everything we know. We cannot conceive of him as active in relation to any

finite existence without compromise, in some form, of his absolute ness. The result is that gradually men come to view him as a simple monad, an indefinable and intangible bare unity lifted far above all finite forms. He is like the dot above the i, and unrelated to it. Or else he is conceived of in a pantheistic way which cancels the meaning and validity of all finite beings, including human personality. Thus God is absorbed in the world like water in a sponge. The philosophic thought which takes either of these directions is fatal to all our higher interests. We are plunged in hopeless agnosticism, or else we are swallowed up in the All which devours ruthlessly every form of finite life.

Now the Christian Trinity recognizes that finite being is not the negation, but in part the expression of God; that the universe is a clue to the meaning of the divine Being, not a veil to hide him from view; that human personality is a reflection of his image, not a passing phase of being. It shows that God's own life may find expression in a finite human life through the incarnation of his Son; that the infinitude of his being as Father does not prevent his gift to us of his Spirit, who teaches us to say, " Abba, Father."

We may sum up the matter by saying that we must find in God himself the ground for all that we discover in his works. God sustains relations to man and nature. Hence we are not surprised to find him revealed as having relations within the divine nature itself.

3. There are several forms of statement which men have employed to show the necessity for distinctions in the Godhead. It is said, for example, that as thinking subject God needs and requires an object. If the universe is created and finite, God can only find an eternal object in himself, that is, in one of the persons of the Trinity.

Again, it is urged that as infinite will God must have a corresponding object for the action of his will. This he finds in the Son and the Spirit.

More attractive than either of these is a third statement, *viz.,* that as eternal love God must have an object which is also eternal. His Son and his Spirit are such objects. Thus it appears that the eternal Fatherhood of God and the eternal Sonship of Christ supply us an infinite ground for love as it is manifest in the world.

Whatever may be said of the first two suppositions, the last must appeal powerfully to every thoughtful mind. We place righteous love at the apex of the divine attributes. It is the crown of all. And yet apart from immanent distinctions in the Godhead it is a finite quality. In a sense it is a derived and dependent quality rather than inherent and essential, since it arises only after God has created finite beings.

A fourth statement is that God as a moral being generally is dependent on immanent distinctions in the Trinity. We can think of God as enacting a moral law, objective to himself, and establishing a moral system for the benefit of his creatures, but it lowers the ethical values very greatly if they be conceived as a mere positive ordinance of God based on expediency and not grounded in his eternal nature. If we eliminate the ethical ideal from the divine nature, it is difficult to see how we can ever give such a system the necessary motive and sanction. It would reduce God to a merely intellectual being without any wealth of moral content. On the other hand, to conceive God as eternally ethical involves relations in the Godhead. At the same time it gives an infinite sanction to the moral ideal among men, and greatly exalts its meaning.

A fifth statement is that the ideal of personality itself involves relationships to others. We remain mere individuals so long as our lives are apart from other lives. We realize our true personality only in our connections with other lives. Love is necessary for us to attain the goal of our being. No truth has become clearer than this is in modern times. Yet a non-Trinitarian view of God leaves the most essential element in our self-realization as personal beings without an adequate basis in the divine nature.

Finally, the Trinitarian view helps us to understand the end of God in the creation of nature and man. A moral kingdom of persons redeemed through Christ is the end set before us in

o

Scripture. The Trinity shows how this kingdom is grounded in God himself. It shows how the universe is the expression of God's nature which is righteous love. The very type and ideal of all that is highest in our individual and social development are found thus in the Godhead itself. Physical nature is a means to this personal, moral, and social end. The image of God in man thus appears in its final and perfected form in a holy society of men who have been recreated in Jesus Christ.

III. The Practical Religious Value of the Doctrine of the Trinity

It was previously stated that the Christian teaching as to the Trinity is not the result of an effort to solve a speculative problem. It is a revealed truth, and its grows out of religious experience. Observe some of the elements of value contained in its meaning as to God and man.

Through it God becomes for men forever a personal being. Jesus, who reveals him in the incarnate life, writes this truth across the face of history. God is a person. He is also paternal. God is our Father. This conception exalts religion to the highest possible level. It is fellowship between the Father and the Son.

As to Jesus Christ, the Trinitarian teaching connects his Saviourhood with the divine nature itself. His incarnation becomes for us the token of God's capacity for sacrifice. Sacrifice on our part becomes the imitation of God. As Saviour Jesus is armed with infinite resources for his redeeming work. He is "mighty to save." This was the experiential conviction of the early Christians in their definitions of Christ's person. His deity and Saviourhood were indissolubly bound together.

As to the Holy Spirit, the Trinitarian doctrine defines him first in relation to the Godhead and then in relation to the work of Christ in and for believers. The material with which the Spirit works is the truth as it is in Jesus. His sphere of action is the consciousness of men. He makes the historic manifestation, the life of Christ, a continuous factor in man's religious life and in history. The outward historic revelation of God in Christ becomes thus the inward revelation of God through the Spirit.

As to believers themselves, the Trinitarian doctrine saves them from unfruitful views of God as above the world on the one hand, and as identical with the world on the other. The Holy Spirit creates the spiritual union between the believer and Christ by his regenerating act. He forms the Christian consciousness in terms of fellowship with God, of sonship, of growing moral likeness to God in Christ. He sustains the inner life of Christians in all stages of its development from beginning to end. In a word, the Holy Spirit makes the historical revelation in and through Christ morally and spiritually effective in the life of believers. His work is absolutely essential to the success of the gospel. In view of this, it is easy to understand the saying of John the Baptist to the effect that the work of Jesus which was to distinguish him in a peculiar manner was that he was to baptize men in the Holy Spirit. The saying is given in all four of the Gospels. It is repeated by the Master himself. The gift of the Holy Spirit at Pentecost is the fulfilment of this promise of Christ. (See Matt. 3 : 11; Mark 1 : 8; Luke 3 : 16; John 1 : 33; Acts 1 : 5.) In the light of these passages, then, we may say: (a) that the relation of Christ to men after his ascension was a relation created and maintained by the Holy Spirit; (b) that the outpouring at Pentecost was the permanent baptism of the Holy Spirit; (c) that the Spirit remains as the guide of Christ's people through all the gospel age; (d) that the Spirit's distinctive work is to carry forward the work Christ began; (e) that Christ's activity on earth is thus continued in and through the Holy Spirit. (Acts 1 : 1.)

IV. OBJECTIONS

In the preceding discussion most of the usual objections to the Trinity have been met in the positive statements made. There are four others to be named. The first is that some of the ethnic religions have forms of Trinitarian belief, from which it is inferred that the Christian Trinity must be false. The reply is that it is a reversal of the proper method of inductive logic to declare that a thing is untrue because there are so many examples of it. The contrary is the true method. The greater the number of examples, the greater the force of the verifying evidence. As in so many other particulars, Christianity is the ideal toward which the ethnic religions pointed. Their trinities are far below the Christian in their appeal to man's religious craving in their ethical quality, and in self-consistency and harmony with the divine unity. The Christian Trinity is a revealed truth which is abundantly verified in our experiential religious life.

A second objection is that the doctrine of the Trinity is self-contradictory in asserting that God is three and one at the same time. The reply is that manifoldness of life is not a self-contradictory idea. A barren unity of being would be far more difficult to conceive. Besides, the objection is groundless in that the three-ness and one-ness of God are asserted with reference to different aspects of his being. God is three in one respect, and one in another, as man is two in one respect, and one in another. He is body and spirit. But he is one person.

A third objection is that the Christian doctrine of the Trinity is unthinkable. This objection sounds very formidable. But it is quite vague. What is thinkable depends on the thinker. Implied in the objection is the assumption that reality must conform to our thoughts about it. On the contrary, our thoughts are bound to conform to reality if we are to have true thoughts. What God is in himself, God alone can make clear. God's revelation of himself in Christ and in our experience of him through the Spirit, is his answer to our theories of knowledge. We must remake those theories if they contradict the given facts. As to the unthinkableness of the Trinity, we need only reflect a moment upon modern philosophic thought to be reminded that in its better representatives it tends to confirm the Trinitarian teaching. Mention may be made, for example, of certain forms of personal idealism in which personality is made the ultimate reality and in which all persons are conceived as having an eternal basis in the infinite life of God.

Another objection is that the Trinity is a metaphysical doctrine and is to be rejected on this account. The answer is that the doctrine of God is metaphysical in the same sense.

There is no way to avoid some metaphysics in religion. The modal and economic trinities are all metaphysical doctrines. In fact all world-views are metaphysical. Yet there is a great variety of them claiming the field, even by those who in some instances object to the Christian Trinity on metaphysical grounds. Indeed, agnosticism itself is a metaphysical world-view. It holds a very definite conception of the make of the universe.

We must have some metaphysics. But metaphysics should be well based in facts. Objections to the Christian Trinity on metaphysical grounds rest on a narrowly rationalistic criterion of truth. There are several forms of rationality: logical, emotional, esthetic, moral, religious. A universe emotionally rational implies a supreme object worthy of our love. A universe esthetically rational implies a supreme satisfaction of our faculty for the beautiful. A universe morally rational implies a being who gives supreme sanction and meaning to the moral law. A universe spiritually and religiously rational implies a supreme object of worship who cares for us, reveals himself to us, and creates in us capacity for holy living and fellowship with himself. Metaphysics goes astray when it assumes that the logical faculty of man alone finds satisfaction in the universe. It becomes thus abstract and misleading. The doctrine of the Trinity in Christianity is God's response to the total religious and moral need of man. It also arises out of the facts of the religious life itself. It is thus the best possible answer to our craving for a completely rational universe. Rationality in all its forms, emotional, esthetic, ethical, logical, and religious, is satisfied in it as nearly as this is possible under present conditions.

CHAPTER IX

THE GOD OF OUR LORD JESUS CHRIST

WE have reserved the discussion of the character and attributes of God for the present section for the reason that we can best understand the God of our Lord Jesus Christ in the light of the teachings of the gospel and our experience of God's gracious power in redemption. In other words, we can best understand the relation between this central doctrine of theology and the realities and facts of religion after we have given a general survey of the facts. In preceding sections we have defined the knowledge arising out of our experience of salvation. We have shown our dependence upon the Scriptures as the authoritative source of our knowledge of God's supreme revelation in Christ. We have pointed out the reasons for accepting Christ as that sufficient revelation of God to us. We have also seen how it is made effectual in us only through the operation of the Holy Spirit. We pass next to the consideration of the infinite and holy God thus made known and thus mediated to us. After this we shall be prepared to consider the great themes which deal with God's work and purpose in Creation, Providence, and Redemption. In this way we are enabled to rise from our most intimate personal relations to God known in experience, to an understanding of his great plan and purposes for the universe. In this way also God is for us a living reality and not an abstraction of the reason.

I. DEFINITION OF GOD

We begin with a definition of God, as follows: God is the supreme personal Spirit; perfect in all his attributes; who is the source, support, and end of the universe; who guides it according to the wise, righteous, and loving purpose revealed in Jesus Christ; who indwells in all things by his Holy Spirit, seeking

ever to transform them according to his own will and bring
them to the goal of his kingdom.

This definition contains the following elements necessary to
the Christian conception of God: (1) what God is in himself;
(2) in his attributes; (3) in his relation to creation; (4) in his
purpose in Christ; (5) in the progressive nature of his kingdom;
(6) in the kingdom's relations to the Holy Spirit; (7) in the
kingdom's consummation and end.

By way of contrast we add two very much briefer definitions.
Dr. A. H. Strong in his " Systematic Theology " defines [1] God as
" the infinite and perfect Spirit, in whom all things have their
source, support, and end." Dr. William N. Clarke defines [2] God
as " the personal Spirit, perfectly good, who in holy love creates,
sustains, and orders all."

Both these definitions are admirable for their conciseness and
clearness. If one cares most for brevity in a definition, it would
be difficult to improve upon these. The chief objection to them
is that they lack the distinctive Christian elements in the idea
of God. Of course the idea of God which these writers present
in their later discussions is not lacking in the Christian elements.
But their definitions imply rather than state them, and a non-
Christian might accept either definition as his own.

In general we may remark that there are a number of objections to the very brief definitions of God given in many works on
theology. First, they are too often abstract and philosophic rather
than warm and living conceptions of God. Secondly, being thus
colorless they appeal rather to the intellect than to the feelings,
the moral nature, and the will. Thirdly, they are usually not
vitally related to the doctrinal views presented in the later discussions of their authors. The philosophic conception is set aside
for the New Testament revelation of God when the doctrinal
system is developed. Fourthly, the brief, abstract definition is
usually better suited to apologetics than to theology. In defending
theism against the non-theistic world-views, one may need only

[1] " Systematic Theology," Vol. I, p. 52.
[2] " Outline of Christian Theology," p. 66.

[215]

to contend for a bare theism. The conception of God may thus become a dim outline with one or two distinctive features. But for the purposes of Christian theology far more is required. In other words, the length of the Christian definition is due to the wealth and fulness of the Christian idea of God. A fifth objection to the brief abstract definitions of God is that they are usually derived from the field of natural rather than that of biblical theology. For the Christian theologian the revelation of God in Christ is primary and fundamental. We come to nature through Christ, not to Christ through nature. While nature presents very strong evidence for God's existence it tells us very little about God's character. We attach due importance to all that nature can teach us. But the corner-stone of Christian teaching is God's revelation in Christ.

II. THE CHRISTIAN DEFINITION

We proceed next to develop more fully the contents of the Christian definition of God. This entire volume is indeed an unfolding of the definition we have given. But before we deal with God's relations with nature and history, and before setting forth the meaning of his redemptive purpose and his moral kingdom, it is necessary that we present the Christian teaching as to God's character and attributes.

1. We note first that God is Spirit. He has not a body. Matter is limited and changeable. It is made up of parts. God is not compounded of parts. He has none of the limitations of matter. In the Scriptures God is often described as having hands, feet, arms, eyes, a mouth, and most of the bodily organs. But these are anthropomorphic expressions designed to set forth his actions in a vivid human way for our apprehension. He is also described as having wings, and in many other ways figures of speech are employed to describe God. These representations are in no way opposed to the spirituality of God.

There are four chief reasons for ascribing spirituality to God. First, our own higher nature is spirit, and from it we deduce the spirituality of God; secondly, our spirits have fellowship with God as Spirit, and thus we know him immediately; thirdly, Spirit is the highest form of existence known to us, and we naturally think of God as a spiritual being; and finally, God's spirituality is clearly and repeatedly taught in Scripture. Jesus said to the woman at the well,[3] " God is a Spirit, and they that worship him must worship him in spirit and in truth."

2. We remark next that God is a person. A personal being is one who is intelligent, self-conscious, self-determining, and moral. Perhaps the qualities by which we distinguish personality most clearly are self-consciousness and self-determination. Self-consciousness is the consciousness of self. A personal being can make himself an object of thought. He knows himself as distinct from other persons and other forms of existence. Self-determination is the activity of the will. Our freedom inheres in the capacity for self-determination. It means that we are determined from within rather than from without. God possesses these attributes of personality in the highest possible degree of perfection.

(1) We show the truth of God's personality in several ways. First, we infer it from our own human personality. Surely God is not below man in the qualities of his being. Personality is the highest we know, and we attribute to God a corresponding fulness of being. Secondly, we infer God's personality from man's religious life. Psychology and comparative religion point out the fact that religion, as it is found among men generally, is carried on in personal terms. We address God and have fellowship with him as a person. A moment's reflection shows that it is inevitable that this should be true. Every valuable element in religion arises from the conception of personality in God. Transgression, confession, thanksgiving, adoration, faith, hope, love, and all the ethical ideals of religion arise out of the conviction that God is a person, and that we have personal dealings with him. In the third place, the biblical teaching about God uniformly is that he is a person. The God of the patriarchs, of the prophets,

[3] John 4 : 24. The marginal reading, which is preferable, reads, " God is Spirit."

[217]

of the apostles, and of Jesus Christ, is a personal God. This lies on the surface of Scripture everywhere. The pantheistic conception of God as an impersonal principle, or force, or substance, or law, fails in all essential respects to meet the requirements of man's religious life.

(2) Objection has been raised to the idea of personality in God. Personality, it is urged, implies limitation. There is the distinction between the self and the not-self; between the knower and the thing known; between the will and the object of the will. If God be regarded as infinite, it is asked, how can we ascribe to him these finite modes and forms of activity?

The reply to this objection may take several forms. For one thing it is based on an inadequate view of personality. Our human personality is as yet imperfect. Its limitations are not to be attributed to God. Our objects of thought usually lie outside of us in space. But God is not located in a particular point of space. He is not a spatially extended or limited being.

Again, the objection is based on a wrong view of the infinite as we shall presently see. When we think of the infinite as the negation of everything known to us, we thereby assert that God cannot be known by us. If God is wholly unlike man, there is no standard of measurement by which we can ever know God.

The objection also overlooks the fact that man can make himself an object of thought. The qualities of personality may thus appear apart from spatial objects around us. The doctrine of the Trinity also aids us in conceiving an object of thought for God within the Godhead itself.

In the fourth place, we reply to the objection by recalling the biblical teaching that man is made in the image of God. Man's likeness to God cannot consist in bodily similarity. It can only be in spiritual qualities. The image of God in man can only be in personality and the qualities which belong to it.

It is sometimes urged that God is more than personal. The object of this is to avoid the difficulties involved in the imperfections and limitations of human persons in our thoughts about God. Now if the assertion means simply that God is free from all that limits and thwarts man, it is true. He is the transcendent personality, far above all the imperfections of the highest human persons. But if the assertion is made in the sense that God is devoid of self-consciousness and will, if he is without intelligence and purpose, then it is to be rejected as meaningless. To assert that God is " above " personality in this sense is to assert nothing definite about God. Or rather it is to assert that God is unknowable. This would be contrary to all religious experience, contrary to reason, and squarely opposed to the biblical doctrine of God.

3. As personal, God is also the living God. Life is a term which cannot be fully defined. Science defines it as correspondence between organ and environment. But it must mean far more as applied to God, since God has no environment. The life of God is his activity of thought, feeling, and will. It is the total inward movement of his being which enables him to form wise, holy, and loving purposes and to execute them.

4. God is the supreme personal Spirit. The word supreme is used to define God instead of some other terms which grow out of philosophical speculation. When we say God is supreme we mean that there is no being above or beyond him, and that in his nature and power, and in the qualities of his being, none other can be conceived of superior to him.

5. The word infinite when applied to God, if properly understood, conveys the same idea. But this word has often been used by philosophers as expressing the notion that God is removed in his essential being from the sphere of all our knowledge. As infinite he is opposed to all that is finite or limited. It has been asserted, and argued, indeed, that God is so far removed from us in the infinitude of his nature, that we can have no knowledge of him.

Such a view of God's infinity is mere negation. If when we look at physical creation or any part of it, and say God is not that, nor in any way like that; or when we look at man or any quality in him, if we say God is not that nor like that, it is clear that we make no positive statement about God. We simply deny thus that any of the things known to us give any real knowledge of God.

But this is not the correct meaning of the word infinite. The God whom Christ reveals to us, and who makes himself known to us through nature, is infinite in a far richer and more fruitful sense of the word. In the qualities of wisdom, goodness, power, and in many others which we know through man and nature, we see qualities which belong to God. But they belong to him in infinite degree. There is, in other words, no limit in him to the abounding fulness of these qualities and powers. The infinitude of God, then, is not to be understood simply as a negative way of thinking of God, but as expressing the largest possible amplitude of excellence in God's nature.

The word infinite is sometimes understood as mere physical greatness. In this sense the mind conceives of God as if he were illimitably extended in space, or indefinitely extended in time. But the word infinite as applied to God is not primarily spatial or temporal. We shall speak afterward of his omnipresence and eternity and related attributes. These indeed arise out of the infinity of his nature. But we mean chiefly by the infinity of God that he is not bound or restricted in his action by time and space. Our own spirits, in relation to our bodies, in some faint manner suggest God's relations to space. Our spirits are not spatial or extended, yet they are related to space. They are capable also of forms of activity which have no necessary relation to space. In our personal spiritual life we transcend space. Yet we may be and are in most of the forms of our activity related to space. Thus God's infinity means that as the supreme personal Spirit he rises above space while yet able to relate himself to it.

Thus the infinite God transcends nature and yet indwells in nature. He is immanent in the world he has made, carrying it forward at every stage to its predestined goal.

The above method of arriving at the idea of the infinity of God is practically very important. We do not make the infinite the same as the inconceivable or the incomprehensible. It is rather the conceivable and the comprehensible raised to the highest power. We never fully understand God; but we do really know him. This is one important result of the method. God is placed among knowable objects for our minds and hearts. It is also suggested thus that God is capable of limiting himself in order to carry out given purposes or ends. The universe and man are forms of manifestations of God's wisdom, holiness, love, and power.

This further outcome is to be noted: created things have capacity for the divine. Man made in God's image may progressively manifest him. There is then no end to human knowledge or to the growth of the human personality. All the way from the present finite stage of human growth up to the divine level itself is open to man for achievement and progress.

Jesus Christ has disclosed to us at once the infinitude of God in all gracious attributes and man's unlimited capacity for God. The Scriptures, especially the New Testament, emphasize this: "For of his fulness we all received, and grace for grace" (John 1 : 16). In Ephesians Paul prays that grace may abound in knowledge. (Eph. 1 : 7-9.)

6. God as the supreme personal Spirit is one. There is and can be but one supreme, infinite, personal Spirit. The unity of God carries with it the denial of dualism or the existence of a good and an evil principle of equal power contending for the mastery in the universe. It denies polytheism, or the existence of many gods. The unity of God is not against the Christian teaching as to the Trinity since the latter doctrine does not mean three Gods, but only a threefold distinction in the one divine nature.

Two other terms, which are sometimes applied to God, we may mention here. These are more or less philosophical in character, and have not the practical value possessed by those we have been considering.

7. One of these is the word *absolute*. It means that which is not relative or dependent. When we apply it to God we mean that he is independent of all created objects.

The word *unconditioned* is similar to the other. By it we

declare that God is not subject to conditions in his actions and purposes as we are. He is not limited and thwarted by external objects in carrying out his plans and purposes.

These words have a certain value in theological discussion, but they are objectionable in some respects. The meaning of both of them has varied from time to time. Philosophical speculation has sometimes emptied them of all positive contents and left them as mere empty shells of thought. They have thus become abstractions of little or no value. For example, it has been alleged that God is the absolute and unconditioned in the sense that he is wholly apart from the world, unrelated to it, and hence unknowable by us. As thus defined the words are without practical value, and they are untrue. God is not thus apart from the world, and he is knowable in some measure by us.

Most of the meaning implied in these terms is expressed by the word infinite as already defined. Hence we are not greatly dependent on them in our thinking and speaking about God.

III. The Attributes of God

The attributes of God have been classified in various ways. They have been divided into communicable and incommunicable, or attributes which can and those which cannot be communicated to his creatures; into absolute and relative, or those which belong to God independently of all relations, and those which relate him to created objects; into immanent and transient, or those which belong to God's inner being and those which pass over to his creatures. These three distinctions are practically one. It is not entirely clear where the dividing line is to be drawn between the attributes falling under the one head and those under the other. Writers differ among themselves on this point. Perhaps in the strict sense we should include only self-existence and immutability under the head of the incommunicable or absolute or immanent attributes of God.

In fact, there is no form of classification of God's attributes which is wholly unobjectionable. For this reason perhaps the simpler the method, the better will be the result. Hence we adopt the distinction of the natural and the moral attributes of God. Of course the moral attributes are also natural to God, and the natural are active when he exercises his moral qualities. Nevertheless, the distinction between natural, as pertaining to God's nature, and moral, as pertaining to his moral character and relations, is clear and practically valuable.

1. The Natural Attributes of God

These are self-existence, immutability, omnipresence, omniscience, omnipotence, eternity, immensity.

(1) When we say that God is self-existent we mean that he derives his being from no outside source. He exists in and of himself. He did not will himself into existence. His existence is grounded rather in his nature. He necessarily exists by reason of what he is in himself.

(2) By immutability we define God as unchangeable in his nature and purposes. This does not mean immobility or inactivity. God is infinite in energy and ceaseless in his activity. It does not mean that God cannot make free choices. The ability to choose ends and the means for realizing them belongs to God in the highest degree. God is infinitely free in his choices of both ends and means. Immutability in God does not mean that he cannot make progress from stage to stage in the unfolding of his plans and purposes. God is constantly lifting creation from lower to higher stages of development. Immutability does not mean that God cannot change his method in carrying into effect his purposes. He frequently changes his method, as in the successive dispensations and periods of Old Testament and New Testament history.

Again, immutability does not mean that God cannot feel. Immutability does not mean impassibility. God has capacity for sorrow and sympathy with the suffering and for indignation and wrath against evil, not because he is deficient in his nature, but because of his abounding fulness of life.

We may best think of the immutability of God, then, as that

self-consistency which runs through all his activities. He is changeless in wisdom, holiness, and power. For this reason he is infinitely flexible and adaptable in the execution of his purposes. His ability to change his method to meet an emergency in dealing with free creatures is a mark of his immutability, not of its lack. His infinitely wise purposes can be carried into effect only as he has power to meet each new situation as it arises.

When sin arises he cannot deal with the sinner as with a sinless being. When he answers prayer it is because he provided for prayer and its answer in his plan for the world. The incarnation was not a change in God's nature or purpose. It was simply a change in the method of his redeeming activity. The New Testament miracles, like the incarnation, were a form of his redeeming activity. All these forms of the divine activity are in accordance with God's immutability. They are, indeed, required by his self-consistency in dealing with men. The apparent changes in God are simply his unresting desire to bless men. They are the ceaseless importunity of his love. They are the unquenchable passion of his righteousness seeking to communicate itself to his creatures. They are not signs of a fickle or limited nature striving in vain to realize its ends. They are rather the expression of the infinite fulness and resourcefulness of God who will not be defeated in his purposes. He pursues men in all their devious ways because he is righteous love. If we think of God as a free personal being, dealing with free personal beings, we have the key to his immutability and to the variety of his methods. There is nothing arbitrary in God's action. The highest motive is always behind his dealings with men. We may sum up the meaning of his immutability then when we say it is his moral and personal self-consistency in all his dealings with his creatures. The tune of a simple song like "Home, Sweet Home" may be played on an instrument "with variations." But through all the variations the tune runs in self-consistent unity to the end. God's immutability is like the tune. It is his self-consistency manifesting itself in endless variations of method.

(3) When we assert the omnipresence of God we mean that God is not confined to any part or parts of the universe either in time or space. He is not present in this or that point in space and absent from some other; nor in this or that moment of time and absent from some other. But he is present in all his power at every point of space and every moment of time. When we speak of the divine immanence we mean this indwelling of God in space and time. When we speak of the divine transcendence we assert that God is not limited by time and space. God's indwelling in the world is not necessary, but free. He is not in the world as a substance, or physical principle, or law, but as a free personal spirit.

(4) Two other words need to be mentioned here—immensity and eternity. These define God as superior to space and time. By immensity we do not mean that God is unrelated to space. We mean rather that God is not a spatially extended being. He is not confined to or limited by space. Spatially extended objects and the relations of these objects to each other in space are seen and known as real to the mind of God. But he is not confined in space nor does he include space in himself as if he were a greater space including a less, a larger circle outside a smaller one. His immensity means rather that his mode of existence is not spatial or extended, and that he is not subject to the laws of space.

(5) In like manner the eternity of God sets forth his relation to time. God had no beginning and will have no end. He knows events as taking place in time, but he is not limited by time in any way. He recognizes some events as past and others as future in relation to present events. But past, present, and future are equally known to him. We tell of events one by one as they occur. God sees all events in a connected whole as if they were one. The difference has been illustrated by the two ways of seeing a street procession. If you stand in a doorway on a street, you see it a little at a time. From the top of a steeple you would see all the procession at once.

There has been much subtle speculation about time and space

among the philosophers since Kant's day. The debate has been chiefly over the point whether or not objects exist really in time and space. Some assert and others deny this. Those who deny claim that space and time are simply subjective forms of human experience. They hold that we must needs think in terms of time and space because our minds are so made, not because time and space are objective realities.

It is not necessary to discuss the point. All that has been said is true upon any view. Time and space are real to human experience whatever may be true as to their objective reality. All that has been said as to God's relations to time and space also remains. For he recognizes them as real forms of human experience while not subject himself to their limitations.

(6) The omniscience of God describes his knowledge. That God knows all things is implied in his omnipresence. The universe as the expression of God's thought and plan suggests his omniscience. Instances of prophecy in Scripture indicate his knowledge of future events. His omniscience is a part of his spiritual perfection.

a. As to God's method of knowing we may assert several things. It is immediate, without processes of thinking, of reasoning, or inference. It is distinct, without vagueness or confusion. It is complete, including the whole and never a part merely of the objects of knowledge. It is inclusive and simultaneous, in that all objects in space and all events in time are direct and immediate objects of knowledge to him.

b. The extent of God's knowledge has already been indicated. It is necessary to add the following statements. God knows not only all actually existent things, but also all future events. He knows all necessary events due to the operation of physical causes. The whole course of nature is an open book to him. He knows also all the free choices of moral and intelligent beings before the choices are made.

Some have discussed the question whether or not God knows all possible events. Does he know all the possible choices of all actual and all possible free beings? Does he know all the possibilities of all possible worlds? In reply it may be said that queries of this kind are not particularly valuable or fruitful of results. It is not necessary for us to suppose that God carries in his mind the useless knowledge of an infinite number of possible free creatures and physical creations. It is only important to assert that God's knowledge is without limit, and that it relates to all objects of knowledge.

He has full knowledge of all things which exist or will exist actually, and of all possible things or events which are in any way involved in his thought and plan for the world as he has made it. There is no need to go beyond this.

c. There are two important questions as to God's omniscience to be mentioned here. First, does God's foreknowledge of an event predetermine the event or necessitate its occurrence? The answer must be in the negative. God's foreknowledge of the sinful choices of free moral creatures does not predetermine those choices. If they were predetermined by God as events in nature are predetermined, they would not be free choices at all. We can only say that God's general plan included these free choices. He does not interpose to prevent them. He permits them in the sense, not of approving them, but of allowing them to take place, as a part of his general plan.

The second question relates to the possibility of God's foreknowledge of the free choices of his creatures. If God does not predetermine in the sense of causing these choices, can he know them before they take place? Some assert that he cannot thus know them. A free choice, it is said, is never caused by a chain of antecedent causes as an event in nature. Hence it cannot be foreknown even by God himself. Even if God knows the motives which influence a man in his free choice, this does not necessarily bring knowledge of the choice itself, for sometimes men unexpectedly refuse to be governed by motives which have previously controlled them.

On the other side, we urge that God does know in advance the choices of his free creatures. We deny that God derives his knowledge by reasoning or inference. Hence the question of motives or conditions prior to free choices is not pertinent. God knows immediately and directly without the need of inference from antecedent motives. We cannot think of the infinite and perfect Spirit as devoid of knowledge of his creation in any respect. A God without a knowledge of all the choices of his free creatures would be without power to guide or control the universe. He would have to sit helpless and await the outcome. Other wills, not his own, would fix the course of events and the destiny of his creatures. The Scriptures in many forms teach the omniscience of God in respect to all the acts of all creatures. The difficulty connected with God's foreknowledge of the free choices of his creatures is a part of the general problem of freedom in relation to the divine sovereignty. In some of its phases that problem is insoluble by us at our present stage of knowledge. The existence of purpose and the orderly progress of nature and human society from lower to higher stages require us to assert that an intelligence which knows the end from the beginning presides over the course of events.

(7) By the omnipotence of God we mean his unlimited power to do any and all things consistent with his nature and purpose. That God possesses such power is clearly seen from its manifestation in many forms in nature. It is also abundantly taught in the Scriptures.

a. God's omnipotence is manifested in many ways. For one thing there is no obstacle which he cannot overcome in the carrying out of his purposes. Again, he has command of all possible ways and means for doing what he wills. Nor is he limited as to the use of means. He can act directly without means in the pursuit of his ends.

b. The universe as we know it is the supreme evidence of God's omnipotence. In creating, sustaining, and guiding it, God exhibits his boundless resources of energy. The universe also shows God's ability to limit or restrain himself. He chose to make it as it is rather than otherwise. He chose to make man free and leave him so. The universe does not exhaust God. There are always in him reserves of wisdom and power.

c. The only limitations in God's power are such as are self-imposed. He cannot perform acts out of harmony with his nature and purposes. Nor can he violate the constitution of the world which he has made. All this is but to say he cannot deny himself. God cannot lie or do wrong in any way. He cannot make wrong to be right. He cannot undo what has been done. He cannot do things which are self-contradictory. He cannot abolish the laws of mathematics so that two and two would make five. But all these limitations in God's power are not defects but forms of perfection. They simply proclaim him as a self-consistent being. His actions all accord with his nature and his purposes.

2. Moral Attributes

(1) Holiness. The most general and inclusive of the moral attributes of God is holiness. This is often defined as moral purity, or God's self-affirmation against evil in contradistinction to his love or self-communication to others. But this definition is not an adequate expression of the biblical meaning of the word. In order to understand the biblical usage it is important to keep in mind the truth that revelation is progressive.

a. There is some obscurity as to the derivation of the Hebrew word holy. The most probable view is that it is from a root which means to cut off, to separate, and hence to exalt. It thus describes God as a being exalted above men and above common things. In the earlier Old Testament usage it describes the divinity or Godhead of Jehovah. The holiness of God means simply his divinity, or acts which reveal his divinity, in certain passages. (Exod. 15 : 11, 13, 17; Isa. 43 : 15; Hosea 11 : 9; Heb. 3 : 3; Ps. 89 : 18; Isa. 1 : 4; 12 : 6; 43 : 3.)

Like all important biblical words, however, this one received new meaning as the revelation proceeded and men grew in knowledge. Holiness thus came to mean devoted or separated unto God, whether applied to things or people. "Ye shall be holy, for I am holy," was God's word to the covenant people. (Deut. 28 : 9, 10; Lev. 11 : 44; 20 : 26.)

The Christian Religion in Its Doctrinal Expression

As we have said, holiness designated the divinity or Godhead of Jehovah. We find accordingly that it is connected with any act of Jehovah, or any attribute wherein his divinity appears. It is found sometimes in connection with the exercise of his natural attributes. But usually holiness is the manifestation of the moral qualities of God. It is thus a general term descriptive of the moral perfection of God. These moral perfections appeared in the course of God's dealings with Israel until in the later prophets we find all the fundamental moral qualities present in the activities of the " Holy One," or " the Holy One of Israel." [4]

In the New Testament the attribute holy is used with reference to God much less frequently than in the Old. But the usage in the New Testament confirms what has been said as to the comprehensive meaning of the word. The holiness of God, then, is his supreme moral excellence in virtue of which all other moral attributes have their ground in him. Holiness may be defined as the sum of other moral qualities, or perhaps better still, as their source and ground.

b. There are three moral attributes central in God which are grounded in his holiness. These are righteousness, love, and truth.

Holiness manifests itself in righteousness. The following passages will make clear the connection between righteousness, or moral purity, and holiness. In Amos 2 : 7 God's holy name is profaned by immoral practices. In Isaiah 1 : 4 the prophet arraigns the people as a " sinful nation, laden with iniquity," because they have " despised the Holy One of Israel." In Isaiah 6 : 3-7 the same ideal of moral purity as required by the holiness of Jehovah is set forth in the prophet's call to his office. (See also Hab. 1 : 12, 13.)

Holiness manifests itself also in the form of love. In Ezekiel 39 : 25 Jehovah declares that he will bring back the captivity of Jacob because he is " jealous for his holy name." Again, in

[4] God is not described as " the holy God " in the Old Testament. But the adjective is frequently used as a noun, and translated " the holy one." Of course the noun holiness frequently appears.

Ezekiel 36 : 22-31, there is an extended description of the mercies which Jehovah will bestow upon the people because of his " holy name." In Isaiah 54 : 5 it is declared for the comfort of the people, " the Holy One of Israel is thy redeemer." These passages might be indefinitely multiplied. In Isaiah and Ezekiel and elsewhere God's redemptive love is constantly declared to be a manifestation of his holiness. God's redemptive activity indeed takes the form of judgment against the nations and salvation for Israel. In both respects it is " the Holy One of Israel " who is at work. In the New Testament the holiness of God is represented as the basis of his love. In John 17 : 11 Jesus prays, " Holy Father, keep them in thy name which thou hast given me." Thus holiness appears as peculiarly the attribute of God as Father, and an act of love on God's part appears as a fit expression of his holiness. So also in Luke 1 : 49 Mary exclaims, " And holy is his name," in a context wherein the overflowing mercy and grace of God are praised.

So also is the attribute of truth grounded in the holiness of God. This comes into view particularly in the New Testament. In John 17 : 17 Jesus prays to the Father : " Sanctify them in the truth : thy word is truth." Here the word sanctify has the same root as that which signifies God's holiness. As the Holy One he makes believers holy by means of truth and in the truth. This shows how closely truth and holiness are bound together in God's nature and activity. Again, in 1 John 2 : 20 are the words, " Ye have an anointing from the Holy One, and ye know all things." In verse 27 again it is declared that this " anointing " gave them ample knowledge so that " ye need not that any should teach you." Clearly in these passages the " Holy One " is the source of truth. In another striking passage the same relation between truth and holiness appears. In John 14 : 26 Jesus declares that the Father will send the Comforter to the disciples. But he further defines the Comforter as " even the Holy Spirit, whom the Father will send." Then he adds, " he shall teach you all things."

Thus it appears that the holiness of God, while originally referring to his divinity, came gradually to stand for any manifestation of that divinity, and through his dealings with his chosen people it came at length to express especially the moral perfection of God. We have seen that the three central attributes of moral perfection, righteousness, love, and truth, are all grounded in the holiness of God, or are to be regarded as expressions of that holiness. We have a powerful confirmation of this view in the name which all the New Testament writers give to the Spirit of God. He is uniformly called the Holy Spirit. According to New Testament teaching the Holy Spirit is the transforming inward power, the principle or law of the spiritual life of Christians. His operations in the hearts of men are inclusive of all phases of Christian experience. There is no difficulty at all in showing the truth of these statements. In many passages the moral qualities we have named, righteousness, love, and truth, are traced to the Holy Spirit. It is needless to dwell at length upon these passages. We recall that when Ananias and Sapphira kept back a part of the price of the land, Peter said that they had lied to the Holy Spirit. (Acts 5 : 3.) Certainly righteousness in man is directly the product of the Holy Spirit. We recall also Paul's expression, " The love of the Spirit " (Rom. 15 : 30), and the beautiful saying in Romans 5 : 5 that "the love of God hath been shed abroad in our hearts through the Holy Spirit." Certainly the Holy Spirit is the author of love. What we have already seen as to the Holy Spirit's relation to truth is confirmed by the teaching throughout the Epistles. Everywhere he is the teacher and guide, the revealer of truth to men.

We have shown that righteousness, love, and truth are manifestations of the holiness of God. It is necessary to set forth the meaning of each of these more fully.

(2) Righteousness. *a*. The righteousness of God may be understood better if we note first its meaning as applied to men. There are various phases in the significance of the word as thus applied. But the underlying and essential meaning is twofold: Positively, it means perfectly answering to the requirements of God; and negatively, free from all defect and taint of character.

The God of Our Lord Jesus Christ

In a word it means morally pure and free from guilt and stain. In a man righteousness defines a relation to God and also relations to other men. We may now define the attribute of righteousness in God. By righteousness we mean the self-affirmation of God in favor of the right as opposed to the wrong, the pure as opposed to the impure. As affirmation it calls into exercise the will of God. As self-affirmation righteousness is grounded in his nature. As favoring the pure and right as opposed to the impure and wrong, righteousness is a part of the moral perfection of God. (See John 17 : 25; Rom. 3 : 21, 26; 2 Tim. 2 : 13; 4 : 8; 1 John 1 : 9; 2 : 29; 3 : 7; Rev. 16 : 5. In the Old Testament also, in many passages: Ps. 51 : 6; 145 : 17; Neh. 9 : 8; Isa. 34 : 16.)

b. The manifestations of God's righteousness are various. In general we define them as mandatory, punitive, and redemptive. God's mandatory righteousness is expressed in the moral laws which he prescribes for the conduct of men. Those laws are stamped upon the moral constitution of men as made in God's image. They find expression in the Mosaic laws of the Old Testament, especially as given in the Ten Commandments. They are also seen in the requirements of the higher righteousness of the New Testament. (Rom. 1 : 17; 2 : 14-16; 8 : 4; 10 : 5; Gal. 2 : 21; Phil. 3 : 6; 1 John 2 : 20; 3 : 7; Ps. 119 : 3, 7, 40, 142, 144, 164.)

The punitive righteousness of God leads him to administer the affairs of his kingdom in accordance with strict justice. He punishes the guilty for their transgressions. His wrath is aroused by the iniquity of men, and he will mete out to transgressors the due reward of their sins. (Gen. 18 : 25; Deut. 32 : 4; Rom. 2 : 6-16.)

In addition to the mandatory and punitive righteousness of God we note also what is best described as his redemptive righteousness. By this is meant the exhibition or vindication of his righteousness in his redeeming activity for men. This is a striking and most impressive aspect of the divine righteousness set forth only in the Bible. In the exercise of his redeeming love toward men, he preserves his self-consistency and the inviolability of his moral

[233]

law. This appears in several Old Testament passages, as in Psalm 85 : 10. In the second half of Isaiah especially is God's redemptive activity for Israel constantly declared to be " in righteousness." (See Isa. 41 : 2; 45 : 13; 41 : 10, 11; 43 : 6; 51 : 5; 42 : 6.) It is not always clear precisely what the phrase means in these passages. But the general truth appears that in all his saving work for his people, God operates on principles of righteousness. Perhaps in these Old Testament passages the prevailing thought is that of God's fidelity to his promise, his self-consistency in the execution of a purpose toward Israel.

In the New Testament, however, the redemptive righteousness of God appears in his moral self-consistency in the redeeming work of Christ. In Romans 3 : 26 he is declared to be " just " and " the justifier of him that hath faith in Jesus." In 2 Corinthians 5 : 21 Paul says: " Him who knew no sin he made to be sin on our behalf ; that we might become the righteousness of God in him." So in 1 John 1 : 9, " He is faithful and righteous to forgive us our sins "; and again in 1 John 2 : 1, " If any man sin, we have an advocate with the Father, Jesus Christ the righteous." All these passages of course relate to the atoning work of Christ. Our interest in them here is to observe the manner in which God's righteousness is bound up with his redeeming love for men. The interests of righteousness are never neglected in God's pursuit of his redeeming purpose.

c. The relation of God's righteousness to his nature may now be noted. The chief point at issue is whether the moral law is to be traced merely to the will of God, or is the expression of his nature. Is a command right because God wills it, or is it right because God is what he is? Beyond a doubt the Scriptures favor the latter view. Of course whatever God wills is right. But the prior question is why his will commands one particular act as right and forbids another as wrong.

We mention three considerations which justify the statement that righteousness is grounded in the nature rather than in the will of God. (a) The first is a fact of psychology. A man's will is a function of his nature. Men are indeed free in the exercise

[234]

of their wills. They are self-determined. They are autonomous beings. But the will never acts independently of the nature since it is a part of the nature. As in man, so also in God, the will is the expression of the nature. (b) The second consideration is ethical. The only permanent and satisfactory ground of ethics is to be found in the divine nature. Utility, happiness, the pursuit of pleasure in its lower or higher forms, for the individual or society, can never constitute an adequate explanation or ground of moral obligation. Moral obligation grounded in mere utility would thereby cease to be moral obligation. Its distinctive element as moral would be wanting. It would have little power to grip men and hold them stedfast in their loyalty to the moral ideal. It could never explain the higher forms of human loyalty to those ideals. (c) The third consideration is the teaching of Scripture. Here there are several points to be noted. The first is that God is declared by Jesus to be the only being who is absolutely good: " None is good save one, even God " (Mark 10 : 18). The second is that man's relation to God is determined by what God is: " Ye shall be holy; for I am holy " (1 Peter 1 : 16). The third point is that moral perfection in man is grounded in moral perfection in God. Jesus said, " Ye therefore shall be perfect, as your heavenly Father is perfect " (Matt. 5 : 48). Finally, it is declared that our moral transformation is due to the fact that we have " become partakers of the divine nature, having escaped from the corruption that is in the world by lust " (2 Peter 1 : 4). It thus appears that our relation to God as his redeemed people, our moral attainments, and our renewed moral nature, are all grounded in the nature of God who alone is the absolute good. All these considerations unite to establish the view that righteousness is grounded in the nature and not merely in the will of God.

(3) Love. In the New Testament revelation through Christ we obtain the only sufficient definition of the love of God. God's love appears in many ways in his dealings with Israel in the Old Testament. There are certain passages in the Psalms, Isaiah, and elsewhere in the Old Testament, in which the love of God is

described in terms of exquisite power and beauty. (*E. g.,* Exod. 34 : 6, 7; Ps. 33 : 5; 119 : 64; 145 : 7-9; Isa. 45 : 8; 61 : 11.) But the complete revelation comes only in Jesus Christ.

Love may be defined as the self-imparting quality in the divine nature which leads God to seek the highest good and the most complete possession of his creatures. Love in its highest form is a relation between intelligent, moral, and free beings. God's love to man seeks to awaken a responsive love of man to God. In its final form love between God and man will mean their complete and unrestrained self-giving to each other, and the complete possession of each by the other.

It is impossible to state in an exhaustive way all the contents of the idea of God's love in Scripture. The following statements give a general outline.

a. Love is grounded in the nature of God. The supreme utterance of the New Testament regarding God's love is that in 1 John 4 : 8: " God is love." In Matthew 6 : 1-8 and 25-32 God's love is described in terms of Fatherhood. In Matthew 11 : 25ff. God's peculiar relation as Father to Jesus the Son is set forth. In John 17 : 24 Jesus declares that the Father loved him before the foundation of the world. This is the immanent love of God which finds its object in the Godhead itself. God is eternally love because there is an eternal object of love. His love is not conditioned upon the temporal and finite, although in these objects his love finds a sphere for its exercise.

b. God's love desires the supreme good of its object. This statement scarcely needs extended proof. It lies on the surface in all the references to God's love in the New Testament. He desires to seek and to save those who are lost. He seeks to reclaim those who wander from him. He strives to create the conditions of fellowship with himself in the hearts of the redeemed. He strives to enlarge their capacities for his love and grace. He cleanses and purges them by discipline and trial that they may become morally pure. He seeks to produce in men the conditions of a perfect society founded upon love to God and a corresponding love to man. He seeks as the goal of his dealings with men that they be worthy of admission into eternal fellowship with himself and into blessedness through Christ in his eternal kingdom.

It thus appears that the love of God is not merely amiable good will or moral indifference. Love exacts the highest from us because it is love. If God's love should let us off with what is below our possibilities in moral attainment, it would leave room for us to reproach love at the end. God's love will leave no room for any of its objects to reproach it in the final retrospect. He loves us too well to be content with anything but the best there is in us. Hence the system of means by which in this life he seeks our moral and spiritual development.

c. God's love desires to possess its objects. In the Old Testament the covenant between God and Israel was the basis of all God's dealings with his people. The meaning of the covenant was that God possessed Israel and Israel possessed God. The relation was sometimes described as like that between father and son, and sometimes as like that of husband and wife. Hence the statement so frequent in the Old Testament that God is a " jealous " God. (Exod. 20 : 5; 34 : 14; Deut. 4 : 24; Isa. 54 : 5; 62 : 5; Hosea 2 : 19.) Of course the word " jealous " as applied to God has none of the evil meaning connected with it in common usage. It is simply an intense assertion of God's moral claim and right to the exclusive possession of his people.

In the New Testament God's desire to possess the objects of his love appears in many ways. In a notable passage the apostle Paul says to Christian believers, " all things are yours, and ye are Christ's, and Christ is God's." Again he sets forth the same relation thus: " Ye are not your own, ye are bought with a price. Therefore glorify God in your bodies " (1 Cor. 6 : 19, 20). In the seventeenth chapter of John the possession of believers by the Father and the Son and the wonderful relations of intimacy are set forth in terms of great beauty and tenderness.

d. God's love acts in behalf of its object. This appears throughout the Old and the New Testaments. We need only emphasize here the supreme expression of God's love in the incarnation, life, and death of Jesus Christ. Christ is the only interpreter of the Father to men. For this end he came into the world. " God so loved the world that he gave his only Son " (John 3 : 16). God spared not his own Son. (Rom. 8 : 32.) God set forth his Son to be a propitiation for the sins of men. (Rom. 3 : 25.)

The perfection of God's love is seen in the redeeming activity of Christ in a threefold way: (a) In his capacity for sacrifice. It brings God very near to us when we realize that there is, as it were, a human element in him. Our capacity for sacrifice is but an element in our likeness to God. (Eph. 5 : 2.) (b) In the degree of the love of which this sacrifice was the expression. He gave the supreme object of his love, " his only Son " (John 3 : 16). (c) In the resourcefulness of God's love in the effort to bless. The incarnation is a mark of perfection, not of defect and limitation in God. It shows that he was equal to the demands of the situation brought about by man's transgression and consequent need and helplessness.

Men have sometimes objected to the view that God can suffer. But his capacity for suffering is a necessary element in his capacity for sacrifice. If Jesus Christ who suffered was God manifest in the flesh, then the divine Being can suffer. Christ did not bring us knowledge of an absentee God who sits apart unmoved as he contemplates human suffering. He revealed rather a God of sympathy who came into human life and who has capacity to suffer with and for us. The love which brings our redemption is a love which expresses the highest and deepest sympathy. Sympathy means the capacity of suffering with another because of identification with another. This God possesses in the highest possible degree. God's saving love is not a love which cost God nothing. It was the highest conceivable form of voluntary sacrifice. This point may be made clear by a glance at the possible degrees of sacrifice. First, we may note unconscious sacrifice. Vegetable life yields itself up to sustain the animal life above it. Secondly, there is instinctive sacrifice. The Mexican thrush will fly into the mouth of a snake which threatens her young. There are many beautiful forms of instinctive sacrifice among the lower animals.

Thirdly, there is involuntary sacrifice among men. We are often involved in the sufferings of others against our wills. The unity and solidarity of the race bring this upon us. Fourthly, there is free and voluntary sacrifice for the good of others. This is sacrifice in its highest form. God's self-giving for human redemption is of this kind. The incarnation and atonement are the supreme revelation of the heart of God. It was sacrifice freely chosen and deliberately carried out to redeem men. The reproduction in men of this kind of free and voluntary sacrifice is the central aim and choicest fruit of the gospel.

e. God's love manifests itself in various ways, according to the character and conditions of its objects. A number of terms have been employed to express this variety. When God's love terminates upon an object which meets his approval, it is the love of complacency. When it takes the form of good will toward all creatures, regardless of moral character, it is the love of benevolence. When its object is in distress, it is the love of compassion. When there is a relation of special intimacy between God's love and its object, it is the love of affection. When it goes out toward the guilty, it takes the form of mercy. Mercy alone, however, does not express the fulness of God's love to the sinful. In the New Testament this love is called grace. Mercy is the withholding of penalty, the pardoning of the transgressor. Grace goes farther and bestows all positive good. Mercy and grace are the negative and positive aspects of love toward the sinful. Mercy takes the bitter cup of penalty and pain from the hand of the guilty and empties it. Grace fills it to the brim with blessings. Mercy spares the object; grace claims it for its own. Mercy rescues from peril; grace imparts a new nature and bestows a new standing. Mercy is God's love devising a way of escape. Grace is the same love devising ways of transforming its object into the divine likeness and enabling it to share the divine blessedness.

f. God's love is inclusive of all mankind. There is a certain particularism in both the Old and New Testaments which has led some to lose sight of the universality of God's love. Israel was the chosen people and peculiar treasure of Jehovah. The elect in Christ are the special objects of God's favor in the New Testament. But the particularism in both cases is a stage toward a wider universalism in God's plan. This may be briefly shown in the following way.

(a) As to the case of Israel in the Old Testament, two points will make the matter clear. (aa) In the call of Abraham and the founding of the commonwealth of Israel the universal blessing of mankind was the expressed purpose and plan of God. A part of the promise in Genesis 12 : 1-3 was, "In thee shall all the families of the earth be blessed." (bb) In the later prophets, when the nation has gone into captivity, the teaching is that Israel is to fulfil her mission by becoming the prophet nation. She is to teach all other people the truth as to Jehovah. This is seen in such passages as Isaiah 49 : 1-6. Jehovah makes Israel's mouth like a " sharp sword," and Israel is like a " polished shaft." This is followed (ver. 6) by the promise, " I will give thee for a light to the Gentiles, that thou mayest be my salvation unto the end of the earth." There are many similar passages in the later prophets.

(b) In like manner the electing love of God in the New Testament is a step in the realization of God's plan for the whole world. Here we need only refer to the Great Commission in Matthew 28 : 19, 20; to the comprehensive universality of God's love in John 3 : 16; to Paul's teaching in the eleventh chapter of Romans, that the salvation of the Gentiles was bound up in the calling of Israel; and to his teaching in Ephesians (3 : 6) and elsewhere, that the "mystery" of the gospel, which had been hidden, but was now made known, was the great fact that Gentiles are to share in the blessings of the gospel.

(4) Truth. By the truth of God we designate the quality in him by virtue of which he is the source and ground of all forms of knowing, and all objects of knowledge. God's perfect knowledge of all things we have already described as omniscience. God's knowledge of himself is the exact expression of his nature as truth. His knowledge arises out of his nature. So also all

forms of knowing in created beings are grounded in the truth as
it inheres in God's nature. Again, all objects of knowledge are
constituted as knowable to us by their derivation from him.

Two conclusions follow from the preceding definition. The
first is that there is no standard of truth outside of God. He is
himself the ultimate reality of truth as of other forms of being.
The second is that truth is truth, not because God wills it merely.
God wills truth because he is true. Being conditions will. What
he wills he wills freely, but to will freely is also to will truly.
He cannot will falsehood or error or sin or self-contradictory
things. This is because he is truth.

All spheres of the truth are grounded in God's nature as truth.
Nature at every level is a realm of truth. Mechanical nature
is the lowest level. Biological nature is the next stage. Sentient
nature is the next, and the rational moral nature of man is the
highest known to us. As all these spheres of creation are constituted in truth, we have the sciences in an ascending scale.
There are the mathematical, biological, and moral sciences, and
the science of comparative religion, and many others. These
sciences or forms of knowledge are possible to us for two
reasons. One is that we are constituted for truth; the other,
that these spheres of knowledge are constituted in truth. Our
capacity to know and their capacity for being known are both
grounded in God, who is truth.

Out of God's nature as truth arise his veracity and faithfulness and wisdom. Veracity in God relates to what he says. God
speaks only truth. His messages to us are always in accord
with his own nature, and with the nature of created things. The
truths revealed to us in nature are consistent with each other. In
like manner the truths revealed in Scripture are a self-consistent
whole. It is, of course, necessary for us to use our intelligence
in interpreting nature and the Bible. But when we find God's
messages to us in these, they are all in accord with each other,
and with his own eternal truth.

By the faithfulness of God we express his fidelity to his promises and his unswerving loyalty to his own nature. He does not

raise expectations in the realm of nature or grace which he will not fulfil. He completes what he begins. He does not change his purposes or take back his promises.

The wisdom of God designates his knowledge and choice of the best possible ends and the best possible means for the realization of his ends. At certain points in nature and in his dealings with men he seems to be making experiments, as if he were trying out different ways of doing things. But properly understood, these are simply stages in the unfolding of his larger purposes. They are the necessary steps in his progress toward a goal. His wisdom is never at a loss for the best means for the attainment of the highest ends.

Many practical considerations arise from what has been said as to the attribute of truth in God.

a. In virtue of his truth God's personality is manifest. Truth is a meaningless term as applied to an impersonal force or energy or influence. Things have meaning only to personal beings. If God has meaning for us, or for himself, it is because he is a person and because we are persons.

b. The attribute of truth in God gives meaning to the conception of error. One statement is true and its opposite false because the world has a definite constitution. The various parts of created being cohere in particular ways. They are subject to uniform laws. These laws owe their origin to God, who is truth. Error in thought or speech is departure from reality in the constitution of man or nature or God.

c. Again, the attribute of truth in God gives rise to an element of knowledge in faith. Some have held that faith is the antithesis of knowledge. They have said, " We have but faith, we may not know " in things pertaining to God. This position is untenable. It is not difficult to perceive the reason why. Faith or trust joins us to God. Through this union God manifests himself to us. Since God is truth, his self-manifestation to us involves the communication of truth to us. Above all, God's revelation of himself to us in Christ is a communication of knowledge, " the treasures of wisdom and knowledge " (Col. 2 : 3).

d. The attribute of truth in God also makes inevitable the element of doctrine in man's religious life. There is always the peril that doctrines as intellectual systems may supplant vital faith. Theology when held as a mere logical or philosophical system may be hurtful to the religious life. We should not confound religion with theology. But it is equally absurd to attempt to maintain a strong religious life without doctrines. Religion has to do with facts about God and man, and the relations between God and man. Doctrines are simply the expression of the meaning of these facts and relations. Hence the two elements which are so conspicuous in the Bible. It is at once a book of life and a book of doctrines or teachings about life. Here again the explanation is found in the fact that God is truth. All true statements of doctrine are grounded in the nature of God, and doctrines inevitably arise in religion because God is a being of truth.

3. *The Attributes and the Divine Personality*

Men have often thought of the nature and attributes of God in a manner too abstract and mechanical. God is a person. His attributes are the qualities of his being as personal. They are not attached to him from without as if they were separate from his nature. They are not independent of each other as if one could be active without the others. They are not in conflict with each other as if there could be schism in the divine nature. There are not gradations among the attributes as if there could be a hierarchy of powers within God himself. It is possible to think of the attributes as if there were many gods rather than one God.

Let us keep in mind the truth that God is a unitary being, harmonious in all his qualities. When God feels, his feeling is qualified by his righteousness and his omniscience. When he thinks, he thinks righteously, truthfully, lovingly. When he wills, he wills according to infinite wisdom, love, and truth. When he punishes the guilty or redeems the lost, he has respect for every quality of his being. He never suspends the operation of his love, nor of his righteousness. But each is exercised according to the character and circumstances of the object.

Errors to be Avoided

If we keep in mind what has just been said as to the unity and harmony of God's attributes, we may avoid several errors:

The error of merging the attributes of God in one attribute.

The error of making one attribute superior to all others.

The error of thinking of the attributes as in conflict with each other.

The error of attributing to God arbitrary or capricious or whimsical action of the will.

We discuss these four points briefly.

(1) We consider first the error of merging all the attributes in some one attribute. Here we leave out of consideration the holiness of God. For, as already shown, holiness is a term descriptive of the moral perfection of God rather than a separate attribute.

Some make love the all-inclusive attribute of God and reduce all the others to some form of love. Again, righteousness, or God's self-affirming quality, is made inclusive of all others. There is no gain and much loss in efforts of this kind. The Scriptures afford no warrant for them. It is highly confusing to define love as God's self-imparting and righteousness as his self-affirming attribute, and then at once proceed to identify the one with the other. The very object of defining the attributes of God is to set forth the manifold riches of the divine nature. The thought of God grows pale and distant when we pass from definite and concrete descriptions of his nature to abstract and vague terms in which all the elements of his being are reduced to one.

(2) The second error to be avoided is that of making one attribute superior to all others. Here the attributes remain, but an effort is made to define them in an ascending order of importance. It will be sufficient for our purposes if we notice the controversy as to the relative places of love and righteousness

among the moral attributes. Some would make love, and others righteousness, the most fundamental attribute of God. Now it is possible to present arguments for either view, based upon a partial use of facts and of Scripture texts which seem conclusive. In favor of the view that love is the fundamental attribute, we are reminded that Jesus makes love to God and man the sum of human obligation; that Paul places love above all other Christian graces; that John declares that " God is love," and in general that the incarnation and atonement of Christ are the revelation of the nature of God as essentially love.

In favor of the view that righteousness is fundamental, our attention is called to such passages as Psalm 97 : 2, where " righteousness and justice are the foundation of his throne "; to the operations of our own consciences, which are supreme over other impulses of our nature; to the fact that God's righteousness limits and controls the exercise of his love; to the moral necessity in the divine nature which was met in the atonement of Christ; and to the inexorable justice of God's dealings with mankind in the course of human history.

It is not possible to establish either of these two views. The correct statement is that righteousness and love are coordinate and equal attributes of God. There is no sufficient ground for placing either above the other. This will appear if we notice briefly the replies to the arguments in favor of giving the primacy to righteousness.

a. It is urged that righteousness is fundamental because the Scriptures make it more prominent than love. But we have already noted the prominence given to love also in the New Testament. Special attention is called to the passage in the book of Revelation where the heavenly beings exclaim, " Holy, holy, holy, is the Lord God Almighty " (Rev. 4 : 8). It is argued from this that in heaven holiness is regarded as the chief attribute of God. But in reply we need only remember our explanation of the biblical meaning of holiness as applied to God. It does not mean righteousness as distinguished from love. In both the Old and the New Testaments it is a general term descriptive of the moral perfection of God. In some cases righteousness is prominent, in others love, and in yet others the truth of God is in view when the term is employed. Sometimes no one attribute is conspicuous, but rather the perfection of God in general. This is true of the passage before us. The term is applied to God because he created all things, and because he is the God " who was and who is and who is to come." There is no passage of Scripture which warrants us in subordinating love to righteousness or righteousness to love.

b. Again, the supremacy of righteousness over love is argued from the supremacy of conscience in ourselves. But surely we are not warranted in inferring what is normal in God's character from the abnormal state of our own. We are tainted and warped by sin and guilt. The sting of conscience attends our struggle for perfection all along the way. Conscience rings the alarm-bell so constantly because we so often do wrong. Of course we may deduce the righteousness of God from conscience. But we cannot deduce from our own spiritual life the relations between righteousness and love in him until we have made greater progress in love ourselves. When we are perfected in righteous love, our own nature may be a better guide to the relations between the two attributes in God.

c. It is argued further that love is optional, but that righteousness or justice is obligatory with God. The statement is, " God may be merciful, he must be just." In reply we say that the argument confounds love as a divine attribute with mercy, a particular form of its manifestation. Mercy is love expressing itself in forgiveness and remission of penalty from the guilty. But love is good will toward all creatures and the desire to bless them. The exercise of mercy is conditioned upon the repentance of the sinner. But God's good will toward all creatures is conditioned upon nothing outside his own nature. As we have seen, God's love is grounded in his nature. If he ceased to love, he would cease to be God. We may admit that mercy is optional with God, therefore, without admitting that love is optional. Love manifests itself in a variety of ways according to the circumstances of its object. But the principle of love in the divine nature, the desire to bless, never ceases its activity. Men, by their rebellion, may prevent its taking certain forms, such as mercy and forgiveness, but they cannot destroy it. If love were optional with God, we might conceive of him as dealing in a perfectly loveless way with the unfallen and pure angels. But such a conception would bring him to a level far below that of the God revealed to us in Christ.

d. Again, it is argued that the righteousness of God is an attribute of being, while benevolence is an attribute of action. The conclusion is drawn that if righteousness or justice should cease to be exercised, it would cease to exist, while benevolence might or might not be exercised according to circumstances. The reply is that here again the error is committed of taking a manifestation of love for the attribute of love. Love is as truly an attribute of being as righteousness. The exercise of both toward intelligent and free creatures must always be understood in the light of the attitude of those creatures toward God. Toward the morally perfect creature justice is quiescent, and love is complacent, but intensely active. Toward the guilty justice may be restrained while love seeks to redeem; or love may be under restraint and justice flame forth when iniquity is ripe. But whether God's action take the form of mercy or justice, God's attributes of love and righteousness remain the same.

e. Again, it is urged that righteousness is superior to love because love requires a norm or standard, while righteousness does not. This is the claim that love must act with reference to something other than itself, that is, righteousness; whereas righteousness is its own standard. But this position is also without adequate support. It carries with it the notion that God's attributes are parts which may be held together or taken apart. It is true that love always acts with reference to righteousness. Love is not an independent or detachable quality in God. But this is also true of righteousness. There is no conceivable act of righteousness or justice on God's part unaffected by his love. He is not two Gods, who stand forth at one time as righteousness and

at another as love. He is always righteous love, or loving righteousness. Love and righteousness are both ascribed to God in
his supreme manifestation as Father by the Lord Jesus in John
17 : 25, where he addresses God in the words, "O righteous
Father."

f. It is also urged that righteousness is superior to love because it controls in the exercise of love in the atonement of
Christ. It is insisted that since it was a demand in the divine
nature that must be met by the atonement, and since in his eternal purpose God planned to meet that demand, we must hold
that righteousness outranks love in God's nature.

But this is an arbitrary placing of one attribute above another.
It was God's love which prompted the atonement. His desire to
bless and save is the ruling motive throughout the incarnation
and atonement of Christ. It might with equal reason be urged
that love is superior to righteousness in God because the love
which provided the atonement overcame the justice which demanded the punishment of sinners.

It is quite possible to argue the case either way with equal
plausibility. If the Judge descends from the bench to become
Redeemer, is he not greater as Redeemer than he is as Judge?
Or we might ask, if the Judge carries the bench with him, as it
were, in redeeming, is he not greater as Judge than as Redeemer?
As a matter of fact, neither question can be answered correctly
in the affirmative. For if God both requires and makes atonement, how can we exalt him above himself in either respect?
We conclude then that righteousness and love are coordinate and
equal attributes in God. Love is as exacting as righteousness because it cannot endure the presence in its object of the sin which
injures and mars it. Righteousness is as patient and forbearing
as love in God, because only by a slow process of cleansing can
the moral ideal be realized.

Love is the sinner's fear as well as righteousness, because love
can only repudiate the sin to which the rebellious heart cleaves.
Righteousness is the sinner's hope as well as love because the goal
of a perfect character and final bliss can only be attained by the

extirpation of sin from his character. Gerald Stanley Lee has said:[5] "God is love, and law is the way he loves us. But it is true also that God is law, and love is the way he rules us."

(3) The third error which arises from failure to recognize that God is a unitary Being harmonious in all his attributes, is that of thinking of the attributes as in conflict with each other. What has been said about righteousness and love as exemplified in the atonement shows that we are not to imagine God as divided against himself, his righteousness being on one side and his love on the other. There are those who, by means of caricature, have sought to make the atonement objectionable. Some have even charged that the doctrine of the Trinity was invented to explain the atonement. God was on one side and Christ on the other. The Holy Spirit came in as the reconciler and harmonizer. This is mere caricature of the New Testament teaching. Christ did not purchase God's love for us by what he did. What he did was the expression of God's love. God's love was the cause, not the effect of the atonement. "God so loved the world" that he gave his Son. The atonement of Christ was the harmonious expression of both the love and the righteousness of God.

(4) A fourth error to be avoided is that of attributing to God arbitrary or capricious or whimsical action of the will. It has often been the fashion in abstract systems of theology to exalt the sovereignty of God by attributing all sorts of mysterious and arbitrary actions to him on the ground of his "mere good pleasure." The phrase, "the mere good pleasure of God," is misleading unless duly qualified. No one objects to the thought of God's sovereignty if it is understood that it is a righteous and loving sovereignty. But when his "mere good pleasure" is detached from these qualities of his being we have the picture of an Oriental tyrant, not of an infinitely wise Father. The sovereignty of God is a doctrine of priceless value. It would be fatal to surrender it. But we should avoid thinking of it as a sovereignty of sheer will. God is far more than a predestinating omnipotence. The best of reasons and motives are behind all his

[5] "The Shadow Christ," p. 38.

[249]

actions. He is a unitary Being, who is a Person, and in him all forms of perfection meet and are harmonized.

At this point we reach the highest possible conception of God. It is that presented to us in the revelation of Jesus Christ. It is the radiant image of God the Father Almighty, maker of heaven and earth. In this supreme revelation of God all other valid conceptions unite. Christ combined the scattered bits of truth about God, like fragments wrought into a mosaic. But he added his own distinctive revelation. The thought of God as first cause leaves us cold. The thought of God as a personal being warms us a little. The thought of him as a personal being with a holy purpose stirs us more deeply. The thought of this personal being as one who cares for us individually, numbering the very hairs of our heads, grips us mightily. But when all these thoughts are combined, and the first cause who is personal, and purposive, and holy, and individualizing, and loving, is recognized also as an infinite and mighty and gracious Father, all the joy-bells of the heart begin to ring. Now it was to reveal such a God that Christ came.

If we would avoid error in thinking of the attributes of God, four things are necessary: First, that we conceive of righteousness, love, and truth, not as abstractions, but as qualities which are unified and harmonized in an infinite person; secondly, that this person is the glorious God and Father of our Lord Jesus Christ; and thirdly, that in his dealings with men he has respect to them as free moral beings; and fourthly, that in himself he does not change, whatever be the necessary variation of manifestation due to the circumstances and actions of his free creatures.

CHAPTER X

CREATION

I. DEFINITION

BY creation is meant all that exists which is not God. This includes nature and man and all other forms of being other than God himself. The problem of creation is one of the most difficult of all those with which the unaided reason of man deals. Modern physical science has given it acute form in its doctrine of the transformation of energy. Everything in physical nature is the transformed result of something prior in the causal series. The outcome is an endless regress of physical causes. Through it we never rise to a spiritual cause.

At this point is seen clearly the contrast (though not contradiction) between the method of physical science and that of religion and theology. In the former causation is expressed in terms of matter and energy; in the latter, in terms of spirit, freedom, and personality. The difference between physical and free causation must be held clearly in mind.

The Christian doctrine of creation, then, is not dependent on the conclusions of physical science as these may relate to the origin of the universe. It begins rather with the new spiritual creation of God in Christ in the redemptive experience of Christians, and finds it easy to accept the Scripture teaching that God created all things. In our religious experience we know ourselves as dependent on God. We know our new life in Christ to be derived from him. We know him as spiritual Creator and ourselves as "new creatures" in Christ. We know physical nature as adapted to promote our spiritual life under God's guidance. We see in nature the evidence of progress toward a goal and end. In man we see the crown of nature. In Christ and his kingdom we see the spiritual end of God in creation. From these things we infer that the universe is dependent on God;

[251]

that he brought it into being and preserves it for his own spiritual and holy purpose. In other words, the Christian does not pursue the physical series of causes and effects, nor the philosophical series of logical concepts, to prove that God created the universe. He rather pursues the personal and spiritual series given in the religious experience of men.

The latter, however, finds strong confirmation in the scientific and rational processes. Science confirms the view especially if we consider the development hypothesis. Its distinctive mark is progress from lower to higher forms. This progress implies purpose. At the beginning, the middle, and the end this purpose implies a divine Creator of the world. At the beginning, because the downward steps into the past carry us to a beginning in time for the first and lowest stage of the process. Physical science expressly precludes a self-originated beginning of all things. Hence a Creator is needed. The middle of the process calls for a guide and Creator since the material of the universe is used at every stage for an end above and beyond present attainment. It is thus dependent on a beginning through an intelligent Creator. The end implies creation, because beginnings can only be understood in the light of endings. The outcome reveals the hidden purpose of the origin. If a spiritual kingdom of free persons living together in eternal bonds of righteous love is the goal to which the entire movement leads up, then that kingdom was the primary purpose of the whole. The complete dependence of the spiritual kingdom on the grace of God in Christ carries us back, therefore, to his creative act as the source and origin of all things.

The logical and philosophical process also confirms the view. The reason calls for an uncaused cause of all things, which nature never yields. The human will suggests the only solution. The will of man is in a relative sense an originating cause, and from it we infer a spiritual first cause who brought the universe into being.

We may sum up the Christian doctrine of creation, then, in the following statements: First, the universe, while distinct from God, originated in his act and is dependent upon him. Secondly, in creating the universe God acted freely and not under necessity or compulsion. Thirdly, in creating the universe God had in view a moral and spiritual end. Fourthly, the end of God was the communication of his own life and blessedness to created beings. His supreme desire was to make vast spaces for the habitation of sentient and intelligent beings; to people these spaces with such beings, and to fill them with the life and holiness, the blessedness and peace of his own nature. His end was to produce a kingdom in which his own image should be reflected, in which his own glory should appear. Fifthly, the end thus defined was an end begun, carried forward, and to be completed in Jesus Christ. (See Col. 1 : 15-17; Eph. 1 : 3-5; Rom. 8 : 21.)

II. Opposing Views

Several theories have been proposed as against the view that God called the universe into being by his creative act.

1. A brief reference may be made to the theory that matter alone is eternal and that all forms of mental and spiritual life are derived from matter. This is materialism and is rapidly passing away as a philosophic theory. It ignores all the most significant elements of being, mind and will and conscience in man. It has failed in every attempt to show that mind is derived from matter. It takes the lowest form of existence and supposes that the highest are derived therefrom. It is directly contrary to all moral progress and religious and spiritual aspirations among men.

2. The second to be noticed is dualism. It holds that there are two eternal and self-existent principles, God and matter. God did not create matter, but used it for his ends. This theory arises out of the difficulty of conceiving how God could bring matter into existence. There are several serious objections to it. One is that it is a self-contradictory view. Two absolute or eternal existences cannot be held together satisfactorily in our thought. The mind carries in itself a fundamental demand for ultimate

unity. Another objection is that the view does not explain how God ever comes into relations with the eternally existent matter. If it existed eternally apart from him, how did he ever come to possess power over it? A third objection is that matter in all the forms known to us, is stamped with the marks of intelligence. Idealism has emphasized this fact. We know of no form of matter which could form a basis for belief in any origin other than in the will of an intelligent creator. A fourth objection is that dualism increases rather than decreases the difficulties of the mind in trying to conceive of creation. It multiplies problems. If it is difficult to think of God as self-existent, how much more difficult to think of a self-existent matter without intelligence or will? The mind inevitably gravitates to the view that the highest thing we know, intelligent and free personality, is the only sufficient clue to the origin of all things.

3. A third theory is that the universe is an emanation from God. In its older form, as held by the Gnostics in the early Christian centuries, we need not consider it. In its more recent forms, it is either pantheistic as with Spinoza, or idealistic as held by Hegel and some of his successors. Spinoza conceived God as the one eternal substance, and extension and thought as its attributes. Hegel conceived him as an absolute being of whom all finite appearances are merely phases. A logical process is the immanent principle of development. Both the Spinozan and Hegelian views are monistic. God and the universe are one.

The objections to the view in either form are very serious. It takes away freedom from God, because the universe is conceived as the necessary unfolding of a principle in the divine nature. It ignores the radical differences between matter and spirit and fails to harmonize them. It makes God the author of evil, because evil remains an essential phase of the process of development. It destroys human freedom, personality, and immortality, because man is merely a passing phase of a logical process which will be transcended in the course of time. In short, necessity rules at every stage of the process and the whole moral and personal realm collapses. All this is in direct conflict with the deliverances of our own moral consciousness and of our Christian experience.

4. A fourth theory of the origin of the universe is that it is the eternal creation of God. The difficulty of explaining why God should have remained idle through an eternity before beginning to create has led to the view. But the objections are greater than the supposed advantages. It tends toward the necessitarian conception whereby God is supposed not to create freely, but by necessity; or else it tends to the theory of the eternity of matter. It is impossible, indeed, to conceive in a satisfying manner the relations between time and eternity. But this theory does not succeed in doing so better than others. We cannot lift the universe out of time because we know it only as subject to temporal conditions. We cannot conceive it as independent because, in all the phases in which we know it, it is dependent. It is best to interpret it in view of the data of our own experience of it and not in an abstract way to meet hypothetical difficulties. As God's free act, with a moral end in view, we can think of the creation of the universe in a manner satisfactory to faith, since in our own experience of him we know ourselves as his new creation, dependent upon his gracious and free action in Christ.

III. THE CREATION OF MAN

We cannot understand creation except by viewing it as a whole. Man is its crown and goal. Looking forward from the last stage prior to man we should expect man to appear. Looking backward from man we can best explain the earlier stages. Science and Scripture agree remarkably in placing man at the end of the series of gradations in nature. All the lower stages precede man in the account of Genesis. According to science, man sums up all the past in himself and then goes far beyond all lower stages. Man was not, therefore, an afterthought, but a forethought of God. In man creation attains a moral and spiritual level. We thus infer that the lower stages were designed to serve the ends of the higher.

In view of the above we are warranted in making the following assertions about man:

1. He consists of a physical and spiritual part, body and soul. As to the physical, he possesses a body in many respects like the bodies of the lower animals. Some Christian evolutionists interpret the Genesis account of the creation of man as implying that the human body was derived from the lower animals, while the soul was God's direct creation. In Genesis 2 : 7 we read, " And Jehovah God formed man of the dust of the ground, and breathed into his nostrils the breath of life." Here was the use of a means in creating the body, and an immediate and direct act in creating the soul.

Two or three remarks may be made as to this matter. The first is that for the Christian religion the vital point is that man is God's creation. He is not the product of material elements. This is placed beyond all doubt by the Genesis account. The second remark is that there are at least two difficulties in supposing an animal origin for man's body. One is the wide chasm between the human brain and that of the highest animals below man. Certainly no known skull of these animals can accommodate the human brain. The other difficulty is in the necessary relation between the brain formation and the indwelling mind. The relation is most intimate in human development from infancy to manhood. It seems most natural to think it has always been so. To take an animal brain and put into it a human mind seems to be an impossible proceeding. The later phase of the evolutionary hypothesis known as the mutation theory is more favorable to the idea of an animal origin for the human body. It teaches that progress is made by sudden and unexpected advances in living organisms. The causes are not known. This would accord with the view of theistic evolution more closely than the older conception of progress by infinitesimal stages of growth. But in any case the chief point is God's agency in the ongoing of the world. It is doubtful whether even the mutation theory can account for the wide chasm between the animal and the human skull. The third remark is that we should not raise a false issue here. Theology can well afford to let the science of biology work out its own problems as to origins. Mutual respect and patience will bring harmony in due time. There are serious enough difficulties for the intellect on any view. Meantime, two truths are to be held tenaciously. One is that man was made a spiritual being in God's image and not as the product of matter. The other is that when we fully understand them and correctly interpret them, the Scriptures and natural science will not bear discordant witness.

2. Now a striking peculiarity of man is that he is the connecting link between the physical and the spiritual universe. His body is the connecting link between man and the physical universe, just as his soul is the connecting link with the spiritual universe. Man is body and soul.

3. The spiritual nature of man is sometimes referred to in the Scriptures as both " soul " and " spirit " (1 Thess. 5 : 23). But a survey of all the biblical teachings shows that the writers were using popular rather than scientific language, and that soul and spirit were the aspects of the one undivided spiritual life of man rather than a scientific distinction of parts. Many passages refer to the spirit only. (1 Cor. 5 : 5; 6 : 17; 7 : 34; Gal. 6 : 18.) The words employed in the Old Testament in reference to man are soul (*nephesh*), spirit (*ruach*), and flesh (*basar*). The words in the New Testament correspond. They are soul (*psuche*), spirit (*pneuma*), and flesh (*sarx*). Man's nature then is twofold. He is spirit and he is body. Both are necessary to him as man. As mere physical organism he is not man. As disembodied spirit he is not fully man. He is man only in the unity of a personal life combining both body and soul. " Soul " then means usually the individual person as in " the soul that sinneth " (Ezek. 18 : 4). " Spirit " means the principle of life as contrasted with body. " Body " means the physical organism.

4. The biblical account makes it entirely clear that man was created by God in the divine image. It is also clear that the divine image in man relates to his spiritual rather than to his physical nature. God is not physical. God is Spirit.

R

[257]

The Christian Religion in Its Doctrinal Expression

In what respects then does man bear the divine image? These may be summed up in the following statements:

(1) Man resembles God in his possession of a rational nature. Man's capacity in this regard is the source of all scientific knowledge. He reads the meaning of nature and discovers that it is stamped with the marks of reason. Man understands God by reason of the marks of intelligence in the world about him. Reason in man answers to reason in God.

(2) Man is like God in that he has a moral nature. He knows good and evil. The moral law, ethical ideals and systems, are all based on the moral nature of God. In man that moral image is reproduced. Conscience is in a real sense God's voice in man. It is the sure index to man's moral constitution. It is not uniform in its action in mankind, but it is universal and persistent.

(3) Man resembles God also in the possession of an emotional nature. He is capable of feeling. His highest feeling is righteous love. This is derived from the same quality in God himself.

(4) Man is made in God's image also in his possession of will. Here we come upon a wonderful endowment of man. Will is totally distinct from all forms of physical causation as known to us. Some have even gone so far as to call it a " supernatural " power. In any event it belongs to an order above the physical. It cannot be explained by the law of the conservation of energy. It is in a true sense an originating cause.

(5) Again, man is made in God's image as a free being. Freedom means self-determination. Man is not a being whose actions are all predetermined for him by external forces. Nor is he in a state of indetermination, as uninfluenced by motives derived from the past, or from without. Freedom in man does not imply exemption from the operation of influences, motives, heredity, environment. It means rather that man is not under compulsion. His actions are in the last resort determined from within. He is self-determined in what he does. Some hold that freedom in man means ability to transcend himself and act contrary to his

[258]

character. The will is thus regarded not as an expression of what man is in his essential character. It is free in the sense of being capable of choices unrelated to past choices, acquired traits, and hereditary tendencies. This is an untenable view of freedom. It makes of the will a mere external attachment to man's nature rather than an expression thereof. Freedom excludes compulsion from without. It also excludes mere caprice and arbitrariness. Freedom is self-determination. The acts of a free being are his own acts. The mere capacity for choosing between good and evil is not the most important aspect of man's freedom. It is one phase of it only. But if he were confirmed in holiness with no temptation to sin, he would still be free. God is self-determined to holiness, yet he is free. Our moral consciousness and our religious consciousness, especially as conditioned by our experience of God in Christ through our own free choice, are indelible marks of our freedom. They are at the same time tokens of the divine image in man. The above traits in man are not to be regarded as altogether distinct from each other. They are all merely aspects or functions of man's unified personal life. They are mutually interdependent. They are elements in the organic unity of his personality.

(6) Again, the divine image in man appears in his original freedom from sin and inclination to righteousness. We should not here confound perfection in the sense of character achieved through long periods of trial and conflict with the sinlessness of man's original nature. Even Christ was made perfect through sufferings. (Heb. 2 : 10.) The perfection of the first Adam at the outset could not have been that of the second Adam at the close of his earthly life. The cumulative growth of knowledge, along with moral and spiritual power, is due to a life lived under the conditions of time. Complete development in all spiritual qualities could only come gradually. But man was created without sin, and as thus endowed he was capable of sin and a fall.

(7) Another mark of the divine image in man was the dominion over the lower orders of creation, given him by the

Creator. " Have dominion over the earth and subdue it " was God's command to him. All human progress is but the fulfilment, in one way or another, of this ideal.

(8) Immortality is a further mark of the divine image in man. The spirit of man survives bodily death in an endless existence. The facts regarding the future life are incapable of proof which will leave no possibility of doubt. This is because they lie beyond the range of present experience. But the natural reason of man and his religious experience combine in a remarkable way to establish belief in immortality. We give the chief arguments in brief outline.

We note first those drawn from the natural reason:

a. First of all, immortality is a necessary inference from a progressive creation. Nature reaches an anticlimax in man if he ceases to exist at death. The movement toward an end is thus defeated.

b. Again, the belief in immortality in some form is practically universal among men. It is a part of the general religious life of mankind. It is like the universal belief in God. This suggests an analogy with the life of the physical organism. It is maintained by means of the correspondence between internal and external relations. The universe responds to the call of its creatures. The fact corresponds to the craving, as the structure of the eye implies the existence of light.

c. Again, modern physiological psychology favors belief in immortality in that it proves clearly a parallelism between mental and physical states, but not a causal connection. Brain states are parallel with mind states, but the brain does not produce thought.

d. Once more, the phenomenon of death suggests immortality. The body as we know it is contrasted in all points with mind as we know it. Bodily decay, therefore, suggests an undecaying spirit. Certain forms of modern idealism have insisted that mental phenomena are simply phases of eternal being, and that by its very nature thought is lifted above the physical and placed in the eternal order. In any event the marked and radical contrasts between matter and spirit remain.

e. Immortality is also urged on the ground of the inequalities and wrongs of the present life. We are all subject to conditions in which men fail to find exact justice. The innocent frequently suffer. The guilty often escape. A future life would provide opportunity for correcting these conditions.

f. Closely connected with the preceding is the further fact that we are conscious of powers greater than our present opportunities. Man is capable of indefinite, indeed possibly infinite, growth. He beats against the bars of present limitations and longs for a wider range of activities. Immortality is a natural inference from this fact.

We note next the biblical teachings:

a. The Old Testament in its earlier stages has no very clear deliverances on the immortality of the soul. Existence after death in Sheol, or the realm of the dead, in a conscious state, is the view underlying the Old Testament belief. In some of the psalms and later prophets strong assertion of immortality are found. (2 Sam. 22 : 6; Num. 16 : 30; Ps. 16; 17; 49; 73; Job 14 : 13ff.; 16 : 18; 17 : 9; 19 : 25f.)

b. In the New Testament the doctrine finds abundant warrant. The resurrection of Jesus is the historical fact of greatest significance. But the entire teaching of Jesus implies the eternal destiny of man. The gospel rests on the infinite worth of individual men. Human personality is the supreme value for God. To redeem it was the end of Christ's mission. Only as immortal was it worthy of such an end.

c. In strict agreement with Christ's revelation is our own religious experience of God in Christ. Through him we are reconciled to God and enter into relations of spiritual fellowship with him. The form which this fellowship takes is that of Fatherhood and sonship. We have the Spirit of adoption whereby we cry, Abba, Father. The worth of man in God's sight is thus the eternal worth of a son. The power by which we realize this fellowship and sonship is the Holy Spirit who raised Jesus from the dead. The measure of the energy working in us is the measure of the power which raised Christ from the grave. (Eph. 1 : 20.)

The Christian thus finds the complete and satisfying answer to the natural craving for and universal belief in immortality. The value which natural religion teaches and natural reason infers is met by the reality which Christianity creates. Immortal life has already begun in the soul when God reveals Christ in us. One of Paul's favorite forms of teaching is that the present life of believers is a resurrection life. (Col. 2 : 20; 3 : 4.)

IV. THE ORIGIN OF SOULS

One question regarding man relates to the origin of the individual soul. Several views have been advanced on the subject. The whole question is more or less speculative, but a few paragraphs may be devoted to it. We note three theories:

The first is the theory of preexistence. Souls have existed in a previous state. The soul enters the human body at some point in the early stages of the development of the body. Some have urged the view to account for the coming of sin into the world. It is supposed that the sin was committed in a previous state of existence.

The idea, however, is foreign to Christianity, and has no warrant other than the speculation out of which it arises. It offers no solution of the problem of sin. It simply transfers it from the present to the past. It does not solve the problem any better than other theories.

The second theory is that each soul is an immediate creation of God. It enters the body at an early stage in the development of the body. The body itself is of course produced by natural generation. The chief object sought by advocates of this theory is to preserve the spiritual character of the soul. It is supposed that if souls are propagated, it implies that they are material.

There are several objections to the view. The biblical teaching does not support it. According to it, God's usual method since the first creation is mediate rather than immediate creation. God rested from his creative labors on the seventh day. The new spiritual creation in Christ partakes of the quality of the original creation in some respects, but it is not identical in kind with it. The new creation in Christ arises out of man's need because of sin. The origin of Christ's human nature is excep‚ tional for similar reasons.

Apart from the biblical, there are two other serious objections to the doctrine of immediate creation of souls. One is that men often resemble their ancestors in spirit as well as body. If heredity explains similar bodily traits, it more satisfactorily accounts also for the spiritual resemblances. The other objection is that the theory of immediate creation fails to account for the tendency to sin in all men. Sin inheres primarily in the spirit, not the body. We cannot accept the view that God directly creates the soul with sinful tendencies.

The third theory is known as traducianism. It holds that spirit and body are produced by natural generation. It is the view which best satisfies the reason and explains the facts. The universal tendency to sin is thus accounted for. The transmission of traits of character from parent to child is explained. The view best explains also the unity of the race. Men are bound together in a common life in spirit as well as body. The view also accords with God's usual method. His present method of working is in general through the law and processes of nature. He is as truly present as on the immediate creation theory. God indwells in all the processes of nature. Life is his gift. But it is his gift through natural generation.

The objection that this view makes the soul material does not hold. God's presence in the process of generation is the guaranty against this. The relation of spirit to body is a profound mystery in the nature of every individual. We can only accept the obvious fact that the two coexist in closest connection in each of us. We cannot explain it. The transmission of both elements of our nature from parent to child is simply a particular phase of the general problem of the relation between spirit and body.

In the absence of direct Scripture teaching on this subject we are without means of setting forth more than a probable conclusion. Theoretical proofs one way or the other are more or less precarious. We must maintain under any view man's spirituality and immortality. If we do this no great consequences can be involved in the theories formed with a view to satisfying the reason.

CHAPTER XI

PROVIDENCE

I. DEFINITION

BEFORE the subject of Providence is discussed it is proper to refer briefly to God's preservation of the world. By preservation is meant God's action in sustaining the universe he has made. We are not to think of the universe as a machine created and left to itself by the Creator. This is the deistic view which virtually excludes God from all human experience as well as from physical nature. Neither are we to think of the universe as God's continuous creation. This is virtual pantheism. It leaves no room for any degree of independence or freedom in nature or man. Thus it would destroy moral and spiritual values along with the idea of natural law. God has created the universe in the past. He now preserves it.

God's present relation to the world is one of immanence and transcendence. As immanent God indwells in nature and man, sustaining both in their natural qualities and powers. His preservation of nature is in harmony with the operation of natural law, and his preservation of man accords with human freedom. As transcendent God is not confined to the created universe. He is more than nature and man. These do not absorb God. He is infinite Spirit and is greater than all created things. He is free in his action and not exhausted by his present activities.

By the providence of God we mean his control or direction of the universe toward the end which he has chosen. There are a number of important truths contained in the general doctrine of God's providential control of the world. We proceed to discuss them.

1. First, God's providence implies a divine purpose in the control of the universe. By tracing the process from lower to higher

stages of creation we discover God's purpose. Man, the free spiritual being made in God's image, is the crown of creation. From this we conclude that God's end has to do with personal and spiritual beings. He is seeking to reproduce himself in a kingdom of free spirits. As Father he is seeking to bring many sons to glory.

This conclusion is in strict accord with the revelation of God in Christ. The Old Testament shows how the foundations of God's moral kingdom were laid in the long history of Israel. The New Testament brings the final revelation of God's purpose in Christ. It culminates in the disclosure of an everlasting kingdom of holy love, in which Christ's people are conformed to his moral and spiritual image in fellowship with one another and with God.

Central in the teaching of Jesus is God's care of the individual as well as the spiritual society. Christian experience affirms with great energy God's care and guidance. The redeemed man knows the superintending care of a loving Father. The evidences of such care are too manifold for him to doubt. It is therefore easy for him to accept the doctrine of Providence. He needs only to generalize his own personal experience along with that of other Christians to express the meaning of this great truth. Here again reason, Scripture, and experience combine to produce certainty in our thinking.

2. The providential control of God implies the divine sovereignty. The sovereignty of God has too often been made a hard doctrine by being presented in a manner too abstract. The decrees of God are defined as the expression of an eternal purpose by which he foreordains all things whatsoever that come to pass. The statement is true only if we bear in mind several other statements. One is that foreordination must not cancel human freedom, else God is responsible for man's sinful acts. Another is that man's sinful acts are foreordained in a permissive sense only and not efficaciously. Again, for us the chief thing in God's purpose is not " all things " in general, but rather the establishment of his spiritual kingdom in Christ. Men do

not object to God's sovereignty if it is seen that we have to do with a righteous and loving God, and not a merely arbitrary and omnipotent being. God's sovereignty means, then, that he keeps the reins of government in his own hands. He guides the universe to his own glorious end. That end embodies the highest ideals of holiness and love. We rejoice that it is so and gratefully trust him and cooperate with him. We shall return to the subject of God's sovereignty when we consider his method in saving men. Here his sovereignty is defined simply in relation to his providential control of the world.

3. God's providential control of the world is in accordance with the presence of law in the physical and moral realm. Little need be said about physical law. Science has demonstrated in a marvelous manner that nature is a realm of law. This is one of the most beneficent arrangements of God. Many if not all forms of human well-being are based on the operation of law. Health of body may be conserved; the ground may be tilled; a thousand forms of human activity are possible by reason of the presence of law in the physical realm.

Law prevails also in the moral realm. The moral kingdom is a reproduction among men of eternal principles of right as these exist in God. Conscience bears witness to the law of right and wrong written in the constitution of human nature. The rewards of righteousness and the penalties for transgression in the individual life bear witness to the reign of moral law. The course of history is an illustration on a grand scale of these same laws. The career of Israel and the teachings of the prophets are God's revelation of his righteousness and love. It is God training a nation in the laws of his eternal kingdom.

The Scriptures do not trace the whole course of the race in moral development, nor do they dwell on abstract questions regarding conscience. But one thing is clearly recognized. It is that moral law is not based on expediency merely. Utilitarian theories do not account for man's moral constitution. The Ten Commandments and the moral law generally are grounded in God's nature.

[267]

4. God's providential control of the world respects human freedom. Man is distinguished from physical nature by the possession of free personality. The laws of nature are fixed and may be expressed in mathematical formulæ. God controls nature in accordance with these laws. But man is on a higher level. God has limited himself in his methods with free beings. Here compulsion is out of the question. Sovereignty and predestination do not annul freedom. If they did so, man would be reduced to the physical, or at least the brute, level. God does not indeed surrender the destinies of the universe to his free creatures. But his control is through means which have respect for their freedom.

5. God's providential control of men makes use of the unity of the race. Heredity is a universally recognized law in modern scientific circles. Each individual is the product of all his ancestors. We inherit traits and tendencies which are physical, moral, and intellectual. The tendency to sin, which always manifests itself in actual sin in every person who attains to a state of moral consciousness, is an inherited tendency.

A great mass of evidence supplies ample grounds for the belief in race unity and solidarity. The Scriptures clearly teach it. This appears in the Genesis account of man's origin and in the New Testament teachings as to the incarnation and its benefits for mankind. Confirmation of the biblical teaching appears in several forms. These can only be referred to briefly. The history of mankind points to a common origin somewhere in Asia. Modern ethnologists are in substantial agreement on this point. Comparative philology points strongly to a common origin for the chief languages of the world, with no evidence against such origin for all languages. Psychology bears witness to common mental characteristics, common moral and social capacities and religious tendencies. Christianity through missionary effort has shown itself capable of meeting the universal religious needs of men, and this indirectly points strongly to race unity. Comparative physiology shows that men are one in their organic physical peculiarities. In the formation of the head, teeth, bones, nervous system, and in other ways all men are essentially alike. Varieties appear in size, color, and other divergencies. But these are traceable to external causes, such as climate and conditions of the environment. They do not alter the fundamental likeness.

The principle of race unity and solidarity in one aspect is dark and forbidding. Through it the tendency to sin is transmitted. Disease, crime, and various forms of physical disability may in some measure result from its operation. Generations may thus be bound together by its action. But, on the other hand, it is marvelously beneficent when it operates normally as God intended. The good results of human attainment may also be perpetuated thus. The cumulative effects of human struggle through history may be floated on the stream of heredity to remote generations. Racial unity and solidarity are vitally connected with the spiritual headship of Christ. The benefits of his mediatorial work flow out to men because he is one with mankind.

6. God's providential care extends to individuals as well as to the race as a whole. We have already indicated the operation of moral law in history. God has been leading the race from stage to stage of progress. Nations are employed to render services of various kinds. Ancient Greece led the world in philosophic thought and general culture. Rome was preeminent in organization and government. Israel was God's organ for the redemptive self-revelation of God. All these and other nations served a great world-end in God's plan.

But God's care extends also to the smallest details of the individual life. The very hairs of our head are numbered. Not a sparrow falleth without God's notice.

God's providence is special in that it extends to the smallest events. It is general in that it extends to great events and to the general ongoing of the world. But special providences are general in that they are part of God's general plan. General providences are special because they are the sum of the special providences. The distinction between ordinary and extraordinary providences is also sometimes made in view of the fact that God has employed miracles and prophecy and other unusual methods as well as those belonging to the normal forces of nature and history. Again, the distinction between physical and spiritual in God's providential action is based on the difference between his method in dealing with nature where physical law is employed and in dealing with man according to his free moral nature.

7. God's providential action has sometimes employed miracles as a means for advancing his kingdom. There are several statements which may be made regarding the place of miracles in God's care of the world.

(1) The first is that the whole question of miracles should be taken out of the region of theoretical abstractions and brought over to the region of fact and evidence. No *a priori* or abstract objection can possibly hold against a fact of any kind. We cannot assert without more ado how God must govern the world. We can only observe how he actually governs it.

(2) A second statement is that, for the Christian, the fact basis from which he regards the whole question of miracles is his own experience of God in Christ. He knows a supernatural power in his own spiritual life. It is an easy transition from this experience to acceptance of the recorded miracles of Scripture where the evidence is sufficient to justify their acceptance.

(3) A third statement is that the fundamental rational ground for belief in miracles is the Christian world-view. That worldview holds that God is a personal free Spirit, greater than the world, who has a loving and holy end in view and seeks to bless his children. The unity of nature is then not merely that of a mechanical system of physical causes and effects, but a free system of divine ends. If God were limited and confined within nature, he would be under the operation of necessity. But being transcendent as well as immanent in the world, God may use natural agencies for spiritual ends.

(4) A fourth statement is that the use of natural forces for spiritual ends is not necessarily a violation of natural law. The miracles of Jesus were often restorations rather than violations

of natural processes. Sin brought the violation through man's abuse of his freedom. God's grace in the gospel is a restoration on a scale of great magnitude and glorious effectiveness. Jesus healed the sick, restored the blind, cast out demons, fed the hungry by means of his miraculous deeds. These were restorations, not violations; disease, sin, blindness, demoniac possession, hunger, were evils he came to remedy.

Thus it appears that Jesus employed natural forces in higher ways and for higher ends. In ordinary human affairs the action of will and personality often modifies natural causes and changes the result. Firemen extinguish burning buildings, medical science reduces disease, and in a hundred ways men change the course of natural events. These are not miracles, but they involve the principle of miracles. Will is higher than physical causation. God is greater than nature.

(5) A fifth statement is that from the highest point of view miracles may be regarded as natural events. We call them supernatural. This is correct when we define the natural as merely the mechanical. But if we include in the natural all that pertains to the nature of God and man as well as physical creation, then the miraculous is also natural. God is not a foreigner in a strange country when he works in the physical order. Its laws are his laws. As the players use ball and bat in a game of baseball, so God meant that men should employ matter, force, and motion to exercise their spiritual powers, to develop their individuality and personality in playing the game of life. In short, the physical is subordinate to the moral and personal order. Uniformity of nature is the established method. When God works through miracles he shows the unity of all things under himself. But he also shows thereby his beneficent purpose toward his free creatures.

(6) A sixth point regarding miracles is that they do not disturb, but rather establish, the higher continuity of the world. Physical science has sometimes regarded miracles as impossible because they seemed to disrupt the continuity of physical causes. But if the world is ultimately spiritual and personal we expect God to

manifest himself in convincing ways when there is need. His ultimate purpose is to develop sons of God in a divine kingdom. The incarnation and resurrection of Christ are God's miraculous self-disclosure toward this supreme end. His movement through Israel's history exhibits the preliminary stages of his unfolding purpose. Christian history marks its continuance. His new spiritual creation of the community of believers through Christ is the crowning act of his first creation of the race. Thus the personal, moral, and spiritual ideal is seen to govern all his actions. This is the true continuity of the world of which the supernatural forms the most significant part.

(7) In closing the subject of miracles a few things may be added to the distinction between the natural and the supernatural. Many people look with certain doubt upon the natural order as if God were wholly absent from it. They think of the supernatural as if it were a power apart from nature, breaking into it and disturbing it. Thus they think of the natural and supernatural realms as if they were opposing systems, God being present in one and absent from the other. Nature is regarded as a self-running machine, and God as apart from it and able to enter it only by " violating " it in some way. Hence the alleged conflicts between science and religion. There is no conflict except when there is confusion of thought. All that is needed is to keep in mind two or three fundamental truths and hold them in their proper relations to each other.

a. The scientific man justly insists that his task is to trace out the rules or laws under which natural events occur. He simply describes their coexistences and sequences and uniformities. He does not ask as to the original or first cause, nor as to the ultimate underlying and sustaining cause, nor as to the final cause or end of all things. All these questions would divert him from his proper task. That task is a limited but very important one for human welfare.

b. The philosopher's task is also distinct. He uses the facts which science presents. But he goes farther. He asks, What was the first cause of all things; what is the underlying, unifying, and sustaining cause; and what is the final cause or purpose of the world? He seeks a rational account of the universe. He justly insists that scientific explanations are not ultimate. They simply define how things act, how physical events come to pass. They never explain why they act in this or that way.

c. The religious man goes a step beyond philosophy. He seeks redemption through divine power, fellowship, and blessedness. He seeks the eternal Person. He desires above all to find God. We may sum up by saying that the scientist works with the principle of causality; the philosopher with the principle of rationality; and the religious man with the principle of personality. Now conflict and confusion arise when these distinctions are overlooked. A scientific man is not bound to stop along the way from time to time and tell what physics, or chemistry, or geology, or physiology teaches about God. But his science in no sense warrants him to silence the philosopher when the latter seeks ultimate causes. Nor can the philosopher forbid the religious man's act of faith through which he finds the personal God. But having found God, the Christian comes back to nature with a new sense of God's presence and purpose in it. For him the causal relation which the scientist studies, and the rational process which the philosopher expounds, are both ways of God's working, methods of his providence and grace. Nature is not a self-running machine. God is everywhere present in it. It is a means for realizing a gracious end. Hence the Christian man avoids the error of a false naturalism which banishes God from nature, and the error of the false supernaturalism which makes of the miracle an intrusion of God into a sphere where he does not belong. So also he grasps the following truths: first, that God is immanent everywhere in nature; that it is none the less God's work, though it be accomplished by slow operation of natural law; that personality is supreme, not law; that the true continuity is in the divine purpose, not in mechanical forces; and that God can work suddenly as well as slowly; that his supreme interest is the realm of free personal beings, and that whatever is needful for their welfare he can and will perform. Whether

S

or not he works miracles, therefore, can never be prejudged on abstract grounds. The facts alone can answer the question. There can be no question as to the biblical witness to his supernatural working.

8. God's providential methods provide for prayer and its answer. Many have found difficulty in reconciling the idea of answered prayer with God's unchangeableness and eternal purpose. But the difficulty rests upon a view of God's plan and purpose which is too narrow. The following considerations will help to make the matter clear:

First of all, God's unchangeableness is simply his moral self-consistency. God always acts in harmony with his character. If the answer to prayer is required by his moral self-consistency, then it is to be regarded not only as possible, but necessary in his providential government.

Secondly, God's eternal purpose, as we have seen, included the creation of free beings capable of fellowship with himself.

Thirdly, religion is the supreme expression and completion of the relationship between God and man. Religion involves intercourse. God speaks to man, and man speaks to God.

Fourthly, prayer is the central and most characteristic mark of religion. In it are involved all the religious elements—trust, sense of dependence, penitence, adoration, desire for moral likeness to God, triumph over sin and death, yearning for eternal life and perfect blessedness in him.

Fifthly, in Christianity religion takes the form of Fatherhood and sonship. This implies the utmost freedom of intercourse between God and man. The divine Father wishes the son to be worthy of his royal lineage in his desires. If the son is to rise to the level of sonship, he will seek many things he does not possess, which only God the Father can give. In prayer he will interrogate God about all of them. His attitude as son will lead him to renounce wrong things as promptly as it will impel him to ask for right things. Now God's fatherly desire toward his children, his aim in " bringing many sons to glory," finds its progressive fulfilment chiefly in the birth of new and greater desires in the hearts of his children. Nothing pleases him more than to see the growth of a truly spiritual ambition in his sons. Coupled with this is their sense of dependence on him, which finds its best expression in prayer and petition. The joy of the Father is to hear the prayers of the aspiring son and to grant his petitions. It thus appears that the answer to prayer is not a thought alien to God's unchangeable purpose and plan, but rather inwrought in its very texture. The play of freedom, of love, of holy purpose, is provided for in God's plan of the world.

Sixthly, the material sphere is not excluded from the operation of God in answer to prayer. Material gifts may be an element in the spiritual end of God in the ongoing of his kingdom. " Give us this day our daily bread " is a petition in the Lord's Prayer. The material and spiritual spheres are not to be conceived of as opposed to each other here. It is an error to think of God as unable to employ material agencies in blessing his children. It is also an error to think of material goods as the supreme gifts of God to men. Nature is subordinate to grace. The supreme gifts of grace are spiritual.

With the above considerations in mind we conclude that the doctrine of prayer and its answer as set forth in the New Testament gives us the only worthy view of God and his purpose. When Paul says, " All things work together for good to them that love God," we understand him to include nature as well as grace. The very make of the universe had in view from the beginning the good of God's children. Prayer is the child's expression of his love and trust and of the firm persuasion that the world is God's world. It is his Father's house, not chaos, or the sphere of action of a blind fate. When Jesus says, " Ask and ye shall receive, seek and ye shall find, knock and it shall be opened unto you," we hear the voice of one who could see behind the veil and knew that God's moral self-consistency as Father impels him to hear and answer prayer. Again, when Paul says, " The Spirit maketh intercession for us with groanings that cannot be uttered," our experience as Christians echoes his words. We understand how God's indwelling Spirit is trying to teach us the supreme art of prayer, and trying to awaken in us a holy daring which will humbly aspire to the highest achievement and attainment.

9. God's providential care of the world admits of the presence of pain and suffering among men. This is what is commonly known as physical evil as contrasted with moral evil or sin. The problem of physical evil is closely related to the problem of sin, which will be considered under a separate head. Meantime, two or three general statements may be made.

The first is that the modern development theory assigns a very important place to the processes of pain and death among the lower animals. It is thus that the species are perfected.

Secondly, in the New Testament suffering is glorified, not as a good within itself, but as a means to spiritual growth. Pain may and indeed often does follow as a result of holy living in a sinful world. In all its forms it is for the Christian a means of growth in the divine life.

Thirdly, the universal experience of believers in Christ confirms the above estimate of suffering, of pain, and conflict. By faith it becomes for them a means of grace.

II. ANGELS

In connection with the subject of Providence we add a brief discussion of angels. One fact is to be noted at the outset. It is that while very little is said in Scripture about the origin of angels, their existence and activity are everywhere assumed in both the Old and New Testaments.

Two unwarranted assumptions against the reality of angelic beings should receive attention here. One is that the belief in angels is merely a survival of heathen beliefs, and that a scientific age can no longer accept it. In reply we admit that belief in such beings is quite common among the races of mankind. But as in so many other instances of religious belief, its universality is not an evidence of falsity. It may imply a fundamental truth. Certainly the scientific assumption that man is the only intelligent being God has ever created is a most violent one. Referring to this subject Dr. William Adams Brown remarks: [1] " We are less ready than earlier generations to dogmatize about the unseen world. But surely no more flagrant example of dogmatism could be found than the assumption that apart from God man is the only moral and reasonable being in so vast a universe, and that the only spiritual meaning which it contains is that expressed in God's relations to us. What moral purpose and spiritual communion God may have with other beings in the boundless reaches of space and time which modern science has brought within our ken, we do not know. Our faith is simply that the meaning of all life everywhere is to be found in its relation to such a wise, holy, and loving Father as Christ has revealed; and that the interest, the wonder, and the joy which we, with our imperfect faculties and narrow insight, feel in our communion with nature, and in our relation to the so-called lower orders, must exist for God supremely."

Another assumption which cannot be admitted is that the authority of Jesus is against belief in the existence of angels. It is held by some that everything in the Gospels bearing on the subject, which comes from his acts and teachings, is to be understood as an accommodation to Jewish belief. We do not propose to review the evidence here. It is very abundant and appears in his dealings with those possessed of evil spirits, his references to little children and " their angels," and to Satan or Beelzebub, and in other ways. In fact, these references are so numerous and explicit that it seems incredible that Jesus could have personally held a view contradictory to that which was so manifest in his words and deeds. We may well admit that our knowledge about angelic beings is limited and that our only source of information is the Scriptures. But we may at least gather up the teachings about them as there recorded. We may set forth a brief outline of biblical teaching in the following statements:

1. The existence and activity of angels are assumed as accepted truths in both the Old and New Testaments. In the Old Testament they are present and " shout for joy " at the creation

---

[1] " Outline of Christian Theology," pp. 199, 200.

of the world. (Job 38 : 7.) As a rule, they bear human form and appear as men. (Gen. 18 : 2, 16; Ezek. 9 : 2.) In Genesis 19 : 13 angels are commissioned to destroy Sodom. An angel appears to Balaam. (Num. 22 : 22ff.) In the New Testament there are frequent references. Angels appear in dreams to Joseph. (Matt. 1 : 20; 2 : 13, 14.) An angel appears to Zacharias and Mary. (Luke 1 : 11-37.) Angels come to Jesus in the temptation (Matt. 4 : 11) and in Gethsemane. (Luke 22 : 43.) Jesus declares that there is joy among the angels over a penitent sinner. (Luke 15 : 10.) Jesus will confess or deny those who confess or deny him in the presence of the angels. (Luke 12 : 8f.) In frequent passages Paul refers to angels. (1 Cor. 6 : 3; 11 : 10; Col. 2 : 18; 1 Tim. 5 : 21.)

2. Little is said as to the origin of angels in the Bible. But it is clear that they are regarded as created beings. In Psalm 148 : 2-5 this is manifest. They are called upon to worship God. They are the heavenly host (1 Kings 22 : 19; Dan. 7 : 10; Ps. 103 : 21; 148 : 1ff.) who praise and glorify their Maker.

3. As to the office of angels two or three statements may be made. Our English word is from the Greek word *angelos,* meaning one sent, a messenger. This Greek word is a translation of the Hebrew word *mal'akh,* which also means messenger. Angels, then, are God's servants or messengers. They do his will in many ways. They are also servants of the saints of God on earth. They are sent forth to do service for the heirs of salvation. (Heb. 1 : 14.) There is no warrant for a belief in "guardian angels" in the sense that each individual believer is attended by an angel who protects him. Still less is there warrant for praying to angels or thinking of them as coming between the soul and God. In Scripture they are employed for particular purposes under exceptional circumstances, but always as servants of God or men except in the cases of evil angels.

4. The Angel of the Covenant is an outstanding figure in the Old Testament teaching as to angels. This angel possesses characteristics which bring him into closest relations with Jehovah himself. His special designation as " the Angel of the Covenant "

or " the Angel of the Lord," is itself suggestive. Some remarkable statements are made about this angel which in some sense identify him with Jehovah. In Genesis 31 : 13, the angel says to Jacob: " I am the God of Bethel, where thou anointedst a pillar, where thou vowedst a vow unto me." Again, in Genesis 32 : 30, after wrestling with the angel, Jacob says, " I have seen God face to face, and my life is preserved." Pardoning power is attributed to the Angel in Exodus 23 : 20, 21. Jehovah says: " Provoke him not; for he will not pardon your transgressions; for my name is in him." In response to a prayer of Moses God says, " Behold mine angel shall go before thee." Later he says, " My presence shall go with thee, and I will give thee rest " (Exod. 32 : 34; 33 : 14). We cannot review all the passages referring to this Angel. (See Gen. 16 : 7; 22 : 11; 24 : 7, 40; Exod. 3; Acts 7 : 30ff.; Exod. 13 : 21; 14 : 19; 23 : 20; Josh. 5 : 13; 6 : 2; Judg. 2 : 1-5; 6 : 11.) It is clear from the preceding that divine functions are attributed to him and that he is identified with Jehovah himself in some passages.

Some have seen in the Angel of the Covenant a manifestation of God in the form of the eternal Logos, or of the second person of the Trinity. Perhaps it is enough to say that there are Messianic elements in the Angel, that is, a special self-manifestation of God. We are scarcely warranted in ascribing Trinitarian views to the Old Testament writers themselves. Looking back from our standpoint, in the light of the full self-disclosure of God in Christ, we are likely to see more in this angelic manifestation than the people of Israel saw. It remains true, nevertheless, that there was something unusual and exceptional in this particular Angel which separates him from ordinary angels.

5. We add a few statements as to Satan and the fall of angels. As to a fall of angels there are a few references in the Scriptures. Angels were of course created holy. All God's works were good and not evil. In the sixth verse of Jude a reference is made to " angels that kept not their beginning." This seems to refer to a fall from holy character. As contrasted with sinful angels we have in Mark 8 : 38 a reference to " holy angels." In 2 Peter

2 : 4 there is clear reference to a fall of angels: " If God spared not angels when they sinned, but cast them down to hell," etc. Again in John 8 : 44 there is a very clear word from Jesus as to the devil and his sin: " Ye are of your father the devil, and the lusts of your father it is your will to do. He was a murderer from the beginning, and standeth not in the truth, because there is no truth in him."

6. The devil, or Satan, is the chief of evil spirits. In the book of Job he appears among the sons of God as the accuser. He is given permission to tempt Job. Some question whether or not his character as the fully manifested spirit of evil appears in the passage in Job. (Job 1.) But while all the traits which appear in the later history, especially in the New Testament, do not appear in this earlier period, the essential qualities begin to show themselves in germinal manifestation. The word Satan means " the adversary " or " the accuser." The word devil means " slanderer." References to Satan are numerous in the New Testament. The enemy that sowed tares in the field is the devil. (Matt. 13 : 39.) In 1 Peter 5 : 8 he is referred to as " your adversary the devil." In Revelation 12 : 10 John says, " the accuser of our brethren is cast down, who accuseth them before God night and day." Paul says he desired to go to Thessalonica; " but Satan hindered us," he adds. (1 Thess. 2 : 18.) That there is a great number of evil spirits under the leadership of Satan appears in many forms of statement. The lake of fire is prepared for " the devil and his angels " (Matt. 25 : 41). In Mark 5 : 9 the demoniac says: " My name is Legion, for we are many." In Ephesians 2 : 2 Paul refers to " the prince of the power of the air," and in 6 : 12, to " the spiritual hosts of wickedness."

7. We have no clear teaching as to the cause of the fall of angels. It is usually held to be pride. This is inferred from Paul's words to Timothy, in which he is speaking of the qualifications of a bishop: " not a novice, lest being puffed up he fall into the condemnation of the devil " (1 Tim. 3 : 6).

CHAPTER XII

SIN

GOD'S providential government of the world takes account of sin and its consequences. Because of its importance we give it treatment in a separate chapter.

A number of topics call for discussion under the general head of Sin. The first relates to

I. THE ORIGIN OF SIN

No explanation of the origin of sin has ever been given which is free from difficulties. The old objection against Christian theism is familiar. It takes the form of a dilemma: If God was good and failed to prevent sin, he must have been lacking in power. If he possessed the power and refused to prevent it, he was lacking in goodness.

This sounds very simple and convincing until examined. But it ignores the abundant evidences of God's goodness and power all about us and within us. It ignores the possible uses of sin in a universe of free beings. It ignores the operations of God's grace in human experience, and the redemption God has wrought in and through Christ. It leaves out of account the vast demonstration through historical time of a divine purpose of love in a spiritual and eternal kingdom among men.

Theories of the Origin of Sin

1. Some have urged the theory that sin is due to man's possession of a material body, that all sin arises out of sensuous desire, and that the only way to be rid of sin is to be rid of the body.

The theory is untenable. The ancient Gnostic heresy was based on the belief of the inherent evil of matter. But the

[281]

The Christian Religion in Its Doctrinal Expression

Scriptures nowhere support the view. Matter as such has no moral quality. " The flesh " in the Scriptures does not, when used in an ethical sense, refer to the body, but to the fleshly mind and will. (Rom. 8 : 6, 7.) Some of the worst sins are not sins of the flesh, but of the spirit, such as strife, jealousy, envy, and other familiar forms of sin. (Gal. 5 : 20.) Men are commanded to present their bodies as living sacrifices unto God (Rom. 12 : 1) and to glorify God in their bodies. (1 Cor. 6 : 20.) It is clear from this that a material body is not inherently sinful.

2. Another theory asserts that sin is human limitation. Man is sinful because he is ignorant and finite. Sin is not a positive thing, but only the negation of good.

The reply is that the theory changes by its definition the nature of sin itself. It confounds other things with sin. Sin cannot be defined as ignorance merely, because an element in sin is the conscious choice of evil instead of good. Growth in knowledge does not necessarily cure men of sin. Sin is not negation merely, because there are forms of it which are very malignant and aggressive.

This theory of sin is based on a form of idealistic pantheism which cancels all finite forms of experience in an Absolute which ultimately swallows them up. Man and his sin are simply finite modes of the infinite and absolute being. They have only a relative reality and value, and will gradually give way to the higher forms of being. This form of pantheism is self-contradictory because it makes the Absolute holy and sinful, omniscient and ignorant, at one and the same time. It certainly contradicts man's moral sense, which pronounces him guilty when he does wrong. It is contrary to the belief in personality and immortality. It has no basis of biblical support whatever.

3. The most satisfactory view of the origin of sin is that which connects it with the creation of free intelligent beings with the power of contrary choice. Historically, we have the record of the origin of human sin in the Genesis account of the fall of man. There has been much discussion of the point whether the writer there meant some elements of the account to be taken in

---

Sin

a symbolical sense. But the essentials of the story are almost self-evidently true to any one who reflects upon the nature of human choices and of sin. Alternative courses of action are presented. Intelligent free creatures are urged to choose the one and refuse the other. The desire for knowledge; the moral struggle within; the subtle urging to the evil choice by an outside agency; the gradual yielding of the will; the subsequent shame and degradation—all these are true to human experience as men know it to-day, except that in the first instance there was no preceding sin. Sin here was the perversion of the good: the desire for food, the craving for knowledge, and the love of the beautiful. (Gen. 3 : 6.)

(1) We have little light upon the question of a fall among created intelligences prior to the fall of man. There are allusions in Scripture which seem to point to such a fall. Satan, the prince of evil spirits, is represented as a malign influence ruling the world and holding man in his power. His agency in the fall of man is clearly implied in various biblical teachings.

(2) We are here concerned chiefly with man's sin and its results. As we have seen, man as created in God's image was a free, moral, and intelligent being. He had capacity for independent action in the exercise of his freedom. The capacity for sinning was an element in his freedom. Of course the actual commission of sin was not necessary to freedom. But the ability to make an evil choice was necessary. The alternatives were: first, to create man without the capacity for discerning good and evil, which would have left him on the level of the lower animals, with instinct merely as his guide; or secondly, to create him with capacity for moral and spiritual discernment, but with no capacity for evil choices, which would have been enforced righteousness. This would have left him without real freedom and responsibility. His righteousness would not have been freely chosen, and hence would have been lacking in the most valuable element in real righteousness.

(3) The mystery of sin, then, is not entirely cleared away, but it is in some degree relieved of its dark aspects when we find the

[383]

key to it in the dignity and greatness of man as originally created. Moral freedom is the mark of man's elevation in the scale of being. Sin and the fall were not thus made necessary, but they were made possible. A universe in which they were possible was better than a merely mechanical universe in which free action of the creature had no place. Only in such a universe could a moral kingdom arise, possessing the highest manifestations of God's grace and human attainment. No theory which derives man's body from preceding physical forms or places him at the end of an ascending series in creation can change the above conclusion. He became man when he attained moral and spiritual consciousness. Sin remains sin under any theory as to the origin of the body. The fall and its consequences remain. They cannot be explained away.

(4) Observe then that sin and the fall afforded an opportunity for God and for man. For God, in that his grace alone could meet the situation. What was required was not that man be rescued merely from the consequences of an accident, or mistake, or unavoidable calamity. This would have called for a measure of divine compassion and power, but not the supreme act of grace in redeeming man from sin. Man's offense did not call for rescue from any kind of human act which was neutral or unmoral in quality. His act was sinful, and it was hateful to God. He was guilty and corrupt in consequence of his deed. But the resources of love were equal to the occasion. No other kind of provocation could have called for such a display of divine love. As Paul says, "Where sin abounded grace abounded more exceedingly." Through sin and the fall the depth of the riches and glory of the divine nature became manifest.

(5) Again, the fall afforded man an opportunity to respond freely to the call of God, and to yield to his grace. It was now possible for him to choose freely the divine righteousness, to work out the salvation God was working in him, through his grace in Christ, and to achieve a righteousness which would entitle him to an eternal reward. It is idle to speculate what the results would have been had man chosen freely the right instead

of the wrong in the first instance. We must deal with the facts
as we have them. Sin and grace are the poles of the human and
divine relationship. Each conditions the other. No other conception of the dealings of God with man can possibly do justice
to the gospel of Christ. Its meaning in large measure loses its
force under any other view.

II. Christ's Natural and Spiritual Relationship to the Human Race

At this point it is well to develop a truth which bears an important relation to a number of important doctrines. It is the
distinction between the natural and the spiritual relations of
Jesus Christ to the human race. It is a clear teaching of the New
Testament that Christ was the medium and goal of all creation.
" All things have been created through him and unto him." " In
him all things consist," or hold together. (Col. 1 : 16, 17.) By
him God made the worlds. (Heb. 1 : 2.) He is the source and
ground of all man's natural powers. " He is the true light which
lighteth every man coming into the world " (John 1 : 9). The
divine image in man's original constitution was derived from
Christ. Christ sustains nature and man in all their activities.
Our natural powers of reason, of will, of conscience, of emotions,
are derived from him.

1. This relation of Christ to us as human beings in our natural
state is the key to the meaning of many things in human history
and experience. It explains conscience. Man's ineradicable sense
of right and wrong, his moral constitution, in short, with all its
variations and divergencies, comes from his original relation to
Christ. Man's ability to perform many forms of duty on the
natural plane is traceable to the same source. Again, man's
rational capacity is due to the eternal Logos, the divine reason as
revealed in Christ whereby man was constituted in the image of
God. From the same source is derived man's irrepressible longing to know God, and the universal manifestation in one form
or another of the religious instinct in man.

2. This truth, which is beyond all question a teaching of the New Testament, has sometimes been taken in a sense which is foreign to another group of New Testament teachings. The natural has been substituted for the spiritual relationship of Christ to mankind. The result has often been an eclipse of the central truths of the gospel itself. Man's natural constitution in God's image has been taken as the essential if not the sole element in man's sonship to God, and the original creative act as the sufficient explanation of God's Fatherhood. All religions are placed on a common level and the supernatural revelation of God in Christ is ignored. Man's natural quest for God, and his moral activities in certain respects are made the basis of a claim that he is naturally capable of all possible growth and spiritual achievement. Thus the necessity for the new birth by the action of God's Spirit is set aside. Salvation thus becomes a natural evolution from lower to higher forms, an unfolding merely of man's natural powers, and destitute of the redemptive elements so clearly taught in the New Testament and so sharply defined in Christian experience. The divine immanence is invoked to enforce the view, and the methods by which the gospel produces its results in the world are radically changed and in large measure rendered ineffective.

3. An illustration will make clear the above statements. It relates to the status of infants according to the teachings of the gospel. Are they in the kingdom of God when they are born? Or must they voluntarily choose the kingdom as responsible individuals when they are capable of doing so in later years? It is not a question whether infants dying in infancy are saved. All schools of theology admit that they are. The provisions of Christ's atoning work extend to them, and God works in them the needed change. But the facts of a hereditary bias to sin and of actual sin in all children as they become morally responsible, show the need of something more than natural birth in order to membership in the kingdom. Especially is this need shown in the universal requirement of free moral choice on the part of every one who is capable of such choice as a condition

of such membership. The very essence of discipleship is the voluntary acceptance of Christ. To them who " received him he gave the right to become the children of God " (John 1 : 12). In other words, the kingdom of God is constituted not on the principle of natural propagation, but of moral and spiritual sonship which is the result of a divine inworking upon condition of faith. Our own free response to the gospel and our own life of voluntary self-renunciation are the core and center, the golden heart of our religion. The natural relations and status of all men are simply a precondition of the spiritual relation and status. This voluntary element appears in the words of Jesus, even in the passage where he employs the little child as a type and symbol of the attitude of all toward the kingdom. Men must be converted and become as a little child in order to enter into the kingdom. A warning is added for those who would cause " one of these little ones who believe on me to stumble. " (Matt. 18 : 1-14; see also Mark 9 : 33-37; Luke 9 : 46-48; 18 : 15ff.; Mark 10 : 13-16; Matt. 19 : 13-15.) Faith in Christ is necessary. We conclude then that any interpretation of the natural relation which puts it in the place of the moral and spiritual, robs Christianity of its ethical and personal qualities. It substitutes biology and natural law for freedom and grace. It takes away the highest and most distinctive elements of the gospel.

4. We do not deny, of course, but affirm the truth that the human race is naturally constituted in and through Christ. This is the major assumption in the gospel of God's grace. The moral, mental, religious, and emotional elements in man are the natural basis on which the gospel operates. But the presence of sin has changed the conditions and has given rise to the need of a new approach of God to man. The incarnation of God in Christ is the outstanding mark of this great truth. The new creation of man in and through Christ lifts him above the natural level to the spiritual. The new sonship and Fatherhood possess elements which are not present in the earlier natural relation. The new moral kingdom is not effected merely through the immanence of God in the natural order. It required the coming of the Son

of God from without into human conditions. First that which is natural, then that which is spiritual. There is harmony between the two orders of creation. But it is to empty the spiritual creation of most of its meaning if we confound it with the natural. God in Christ is lifting the universe to a higher level. He is completing creation in and through Christ. But we must not forget that it is a new creation and not merely an unfolding of the natural order.

Thus it appears that God's good will toward men has taken the form of grace, because sin has radically altered man's relations to God. The gospel is the divine initiative for man's salvation because sin has created the need. The coming into human life of a new creative force from without was the only means for bringing about the result. Christ's original relation to the race is what made possible his redemptive relation. He could become one with humanity and act for humanity, because humanity had already been constituted one through his creative act.

III. THE BIBLICAL TEACHING AS TO SIN

We cannot treat the subject exhaustively, but give the essential points. A few definitions of sin may be noticed at the outset. Sin has been defined as selfishness. This is certainly correct as far as it goes. But taken by itself, selfishness is too indefinite a term to cover certain meanings which enter into the definitions of sin. Sin has also been defined as lack of conformity to God's moral law. This also is correct as a partial definition of sin. But lack of conformity to law is not an adequate definition. John indeed says that sin is transgression of the law, or, as in the Revised Version, " sin is lawlessness " (1 John 3 : 4). Paul teaches the same in numerous places. (Rom. 7 : 8, 9, 13, 23, 25.) But elsewhere he develops other phases of sin. Law as such does not lead us to the root of sin. Behind the law is the personal God. Sin is a breach of our personal relations with God. Again, sin has been defined as an act, disposition, or state which is morally wrong. This is certainly an element in human sin.

[288]

Not merely our separate acts, but our moral bias, the bent of our nature, constitutes a real part of the sin of man. But this also needs rounding out with other truths in order to render it acceptable as a definition of sin.

1. In the Old and New Testaments alike, sin is thought of chiefly as a breach or rupture of relations between the sinner and the personal God. We look briefly at the Old Testament teaching. Sin manifests itself in many ways, but the ruling thought in them all is the departure of the sinner from Jehovah's will. There was indeed transgression of law, but it was Jehovah's law. There were many forms of selfishness, but these were in their essence the exaltation of self against Jehovah. There was the sinful disposition, the wrong motive, but it consisted chiefly in alienation of heart from Jehovah. In the story of the fall man's sin is direct disobedience to Jehovah's command. In Genesis 5 : 24 a righteous man is described as one who " walked with God." Thus righteousness is personal fellowship, and by implication, unrighteousness is the lack of such fellowship.

(1) Sin is a breach of covenant relations between God and the people. God made many covenants with Israel. The Mosaic covenant best expresses the covenant idea. That idea was a nation in religious fellowship with God. Here all the provisions of the law, ceremonial and moral, related to men inside the covenant. Sins of ignorance, or infirmity, or inadvertence, were provided for. When these were committed fellowship with God was restored by means of offerings. But sins " with a high hand " were not recognized in the covenant legislation. Idolatry, for example, was visited with the extreme penalty of death, because it was the deepest of sins against God.

(2) The personal relation involved in sin became clearer in the course of the history. David committed a grievous sin against his fellow man, but in the psalm which expresses his deep penitence, he exclaims, " Against thee only have I sinned, and done that which is evil in thy sight " (Ps. 51 : 4). The prophets especially emphasize the deeper moral and spiritual aspects of sin. With Amos sin is injustice and wrong as be-

tween man and man. With Hosea sin is sin because it is alienation of heart from God. It is sin against his love. Thus we see that while the Old Testament never loses sight of the moral law and man's duty to his fellows, yet it couples transgression of law in this regard with the more fundamental religious aspect of sin.

(3) The Old Testament is rich in its ethical terms and the variety of its definitions and descriptions of sin. The Hebrew *pethi* means the simple undeveloped man. *Kesil* means the sensuous man. *Nabhal* means the fool, or man destitute of wisdom, not only in the intellectual, but in the religious sense. These are secondary meanings. More fundamental are the following: *Chata'* means to miss the mark, and is like the New Testament word *hamartano*. *'Aven* means crookedness or perverseness. *Tsedeq* means linear straightness, which then comes to mean righteousness. Sin is its opposite. *Ra'* means violence or breaking out as of evil.[1]

As indicative of the wealth of moral ideas in the Old Testament and the deep sense of sin, Doctor Davidson says:[2] " Here we see that, in the sphere of religion, sin is idolatry; in the sphere of speech, truth is righteousness and sin falsehood; that, in the sphere of civil life, justice is righteousness, and sin is injustice; and that, in the sphere of the mind of man, sin is the want of sincerity, either toward God or man, guile; purity, the opposite to this, being purity of heart, simplicity, openness, genuineness."

2. Sin in the New Testament Teaching

There are two or three general statements as to the teaching of Jesus. First, Jesus portrayed the ideal human life as a life of fellowship with God the Father. Sin is the want of this fellowship. The conceptions of heaven and hell are thus transfigured. Hell in its worst element is alienation from God. Heaven is the blessedness of communion with the Father. Secondly, Jesus traces sin to the inner motive of men. The sinful

[1] Cf. Davidson, " Theology of the Old Testament," pp. 207ff.
[2] " Theology of the Old Testament," p. 231.

thought is in quality the same as the outward act. Thus Jesus greatly deepened the sense of guilt. Thirdly, the exalted standard of his own life became the measure of human obligation and at the same time the criterion for judging sin and guilt.

(1) Jesus called sinners to repentance. He was the friend of publicans and sinners. (Matt. 11 : 19.) He did not regard all men as equally bad, nor did he consider them as wholly destitute of all good. (Luke 7 : 9; 19 : 1-10; 23 : 42, 43; Mark 10 : 21.) But he did regard men as lost. He came to seek and to save that which was lost. Men were of priceless value in God's sight, notwithstanding their sin. The mission of Jesus was to bring them back to God. In his teaching sin is universal. All men need to be saved.

(2) In the Fourth Gospel sin is represented in various ways. It is darkness as opposed to light. Men are represented as wilfully blind to the truth. (John 9 : 41.) It is bondage as opposed to freedom. (John 8 : 34.) Men are the willing captives of sin and Satan. Jesus contrasts flesh and spirit in the Fourth Gospel and teaches that the spiritual birth from above is necessary to all men. (John 3 : 6.) The world as the sphere of the operation of sin and Satan is regarded as sinful and corrupt. (John 18 : 36; 17 : 25; 14 : 17; 12 : 31.) Sin is also summed up as unbelief. (John 16 : 9.) This expresses an attitude of resistance to truth and to the Spirit of God. Unbelief is the inclusive sin, the root sin. Because of it men are morally and spiritually blind. The duty of men is to believe. Jesus is the revelation of God to men, and their attitude toward him becomes the basis of judgment. (John 3 : 19-21.) Now it is clear that in all the preceding the moral and spiritual likeness of God resulting in true fellowship with him is the ideal of Jesus. Sin is the lack of such character and fellowship.

(3) In Paul's teaching as to sin several points need emphasis. One is his use of the word "flesh." With Paul the use of this term flesh is based on the Old Testament. It refers first to the fleshly as distinguished from the spiritual element in man as weak and infirm, and the seat of evil desires and pas-

sions. But there is no dualism of a philosophic kind in this. Paul does not regard the body as evil because it is material. As matter simply it has no moral quality. But as the body is the source of certain impulses which lead to sinful motives, desires, and acts, the term "flesh" came to be used by Paul for the lower nature as contrasted with the higher. But the sinfulness of men inheres in the mind and will, not in the material body as such. The "carnal mind" is enmity against God. The "mind of the flesh" is that which cannot please God. (Rom. 8 : 1-11.)

Paul represents men as dead in trespasses and sins, and exposed to the wrath of God. (Eph. 2 : 1-3.) He does not mean by this a merely passive state. Sinners are often intensely active and aggressive. Nor does he mean that men naturally are wholly destitute of moral light. For he declares that men by nature do the things of the law, since they have the law written on their hearts. (Rom. 2 : 14, 15.) Paul is simply recognizing here the natural morality of men as contrasted with their spiritual life in Christ. It is the same fact which Jesus observed in the case of the young ruler. "He looked upon him and loved him" because of his moral attainments. But the man was lacking in the higher spiritual life as appears from his moral failure under the test of Jesus. (Mark 10 : 17-22.) It is in instances like these that we see sharply distinguished the difference between the natural and the spiritual relations of Christ to men. As we have previously pointed out, men are naturally constituted in and through Christ. Their natural powers are all traceable to him. But sin has changed man's attitude to God. Christ came to recreate men in the divine image and establish a higher spiritual life in them.

Paul discusses sin in relation to the law. He means usually the Mosaic law. His conclusion in general is that the law was meant to lead men to Christ. It operated thus: When the commandment came, sin was aroused in man and he died. The law was not in itself weak or bad. It was ineffective only through the sinfulness and weakness of the flesh. Human ability was thus shown to be unequal to the requirements of the law. A sense of sin, of corruption, and of guilt was awakened. The need of a redemption through divine power was made manifest. Thus the law became a schoolmaster or tutor (pedagogue) to lead to Christ. (Gal. 3 : 24.)

Paul teaches that deliverance from sin is through faith in Christ. This introduces a new spiritual energy in the soul. " The old man " is crucified with Christ. An ethical-mystical death and resurrection takes place. The law of the Spirit of life in Christ now emancipates from the law of sin and death. (Rom. 8 : 2.) The power of sin is broken by new power that is greater. The new life in Christ is not the blossom, so to speak, on the stalk of the natural moral life of man. It is a new life with higher aims and ideals. It is not a natural development. It is a new creation. The natural was the antecedent condition of the spiritual, but new elements are introduced which exalt and transfigure the natural life. Man now transcends his old self. He finds himself anew in his new resurrection life in Christ.

Paul traces human sin back to Adam. " As in Adam all die, so in Christ all are made alive " (Rom. 5 : 12-21; 1 Cor. 15 : 22.) Paul does not give us an elaborate theory as to how Adam's sin is imputed to mankind. There is no clear evidence that he held the view that Adam was the " official " head of the race and that we sinned through him because he represented us in a covenant relation. Nor does he assert that we sinned in Adam because we were actually present in him when he sinned. This theory is based on the supposition that since the race has come out of Adam, we may properly assert that the race as a whole was in Adam. These are speculations about Paul's teaching rather than interpretations of it.

Paul clearly recognizes the principle of heredity. Adam was the natural head of the race. Our tendency to sin is derived from him. All men are affected by his act through the medium of natural propagation.

This is a fact strongly emphasized by modern science. The solidarity of the race is a profoundly significant truth. We cannot escape our relations to our progenitors. But as we shall see later, in so far as we were under condemnation for the sin of Adam, Christ has removed that condemnation. He too bears a relation to the race as a whole. Solidarity and heredity are beneficent principles when acting normally.

IV. The Consequences of Sin

1. Sin Universal

It is clear from the facts which show the unity of mankind, and the moral and spiritual history of the race, as well as from the teachings of Scripture, that human sinfulness is universal. "There is none righteous, no, not one" (Rom. 3 : 10-18).

The phrase "total depravity" has been employed in theology to describe the sinful state of men. But it needs careful defining lest it lead astray. In brief, it means that all the parts of our nature have been affected by sin. It does not mean that men are as bad as they can be, nor that all men are equally bad. It does not mean that human nature is destitute of all good impulses in the moral sense. It means rather that human nature, as such, and in all its parts in its unregenerate state, is under the dominion of sin.

The question arises here as to man's ability or inability. Man is sometimes declared to possess "natural," but not "moral" ability in things religious. By natural ability it is meant that he possesses all human faculties and powers, including will and the power of contrary choice. He is self-determined and not compelled in his actions. He is responsible and free. He is guilty when he does wrong. He could do right if he would, because he is equipped with the faculties for moral action.

On the other hand, it is asserted that man lacks "moral ability" because he cannot change his own nature. He cannot radically alter the bias of his will. The regenerating power of God's Spirit is required. He must be born from above.

Now as we have defined these phrases both are true. But it is doubtful whether their use is not misleading despite the definitions. In our thought processes we sometimes are driven to such distinctions for the purpose of producing orderly systems of truth. But in appealing to men generally it is easy to mislead by their use. If a man is told that he has "natural ability" in religious things, he is likely to overlook his dependence on God's grace. If he is told that he lacks "moral ability," he is in danger of losing his sense of responsibility. The gospel appeal always presupposes the divine initiative in salvation and the necessity for divine grace. The Scriptures do not dwell upon man's "moral inability," but rather upon his unwillingness to repent and believe. Men are exhorted to turn from their evil ways and live. This does not imply that God's grace is not required if they are to do so. It implies rather that God's grace acts through their own free response and choice of the right. The first decisive result of grace in the heart is the free and glad response of the sinner.

2. Guilt and Penalty

Other consequences of sin are guilt and penalty. *a.* Guilt is the ill-desert of the sinner on account of his sin. Here we must keep in mind the personal relation involved in sin. It is transgression of objective law in some cases. It is against the attribute of divine justice. But it is more. Sin is man's personal opposition to the personal God. Guilt thus takes the form of self-condemnation based on a sense of God's disapproval. In conscience guilt is not a sense of transgression against abstract law or justice, but against the divine will. In Scripture also the most intense expressions of the sense of guilt take the form of consciousness of the divine anger at sin. This appears especially in the psalms and prophets. Of course there are degrees of guilt. We have, for example, sins of ignorance and sins of knowledge, sins of infirmity and sins of presumption, sins of partial and of entire opposition to God's will. (Matt. 10 : 15; Luke 12 : 47, 48; John 19 : 11; Rom. 2 : 12; Ps. 19 : 12; Matt. 12 : 31; Mark 3 : 29.)

b. Penalty is the effect produced on the sinner by his sin, whether it be through the operation of natural, moral, or spiritual law, or through the direct action of God. Penalty in any of its forms is God's reaction against sin. Men reap what they sow through the action of the laws of nature or their moral constitution in many cases of transgression. This is the divine reaction against sin as truly as God's more direct action. But God is not limited to these laws. He remains a free Person, capable of employing various means to vindicate himself and his government against wrong-doing. All penalty against sin is based ultimately on the holy nature of God. God is immanent in the world. His laws are not apart from him, like a self-acting mechanism. God acts, his laws act, and God acts through his laws. All these statements are required.

c. A question arises here as to the object of penalty. Does God punish solely as a means of vindicating his justice, or does he have in view the reformation of the sinner, or the good of society? Divergent theories are based on opposing answers to this question. There is, however, no necessary conflict between these various aspects of punishment. As we have seen, the individual man is a member of society. Heredity and solidarity are facts. God has so made the world. As man cannot act apart from his social relations, merely as an isolated unit or atom; so it is inconceivable that God's dealings with him could be without social effects. Moreover, if God really loves all men, we cannot think of his love as being entirely suspended when he punishes. He must desire the good of the sinful even when he visits iniquity with stripes. Again, it is an error to assume that God punishes *merely* to reform the sinner, or for the good of society. His righteousness is an essential quality. He punishes sin because it is sin and because his own nature necessarily reacts against it. Of course the incorrigible sinner is cut off completely from the hope of reformation, and the society of the sinner may be likewise an incorrigible society. But this does not alter the truth that God never loses his good will toward men. Men put themselves beyond the reach of his gracious appeal, and only his vindicatory righteousness can find opportunity for action. We conclude then, first, that because man is responsible and deserves punishment, God punishes him; secondly, because man is a social being, God's penal action on the individual necessarily affects society; and thirdly, because God is essentially righteous, he must needs punish the sinner in accordance with his own nature.

d. The chief penalty of sin in the Scriptures is death, physical and spiritual.

We consider first physical death. In Genesis 2 : 17 God declares to the man he had created that if he partook of the forbidden fruit he would "surely die." In a great number of passages in the Old and New Testaments alike, the death of the body is declared to be the penalty for sin. In Romans 5 : 12 death is declared to have entered the world through sin. In verse 21 Paul declares that sin reigned in death that grace might reign through righteousness unto eternal life through Jesus Christ our Lord. In Romans 6 : 23 we read that "the wages of sin is death, but the gift of God is eternal life through Jesus Christ our Lord." There is little need to give extended references on this point. The New Testament abounds in passages which make it clear that physical death is regarded as a penalty of sin.

The view is held by some that physical death is natural. It is simply the expression of a biological law. Men were created mortal in the sense that the body would die. Death is a beneficent arrangement to prevent overpopulation of the earth, and to enable the race to make progress by allowing room for new generations of men. It is held that a natural law was given a moral and penal significance when sin entered, so that death became also a penal infliction. Man's fear of death and the suffering he endures thus become penalties for sin.

Scripture, however, does not seem to require this view. Enoch and Elijah were translated without tasting death. Those who are alive at Christ's second coming are to be translated, according to Paul. (Cf. 1 Cor. 15 : 51; 1 Thess. 4 : 17.) At any rate, it is conceivable that God might have provided some other means of exit from the world if man had not sinned. Whatever is true as to the lower animals (and we recognize the biological law), we are not shut up to the view that physical death was the only possible ending of the earthly life of a sinless man. We may add, however, that whatever view be held as to the biological law of death as applied to all physical organisms, including that of man, the Scripture teaching that death is a penal consequence of sin remains. Physical death has become a much more terrible thing as the result of man's sin and separation from God. The sense of responsibility and of guilt has transformed it into a formidable enemy. The foreboding and dread with which men regard it has been immeasurably deepened by the reign of sin in our human spirits. Thus a natural process might have been included as a part of the penal consequences of sin by reason of the intimate relation between the two. In Genesis 3 : 14 a part of the curse against the serpent is seen to involve the natural mode of locomotion of the latter: " Upon thy belly shalt thou go, and dust shalt thou eat all the days of thy life." This was not a new mode of locomotion imposed on the serpent, but rather a use of that which was natural as a means of emphasizing the divine anger against transgression.

e. Spiritual death is the chief penalty of sin. This means separation of the soul from God. It was this spiritual death which followed " the day " of the first transgression. In 1 John 3 : 14 we read, " He that loveth not . . . abideth in death." In Matthew 8 : 22 Jesus says: " Follow me ; and leave the dead to bury their own dead." Here it is clear he means those who are spiritually dead are to bury the dead body. Thus Jesus as well as Paul declares that men are dead in sins. In Ephesians 2 : 1 Paul says his readers were once dead in trespasses and sins.

Eternal death is involved in the penalty against sin. It is spiritual death when it has become permanent in the soul. Spiritual death being the absence of spiritual life, separation from God, and loss of fellowship with him and of blessedness which attends that fellowship, it follows that eternal death is the soul's permanent attitude of unbelief and sin, its wilful and final separation from God.

V. SOLUTION OF THE PROBLEM OF SIN THROUGH CHRISTIAN EXPERIENCE

The consciousness of sin is one of the most real and painful of all human experiences. The bondage and helplessness of men who are held in its power are too manifest to be questioned. It is a serious defect of some forms of theology that they make no adequate provision for the fact of human bondage to sin and for the sin- and guilt-consciousness which attends it. Men are told to imitate Christ, or to strive to realize the consciousness of Christ. Or they are told to claim their privilege as the natural children of God, and to begin a new life thus. But a gospel which thus limits itself overlooks certain fundamental truths. Christ's consciousness was sinless. How then can the sinner, under his sense of guilt and condemnation, imitate Christ? He knows that death reigns in him while life reigned in Christ. How can the sinner make the transition from his own consciousness of sin to the consciousness of Christ? How can he claim sonship to God in any satisfying way when the very center of his sin-consciousness is his sense of ethical unworthiness for sonship? To him it is incredible that one whose being is so under bondage to evil can claim the moral likeness to God required by sonship. No gospel which begins with any basal fact save that of man's actual unworthiness and his sense of ill-desert can meet the needs of men. In a word, the gospel of God's grace is necessary to meet the fact and the consciousness of sin.

The following elements enter into the solution of the problem of sin in Christian experience: First, the revelation of God in Christ makes clear God's attitude toward the sinner. He desires his salvation. Secondly, the atonement of Christ meets the rational and moral difficulty involved. Through it the sinner understands how forgiveness and justification and reconciliation are possible, despite his own sense of unworthiness. Thirdly, his own sense of sin is in the first instance deepened rather than removed. The Holy Spirit convicts him, overcomes him with a sense of sin. But as the conviction heads up in unbelief, so also it is seen that faith in Christ is the sole condition of acceptance with God and deliverance. Thus the sinner's moral inability resolves itself into his unwillingness to accept Christ. Fourthly, Christ is formed in the sinner, the hope of glory, and through faith divine fellowship is restored. The law of the Spirit of life in Christ makes free from the law of sin and death. Fifthly, a new consciousness now takes the place of the sinner's own guilt-consciousness. This new consciousness contains, first of all, a sense of reconciliation with God. It contains a sense of ability to make moral progress. Aspiration and desire now become victory instead of defeat. The sense of moral and spiritual loneliness now gives place to a sense of the inner presence of the Great Companion, the Comforter and Helper. Religious desire is no longer a hopeless struggle through human effort alone. It is not a soliloquy now, but a dialogue between the soul and its God. His former cry of despair was, "O wretched man that I am! who shall deliver me out of this body of death?" But now in triumph he exclaims, "I thank God through Jesus Christ, our Lord" (Rom. 7 : 24, 25).

We may now see the contrast between the two theological standpoints in their dealing with the consciousness of sin in man. One seeks to minimize the consciousness of sin and guilt; the other recognizes its reality and validity. One holds that God's anger is merely subjective; the other that it is objective and real. One denies the cause; the other recognizes it and seeks to remove it. One emphasizes the appeal of God's love apart from Christ's atoning death; the other urges repentance on the ground of that death.

VI. Objections to the Biblical Doctrine of Sin

Before concluding the subject of sin, two objections need to be considered briefly. The first is an arraignment of the moral system of God. Men urge that it is unjust to hold men responsible for the working of a system in which they seem to be victims rather than transgressors. The reasoning is as follows: Heredity predisposes to sin; man's earliest consciousness is scarcely moral at all; he is born into an environment which also predisposes to sin. Thus he is, as it were, flung out into a universe where transgression is inevitable by reason of the forces which operate within and around him.

The answer to this objection is not difficult where all the facts are taken into account. It runs thus: Condemnation is not for hereditary sin, but only for actual sin. Christ died for the race as a whole and removed the curse so far as condemnation for the racial sin is concerned. The solidarity of the race is a fact. But environment is not all bad. There are many redemptive influences at work all around us in Christian lands. The infant consciousness, it is true, is without moral discernment. But this negative condition is an opportunity for good as well as evil influences. There are degrees of guilt. Men are penalized according to the light against which they sin. The unity and solidarity of the race is a fact most favorable for moral character when good influences prevail. The individual is buoyed and sustained by ten thousand agencies of good. The aim of the gospel is in part to convert heredity and environment and all social forces into beneficent agencies in a kingdom of righteousness, and peace, and joy in the Holy Ghost. We may well believe that such a system is far better than one in which men would be merely detached atoms. We can only judge God's moral order by its prospective outcome taken along with its present organization. The end will justify the beginning.

The second objection relates to the salvation of infants dying in infancy. If the principle of hereditary sin is true, how can the vast multitudes of infants who die in infancy be saved?

In reply it may be said that there is comparatively little direct teaching in the Scriptures as to the salvation of infants dying in infancy. And yet there is abundant indirect evidence, as we have already seen.

Again, it is entirely clear from the New Testament that Christ's union with the human race made his atoning work efficacious in some measure for all mankind. "As in Adam all die, so in Christ are all made alive" (1 Cor. 15 : 22). This does not teach universalism, but it suggests that there is a similarity between the racial effects of the act of Adam and that of Christ. Christ "died for all" (2 Cor. 5 : 15); or as it is elsewhere expressed, he tasted death for every man. (Heb. 2 : 9.) Men are not condemned therefore for hereditary or original sin. They are condemned only for their own sins. They are called to repentance and faith by the gospel. It is their own act of rejection which is the basis of their condemnation. Infants dying in infancy cannot repent, or believe, or perform works of any kind, good or bad. We do not know how the grace of God operates in them. But we are fully assured that Christ provided for them, and that they are created anew in him and saved.

CHAPTER XIII

THE SAVING WORK OF CHRIST

I. THE THREEFOLD OFFICE OF CHRIST

THE work of Christ is usually summed up as a threefold activity of prophet, priest, and king. Some prefer to describe his atonement as a sacrificial rather than a priestly work. Either term, properly understood, will answer the needs of the case. Christ was both priest and sacrifice. Both elements enter into the proper view of his work.

As prophet, Jesus reveals God to men and he reveals men to themselves. He is the crown of Old Testament prophecy and the perfect prophet. Old Testament teachings in ritual and ceremonial laws, in moral precepts, and in spiritual meaning, all converge upon and unite in him. In his person he is the " truth " as well as the " way " and the " life." His miracles as well as his parables are filled with moral meaning. He gradually led his disciples to the higher conception of his Messiahship and his kingdom. In every act of his life, including his voluntary death, as well as in his words, Jesus taught men the truth. He predicted regarding the future of the kingdom and revealed new truth to his disciples after his death.

The priestly work of Christ was accomplished especially in his atoning death. As the atonement is to be dealt with more fully, little need be said here. Jesus was the perfect high priest and the perfect sacrifice. His work forever abolished the need of priest and sacrifice in man's approach to God. Herein appears an aspect of Christianity which shows it to be the completion of other religions, and also that it is the final religion. The Epistle to the Hebrews develops this thought in a very impressive way.

The kingly office of Christ appears in various ways. The Old Testament Messianic ideal took the form of perfect kingship.

The Hebrew word (*Mashiach*) and the Greek word (*Christos*), translated Messiah, both mean the "anointed one," and this points directly to kingship. In the New Testament, as king, Christ founds the kingdom of God; he claims the obedience of men; he speaks with authority; works miracles; he claims all authority as Messiah; he establishes the ordinances; founds the church; conquers death; commissions the disciples to preach the gospel; ascends to the right hand of God; intercedes for his people; and will reign until all his enemies are subdued.

It is impossible, however, to separate entirely the prophetic, priestly, and kingly offices of Christ. They are interdependent forms of activity and blend with each other at many points. For example, his priestly work of atonement is a vital element in his prophetic work. By his sacrificial death he reveals the nature of God as holy love. Again, as Lord and King, he gives efficacy to the priestly work of atonement as the gospel is preached to men. So also in the salvation of men and in the progress of the kingdom on earth his prophetic office continues because it is his person, teaching, and work which are the contents of the saving gospel. The Holy Spirit takes the things of Christ and shows them to men.

II. The Atonement

Special attention must be given to that part of the saving work of Christ which he accomplished in the atonement through his sufferings and death. This is due to several facts. One is that the atonement is central in the teachings of the New Testament. Another is that it has occupied a large place in theological discussion, and is a vital and essential element in an effective gospel. A third fact is that it has ever been a fundamental element in the experience of Christians.

As we shall soon see, the writers of the New Testament represent the atonement of Christ under various forms. They also employ a number of figures of speech, no one of which, taken by itself, gives an adequate idea of the atonement. In some passages the death of Christ is described as a propitiation. In others it is reconciliation. Sometimes it is simply redemption. In some passages it is described in its effects as securing remission of sins. Sometimes his death is called a ransom. In other passages it is the purchase price paid for our deliverance. So also Christ is declared to have become a curse for us.

In all the above forms of statement and in others which are not mentioned it is abundantly clear that the death of Christ stands in a very intimate and vital relation with the salvation of men. Many theories have arisen in the course of history to explain that relation. Most of them emphasize an element of truth and are defective in what they omit rather than in what they assert. The final view should contain the true elements in all theories. And it will be found that by the simple and direct method of taking the New Testament statements in their proper meaning and constructing a theory out of these teachings we shall arrive at the most satisfactory conclusion. A theory in such case will be simply an interpretation of facts.

There are some who object to any effort to discover the meaning of Christ's death. They insist upon our teaching and preaching the " fact " as opposed to the " theory " of atonement. The reply is obvious. Theory may not be the best word here. But theory simply expresses meaning. It is of course absurd to try to exclude all meaning from the death of Christ. Again, no moral or spiritual fact can be a fact for an intelligent being without a meaning. The fact does not become a fact for intelligence apart from its meaning. A dose of medicine given to relieve physical pain might do its work without a grasp of its meaning by the patient. But in the higher realm of spirit fact and meaning are inseparable. Apart from their meaning religious facts become mere magical agencies. Religion becomes priestcraft under this view and sinks to the old level of superstition and bondage. A third reply is that Christianity cannot afford to abjure intelligence. We must dare to seek the meaning of every part of the religion of Christ. We shall not succeed completely, just as men do not discover all of truth in any other realm. But religion must not plead exemption from the task of searching for

U

meanings and the further task of setting forth the meanings of all its great realities.

III. A Brief Review of Theories

We shall give a very brief sketch of some of the leading theories of the atonement by way of preparing the way for a positive statement.

1. We need only to mention the early patristic view that the death of Christ was a ransom paid by God to Satan to redeem men who were held as Satan's captives. The view is revolting to the Christian moral consciousness. It was based on an effort to express the full meaning of atonement by means of the single figure of a ransom while ignoring various other forms of representation in the New Testament. It was held that if Christ's death was a ransom, it must have been paid by some one to some one else; that there must have been prisoners held by right of conquest and requiring ransom for deliverance; that, as it was unreasonable to think of God paying a ransom to himself, it was the devil who must be paid. Hence the theory arose. No one holds it to-day. It illustrates the partial and fragmentary method of dealing with the Scripture passages bearing on the atonement.

2. A later view set forth by Anselm in the eleventh century put much emphasis upon the idea of divine honor or majesty and the debt of sinful men. Sin violates God's honor. It deserves infinite punishment since God is infinite. Man cannot pay because he is finite and morally bankrupt through sin. Christ in his atoning death paid the debt. This he could do because as divine he could pay an infinite debt, and as sinless and human he could represent men. But as sinless he was not obliged to die. Hence by death he obtained (on the Catholic theory) an excess of merit which could be placed to the credit of sinners. Anselm's view is an improvement on the ransom-to-Satan theory because it connects the atonement with a requirement of God. But it is wrought out in abstract terms of honor, justice, satisfaction,

and merit, apart from regard for the personal relations between God and man, and the specific New Testament teaching. It emphasizes God's honor rather than his righteous love, and leaves the atonement rather an external act than a vital divine deed for human redemption.

3. Hugo Grotius, in the early part of the seventeenth century, propounded what is known as the governmental theory of the atonement. In this view God's government rather than his honor, or his righteousness, is central. To pardon sinners without showing the heinousness of sin and the majesty of violated law would endanger moral government. The death of Christ was God's exhibition of his own high estimate of law and of his condemnation of sin. Christ did not suffer the penalty of man's sin, but demonstrated the penal principle in divine government. His sufferings were substituted for man's punishment. God could thus pardon sinners without peril to his government.

This view is also inadequate. The atonement does indeed respect God's government. But it is a more vital and internal event both for God and man than a mere means of maintaining government. The government of God is the outward expression of his nature. His approach to man is on the basis of his own spiritual nature and the moral and spiritual laws of man's being. The maintenance of government expresses, therefore, not the most central truth of the atonement, but a secondary result, as we shall see. To understand the atonement we must view it in relation to that which is central in God, righteous love, and in relation to the reproduction of that love in sinful men.

4. A fourth theory is known as the Socinian or example theory of the atonement. Modern Unitarians follow Laelius and Faustus Socinus in the sixteenth century in holding this view. The theory is that Christ's death was merely a martyr's death. His example of loyalty to the truth, even unto death, inspires us men to heroic moral struggle and victory. God needs no atonement, and man needs none apart from this. Our sense of sin, guilt, and condemnation is subjective. There is no obstacle to pardon in God. Our repentance is all he requires.

In reply, we need only say that while we recognize the element of truth in the theory, it is nevertheless far short of the whole truth of the atonement. Jesus was indeed a martyr to truth, but far more. The view as stated provides for merely a small fraction of the New Testament teaching on the subject. It is at variance with the Christian experience of the centuries. It is void of the great elements of power in the gospel of God's grace which has been the moving force in Christianity from the beginning.

5. A fifth view of the atonement is best described as the moral influence theory. It has come to be one of the most popular of modern theories and has been held by many leading preachers and theologians. Its chief characteristic is its claim that in the atoning work of Christ no necessity of the divine nature was met. The aim of the atonement was rather to influence men to repent. God was already reconciled. The atonement was the expression of God's love and sympathy for sinful men. The incarnation united Christ to the sinful race, and his death was the outcome of his sympathetic efforts for their salvation. There was no obstacle to forgiveness in God. The only obstacle was man's own unbelief and stubborn will. Its effect is to move men to repentance and loving obedience.

Here again we have a partial truth. The moving power of Christ's death is unquestioned. But it was more than a moving spectacle addressed to men. The theory fails to explain many passages of Scripture which we shall soon consider. It does not satisfy the requirements of Christian experience. There are other elements in justification than those suggested by the moral influence theory. Besides, the theory seems very unreal and dramatic. Spectacular suffering on the part of Christ, merely to touch the human heart, is an irrational conception. A father might be badly burned in the effort to rescue his child which had fallen in the fire. We would applaud such a deed. But we would consider a father lacking in rationality who should call his child to the fireside and then attempt to prove his love by thrusting his hand in the flame. Unless the necessity for Christ's death is found somehow in the nature of things, that is, in the moral constitution of man and in the nature of God, then we come short of an adequate explanation. This theory is in principle much like a perversion of the biblical view to which it is often opposed. That perversion starts with the necessity for "satisfying" justice. But it thinks of justice as an abstraction, a detached attribute of God which is angry. The death of Christ appeases the anger of this detached attribute, and thus love, another detached attribute, can freely act. So that the atonement is thought of as a means of reconciling the two attributes of God which are at war with each other. The error of the view is in its abstract conception of justice and satisfaction, and in its failure to show the necessary connection between Christ's death and its object, the salvation of men. The theory leaves the atonement outside the moral and spiritual necessities of mankind, and unrelated to our need. The moral influence theory is equally abstract. It converts the atonement into a mere dramatic spectacle and appeal, grounded in no great and fundamental moral and spiritual necessities. It involves a suffering and humiliation of Christ having no inherent and vital connection with the end in view, and hence an unworthy view of God. It fails to explain the prayer and agony and bloody sweat of Christ in Gethsemane, and his forsaken cry on the cross. Unless there was more in his death than this theory supposes, Christ was less heroic in his death than some of his followers have been, who have gone singing to the martyr's stake. Early Christianity abounds in such instances.

6. There have been variations of the moral influence theory. McLeod Campbell held that Christ was the representative penitent. He, being one with the human race, by his incarnation shared with men their sin- and guilt-consciousness and actually repented for mankind while remaining sinless himself. On the basis of his representative penitence God forgives sinners.

In reply, we recognize the truth that Christ did repudiate sin, and that he was in organic relations with the race. But it is a strained use of language to say that he repented. Christ could not repent in the strict sense. The view of Campbell is inconsistent with other views of the advocates of the moral influence theory. Those advocates object to substitution on the Godward side in Christ's death. Campbell's view asserts substitution, or at least representation in the sense of substitution, on the manward side. If the principle of substitution is wrong in one case, it is also in the other. The true view recognizes the principle, but defines it in a more adequate way.

F. D. Maurice emphasized the unity of Christ with the race. In his sufferings the race suffered. He thus became the "sinless root" of a new race. By union with him men enter a new life, and in the end will share the sinlessness of Christ.

Here again the unity of Christ with the human race is a vital truth and one essential to a correct view of the atonement. It is also true that Christ became, in a figurative sense of course, the "sinless root" of a new humanity. But this does not approximate, much less exhaust, the biblical teachings on the subject of the atonement, as we shall at once see.

7. Sometimes an effort is made to minimize the historical atoning act of Christ by the assertion that the atonement was an eternal act of God, and that the event on Calvary was a mere incident of the greater reality. It is not necessary to reply at length. The offering of Christ was indeed an eternal atonement in the sense that it was the expression of an eternal impulse of God's love, an eternal desire to give himself for the good of his creatures; and also in the sense that it is eternally efficacious. But it was none the less necessary as a historical act. It was the expression of God's nature, but its historical form was necessary to its operation in the realm of history in order to produce a moral kingdom among men.

IV. GENERAL PRELIMINARY STATEMENTS AS TO THE BIBLICAL DOCTRINE

There are a few general remarks which will prepare for a satisfactory study of the atonement as it is set forth in the New Testament.

1. The first is that it is important to include all phases of the New Testament teaching which may be found necessary to this end. The atonement is a great subject with many sides. It may be approached from many angles. It is easy to be one-sided and fragmentary in dealing with the New Testament material. Care should be taken to include all the vital aspects of the subject.

2. Again, we should be on our guard against fallacies which arise through abstract processes of thought. As one reads the many books on the atonement produced by men of all schools of theology, one is deeply impressed with the tendency to deal with the subject in an abstract manner: almost every leading word and idea has been so conceived: the idea of law, as some vague abstraction which Christ satisfied; the idea of penalty so stated as to involve Christ himself in actual sin; the wrath of God conceived as fierce anger poured out on Christ instead of its true New Testament meaning as God visiting sin with its just penalty; the idea of substitution conceived as if the transfer of sin and righteousness were physical acts instead of moral and spiritual deeds; and the idea of salvation as if it were a mere matter of bookkeeping with a debit and credit side of the account—this and nothing more.

In like manner the tendency to abstract modes of thought has led to fallacies about God and the persons of the Trinity. For example, the attribute of justice has been thought of in conflict with the attribute of love, and men have thought of a war of the attributes which ended with the atonement. Or the Father has been conceived of as if he were angry with men until Christ died and then for the first time began to love them. Thus men have thought of a conflict in the Godhead between Father and Son. Such conflict has at times seemed to be implied in the statements of those who hold the essentials of the New Testament view, or it has been alleged against them by their opponents.

Another example of the tendency to abstract modes of thought about the atonement has been the exaltation of some one attribute or quality of God to the supreme place. We name two or three instances. Some have thought that the mere will of God apart from his nature, his righteousness or love, is the ground of the saving value of Christ's death. There was no inward necessity in the nature of God or man, but only the divine appointment. This view is wholly untenable to all who understand the relation of will to nature. The will is the expression of the nature Others make the love of God the sole moving power in atonement. Righteousness is held to be subordinate to love. Yet others make righteousness fundamental and assert that the exercise of love is optional with God while righteousness or holiness is imperative in its demands. Now it is difficult to see how any act of God can be unrighteous or unloving, or how God's will can ever be properly conceived as acting apart from his nature. Outward conditions among free beings will lead to variation in God's methods, but not to suppression of any quality in his nature. He always acts as a free personality in the totality of his being and not in separated parts of his nature. We cannot understand the atonement unless we keep this in mind.

3. A third general statement is that the best guide to a clear understanding of the atonement is a direct study of the facts involved. These are recorded in the Gospels and Epistles of the New Testament, and they are reflected in modern Christian experience. This direct study is the scientific method of approach. If faithfully pursued, it will save us from many errors and reduce to clearness much that has been complicated in discussions of the atonement. Thus our doctrine will rest on a basis of fact.

4. A fourth general statement relates to the New Testament teaching as to law in connection with the atoning work of Christ. This refers particularly to the writings of the apostle Paul. Many have sought to show contradictory elements in Paul. They have claimed that there are juridical, or forensic and outwardly legalistic elements in Paul's writings side by side with others which are vital, spiritual, and inward, and these diverse elements remain unreconciled. The view is that Paul as a Christian never overcame fully the Jewish standpoint.

Now we recognize fully the inward and spiritual nature of Christianity. But Christianity is not a lawless religion. Its laws are not statutory and outward, but vital and inward and personal, written indelibly in man's constitution and in God's nature. This truth appears everywhere in Paul's writings. For him the gospel is " the law of the Spirit of life in Christ Jesus " (Rom. 8 : 2).

But Paul deals with law in the outward sense in certain connections. Statutory law as taught by Moses, the law of outward commands as recognized by the natural conscience and embodied in human codes generally, are treated by him. But it is a serious misreading of Paul to assert that this element in his teaching contradicts the spiritual element. On the contrary, the real key to the interpretation of Paul is the recognition of the uniform manner in which he asserts and proves that in the gospel all outward and statutory law becomes inward and spiritual. In his gospel he digests and assimilates, as it were, all forms of righteousness as expressed in outward commands. He transfigures and glorifies them through their relationship to Christ. This will become very manifest in his doctrine of atonement and justification. In these the law of Christianity is the law of the Spirit and the law of Life. The merely formal and outward, the merely juridical and statutory, is abolished.

V. THE BIBLICAL DOCTRINE OF THE ATONEMENT

We need to keep in mind the preceding general statements in considering the biblical teachings as to the atonement. Otherwise we are likely to import much into these teachings which comes from human speculation. We should keep strictly to the biblical facts and their clear meaning.

1. We consider first the motive of the atoning work of Christ. The motive is the love of God. This is abundantly evident from many New Testament passages. In the epitomized gospel in John 3 : 16 we read that " God so loved the world, that he gave his only begotten Son." In the next verse we read: " For God sent not his Son into the world to judge the world; but that the world should be saved through him." Again in Romans 5 : 8: " But God commendeth his own love toward us, in that, while

we were yet sinners, Christ died for us." It is needless to multiply references. These and many other passages show clearly that God does not love us because Christ died for us, but rather that Christ died for us because God loved us. His life and death are the expression of God's love, not the producing cause of that love. Of course the love which is the moving cause of the atonement is a righteous love. It is the love of the holy God for men. The atonement in all its elements must be understood as the provision and expression of such love. It will be found consistent at all points with righteous love.

2. Observe next the end of the atonement. What did God have in view in the gift of his Son? The New Testament answer takes several forms. We select a few which will serve our present purpose. The most comprehensive general answer is man's salvation. This contains two elements. One deals with the presence and power of sin. The other with the ideal of righteousness. On the side of sin the Gospels and Epistles are in complete agreement. Space forbids an exhaustive array of the passages. In Matthew 26 : 28 Jesus says, " For this is my blood of the new covenant, which is poured out for many unto remission of sins." He had already declared (Matt. 20 : 28) that he had come " to give up his life a ransom for many." In the Fourth Gospel a similar statement is made by John the Baptist. He sees Jesus coming, and says, " Behold the lamb of God, that taketh away the sin of the world " (John 1 : 29). In the Epistles this truth is repeated in one form or another so often that it can only be understood as the universal belief of early Christians. In Ephesians 1 : 7 we read, " in whom (*i. e.,* in Christ) we have our redemption through his blood, the forgiveness of our trespasses, according to the riches of his grace." From those passages we conclude that the death of Christ secured in some way the remission or forgiveness of sins. Of course this carries with it freedom from condemnation and judgment which falls upon sinners because of their sins.

As to the ideal of righteousness the object of the atonement is equally clear. In Ephesians 2 : 10 we read, " For we are his workmanship, created in Christ Jesus for good works, which God afore prepared that we should walk in them." In Ephesians 1 : 4 the purpose of God in Christ is "that we should be holy and without blemish before him in love." The purpose of God as realized in a holy church and a holy kingdom is also made clear in various places. (Eph. 3 : 10; 5 : 25-27; Rom. 14 : 17.) The ultimate end of the mediatorial work of Christ is the manifestation of the sons of God. In Romans 8 : 19 we read, "For the earnest expectation of the creation waiteth for the revealing of the sons of God." In Hebrews 2 : 10 again we read, "For it became him, for whom are all things, . . in bringing many sons unto glory, to make the author of their salvation perfect through sufferings."

Now these texts and many others abundantly show the ethical nature of the atonement in its end and purpose. To sum it up: (1) It is God's method of bestowing forgiveness or remission of sins. (2) It is God's method of producing righteous men and women. (3) It is God's means of creating a holy society. (4) It is God's way of producing a holy society in which Fatherhood and sonship shall be the supreme expression of the relationship between God and men.

With this understanding of the motive and end of the atonement, we shall find less difficulty in understanding the fact itself. We remark, therefore:

3. That the atonement of Christ was the means adopted by God, in the exercise of his righteous love toward sinful men, to secure the full and free activity of that love in bestowing forgiveness and in perfecting individual men and women in a holy society of sons and daughters of God.

As God's means to the above end the atonement of Christ involved the following:

(1) Identification with the race he came to redeem. This point is strongly emphasized in Hebrews 2 : 14-18, which reads in part as follows: " Since then the children are sharers in flesh and blood, he also himself in like manner partook of the same; that through death he might bring to naught him that had the

power of death, that is, the devil; and might deliver all them who through fear of death were all their lifetime subject to bondage. For verily not to angels doth he give help, but he giveth help to the seed of Abraham. Wherefore it behooved him in all things to be made like unto his brethren, that he might become a merciful and faithful high priest in things pertaining to God, to make propitiation for the sins of the people." The same truth appears in another form in Galatians 4 : 4, 5: " When the fulness of the time came, God sent forth his Son, born of a woman, born under the law, that he might redeem them that were under the law, that we might receive the adoption of sons." There are numerous other passages which are equally explicit, such as John 1 : 1-18; Philippians 2 : 5-11; Colossians 1 : 14-20.

The conclusion from these New Testament teachings is that the incarnation was God's method of coming into saving relations with mankind. By this means Jesus became one with the race in a profound and real sense.

Now this unity and identity of Christ with mankind had a backward and a forward reference. The backward reference was to his original relation to the human race. As we have already seen, man was made in the image of Christ. He is the natural bond of mankind. The new spiritual head of that race was the original creative head. In becoming flesh, as John declares, Jesus Christ came to " his own " although " his own rejected him."

The forward reference of Christ's unity with mankind is to his causal action in our salvation. He took flesh, entered human conditions, in order that he might become an effective power for man's redemption. The power of sin rendered man incapable of self-redemption. He could not lift himself above himself. A new power from without was required, and yet a power acting from within according to moral and spiritual laws.

Thus we see that the backward reference of the incarnation connects Christ with God. He was the divine Son. The forward reference connects him with our need, deliverance from the power of sin and the attainment of righteousness. Being one with God and one with man he could act for both.

[316]

One caution is needed here. The unity of Christ with the race in no way affects the other truth of his apartness from the race by reason of his sinlessness. He was one with mankind, but "separate from sinners." Hence in two respects the unity is a qualified unity. As sinless he remained apart from sinful men. As sinless he could do for them what they could not do for themselves.

(2) We remark, in the second place, that as God's means for securing our salvation the atonement of Christ implied a previous life of obedience. The atoning death was itself an act of obedience. Theology has sometimes made much of the distinction between the active and the passive obedience of Christ. But it is a distinction difficult to maintain consistently. The active and passive elements were combined at every stage. In his career as teacher and preacher he constantly suffered. Heroic endurance was the constant task of his holy will against human unbelief and sin and "the gainsaying of sinners." The passive elements entered all the so-called active obedience. On the other hand the so-called passive obedience was also active. One of the most remarkable things about the death of Jesus was its voluntariness. He willed to die. In John 10 : 14-18 he states this truth and emphasizes it by repetition several times. In verse 15 he says, "I lay down my life for the sheep." Again in verse 17, "Therefore doth the Father love me, because I lay down my life that I may take it again." Then in order to bring into sharp and clear expression the fact that his death was the result of his own voluntary act he says: "No one taketh it away from me, but I lay it down of myself. I have power to lay it down and I have power to take it again" (ver. 18). Again in John 19 : 30 it is declared of Jesus on the cross that he said: "It is finished; and he bowed his head and gave up his Spirit." The expression "gave up" may be translated "sent forth," as indicating his own act. Again in Hebrews 9 : 14 the statement is made that Christ "through the eternal Spirit offered himself without blemish unto God"; and in Hebrews 10 : 1-10, in which reference is made to Christ's sacrificial death, the central

truth is declared to be his own moral act of obedience: "Then said I, Lo, I am come (in the volume of the book it is written of me) to do thy will, O God."

Our conclusion is that in every act of his life Christ conformed to the perfect moral law. Or rather we should say he was the embodiment, the incarnation of the moral ideal. It was the moral ideal in its filial form. His life was the perfect answer of the Son to the supreme requirements of the holy Father.

(3) We remark, in the third place, that the atonement as God's means for securing the salvation of men involved the subjection of Christ to the operation of the law of sin and death. The bare historical fact of Christ's death is clear evidence of this truth. Jesus died despite the fact that he was holy. We have already cited Scriptures which teach that remission of sin is thus secured. There is great abundance of material on the subject. A few leading passages will suffice. In 1 Peter 2 : 24 we read, "who his own self bare our sins in his body on the tree, that we, having died unto sins, might live unto righteousness." Again in 2 Corinthians 5 : 21 we read: "Him who knew no sin he made to be sin on our behalf; that we might become the righteousness of God in him." Again, in Romans 3 : 24-26 there are a number of statements made, summing up the essential points in the atoning work of Christ as follows: (a) We are justified freely by his grace; (b) God set forth Christ as a propitiation for our sins; (c) the benefits are available to us through faith; (d) the object in view was the exhibition of God's righteousness, because of the passing over of former sins; and finally (e) that God might be just and the justifier of him that hath faith in Jesus.

The question arises: Why was it necessary for Christ to suffer death in order to redeem sinners? This is the point of chief difficulty in the doctrine of the atonement. Here diverse answers are given. Here controversy arises. And yet if we avoid abstractions about law, and wrath, and justice, and deal with the concrete realities, with the facts themselves, the answer to the question is not as difficult as some have made it. It was a necessary means to a definite end.

[318]

Here we must keep in mind a few cardinal facts. The first is the necessary connection between sin and death. "The wages of sin is death" (Rom. 6 : 23). Death is related to sin as penalty. This means not physical death only, but also spiritual death or separation from God. The connection between sin and death is not an arbitrary appointment of God. It is the expression of an eternal law of the divine nature itself. Our own spiritual consciousness confirms the law. Death, or separation from God in our moral and spiritual consciousness, is the negation of all life and blessedness, of all peace and holiness.

A second fact to be kept in mind is that the law of sin and death was operative in the sinful race. The sin-death principle, as we may call it, held man in its power. It was a racial power affecting all mankind.

A third fact to be borne in mind is that if men are to be redeemed from the power of the sin-death principle, that power must be broken. It must be annulled. This is clearly Paul's view of the matter. He says in Romans 8 : 2, "For the law of the Spirit of life in Christ Jesus made me free from the law of sin and death." In the third verse he continues, "For what the law could not do, in that it was weak through the flesh, God, sending his own Son in the likeness of sinful flesh and for sin, condemned sin in the flesh."

The thought in Paul's mind is this: This sin-death principle operative in humanity must be overcome and destroyed by the obedience-life principle operative in Christ. In other words, Christ's death was God's means of relating himself in a saving way to sinful men. Christ became organically one with men, even to the point of dying for them in order that his righteousness might become a saving power in the race. The law of the Spirit of life in him overcame thus the law of sin and death in them. The atonement was thus a means adopted to secure a definite end. The end and means were not arbitrary appointments. Both arose out of inherent necessities in the moral kingdom. They were grounded in the moral nature of God and man. They are a clear instance of spiritual cause and effect.

VI. ATONEMENT AND THE DIVINE IMMANENCE

Light is shed on the atonement when we consider it as God's method of becoming immanent in a sinful race. God's transcendence is a truth to be kept always in mind. Its correlative truth is God's immanence in the world. God is everywhere immanent (that is, he indwells) in nature. He also indwells in man so far as his body and his moral constitution are concerned. But God is not immanent in man's sin- and guilt-consciousness as he is elsewhere. Sin has separated man from God. Yet God must dwell in man if man is to become God's holy son.

The absence of God from the natural human consciousness is seen in the failure to attain the moral ideal. Man perceives the right as an ideal, but attains the ideal at no point in his experience. The moral ideal transcends him. It is an ideal rooted in God for which man hungers and thirsts, but which he cannot attain.

Jesus Christ is the supreme and perfect embodiment in human form of the moral ideal. The incarnation, therefore, is the descent of the transcendent moral ideal in God into the human race. It is God becoming immanent in the race. It is the transcendent God becoming immanent in the world among free beings, who are held by the power of sin, in order to its salvation. The death of Christ on the cross was thus the God of holy love projecting himself into the life of the race by overcoming the sin-death principle in the race. In other words, God's immanence thus becomes a new law of life, operating in an ethical and spiritual manner for the salvation of men. It is a new life force acting graciously for human redemption. If Christ's approach to man had stopped short of dying, if he had been translated without tasting death, he would have remained apart from man at the point of his deepest need. He would have then disclosed a shining moral goal indeed, but it would have been left suspended in midair with no point of contact for sinners. It would have remained transcendent. Men would have remained powerless to attain it.

The gift of the Holy Spirit was necessary to complete the process of the divine immanence through the atonement. The day of Pentecost was a necessary sequel to the event on Calvary. The life in and through Christ must become a reality in the heart of the individual and in the Christian community. Now the Holy Spirit's work is to take the things of Christ and show them to believers. This means the creation in them of Christ's moral image. The attainment of Christ's moral image is the destiny of all Christians. And the beginning of the Spirit's work in the individual takes the form of a death to sin and a resurrection to righteousness. The sin-death principle is first of all broken, annulled, in the individual consciousness. The cross-principle is cardinal in the new creation in Jesus Christ.

In this way the mystical or spiritual union between Christ and the believer takes place. As Paul expresses it: " I have been crucified with Christ; and it is no longer I that live, but Christ that liveth in me, and that life which I now live in the flesh I live in faith, the faith which is in the Son of God, who loved me and gave himself up for me " (Gal. 2 : 20). In short, Paul is so conscious of the presence of Christ in him and of the death of the old nature that he has become a new person. The old man is dead. A new man has arisen. The new man is simply the growing image of Christ in him. Thus God in Christ has become immanent in Paul's consciousness through the creative activity of the Holy Spirit. Spiritual cause and effect come into clear expression here. The destruction of the sin-death principle on the cross when Christ made atonement, has become a redemptive force in the inner life of Paul through the destruction of the sin-death principle in him. The transcendent moral ideal in God passed through Calvary into the human consciousness. The historic act now issues in subjective experience. Atonement becomes reconciliation within as well as without. In becoming flesh and dying Christ became one with the race of sinners. In regeneration and justification he becomes one with the individual, and through the redeemed individuals he creates a new race.

v

The Christian Religion in Its Doctrinal Expression

VII. The Vital and Legal Elements in the Atonement

The preceding exposition has dealt with the vital principle in the atonement. There is also a legal element. But by legal we do not mean any artificial or merely external or arbitrary arrangement. We mean simply that the vital principle of the atonement is the expression of moral and spiritual law. Most of the errors as to the atonement have arisen through a failure to conceive and treat properly the relation of the vital to the so-called legal element. The atonement is the transformation and glorification of law. In it law becomes the expression of life. Writers have often defined law in an abstract artificial manner and then proceeded to demolish what they called a " legal " or " judicial " atonement. In so doing they failed to grasp the New Testament point of view.

Let us consider now the elements of law in the atoning work of Christ. We can best do so by a series of questions and answers.

1. The first question is, How was the atoning death of Christ the satisfaction of law? The answer is that it was the satisfaction of those laws which were involved in the atoning act itself. The idea of law or justice is not to be conceived abstractly, as if it were something apart from God, a hungry beast, waiting to be satisfied. Christ satisfied law and justice in the atonement because at all points he conformed to the requirements of the eternally Holy One whose laws found expression in the moral order. Christ entered to make atonement. The laws, then, which Christ satisfied and to which in his atoning work he conformed, were simply those laws which he encountered in the saving enterprise itself. There are at least four forms or aspects of law which were involved: (1) The moral law generally, including the Mosaic law. He fulfilled in his person the highest moral ideal. That ideal is grounded in God's nature. His obedience was perfect. It was law embodied in a life. (2) He became subject also to the operation of the law of sin and death. This was also the expression of the divine nature. The death penalty

is the negative aspect of the law of holiness. It is God's reaction against sin, but he became so identified with sinners that he suffered death at their hands and in himself bore the consequences of their sin. (3) He also obeyed perfectly the law of filial loyalty and devotion. The filial ideal is simply the moral law in its highest expression. He was the perfect Son, and nowhere did his sonship please the Father more than in his death for sinful men. (4) Thus also he satisfied the love of God for men. Love prompted the atonement. In it love as well as righteousness was completely fulfilled.

2. The next question is, In what sense were the sufferings of Christ penal? Ordinarily the words penal and penalty refer to personal guilt. Christ did not personally sin. Hence he could not have borne a penalty in the ordinary sense. But he did bear the penal consequences of the sin of the race because of his complete identification with it. Death is the penalty of sin. Christ died. He died at the hands of sinful men, while giving himself freely to deliver them from the power of the sin-death principle operative in them.

3. The third question is this, Did Christ in his death endure the wrath of God? Here again we need to remove a false conception of wrath. With God wrath is not angry passion. It is not vindictiveness or hatred. The wrath of God is his resistance against sin, his reaction against wrong-doing. This reaction expresses itself in penalty. The broadest expression of God's wrath is the death-penalty for sin. In his atoning death, therefore, we are not to conceive of God's wrath as poured out upon Christ's head and directed against him as a personal sinner. Christ endured the wrath of God only in the sense that he permitted the sin-death principle to operate in him. Wrath was already acting against sinful men. Christ endured it because he entered the estate of sinful man and endured death which is the expression of God's wrath and the penalty for their sin. The bloody sweat and prayer for deliverance in the garden, and the cry of the forsaken one on the cross suggest the depths of Christ's sufferings for sinners. God of course did not really

forsake Christ, but in his death there was, in some real sense, beyond our power to fathom, a clouding of his consciousness of God. He entered the region and shadow of death for human sin.

4. A fourth question is, In what sense was the death of Christ a propitiation? The word propitiation signifies a means of rendering favorable. We have already seen that Christ's death did not purchase God's love for us. It did not convert hate into its opposite. But Christ's death was a means of rendering God favorable in that God can now bestow upon the race the riches of his grace in Christ because Christ is now one with the race. In his death Christ became forever identified with men, and in principle all the fulness that dwelt in Christ belongs to mankind. "The law of the Spirit of life" in Christ is now operative in the human race. Christ's death was a propitiation further in that it exhausted the judgment of God against sin. He put an end to the reign of death by his victorious death and resurrection. This was an appeasing of God's wrath against sin. He thus removed the wrath of God from men who were under the power of the sin-death principle. Christ also broke the power of Satan in his death and delivered those who were held in his power. Thus his atonement was a means not of making God love us, but of making the free exercise of his love possible and consistent with his own inherent antagonism to sin.

5. A fifth question is, Was or was not the death of Christ substitutionary? The answer is that in the nature of the case it could not have been otherwise. But here again we must put aside merely commercial and abstract conceptions of substitution and construe the principle in terms of divine spiritual laws and life.

We may conveniently discuss the question of substitution by considering first the fact and then the principle of substitution.

(1) The fact of substitution. The New Testament teaching does not leave the matter doubtful. It is not merely a question of the use of the Greek prepositions *anti,* which means "instead of," and *huper,* which means "in behalf of." The former is

employed in clear reference to Christ's atoning work, although the latter is the prevailing word in such references. But *huper* does not exclude the meaning " instead of," but rather includes it as a possible element in a larger meaning. " In behalf of " does not necessarily mean " instead of," but " instead of " does mean also " in behalf of." The argument, however, does not turn upon the use merely of these prepositions. The idea of substitution is inseparable from the facts, and various passages of Scripture declare it.

Consider the following facts: The sinless died for the sinful. He broke the reign of the sin-death principle in his death and resurrection. The benefits of his obedience and conquest of death become ours by faith. In this work the Saviour can be thought of as sustaining either of two relations to us. We might think of him as our representative. But this is not an adequate conception. We did not appoint him. Man did not send him. He did not bear man's message to God, but God's message to man. Christ indeed becomes our representative after we believe in him, but prior to that our relation to him is one of antagonism. He is our representative only after we approve his work and obey his gospel.

The other possible relationship is that of substitution. What he did for us we could not do for ourselves. We could not, as sinful, die an atoning death for the sinful. As victims of the sin-death principle reigning in humanity, we could not become its conqueror. We could not break the power of death and annul the law of sin and death. But Christ did both these things for us. This is substitution. Various passages make it clear. In 1 Corinthians 6 : 20 we read: " For ye were bought with a price: glorify God therefore in your body." In 1 Corinthians 7 : 23 the same general statement is repeated. The figure of a purchase here is of course not one which can be carried through at all points. But it clearly means that Christ paid something for our salvation which we could not pay. He assumed our responsibility and discharged it in a real and vital way. Observe again, it is not a mere matter of bookkeeping. What Christ did for us does not exempt us from moral obligation. It became rather the new creative force which generates in us power to attain the moral ideal. But he did act and he did achieve for us at a point where we were helpless and thus acted in our stead.

In Galatians 3 : 13 we read, " Christ redeemed us from the curse of the law, having become a curse for us." Some have pronounced this text a remnant of Paul's Jewish legalism. But in this they misread Paul. Beyond doubt Paul's desire here is to clear away Jewish objections. But his whole aim is to go behind the outward Jewish law to the new life principle, faith. The next verse shows this : " That upon the Gentiles might come the blessing of Abraham in Christ Jesus, that we might receive the promise of the Spirit through faith." Thus the end of Christ's work in becoming a curse for us is to create a spiritual religion in place of a legal. Mark this point clearly. Here, as elsewhere, when Paul sets forth the gospel in Jewish or legalistic forms of statement or habits of thought, his aim is to show how legalism and Judaism are abolished. Here he says in effect : The moral consciousness of the sinner knows itself condemned, under the curse of God. This is peculiarly true of the Jew with his training in the Mosaic law. And it is true of him in proportion to his appreciation of the true moral ideal. The law of sin and death is self-evident to the morally enlightened. The atonement of Christ abolishes the legalistic method in God's dealing with men, because in it Christ acted in our stead when he abolished the law of sin and death. He substituted the obedience-life principle for the sin-death principle. He did this by a vital union with men as subject to the law with them. He did it supremely in his atoning work.

Very much the same in meaning is the declaration in 2 Corinthians 5 : 21 : " Him who knew no sin he made to be sin on our behalf; that we might become the righteousness of God in him." Of course this does not mean that Jesus was made a sinner, but it does mean that he acted for sinners in relation to their sin in a manner which enabled them to escape the consequences of their sin.

The Saving Work of Christ

The Old Testament teaching confirms the New Testament. It supplies the background of thought for the New Testament view. John's word, " Behold the Lamb of God, that taketh away the sin of the world! " is rooted in the soil of the Old Testament. It has been held by some that the Old Testament sacrifices do not teach a substitution, but rather that they are a presentation of gifts to Jehovah, or symbolize restored fellowship. In reply, it may be said that these explanations come far short of explaining all the meaning in those sacrifices, although they contain part of the truth. Certain phases of these offerings make clear the ideas of sin and guilt and atonement by substitution. The regulations regarding the day of atonement show this clearly. (See Lev. 16 : 1-34. Cf. Exod. 32 : 30-32.) The scapegoat suggests vividly the element of taking away the sin of the people; and the offering of the blood of the sacrifice in the most holy place reflects the idea of propitiation or expiation. The idea in all these sacrifices is that the blood is the life. Isaiah 53 : 1-12 is an Old Testament interpretation of sacrifice in unequivocal terms. The victim is here a man and not an animal. But substitution is expressed in various forms too clearly to be gainsaid. " He hath borne our griefs, and carried our sorrows " (ver. 4) ; " He was wounded for our transgressions, he was bruised for our iniquities; the chastisement of our peace was upon him; and with his stripes we are healed " (ver. 5). " Jehovah hath laid on him the iniquity of us all " (ver. 6).

(2) We consider next the principle of substitution. There are many modern writers who fail to grasp the spiritual quality in the substitutionary element in the death of Christ, and seek to empty it of that element entirely. Or else they put in place of it a conception of sympathetic suffering designed to set forth the love of God. We do not deny sympathy of course. We only affirm that there was more than sympathy in Christ's death. It contains every form and phase of love.

We may illumine the principle of substitution by showing it in its relations to personality, morality, Christian experience, and the original connection between Christ and the race. This will demonstrate that substitution as applied to Christ's death is not a mechanical artificial transaction, but an ethical living reality.

a. Substitution and personality. Consider a case of physical substitution by way of contrast. A builder might put a block of granite in the place of a block of wood to support the corner of a building, because the latter proved insufficient for the burden. This is simple physical substitution of one body for another. But in the personal realm physical laws do not apply. Here psychic and moral relations control. Whatever takes place is by way of free causation. And yet the human personality has a capacity for changing other personalities, which is well-nigh boundless. The man who struck the revolutionary patriot, James Otis, and silenced him, projected his malign personality into American history, and influenced it profoundly. The murderer of Abraham Lincoln projected his wicked will into the destiny of the nation, and changed the course of events. A child born in an African jungle and destined for savagery is transferred through an act of love to a Christian environment in a Christian land, and becomes a saint. In all these cases we are dealing not with the ordinary power of influence, good or bad, nor with mere sympathetic relations. These are forms of substitution. The personal realm is so constituted that one personality can project itself for good or ill into the destinies of other personalities. Now if this is true of men generally, it is even more true of Christ, to whom we owe our personality. He made us persons, in his own image. We are constituted persons in him. This truth underlies all his mediatorial work for us. It binds him to us in unique ways. It makes possible especially all his redemptive relations to us.

b. Substitution and morality. The moral ideal attains its most perfect expression in love for others. To be just and fair, to speak truth, these are high forms of expression for the moral law. But self-denying love is the highest form. Now the question of substitution is simply a question of how far love can go in the service of others. Christianity teaches that it can take the place of another. Take the case of the New England teacher, Bronson Alcott, who sought to impress the value of law and discipline upon his pupils by requiring the offender to punish their teacher. No wonder the offender was broken-hearted. The exhibition of vicarious love, combined with stern loyalty, was a tremendous moral dynamic. Other instances of this kind are on record. Men deny substitution in the atonement because they do not conceive it in high ethical terms. The highest form of love is substitutionary love.

c. Substitution and Christian experience. Paul's words are: " I have been crucified with Christ; and it is no longer I that live, but Christ liveth in me " (Gal. 2 : 20). Consider these remarkable words. The old personality of Paul died. A new personality has arisen. Paul was never more free, never more conscious of his liberty as a Christian. Yet he says: " It is no longer I that live. Another lives in me. My present personality is his personality. What I am now is all derived from Christ. Indeed it is Christ who lives in me." Here was the substitution of Christ's life for Paul's old life, Christ's personality for Paul's old personality.

Now it was with such an experience that Paul viewed and interpreted the cross of Christ. What had taken place in Paul's personal experience had taken place in a racial way when Christ died. In his atoning death Jesus projected himself as a redeeming power into a sin-laden race. It was easy for Paul to grasp this. His own experience of the substitution of Christ in place of his old pharisaic consciousness made it easy for him to perceive the great truth that Christ's atoning work was also substitutionary in relation to mankind.

d. Substitution and Christ's original relation to the race. The union of deity and humanity in Christ made possible the atoning work. As divine he sustained a relation to God which an ordinary man could not sustain, and as the divine man he could do for men what another could not do. Substitution here is not simply a transfer of moral responsibility from one man to another man, nor was it merely a good man made a substitute for bad men to glut a divine vengeance. This latter form of objection is often raised. It is alleged that it makes the atonement immoral. But it loses its force the moment we recognize Christ's relation to the race as Creator. If human personality can project itself into the lives of others, and if human love can empty self to the point of substitution for other selves, much more can the divine-human Christ project his personality and manifest his love thus. We must never lose sight of the fact that the person of Christ gives its dignity and value to his atoning work.

VIII. The Godward and Manward Reference of the Atonement

We come back to the old question at issue between the various theories of the atonement, *viz.,* whether the work of Christ on the cross referred to God or man or both; whether the necessity for atonement was in God or man. In view of the preceding discussion there can be but one answer to the question. The necessity was in both God and man.

1. We note first the Godward reference. We were not content to say with Anselm that God's honor was maintained, nor with Grotius that God's government was secured by the atoning work of Christ. These are external aspects of God's character. God's honor and government are indeed preserved. But this is because these are outward expressions of God's nature, and not the very inner nature itself. The atonement of Christ was the deepest expression of God's righteous love. The form it took was due to the moral order God established in making man a free being in his own image. What we call moral law is the expression of God's nature. The law of sin and death is simply the other side of the moral law and equally an expression of that nature. The divine necessity in the atonement antedates, therefore, the act itself. It arose when sin entered. Indeed, its ground in God antedated sin. It is an eternal necessity by reason of what God is in himself. In tracing the atonement to its source, then, we do not stop with the divine law, or the divine government, or the divine honor. We pass through these to something deeper, the divine nature. That, and that most of all, is the spring and source of atoning love. The necessity involved in the work of

the Redeemer was perfect conformity to the moral ideal, and subjection to the operation of the sin-death principle in the sinful race of man. This conformity and subjection were required because the nature of man and the moral order in which he sinned was an expression of God's own moral nature. Entering that moral order to redeem men, the Redeemer must needs conform to the laws of its constitution.

From all this then it is clear that the atonement was based on a necessity in God. But it was also God's gift. He gave his Son. It follows, of course, that God accepted it as sufficient for its purpose.

An objection has been urged here to the effect that God could not both demand and provide the atonement. This objection is only apparent. God requires repentance from the sinner and bestows it. He requires all moral perfection and imparts it. Augustine expressed the essential nature of God's relations to us in the prayer, " Give what thou commandest, and command what thou wilt." We are made dependent on God, and we are made free and responsible. The atonement was a fulfilment of both these relations.

Another objection is that God's love could not be free if it required an atonement in order to forgiveness. The objection has already been met in what has been said. The freeness of God's forgiving love is enhanced rather than clouded by the gift of Christ. The same objection would hold against the incarnation itself. The fact is that the love of God never acted more freely than in the incarnation and atonement. It was love breaking down all barriers to reach men. It was " love outloving love." It was grace which superabounded where sin abounded.

2. Consider next the manward reference of the atonement. This reference may be summed up in the following points:

(1) The atonement produces in man an adequate repentance. It reveals the nature of sin, its hatefulness to God and God's judgment against it. Only through it does the sinner understand sin. And only as he understands it can he truly repent. The sinner sees in the cross that God freely forgives, but not without

cost to God. That cost in suffering is as freely provided as forgiveness is freely bestowed. The cost of atonement awakens in the sinner a just appreciation of sin. Thus only does he truly repent. He is forgiven then because the atonement has produced in him a forgivable state. All the truth in the moral influence theory, and more, is contained in the above statement.

(2) The atonement destroys the legal consciousness of the sinner by becoming the ground of his justification. Justification by faith is God's method of enabling sinful men to pass from the legal to the filial consciousness. Many have greatly misunderstood justification and discarded it as a remnant of Paul's Judaism, a merely legalistic conception of salvation. It is exactly the reverse. It is Paul's way of destroying Jewish legalism. If justification be confined in meaning to what occurs in a law-court when a criminal is pardoned, and if faith be restricted in meaning to a bare belief of the bare truth, then justification by faith is Judaistic and legalistic. But this is a perversion of the New Testament meaning of justification and of faith.

In the justification taught in the New Testament, God reckons to us our faith in Christ for righteousness. (See Rom. 4 : 3-8; also 4 : 22-25.) And faith according to the New Testament results in a vital union with Christ. Thus a vital life-union is combined with a formal declaration. The formal declaration is that penalty is remitted, condemnation removed, a new status bestowed. But this formal declaration is not all. A new life-union is established. The justification of the New Testament is lifted clear above all mere legalism by the qualifying phrase, " by faith." The faith principle in justification thus changes the formal and legal side into something vital. At the same time the formal declaration or reckoning of faith for righteousness clears the sinner's mind forever of all doubt as to his standing with God. Until that declaration is made in that justifying act of God in his behalf, he can only have a legal consciousness. The man who knows the meaning of sin and has a sense of guilt and condemnation, can never rise above the wavering doubt, the hesitation, and unrest of spiritual struggle, without a justifying act on God's part. He can never rise to the unclouded filial confidence and love until the problem of sin and condemnation is out of the way.

We conclude, then, that the New Testament doctrine of justification by faith based on the atoning work of Christ promotes moral and spiritual interests in two ways: First, it joins the soul to Christ in a living union which is potential of all moral attainment; and secondly, it provides for the needs of the sin- and guilt-consciousness of men and enables them thus to rise to the filial consciousness of true sons of God. Of course the doctrine of justification may be abused like all other good things. But if we can avoid abstractions about it and keep close to the New Testament modes of viewing it, the abuses will pass away.

It may be objected that the sin- and guilt-consciousness is merely subjective. Man imagines God's wrath which does not exist. He is haunted by the idea of condemnation and penalty when these are mere fictions of his imagination. This objection is common to most theories which seek to weaken the element of cost in the atonement. There are several lines of reply. One is that to explain away the sin- and guilt-consciousness is highly perilous to ethics. Our conscience is central in our moral nature. The sense of guilt is inherent in the sinful consciousness. Penalty goes with guilt both in our thought and in fact. The validity and truth of the guilt-consciousness are established by the fact of penalty in experience. We cannot eliminate suffering, especially death as the consequence of sin, from our experience. Bushnell and Harnack have recognized the fact of our guilt-consciousness and the need of atonement with its " altar forms " of substitution and propitiation while denying the objective need of these forms. But we may well conclude that if the need of the soul is so clearly defined in its consciousness of sin and guilt, the answer to the need must correspond in its foundation in fact.

Besides the above we add that the sin- and guilt-consciousness has as its correlative all the higher moral values. These values are high as their opposites are low. Virtue is exalted in the degree to which vice is degraded and degrading. The filial consciousness of God's sons is noble in a manner answering to the degree in which the opposite of that consciousness is ignoble. If we are to keep ethics pure and high, therefore, we must avoid weakening the sense of sin and explaining away the sense of guilt.

(3) The atonement is a powerful dynamic in human experience. As such it produces various kinds of moral and spiritual results. We can only mention a few.

a. One of these is psychic. The atonement of Christ creates in the saved man an assurance of his standing with God. The reconciliation which Christ effected on the cross, regarded as the ground of the sinner's acceptance with God, imparts to his life the power of an abiding conviction. Christians of course sometimes doubt. But they need not doubt. Moreover, the atoning work of Christ awakens in the believer the deepest springs of gratitude. It also humbles his pride since it awakens in him a sense of boundless obligation to Christ. The deepest springs of loyalty, love, and devotion are thus unstopped. This dynamic quality of the atonement is shown in the experience of Christians in many forms. Paul's own deathless devotion, his sublime loyalty, his sufferings and toils, were born of his deep sense of gratitude to the Son of God who, as he declares, " loved me and gave himself for me."

The same experience is reflected in the hymns of the Christian centuries. A deep sense of indebtedness to Christ runs through most of them. He is the soul's refuge from sin and temptation, its strength in sorrow, its hope for the future. These hymns have been criticized as lacking the " social note." The criticism may be partially just. The gospel properly understood is intensely social. But no efforts for social improvement can ever hope to succeed on a large scale if they lack the dynamic reenforcement of the gospel. Nothing could better promote social effort than a return to Christ's atonement and an interpretation of it in its social relations.

b. The atonement is a powerful dynamic in the moral and spiritual life of believers. The mystical union of the Christian with Christ is, as we have seen, the reproduction of the cross-principle in the spiritual life. The Christian life is summed up in the phrase " Christ in you the hope of glory."

It is here we see the answer to an old objection: " How can you explain the morality of punishing an innocent man that sinners may go free? Both acts are ethically indefensible." The objection is based on a false analogy and does not state the whole case. Christ is not simply " an innocent man." He is the Creator of the human race. When in atonement he assumes its responsibility, it is a part of the original responsibility involved in his creative act. Again, it is not simply a case of letting " criminals go free." Those who are set free through Christ are no longer criminals. He changes them into saints of God. He sustains a causal relation to their moral and spiritual life. He recreates them morally. In a word, Christ's historic act on the cross is also the beginning of a vital spiritual process in human hearts. The two things are indissolubly bound together.

A QUESTION AS TO THE ATTRIBUTES OF GOD IN THE ATONEMENT

We ask: What attribute or quality in God controls in the atonement? Is it righteousness, or is it love, or is it merely the divine sovereignty, which conditions the saving work of Christ? The reply is that it is no one of these alone, but all in combination. The atonement was not the mere appointment of the divine sovereignty, as some have claimed, without reference to other qualities in God. Nor was it a provision of his righteousness to which love was subordinate, nor of his love to which righteousness was secondary. The atonement was not the product of any mere attribute of God. It was the expression rather of the inner being of the righteous and loving God who was sovereign. God drew the world back to himself by a cord which was made up of two strands, righteousness and love. The atonement then was not a mere utilitarian expedient for accomplishing an end which might have been otherwise achieved. It was rather a divine enterprise in which the requirements of righteousness and of love were met at every stage. Here as elsewhere we must think of God as a unitary Being, and not permit the thought of separate attributes to mislead us.

THE EXTENT OF THE ATONEMENT

The atonement of Christ was for all men. His relation to mankind which has been set forth involves the consequence that he died for all. There are numerous passages of Scripture which leave no room for doubt. In John 3 : 16 it is declared that "God so loved the world" that he gave his Son; in Hebrews 2 : 9, "that by the grace of God he should taste of death for every man"; in 2 Peter 2 : 1 it is declared in regard to false teachers, doomed to destruction, that they denied "even the Master that bought them." In 1 John 2 : 2 we read, "he is the propitiation for our sins; and not for ours only, but also for the whole world." In 1 Timothy 2 : 6 again we find the same statement in this form, "Who gave himself a ransom for all." In Titus 2 : 11 we read, "For the grace of God hath appeared bringing salvation to all men." In 1 Timothy 4 : 10 a distinction is made between the race as a whole and those who believe. God is "the Saviour of all men, especially of them that believe."

This last passage makes clear the fact that all men do not share equally in the benefits of the atonement of Christ. Those who remain in unbelief are not saved. Yet even they share many of the common blessings of life through the work of Christ. God's anger against human sin is restrained in order that men may repent. Every motive and appeal is provided in the gospel to induce them to do so.

THE INTERCESSION OF CHRIST

The New Testament teaches that Christ intercedes for us now in the presence of the Father. We do not think of this as spoken prayer. It is rather his continued activity carrying out his atoning work and making it efficacious for men. "He ever liveth to make intercession for them" (Heb. 7 : 25). "If any man sin, we have an advocate with the Father" (1 John 2 : 1). " It is Christ Jesus that died . . . who also maketh intercession for us" (Rom. 8 : 34). Christ intercedes for transgressors (Isa. 53 : 12; Luke 23 : 34), and of course he intercedes for his people. The above passages make clear the latter point. There are many others. (Eph. 1 : 6; Acts 2 : 33; Matt. 18 : 19, 20; Heb. 2 : 17, 18.)

The Holy Spirit intercedes for us in our hearts. He teaches us to pray. He makes intercession for us with unutterable groanings. (Rom. 8 : 26, 27.) The intercession of Christ in heaven and that of the Spirit on earth are in perfect harmony. Here as elsewhere the Holy Spirit takes the things of Christ and shows them unto us.

W

CHAPTER XIV

ELECTION: GOD'S INITIATIVE IN SALVATION

I. GOD'S SOVEREIGNTY

IN a previous section (The Providence of God) we have briefly referred to the sovereignty of God. A number of closely related topics were there also discussed. It is necessary at this point to consider God's sovereignty in its relation to human salvation. This relation is usually expressed by the terms predestination or election. As will appear in due time, however, the question of election and predestination turns upon the question whether God or man takes the initiative in salvation. In this question are bound up all other issues involved in the general problem. Hence we have adopted as the principle to be expounded here God's initiative in the salvation of men. As in creation, so also in redemption, the fundamental truth is expressed in the language of Genesis 1 : 1, "In the beginning God." The motive, the method, and the end of human salvation all arose out of the nature of the infinitely holy God. The initiative was with God, not with man. This in brief is the ultimate meaning of the divine sovereignty as it relates to our salvation. All systems of theology in the end are bound to recognize it as a fundamental truth, despite the fact that many systems have failed to apply it consistently.

1. In approaching the subject we should avoid certain errors in the manner of conceiving God's sovereignty. Chief among these has been the habit of making the sovereignty of God depend upon his "mere will" or "good pleasure." It is the same kind of error which we discussed in connection with the atonement. Many of the same general cautions are necessary here. The danger is the fallacy of the abstract method. We are in danger of taking a single aspect, or attribute, of

quality in the divine nature instead of the divine nature as a whole. We may in our thoughts take God's will apart from his righteousness and apart from his love, and combine it with his infinite power. In so doing we are in danger of conceiving God as an arbitrary despot instead of a being who loves and seeks the good of all. In a word, we must avoid the abstract method and think of God as he is revealed in the Scriptures, and especially as he is supremely revealed in Christ. God is more than will. He is an infinite Person, rich in all moral attributes. He is the eternal Father, as Christ is the eternal Son. We must never, therefore, exalt the mere will of God, apart from his character as so revealed, in our efforts to define his sovereignty.

2. Some forms of the older Calvinism will serve as examples of the danger we are considering. There were two forms of it which may be mentioned. Both arose as the result of applying the rigid forms of logic to the idea of God's sovereignty as inhering in his will alone. One form asserted that God foreordained some men to eternal life for the exhibition of his love, and others to eternal death for the exhibition of his justice, and that he created men with these ends in view. It followed from this that the atonement of Christ was made not for the whole world, but for the elect alone. The other was a somewhat modified form of this view. It held that the purpose to create preceded the purpose to save. But along with this it was held that some were chosen for eternal salvation and others were chosen in the same way for eternal reprobation or damnation. The limited atonement was also an essential element in this view.

3. In these views we have a striking example of the abstract method. They were due to the fact that their authors conceived of God's "mere will" apart from his character, and with this false premise they proceeded by a rigid logic to their false conclusions. Undoubtedly these views contain one truth, which is that the salvation of individual men is to be traced to the initiative of God. He took the first steps and continued his gracious action until men believed and were saved. But it is

not true that God created men expressly in order that he might damn them, for he willeth that none should perish, but that all should live. It is not true that Christ's atonement was limited. It was a universal atonement, as we have already seen. It is not true that God acted in saving and condemning men in an arbitrary manner after the fashion of a human despot. He was and is the personal eternal and holy Father of our Lord Jesus Christ. All his dealings with mankind are consistent with this supreme fact. That it is so consistent was the chief burden of his revelation of himself to us in Christ.

In order that we may understand God's sovereignty in saving men, it is necessary that we trace briefly the biblical doctrine of his eternal purpose toward mankind. It is only in the light of this larger purpose that we can understand his method in saving individuals.

II. God's Purpose Toward Mankind

If we abandon the abstract way of thinking of God's sovereignty and define it according to the teaching of Scripture, we find ourselves at once in a different atmosphere. Sovereignty at once becomes transformed into a glorious manifestation of God's love for the race of man. There are four statements which may be made to set forth this truth.

1. The first is that from the beginning God's gracious purpose has been not national, but racial. He has had in view not one family or nation, but the whole of mankind. There were chosen families and a chosen nation. But these were not only ends in themselves, they were also means toward a larger end. At one crisis in the world's history Noah and his family were chosen as the channel of God's blessing to mankind. Later God chose Abraham, whose descendants became the nation of Israel. God's promise to Abraham was the disclosure of his purpose toward mankind: " I will make of thee a great nation, and I will bless thee and make thy name great; and be thou a blessing; and I will bless them that bless thee, and him that curseth thee will I curse: and in thee shall all the families of the earth be blessed "

(Gen. 12 : 2, 3). This promise was repeated to Abraham many times in substantially the same form. We do not rightly understand the calling of Abraham unless we see in him the manifestation of God's world-wide purpose of grace.

2. The second statement is that the course of Old Testament history clearly shows that the unvarying and consistent purpose of God was the bestowal of his favor upon the world at large through Israel. Israel became a nation, an elect and holy people. In the end it was destroyed because of pride and self-righteousness and spiritual blindness. God had made her an exclusive people for a world-wide end. She became pharisaical in spirit. But the spiritual treasure she bore was not lost to mankind. We need only to read the messages of the prophets in all the great crises of the nation to understand God's all-inclusive plan which he was working out through Israel. Isaiah recalls to Israel the message of Jehovah, " I will also give thee for a light to the Gentiles, that thou mayest be my salvation unto the end of the earth " (Isa. 49 : 6). Again he says: " For behold, darkness shall cover the earth, and gross darkness the peoples; but Jehovah will arise upon thee, and his glory shall be upon thee. And nations shall come to thy light, and kings to the brightness of thy rising " (Isa. 60 : 2, 3). These passages represent a great class of prophetic utterances. When the nation was broken up by the captivity the prophets came with their enlarged conceptions of God as the key to the meaning of the great tragedy.

3. The third statement is that the incarnation and atonement of Christ imply and involve the same world-wide purpose of God's grace. Christ was the " Son of man," and not merely a Jew of the first century. His incarnation made him organic with mankind. As we have already seen, his atonement was for all. The Great Commission expressly includes " all nations " and " every creature " in the destination of the gospel. (Matt. 28 : 19, 20; Mark 16 : 15, 16.)

4. The fourth statement is that the New Testament history and teaching generally confirms the above interpretation of the incarnation and atonement. The book of Acts records the spread

of the gospel among the Gentiles. The choice of the apostle Paul and his mission especially signalize the universality of the gospel. His doctrine of justification by faith was squarely against the Jewish narrowness which would have required converts to become Jews in principle and practice. In Ephesians Paul declares that the universality of the gospel was the secret of the ages now made known through Christ. (See Eph. 2 and 3, especially 3 : 4-13.) The book of Revelation in many places gives us visions of great multitudes from every nation and kindred and tribe and tongue redeemed unto God through the blood of Jesus Christ.

From the foregoing we draw the following conclusions: First, the details of God's sovereign plan for men can best be understood in the light of his larger plan for the race. His method of saving individual men can best be understood only in its context of the larger plan and purpose. Secondly, all that may at first sight seem arbitrary or capricious in God's dealing with men ceases to be so when viewed in the light of his gracious purpose toward mankind. Thirdly, when there are delays in the execution of his gracious purpose it is not due to indifference on his part to human welfare. It arises rather out of the needs of the situation. The New Testament writers, especially Paul, speak of the " fulness of times " as a principle in the unfolding of God's plan. Delay may be essential to the final end in view. A fourth conclusion is that God has never lost interest in the Gentile nations. He has never relinquished his claims upon them. He has ever planned great and gracious things for them. A fifth conclusion is that while logic is good in itself, it may easily go astray if it starts with a false premise, such as the mere " will " of God conceived of apart from his revealed purpose toward all nations, his good-will toward all mankind. This truth must never be overlooked.

III. THE SALVATION OF INDIVIDUALS

We can best discuss the sovereignty of God in the salvation of individuals by asking and answering a series of questions. The first question will deal with the crucial point of difference between opposing theories of election.

1. Does God choose men to salvation because of their good works or because he foresees they will believe when the gospel is preached to them? Beyond doubt God foresees their faith. Beyond doubt faith is a condition of salvation. The question is whether it is also the ground of salvation. The Scriptures answer this question in the negative. The gospel is efficacious with some and not efficacious with others because God's grace is operative in the one case beyond the degree of its action in the other. There are many passages which teach this. We cite a few. Jesus says to the disciples: "Ye did not choose me, but I chose you and appointed you, that ye should go and bear fruit, and that your fruit should abide; that whatsoever ye shall ask of the Father in my name, he will give it you" (John 15 : 16). Observe here that the disciples were chosen not as an end in itself merely, but as a means to fruit-bearing, and that this latter end was to be achieved through prayer. The election included in its scope the good works which were to follow the faith. It included also the power in prayer which was to be the expression of the faith. Salvation is rich in contents. It is not a bare deliverance from sin. The faith which is the condition of justification is also the germ of a fruitful life.

Again, Jesus says: "All that which the Father giveth me shall come unto me; and him that cometh to me I will in no wise cast out" (John 6 : 37). Again he says: "No man can come to me except the Father that sent me draw him: and I will raise him up in the last day" (John 6 : 44). In connection with the preaching of Paul and Barnabas we read, "As many as were ordained to eternal life believed" (Acts 13 : 48). In Romans 8 : 29, 30 Paul joins together God's foreknowledge, his foreordination, his calling, his justification, and his final glorification of the saints in a bond of spiritual unity and traces all back to the eternal purpose of God. And in Romans 9 : 11-13 the apostle refers to the fact that prior to their birth, before Esau or Jacob could know good and evil, and in order that "the purpose of God according to the election might stand," he chose Jacob. In Ephesians 1 : 4 he declares that God chose us in Christ before the foundation of the world.

In close connection with the above truth is the further truth that faith, repentance, and good works are all the gift of God. In Romans 12 : 3 we read as to faith, "according as God hath dealt to each man a measure of faith." Again, in Ephesians 2 : 8, 9: "For by grace have ye been saved through faith; and that not of yourselves; it is the gift of God; not of works, that no man should glory."

As to repentance the same type of teaching appears. In Acts 5 : 31 we read, "Him did God exalt with his right hand to be a Prince and a Saviour, to give repentance to Israel and remission of sins." In Acts 11 : 18 also, "Then to the Gentiles also hath God granted repentance unto life."

The good works of Christians are also attributed to God. In Philippians 2 : 12, 13 we read: "Work out your own salvation with fear and trembling; for it is God who worketh in you both to will and to work for his good pleasure." And again, in Ephesians 2 : 10, "For we are his workmanship, created in Christ Jesus for good works, which God afore prepared that we should walk in them."

It would be easy to multiply passages showing how the calling of sinners effectually to repentance, their regeneration and conversion, are all attributed to God's initiative and grace. (See Acts 18 : 9, 10; John 1 : 13; 1 John 4 : 10; 1 Cor. 1 : 24-29; 11 : 29; Gal. 1 : 15, 16.)

2. The second question concerns the human will and choice: Does God's election coerce man's will, or does it leave it free? The answer is emphatically that the will of man is not coerced, but is left free. In his free act of accepting Christ and his salvation man is self-determined. He would not have made the choice if left to himself without the aid of God's grace. But when he chooses, it is his own free act. God's grace is not "irresistible" as a physical force is irresistible. Grace does not act as a physical force. It is a moral and spiritual and personal power.

Here we confront a great fundamental truth, *viz.*, the moral, spiritual, and personal method of divine grace in saving men. This truth contains several other subordinate truths, as follows:

(1) God's appeal to men through the gospel is addressed to the faculties and powers in man which distinguish him as a moral, spiritual, and personal being. Man has intelligence. The gospel appeal is addressed to the intelligence. As Paul expressed it, "Knowing therefore the fear of the Lord, we persuade men" (2 Cor. 5 : 11). The gospel is a gospel of argument and persuasion. Again, man has conscience. The gospel is an intensely moral appeal directed to the deepest moral consciousness of man. Paul adds to the preceding statement: "but we are made manifest unto God; and I hope that we are made manifest also in your consciences" (2 Cor. 5 : 11). The gospel is thus a moral tonic. Again, man has emotions. The gospel appeals to all proper human emotions. Hope is a large element in it. "For in hope were we saved" (Rom. 8 : 24). Love is aroused to its depths by the gospel message. Nothing else avails if love is wanting. (1 Cor. 13.) The gospel produces godly sorrow: "For godly sorrow worketh repentance unto salvation, a repentance which bringeth no regret" (2 Cor. 7 : 10). And so on through the list of human emotions. The gospel purifies and stimulates all human emotions. Again, man has will. The gospel appeal is addressed to the will. The disobedient will alone prevents the salvation of men. Jesus said to the Jews, "And ye will not come to me that ye may have life" (John 5 : 40). In his words to Jerusalem he said, "How often would I have gathered thy children together, even as a hen gathereth her chickens under her wings, and ye would not" (Matt. 23 : 37). Thus the gospel arouses the will. We repeat then that the gospel of God's grace acts as a moral and spiritual and personal force, and not as a physical force. Men have been ever prone to think of electing grace as if it were dynamite or some other kind of material force compelling men instead of a moral force persuading them. Grace does not become effective until men freely respond to it. The preacher's appeal may be to hope or fear. He may cover the

entire range of human emotions. He may appeal to the reason, the will, the conscience, the imagination. But whatever be his form of appeal, his message aims at a free response of man's will. God's grace acting through and along with God's message aims at the same result. It appears supremely as grace when it produces this free response in man.

(2) A second truth contained in the general truth that God's method is moral and spiritual and personal is this: To reach men through the divinely given powers and faculties, God employs a system of means. Among these the most prominent are the church and its ordinances, the lives of Christians, the ministry, the Bible. In a word, the means and apparatus of the gospel conform to God's moral and spiritual and personal method. It is not a priesthood with exclusive rights to approach God, but a universal priesthood. It is not a church which saves, but a church which is the spiritual home of the saved. It is not sacraments possessing magical power, but ordinances which symbolize the truth for the discerning disciple. It is not human custodians of the grace of God bestowing it upon those who become obedient to the church, but preachers proclaiming a salvation for all who will believe. In all respects the means are thus moral and spiritual. The electing grace of God acts through such means and achieves the salvation of men.

(3) A third truth is that the Holy Spirit acts in conformity with God's moral and spiritual and personal method. The work of the Holy Spirit is to teach, to guide, to lead, to take the things of Christ and show them to disciples. (John 16 : 7ff.) The work of the Holy Spirit is summed up as moral demonstration of the truth of the gospel. This appears in John 16 : 8-11, where his work is described as conviction of sin, of righteousness, and of judgment. It is not proof to the intellect merely. It is not a stirring of the emotions merely. It is not sheer power exerted upon the will of man. It is rather a work which contains all these elements in a conviction or moral conquest in the soul. Paul employs a like form of statement where he declares that his preaching was in " demonstration of the Spirit and of

power " (1 Cor. 2 : 4). God's moral and spiritual and personal method in the gospel thus includes a moral demonstration within the soul by the Holy Spirit of God.

Let us now restate the doctrine of election in the light of these truths. Election is not to be thought of as a bare choice of so many human units by God's action independently of man's free choice and the human means employed. God elects men to respond freely. He elects men to preach persuasively and to witness convincingly. He elects to reach men through their native faculties and through the church, through evangelism and education and missionary endeavor. We must include all these elements in election. Otherwise we split the decree of God into parts and leave out an essential part. The doctrine may be presented as a mere fragment, which leads to many errors.

We may illustrate our answer to the question as to man's freedom at the head of this section as follows: When God saves A. he wills two things, *viz.*, that A. shall be an agent or medium for conveying those blessings to B. In like manner he wills that B. shall be a means of blessing to C., and so on through the entire list. Now God's grace saves A., not by a bare forgiveness and justification. God's grace in saving A. means the love, the sympathy, the prayers, the efforts, and strivings of A. to save B. Grace does not fully work itself out in saving A. unless A. permits grace to awaken in him a desire, yearning, prayer, effort for B. This desire, yearning, prayer, effort is an essential part of the salvation of A. God's purpose in A. comes short unless grace reappears in A. as tender love for the lost, for B. The salvation God brings to men is a far richer gift than men sometimes imagine. It is not the mere plucking of a human unit here and there as a brand from the burning. It is this, but far more. It is a salvation which works through human agents and agencies and which involves a great series of human relationships and influences.

3. A third question about God's sovereignty is this: Can we reconcile the sovereignty of God and human freedom in his electing grace? The answer is in the negative. We are dealing here with

ultimate forms of experience and of thought. God's sovereignty held in an abstract way and apart from our freedom, or man's freedom held in an abstract way apart from God's sovereignty, is a very hurtful and dangerous teaching. We are conscious of freedom as an ultimate fact of experience. We are driven to God's sovereignty as an ultimate necessity of thought. One has expressed it thus: " I am fated; that is false. I am free: that is false. I am fated and free: that is true." The word " fate " is not proper to express any relation to God. But apart from this the above statement suggests the great truth with which we are dealing.

4. A fourth question is: Can we assign any reasons why God should adopt the method of election in saving men? The reply is that we certainly cannot fully understand. But there are some reasons which will shed light upon the matter. We need to remember, first of all, that God is limited in his methods by the moral ends of his kingdom. His limitations are of course self-imposed. But they govern him when once adopted. God is limited in two ways in his dealings with men. First, he is limited by human freedom. He made us free. He will not coerce man in his choices. If he did so he would destroy our freedom. We would cease to be persons and become things. God's problem is to save men and at the same time to leave them free. This is the greatest and most difficult of all problems. It is this problem which explains the system of moral, spiritual, and personal agencies we have been considering. God cannot take the soul by sheer omnipotence. He cannot storm the will and take it by assault, overpowering and crushing it. This would not save it, but lay it waste. Human agents of redemption, persuasion, argument, entreaty, prayer, personal influence—in a word, moral and spiritual forces are the only kind available for the end in view. God is limited by man's freedom.

Again, God is limited in his method by human sin. Sin enslaves men. They are endowed with moral freedom, but their wills have a bias which inevitably leads to the rejection of the gospel except when aided by God's grace in Christ. It is not a question merely of ability, but of inevitability. Man inevitably chooses evil. The carnal mind is not subject to the law of God, neither indeed can be.

Now combine these two thoughts. If man is free, and if he will inevitably reject the gospel unaided by divine grace, what will be the outcome? No one would be saved. But if God interposes, it can only be some form of election. But in adopting the method of election he must work in a moral, spiritual, and personal way on man, the moral, spiritual, and personal being. He must reduce his own action to the minimum lest he compel the will. He must interpose sufficiently to secure the result because the moral and spiritual process is gradual. Character comes by degrees. Regeneration is instantaneous. But the new birth is the beginning only of the new character in Christ. Preaching, persuasion, in short, all the moral and spiritual agencies, require time. If salvation were achieved as a complete whole in a twinkling, if character could arise at one stroke, the case might be different. We conclude, then, that God is limited by human freedom and sin to the method of election, and that in executing his purpose he must, by reason of these limitations, work gradually and through human agents.

5. A fifth question is: Would it not be fairer and more just if God left men to accept or reject when the gospel is preached to them, without any previous choice on his part? The reply is that if the final outcome is the salvation of some and the loss of others, any other system would be ultimately traceable to God's sovereignty and election. Assume that equal grace is given to all. Some are receptive, and some hostile to it. The receptive are saved, the hostile lost. Then God's sovereignty and election operated to provide efficaciously for the receptive only. He did not give grace to overcome hostility. He elected thus the receptive and only the receptive. Assume again that with equal grace to all, some respond and believe because they are better morally, or less stubborn in will, or more believing, or for any other conceivable reason. Clearly if these are saved and the others lost, it is because God elected to offer a gospel

adapted to reach one class and not adapted to reach the other class. As we remarked at the outset, the fundamental truth is that of Genesis I : I, " In the beginning God." If it be assumed that God could save all, but refuses to do so, then any scheme whatever carries with it the idea of an election based on God's sovereignty. Our own view, as we have just stated it, holds that under the moral and spiritual conditions involved in man's sin and freedom, God could not save all. God's choice becomes effective through special grace based not at all on human merit, and on no principle of partiality or arbitrary selection. He chooses rather on a principle which makes possible a rapid movement toward his all-embracing purpose for the human race. No instance of individual election can be fully understood when viewed out of relation to the universal plan and purpose. The next question brings out this point more fully.

6. A sixth question: Is God seeking to save as few or as many as possible? Men have sometimes conceived of election as if it were a plan to save as few as possible. The whole tenor of the Bible is in the other direction. Here we must speak with caution. But there are many indications that God is seeking to save men as rapidly as the situation admits—in view of sin and freedom and the necessity for respecting human freedom. The hostility of the world to Christ and the persecutions of Christians during the first centuries of the Christian era show clearly that an earlier giving of the gospel in its fulness might have been disastrous. In a moral kingdom men must be prepared before great epoch-making advances are possible. First the blade, then the ear, then the full corn in the ear, is the process. The following points will serve to make clear the purpose of God to save not as few, but as many as possible:

(1) The purpose expressed in the call of Abraham. We have clearly seen that God's purpose in that call was twofold, the blessing of Abraham and his seed and through them the blessing of all mankind. This wider purpose never disappears from the Old Testament history. It becomes most explicit in the later history after the exile in the teaching of the prophets.

(2) The land given to Abraham and his descendants sug gests the same truth. Palestine was at the center of the known world on the central sea, the Mediterranean. It was the highway of the nations going eastward from the west, or westward from the east. The Jewish theocracy was like a grain of musk deposited in the very heart of mankind to prepare the whole lump in due time. The Jewish dispersion in all directions was the preparation for the spread of the gospel. The synagogue was usually the nucleus and center of evangelization. Converted Jews bridged the chasm across to the Gentile world.

(3) The unity of the world under the Roman Empire when Christ was born and the facilities for travel to every part of it were parts of divine preparation for the apostle and the missionary with the good tidings of salvation. Thus the good will of God for all the race begins to be manifest in a most striking way.

(4) The spread of the Greek language and culture as a medium for communicating the truth of the gospel is another mark of the universal plan of God. One has expressed it thus: " As the river Nile at a certain season overflows its banks and floods a wide area, leaving its deposit of rich soil for the Egyptian farmer, and then subsides again into its narrow channel, so also in God's providence Greece overflowed the national limits and left its deposit of language and literature and then subsided into its narrow channels." This universal language became the instru- ment for the spread of the gospel over the earth.

(5) The career of the apostle Paul was a notable factor in this great series of secondary causes. This is seen in his message and in his travels. His message was Christianity stated in universal terms and maintained with all vigor against Jewish narrowness and the tendency to make it a mere Jewish sect. His doctrine of justification by faith apart from works of the law proclaimed it as a Gentile as well as a Jewish religion. Paul's travels took him westward, not to the dreamy and inactive people of the East. He planted the gospel in Europe among the aggressive, ambitious, individualistic, inventive races, who in due time

were to recover the early faith from a vast ecclesiasticism and again make it a conquering missionary religion. In our own day we witness a new " fulness of time," in the world preparation for the gospel and a new outburst of missionary life and power. The great war in progress at this writing will no doubt change the face of civilization in many ways. It will prepare for new fulfilments of God's purpose in Christ.

Now this historical survey suggests in a very impressive way that God's electing grace has never been a narrowing, but always a widening principle. He has been ever eager to prepare men for larger blessings than they could receive at the time. His purpose and plan have ripened as rapidly as the moral and spiritual and personal kingdom and its appropriate forces could bring it to pass. His love has ever sought to overleap the barriers which human sin and unbelief have interposed.

7. A seventh question: Can we discover any principle which has guided in the electing love of God? In reply two or three things are perfectly clear. First, men are not chosen because of merit of any kind on their part. This is the constantly recurring note in all Paul's epistles. Salvation is not of works, lest any man should boast. Whatever be the reason for the salvation of men, it is not due to any merit or moral worth in them. Secondly, it is also clear that men are chosen for service in God's kingdom. The Bible nowhere regards men as detached atoms unrelated to other men. This choice for service applied to Abraham as we have seen. It applied to Israel as a nation. The later prophets interpreted Israel's mission as a mission to mankind. Isaiah especially insisted that the " remnant " of Israel was the prophet of God to teach the nations. The apostle Paul conceived of himself as chosen from birth for his apostleship and mission to the Gentiles. Jesus expressly told the disciples that he had chosen them, that they might be his witnesses. They were to await the enduement of power after his departure that they might carry forward his work. In the third place, we may infer that God's election pursues the course which will yield the largest results in the shortest time. Men may be so placed in relations to other

men that their election could easily become an avenue of approach to others, and these in turn to others. There might thus arise a principle of electing strategic men, through whom God's widening purpose might swiftly realize itself. This would not imply merit on the part of those chosen. In some cases, indeed, the strategic man might be among the worst of men morally, and yet so related to others, or so endowed, that he could be employed best for the ends of the kingdom. Paul declared himself to have been the chief of sinners. But for this very reason God's grace obtained a monumental victory through him so that other bad men might hope. In bowling the aim of the bowler is to hit the " king " pin so that it will knock down the other nine. It is not that the " king " pin is in any essential way different from the others in itself, but rather that it is so related to the other pins that to hit it right means the largest results. It occupies a strategic position in relation to the other pins. We may assume, therefore, in the light of God's universal purpose for the race of man, that he has ever pursued this plan.

In view of all the preceding it appears that God's sovereignty in his electing love in no way brings reproach upon the love and grace of God. It is rather a masterpiece of love and grace seeking to bless men. We can never fully fathom the depths of the divine motives in his dealings with men. We can never grasp entirely the significance of all his methods. Especially is this true regarding the doctrine of election. But it is not difficult to see that there is nothing arbitrary in God's ways. Infinite love is behind all his acts as well as infinite righteousness.

IV. OBJECTIONS

Most of the objections to the doctrine of election have already been answered indirectly in the preceding discussion. There are a few, however, which need specific treatment.

1. It is objected that the teaching makes God partial. Why should he save some and refuse to save others. The answer is contained chiefly in what has already been expressed. Election

is his method for realizing a great purpose for all. It is the only method possible under all the circumstances. But we add that election is a universal principle in God's methods. He chooses some plants and flowers to be more beautiful than others. He chooses some birds to be singers while others can only croak. He chooses to endow some men as poets and artists while others are commonplace plodders. The black races in Africa might complain of the partiality of God for the white races of Europe and America. God chose Israel as his peculiar people out of all the races of men. The modern doctrine of natural selection as applied in biology generally is a scientific expression of the same general principle. It is evident that God's ends in the world could not be achieved by means of a dead level of privilege. Life in all its forms, physical, moral, and spiritual, involves differences of various kinds, and these differences imply ultimately a principle of election.

2. It is also objected that election involves insincerity in the offer of salvation to all. The reply is that there is absolutely no barrier to the salvation of any, save their own wills. Christ died for all. God is willing to receive all who will come. God knows that some will not accept. Indeed, he knows that all will refuse unless by his special grace some are led to believe. But invitation and persuasion and appeal and man's free response are the only means available in a moral and spiritual order. Grace can only operate thus. If angels were sent to capture the elect and bring them in by force, this would not be a method in harmony with grace. It would leave the will unmoved and character unchanged. The choicest element in man's spiritual life in God's sight is his own free act in choosing God and returning to him. The gospel invitation makes this choice possible. No other method is conceivable by which it could be so well done.

3. Again, it is objected that God does not desire the salvation of all, or else he would elect all. But the Scriptures expressly declare that " God so loved the world " that he sent his Son, and also that he wishes none to perish, but that all should come to

repentance. (2 Peter 3 : 9.) The objection assumes falsely that there are no moral limitations of any kind in God, and that he can do anything he desires. But human freedom limits God, as does human unbelief and sin. Men cannot be made righteous by sheer omnipotence. God cannot force or compel any one to be good. The situation does not admit of the use of force. It is a situation rather in which a race of men is bent on self-destruction, or moral and spiritual suicide. God interposes by a method which respects their freedom and gradually works out a universal purpose of blessing.

4. It is objected also that election cuts the nerve of Christian endeavor. It is felt that if the number of the saved is fixed beforehand, there is little need on our part to strive for their salvation. But this forgets the meaning of salvation. Our salvation means in part our love and effort for the lost. It means our sharing the redemptive passion of Christ. It means all the forms of self-sacrifice and of moral worth which are required to save others. The objection also forgets that the kingdom of God is a kingdom of human relations. God is perfecting us through our interactions in a moral and spiritual realm. It forgets also that the kingdom is a historical movement in which all the parts are closely related and interdependent.

The objection forgets the alternative of God's election. Our effort would be hopeless indeed without it. We would soon cease all effort because all effort would appear to be fruitless. There is no greater incentive to effort than the consciousness of a divine purpose working in us. All great reformers and evangelists have had the conviction. Revolutions were successful in such large measure because a sense of God's purpose was the impelling motive behind them.

5. It is also objected that an insoluble mystery confronts us when we seek to unite the two ideas of God's sovereignty and man's freedom. The reply is that this is true and should be expected rather than cause surprise. All the relations between the infinite and the finite run back into mystery. The ideas of incarnation and prayer and Providence and all others which

combine the eternal with the temporal, the infinite with the finite, carry us finally into a realm beyond our present powers. But this fact ought not to create doubt. In science and philosophy, just as in theology, the same difficulty exists. The facts of experience, however, are their own best evidence, and in religion these are incontestable.

One point should never be overlooked in considering the doctrine of election. We should bear in mind the importance of proclaiming a universal gospel. We are untrue to the spirit of the New Testament when we fail here. Whatever of mystery or of difficulty remains after all we can say about election, one thing stands out in clear sunlight in the New Testament. And that is that God sent his Son on a world-wide mission, that preachers are not only authorized, but commanded to preach the gospel to every creature, and to give a universal invitation.

Hardening the Heart

6. Before leaving the subject one other difficulty should be briefly considered. Certain passages of Scripture seem to represent God as actively working to harden the human heart and prevent acceptance of offered mercy. In Exodus 7 : 3 God foretells that he will harden Pharaoh's heart. In 7 : 13 it is declared that Pharaoh's heart was hardened. In Exodus 10 : 1 God is represented as saying, " I have hardened his heart." There are many similar passages in other parts of the Bible which seem to attribute directly to God the blindness of sinners, or the hardening of their hearts. It is not necessary to review all of them. The same general principles apply in interpreting them in whatever connections they are found. The following statements supply the needed guidance :

(1) In the Scriptures we find a sense in which any event or act, good or evil, is attributed to God. In Isaiah 45 : 7 Jehovah says : " I make peace and create evil ; I am Jehovah that doeth all these things." The context here shows that Jehovah's sovereignty is expressed by these words. He is in no sense the author of the

wicked deeds of men, but he permits them and overrules them for a higher end. The permissive decree or purpose of God explains his relation to events or acts which involve sin and guilt.

(2) Again, in practically all the passages in question, the context shows that the sin or hardening of the heart was due to the voluntary acts of the men themselves, and not to God. In the case of Pharaoh it is declared repeatedly that he hardened his own heart. (Exod. 8 : 15, 32.) The whole course of events suggests an appeal of the divine mercy and forbearance. The final blow does not fall until every resource has been exhausted to move Pharaoh to repentance. Sometimes he shows signs of temporary change of heart, but the old stubbornness always returns. (Exod. 9 : 27, 28.)

(3) The Scriptures clearly declare that men bring upon themselves a moral and spiritual blindness and insensibility by persistence in sin. This may be attributed to God. But God's agency in it is expressed through the moral and spiritual laws involved We cannot violate conscience without dulling the moral sense. We cannot resist moral and spiritual light without losing our finer appreciation of moral and spiritual realities. This appears in Matthew 13 : 13-15 and in Mark 4 : 11, 12 and Luke 8 : 10. These are parallel passages. In Matthew the explanation is given: "For this people's heart is waxed gross, and their ears are dull of hearing, and their eyes have they closed; lest haply they should perceive with their eyes, and hear with their ears, and turn again, and I should heal them" (Matt. 13 : 15). A judicial blindness or hardening came as a result of their own sin. It was the result of God's action only as expressed in the laws of their moral constitution.

(4) Finally, we must understand all such passages in the light of the uniform teaching of Scripture that God willeth that none should perish. He invites all men everywhere to accept his mercy. No hand that was ever stretched out to him for help in genuine repentance was stayed by him. If he should refuse mercy to the truly penitent it would be a denial of his own nature and a failure to keep his promises. For him to work actively to

prevent the salvation of men would be to undo the gospel and nullify the deepest meaning of the incarnation and atonement. Nothing could be more directly opposed to all that Christ has made known to us than the idea that God could or would hinder men from accepting his grace. The final state of the wicked is their own self-wrought destiny, as we shall see.

CHAPTER XV

THE BEGINNINGS OF THE CHRISTIAN LIFE

I. The Work of the Holy Spirit in Salvation

IN an earlier section the general teaching of the Bible on the subject of the Holy Spirit was set forth. Here it is only necessary to call to mind what was said there, and to add a few points as to the place of the Holy Spirit in the process of salvation. We are now to consider the work of God's grace in saving men. The fundamental and vital relations of the Holy Spirit of God to that work must be kept constantly in mind. To this end we consider the Holy Spirit in relation to God; in relation to Christ; in relation to men; in relation to the means of grace.

1. The Holy Spirit in relation to God.

The Holy Spirit is called the Spirit of God in both the Old and the New Testaments. The term "holy," as applied to him in the New Testament, is found in a very few instances in the Old Testament. (Ps. 51 : 11; Isa. 63 : 10, 11.) No doubt the usage arose out of the deepening ethical sense of the Old Testament writers. In the New that sense reaches its supreme heights, and the term Holy Spirit, indicating the moral perfection of the Spirit as God's Spirit, became the prevailing designation. The Spirit is sent from the Father by Christ, according to John 15 : 26, 27. A controversy arose between the Eastern and Western Churches over the doctrine of the " procession " of the Spirit. The point of controversy was whether the Spirit proceeded from both the Father and the Son, or from the Father only. The Western Church held that the procession was from both Father and Son, while the East held that it was from the Father only. The Scripture evidence for a strict doctrinal definition is very meager on this point. We are not obliged to define exactly the process of the Spirit's coming. The great fact stands forth clearly. He bears a vital relation to the Father and the work of the Son. He is sent by the Son and proceeds from the Father.

2. The Holy Spirit in relation to the Son.

We have already seen that the Holy Spirit acted everywhere upon the incarnate Son of God, beginning at his birth, continuing to his baptism, imparting the equipment necessary for his mission while on earth, manifesting his power in the sacrifice of Christ on the cross (an offering through the " eternal Spirit "), and raising his body from the dead.

What we need to grasp clearly here is the vital and essential relation of the Spirit to the gospel of salvation as it was preached after the ascension of Christ. The coming of the Spirit had been predicted and promised during the earthly ministry of Jesus. (See Luke 24 : 49; John 20 : 22; Acts 1 : 5.) He was to be the great source of life and power to believers. (John 7 : 38.) The disciples were commanded to tarry in Jerusalem until the Spirit came and endued them with divine power. (Luke 24 : 49.) His coming was to impart the qualifications needed for proclaiming throughout the world the gospel of salvation. Jerusalem, Judæa, Samaria, and the uttermost parts of the earth are named as the range of the activity.

Pentecost was the fulfilment of the promise of Christ. It is so interpreted by the early preachers in the book of Acts. Pentecost was the historical fulfilment of the predicted baptism of the Holy Spirit. (Acts 1 : 5.) This seems to have been completed at the conversion of Cornelius, another Gentile. (Acts 10 : 1 to 11 : 18.) After this the baptism of the Spirit is not mentioned. He now abides continually in his fulness with the community of disciples. He remains on earth " forever." He is not withdrawn. (John 14 : 16.) We are commanded to ' take " (*labete,* John 20 : 22) the Holy Spirit. This is a word expressing action, and not merely passive reception, on our part. The Spirit is given, but we must claim and appropriate him by faith. The Holy Spirit is related to Christ's work in the following ways:

(1) He is " another Paraclete," or Comforter, and guide who

takes the place of Christ and carries on his work. He is to carry forward the work of Christ now that Christ is to be absent in body from his people. (John 16 : 7-14.)

(2) His work, however, is all related to Christ. He was to bring to memory the things that Christ had taught. He was to show disciples things to come. (John 16 : 12-14.) He was to teach them additional truths which they could not receive while Christ was with them. Thus he was called the Spirit of Truth. Truth was the instrument with which he did his work. (John 14 : 17.) He was to glorify Christ. (John 16 : 14.)

(3) The entire work of the Spirit is summed up in the task of revealing Christ to men. (John 16 : 14.) But it is primarily a ministry within the human spirit. It includes conviction for sin, regeneration, sanctification, inner witness in the believer's heart, and communion with God the Father, enduement and equipment for service, raising of the bodies of believers, and their glorification.

Now all the above activities are directly related to Christ. The Spirit's work is to reveal Christ to us, to form Christ within us. It may be expressed thus: The sitter for the photograph is Christ. The sensitive plate to receive his image is the human heart. The light which shines upon the sitter is the Holy Spirit. Even this is an inadequate illustration. For the Spirit shines also in our hearts. We may sum up the Spirit's ministry in us as follows: (a) He makes real in us the life-principle which was perfectly embodied in Christ. (b) He makes the spiritual rights and privileges secured for us by Christ, our actual possessions. (c) He makes the ethical ideal which was embodied in Christ our own experience in a progressive life. (d) He makes the victory of Christ over sin and death our victory.

3. The Holy Spirit in relation to the human spirit.

Here, of course, are mysteries beyond our ability to penetrate. There are, however, a few things which are clear. First, the Spirit's action on the human spirit is in harmony with the psychological laws of man's nature. The Spirit of God may act through the subconscious region within us. But his efficient action is manifest also in consciousness. He acts through the emotions, the intellect, the conscience, and the will. His work in us follows thus the lines of our spiritual being.

Secondly, the Spirit acts upon us chiefly through the truth. He is the Spirit of Truth revealing Christ who is the Truth. His action is not magical or sacramental. The ordinances of Christianity are symbols of truth. The Spirit employs them as symbols, and they profit us through our own discernment of the truth symbolized in them.

Thirdly, the Spirit's action in us is moral and personal. He leaves us free. There is no pantheistic absorption of our spirit in the Supreme Spirit. There is no compulsion of our wills. We are never more deeply conscious of our own personality and freedom than we are when the Holy Spirit moves upon our spirits. Thus the Spirit is God immanent in us, not far away from us and apart from his world. There is a profoundly mystical element in our faith through the Spirit's action. But it is not mysticism in the narrower sense of an unethical and non-rational and merely emotional absorption in God. The mysticism of the Christian religion is the mysticism of the practical life in communion with God, of battle with sin and temptation in daily affairs. It is a mysticism which is devoted to truth and its propagation in God's strength. It is a mysticism which has an ethical passion inspiring continuous effort toward the highest ideal in Christ.

4. The Holy Spirit and the means of grace.

God has for the best of reasons chosen to approach men through appointed means. There are two extreme views as to these means of grace which need to be avoided. The first view tends to ignore them altogether. It may lead to a false mysticism which makes religion merely an ecstatic emotionalism, on the one hand, or, on the other, it may lead to "hard-shellism," which neglects all aggressive missionary endeavor by reason of a false view of the divine sovereignty. The second view recognizes the means of grace, but, in the Roman Catholic fashion, converts them into sacraments having in themselves power to impart life. Baptismal regeneration and the doctrine of the "real presence" in the Lord's Supper are examples of what is meant.

Now the fundamental error of both these views is that they overlook the fact that the Spirit of God acts upon the human spirit by means of the truth. He deals with us as intelligent conscious persons capable of understanding and acting upon God's revelation to us. Hence all the means of grace are means for conveying spiritual truth to us. All the means of grace therefore presuppose the truth of the gospel. Everything which may be employed by God's Spirit for reaching and influencing men is in some sense a means of grace. We think first of preaching and witnessing for Christ. Then we think of the Bible, the church and its ordinances and officers, its worship, its activities, as means of grace. We must include also all the providential dealings of God with us, all life's experiences, our fellowships and our struggles, our prayers, our sufferings and losses. All these are means employed by the Holy Spirit to teach us the truth of God.

The question may be asked: Why should there be means of grace? Why could not God accomplish his ends directly upon and within the human spirit without the appointed means? The answer to these questions takes several forms:

(1) It is seen in part in the ethnic religions. Man has always been seeking God in some form or other. He is an "incurably religious" being. And surely God has not been indifferent to men in their search for him. And yet, by reason of sin and moral blindness man's religious struggles present a tragic picture groping in the dark, or striving to follow a divine light. There is great variety in the forms of religion. Some of them are most immoral and debased. It is clear that men needed some medium of communication with God which would lead them surely into the path of true faith and right living. The Christian means of grace are an answer to this need.

(2) The answer is found in part in the philosophical struggles of men. It might be supposed that nature supplied the medium for communion between God and man. Human thought has been grappling with the problem of the meaning of nature through

the centuries. It has not yet arrived at a consensus of opinion. Many systems of philosophy are advocated to-day. Somehow nature does not speak the same message to all. This is not due to anything equivocal in nature, but to the condition of men's minds. God remains, in large part, unknown in philosophy as in the ethnic faiths. Christianity recognizes this situation and offers links of connection with God in the means of grace. They are ladders on which the intellect climbs to God.

(3) The answer as to the necessity for means of grace is found in the incarnation of God in Christ. Jesus expressed the fundamental truth about the matter when he said, " Neither doth any know the Father, save the Son and he to whomsoever the Son willeth to reveal him " (Matt. 11 : 27). So also in John 1 : 18 he says : " No man hath seen God at any time ; the only begotten Son who is in the bosom of the Father, he hath declared him." The prophets of the Old Testament possessed a knowledge of God superior to any other of their times. But even this revelation needed to be completed. The ideas of God, of duty, of immortality, remained too vague and uncertain to triumph fully in the world without an incarnation. And so the Word became flesh and dwelt among us. Jesus Christ was the supreme means of grace to men. Indeed, he was grace itself. " The law was given," he declared, but " grace and truth came through Jesus Christ " (John 1 : 17).

We conclude, therefore, that the necessity for means of grace is based on the necessity for the incarnation. All the means of grace which were mentioned in a previous paragraph are simply means by which the Holy Spirit forms Christ within us. He thus carries on the work of Christ, creating his spiritual kingdom among men. The necessity of which we here speak was due to God's nature as pure Spirit, and to man's nature as spirit and body. The absolute pure Spirit could become known to other spiritual beings, who were also flesh, only by becoming flesh. The incarnate One could become a living power in human souls only through the regenerating and sanctifying act of the Holy Spirit. The Holy Spirit operates most effectively through the

The Beginnings of the Christian Life

use of means. Hence the means of grace are necessary for the effectual propagation of the gospel of the grace of God.

II. The Beginnings of Salvation

Under this head we include calling and conviction for sin. These are prior to God's saving act in the soul. But as preparing the way for it, they need to be mentioned here.

1. Calling is the invitation of God to men to accept by faith the salvation in Christ. It is sent forth through the Bible, the preaching of the gospel, and in many other ways. Nothing can be clearer from the teaching of Scripture than the fact that the call and invitation are universal and that there is a free offer of salvation to all who hear and repent and believe. A very few of many passages may be cited: Ezekiel 33 : 11: "As I live, saith the Lord Jehovah, I have no pleasure in the death of the wicked; but that the wicked turn from his way and live: turn ye, turn ye, from your evil ways; for why will ye die, O house of Israel?" Isaiah 55 : 7: "Let the wicked forsake his way, and the unrighteous man his thoughts; and let him return unto Jehovah, and he will have mercy upon him: and to our God, for he will abundantly pardon." The New Testament abounds in general invitations. Matthew 11 : 28: "Come unto me, all ye that labor and are heavy laden, and I will give you rest." Mark 16 : 15: "Go ye into all the world and preach the gospel to the whole creation. He that believeth and is baptized shall be saved; but he that disbelieveth shall be condemned." Revelation 22 : 17: "And the Spirit and the bride say, Come. And he that heareth let him say, Come. And he that is athirst, let him come: he that will, let him take the water of life freely." Again, in Romans 8 : 30: "And whom he foreordained, them he also called: and whom he called, them he also justified: and whom he justified, them he also glorified." These passages might be indefinitely multiplied. But there is no need of this.

One question may be asked at this point. If the call is universal, and if some accept because God gives them grace to

[365]

accept, and others reject because he does not give them sufficient grace, how can we regard the call to the latter class as sincere?

The answer in part is that many a sincere invitation is given among men where it is known beforehand that it will not be accepted. Foreknowledge of a refusal does not affect the sincerity of the offer. Again, the Scriptures make it plain that responsibility for rejection is upon those who reject the gospel offer, not those who make it, much less upon God himself. Again, it is clear that God desires the salvation of all, although he does not efficaciously decree the salvation of all. How can we explain this divergence between the desire and purpose on God's part? It cannot be due to any conflict in his own nature. It must be due to conditions with which he has to deal. We have already pointed out those conditions in a previous section. Human sin and human freedom are factors in God's problem with man. His grace goes as far as the interests of his moral kingdom admit. His omnipotence does not enable him to do a moral impossibility.

2. Conviction for sin is the result of the Holy Spirit's action awakening in men a sense of guilt and condemnation because of sin, and particularly because of unbelief. In John 16 : 8-11 we have the teaching of Jesus on the subject. Referring to the coming of the Holy Spirit, Jesus says: "And he, when he is come, will convict the world in respect of sin, and of righteousness, and of judgment; of sin, because they believe not on me; of righteousness, because I go to the Father, and ye behold me no more; of judgment, because the prince of this world has been judged."

Two or three remarks may be added. The first is that the word "convict" here means moral demonstration. It carries the idea of convincing the intellect, but it is more than intellectual. It is moral. It involves the personal relations of the soul. Hence it is not an argument addressed to the reason merely. It penetrates the conscience as well. It is moral and spiritual demonstration.

The second point is that the conviction which the Holy Spirit produces refers in all respects to Jesus Christ. It is a threefold conviction, as follows:

a. The sin to which the conviction refers is summed up as unbelief, lack of faith in Christ. This implies that unbelief is the root sin. The Spirit may convict of any particular sin and bring home its enormity to the conscience, such as lying, stealing, etc. But in that conviction all sin is ultimately traced back to unbelief. As faith in Christ is the cure for all sin, so the absence of faith, or rejection of Christ, is an act potential of all other forms of sin.

b. Again, the conviction of righteousness refers to Christ. Righteousness is the opposite of sin. This conviction is the other side, so to speak, of the conviction of sin. But it is the righteousness revealed in the character and work of Christ, a righteousness vindicated and made fruitful in the resurrection: "because I go to the Father."

c. The conviction as to judgment also refers to Christ: "because the prince of this world hath been judged." Christ's anticipated death on the cross is here regarded as the judgment, the condemnation, and conquest of the prince of this world. Compare John 12 : 31, 32: "Now is the judgment of this world: now shall the prince of this world be cast out. And I, if I be lifted up from the earth, will draw all men unto myself."

In the third place, this conviction is the conviction of hope rather than of despair because it refers thus in every instance to Christ. The infinite Spirit of God in a sinful heart, showing the dreadfulness of sin, and the eternal demand of righteousness, and the fearfulness of God's judgment against sin, would indeed crush man's spirit and overwhelm it with despair if it were unaccompanied by the reference to Christ. But the aim of the conviction is to produce faith in the Christ who cleanses from the guilt of sin and breaks its power, whose righteousness is shared with the pardoned sinner, and whose death has already triumphed over the prince of this world. Hence the conviction of the Holy Spirit is a conviction of hope for all who yield to it and turn from their sins.

Before passing from this topic one caution is necessary. The doctrine of conviction should not be made into a stereotyped rule. We are not to suppose that all men are required to pass through a conscious and clearly defined conviction of sin, of righteousness, and of judgment in explicit terms. The language of Jesus simply interprets the meaning of the experience of conviction. Many who have it could not state their own experience in very clear or coherent language. But this does not alter the fact itself. Again, we must recognize varying degrees of intensity in the conviction for sin. With some no doubt it is a deep tragedy of the soul. With others it is rather a sense simply of being out of adjustment with God. Temperaments vary, and the experience will vary accordingly. Children are less powerfully moved by conviction, as a rule, than adults. We must make due allowance for the differences in men and for the variety in the manifestations of the Spirit of God.

III. The Order of Salvation

The act of salvation and the life which follows both involve action on God's part and on man's part. Which side should be presented first? What is the order of salvation? A certain cause is here at work, producing certain effects. The cause acts in a spiritual and free manner in accordance with the nature of spiritual causes generally. The effects in man are produced in the same way. They are moral and spiritual effects. Now in describing this work we may begin with the cause and trace its action in producing the effects, or we may begin with the effects and trace them back to their cause. Perhaps the former would be in the strict sense the more logical method. But from the point of view of our experience of the grace of God, the way in which the knowledge arises in us, the latter method is preferable. We conform here to the order of experience, and deal first with repentance and faith, and later with regeneration and related topics. We are not to conceive of any interval of time between God's work in us and our response to it. Faith and repentance become complete in us when regeneration is complete, and regeneration is an accomplished fact when repentance and faith are complete. So also as to repentance and faith. They are simultaneous experiences. They are the negative and positive aspects of the same fact. Otherwise there might be an impenitent believer, or a penitent unbeliever, which is contrary to the New Testament teaching, as well as our own experience.

1. Repentance

There are several expressions in the Scriptures which describe the first stages of the Christian life. Sometimes it is a turning from idols to the service of God. (1 Thess. 1 : 9.) Sometimes it is a becoming dead to sin. (Rom. 6 : 1-11.) Again, it is described as a putting off of the old man. (Eph. 4 : 22.) Again, it may be an awaking from sleep. (Eph. 5 : 14.) But the word which contains all these ideas, and that which especially defines the renunciation of sin at the beginning of the Christian life, is repentance.

The word repentance is the translation of two Greek words in the New Testament. One of these is *metamelomai*. This word expresses the emotional element in repentance. It means regret. But this regret may be of a godly sort leading to genuine repentance, or it may be a regret which produces no moral change. (See 2 Cor. 7 : 9, 10; Luke 18 : 23; Matt. 27 : 3.)

The other New Testament word translated repentance is *metanoia*. This word means a change of the mind or thought. But the change of mind expressed by this word is more than a mere intellectual change of view. It carries with it the idea of will. (Luke 17 : 3; Acts 2 : 38; Rom. 2 : 4; Mark 1 : 4, 14.)

It is clear, then, that man's spiritual nature as a whole acts when he repents. It is not one faculty or function of the soul, but his entire spirit. Repentance includes three elements.

(1) First, there is an intellectual element. It is a change of thought. A man's view of sin and of God and his relations to God undergo a change when he repents. His thought of sin changes from approval to disapproval. His thought about God

Y

changes from indifference or hostility to reverence and submission. His thought about his relations to God changes from a sense of security to a sense of condemnation and exposure to wrath.

(2) There is also a change of feeling. A penitent man has genuine regret. But this regret is of a godly kind which leads to a real change. (2 Cor. 7 : 9, 10.) It is to be distinguished from the form of regret which has no godly reference. A man may have deep regret for a wrong committed because of the social condemnation which follows. He may be sorry for a crime committed because the consequences are unpleasant. But regret of this kind is not the godly sorrow which works true repentance.

(3) There is also a voluntary element in genuine repentance The will is changed. A new purpose is formed. As a consequence of the change of will and purpose there is an actual forsaking of sin and an actual turning to God. This is the most vital and fundamental element in repentance. No repentance is genuine without it.

Repentance is the result of God's gracious action upon the soul. The goodness of God leads men to repentance. (Rom. 2 : 4.) In Acts 5 : 31 it is declared that Christ has been exalted to give repentance and remission of sins unto Israel. And in Acts 11 : 18 it is declared that God granted to the Gentiles repentance unto life.

God employs a great variety of means for leading men to repentance. The preaching of the gospel; holy living of Christian people; the influence of the church; providential events; in short, any and all channels or means through which the truth of God may reach men are used by him in leading them to turn away from their sins. One or two additional statements may be made about repentance. The first is that repentance becomes a permanent attitude of the soul toward sin. The first act of true repentance introduces the penitent into the Christian life. But this act is not a mere legal transaction which is over and done with once for all. It is a permanent moral process going on every day. Every renunciation of sin, every putting off of the old man, is in essence the repetition of the first act of repentance. Hence it is an attitude of the soul to be cultivated. The definite and positive renunciation of sin in every form should become the fixed habit of the soul. Thus do we pass from infancy to maturity in the spiritual life.

A second statement is that repentance is the identification of a sinful man with God's attitude toward sin. It is not a meritorious work which entitles us to salvation. But when we repent we think God's thought about sin. We renounce it as Christ renounced it. We hate it as he hates it. It is this which indicates the great ethical significance of repentance. When a man from the very core and center of his being repudiates sin, and abhors that which is evil, it is clear proof that moral transformation has begun. Indeed it is proof that he has become partaker of the divine nature. We see from this why repentance is always made a condition of forgiveness in Scripture, whether that forgiveness be human or divine. In God's sight a man only becomes forgivable, that is, he only exhibits a moral attitude which can be forgiven, when he adopts God's point of view regarding sin. That point of view is expressed in and through repentance.

2. Faith

Faith occupies a central place in the religion of the Bible. It is central in the Old Testament as well as the New. It is so rich in its contents, and so comprehensive, so inclusive of the relationships of man that it is easier to describe than it is to define it. All brief definitions of faith come short of the complete reality. Yet the meaning is simple and easy to grasp, in its essential contents. We give first a brief definition and follow this with a more extended description of faith.

Saving faith, according to the New Testament, we may analyze into at least three elements. But it is difficult to separate one of these from the other two.

First, faith contains an intellectual element. We believe the truth of the gospel. We recognize in Christ and his work God's provision for our salvation. We accept thus the historical facts and also the interpretation of their meaning as these are given in the records. But it is clear that this alone is not saving faith. Devils believe in this sense and shudder. (James 2 : 19.)

The second element is assent. The sinner convicted of his sin and need and his dependence recognizes in the provisions of the gospel the divine answer to his needs. This necessarily includes an element of feeling as well as of knowledge. But it is not even yet the faith which is the condition of salvation. Jesus recognized that there were transient or emotional believers. Hence he declared that abiding in his word was the test of true discipleship. (John 8 : 30, 31.) The stony ground hearers belonged to this class of emotional disciples. (Matt. 13 : 20, 21.)

The third element in saving faith is volition. In the last resort faith is an act of will. It is trust in Christ as Saviour, based on the conviction that he is trustworthy. He is trustworthy as God's gracious revelation for man's salvation. He is trustworthy as atoning Redeemer. He is the sufficient offering for sin. He is trustworthy in his wisdom to guide, in his power to deliver, and in his holiness to sanctify. He is trustworthy as Lord of the life. When we trust him, submit our wills to him, obey him, we exercise saving faith in him.

The second of the above elements is almost necessarily a part of the first and third. Assent in some measure goes with intellectual belief. It is necessarily present in the act of trust. Hence it is not incorrect to say that saving faith is made up of belief and trust. But assent may be conceived of as a distinct element in which we recognize in the gospel the provision for our need prior to the act of the will. It thus brings into clearness the fact that our whole spiritual nature is called into exercise in saving faith, intellect, emotion, will.

We may now enlarge upon the foregoing definition of faith by pointing out certain relations it sustains in the Christian life. The following statements will make these clear.

(1) The first is that faith unites us to God. Faith in the saving sense of the New Testament is never mere belief of a proposition

or acceptance of a creed. " The will to believe " is a modern
phrase which expresses a man's right to hold a proposition as
true and the right to act upon the proposition. But such will
to believe is not the saving faith of the New Testament until it
unites the soul vitally with God.

(2) Again, saving faith unites us with God as he is revealed to
us in Christ. For the Christian Christ is the revealer of God.
The God we worship is the God we see revealed in Christ. He is
made unto us the wisdom, the righteousness, the sanctification,
and the redemption of God. (1 Cor. 1 : 30.) As wisdom, Christ
is the truth about God. As righteousness, he embodies the moral
qualities in God. As sanctification, he gradually produces in us
the moral traits of God. As redemption, he is the power of
God for us and in us, breaking the power of sin and death and
removing guilt. Thus Christ ministers the divine life to us in all
necessary ways.

(3) Again, saving faith manifests itself by its works. We are
not saved by works, but by grace through faith as the condition.
Faith, then, according to the New Testament, is never regarded
as a meritorious work which secures redemption for us. And yet,
genuine faith is never thought of by the New Testament writers
as having no relation to works. True faith is a working faith.
Paul makes this clear, although he constantly opposed the Jewish
idea of salvation by works. " Neither circumcision availeth anything, nor uncircumcision," he says, " but faith working through
love " (Gal. 5 : 6). It is important to keep this truth in mind.
Otherwise there is danger of making formal faith or mere intellectual belief the condition of salvation. Works do not save,
but saving faith may be recognized by the fact that it is a working
faith. (James 2 : 17, 18.) It follows that obedience to the commands of Christ is a necessary expression of genuine faith. Faith
is indeed the great fundamental act of obedience which includes
potentially all other acts. We may briefly sum up the meaning
of faith by saying it is willingness to act. Trust in Christ implies
willingness to conform to the will of Christ. This is one of the
best of all tests of the genuineness of faith.

(4) We remark further that saving faith is a form of knowledge. An error has long prevailed on this point in some quarters. Men have said, " We have but faith, we may not know," as if knowledge were incompatible with faith and faith destitute of knowledge. A hurtful error lurks in such assertions. Faith deals with the invisible, while the ordinary scientific forms of knowledge deal with the natural and visible world. But the distinction between the invisible and visible does not involve a contradiction between faith and knowledge. Scientific knowledge of material things is grounded ultimately in faith. The uniformity of nature, the universal law of causation, and all the great ultimate truths of science are not demonstrated truths. They are great acts of faith. On them the fabric of knowledge is built as upon an enduring foundation. Physical science deals with the realities of the physical universe. But there are other realities. Faith deals with realities as truly as does physical science. The realities of faith are invisible and spiritual; but they are none the less real on that account, but rather more so. We know God in the experiences of faith. Christ enters our souls through his Spirit. He is created in us the hope of glory. We know him as a transforming cause producing spiritual effects in us. Theology is our effort to interpret the meaning of his presence in us in the light of the New Testament. The New Testament constantly recognizes the reality of the knowledge which arises in us through faith. (Heb. 11 : 1; Eph. 1 : 8, 9, 18; 2 Tim. 1 : 12.) No form of knowledge is more genuine.

(5) Again, saving faith is the germinal grace of the Christian life. It is God's gift to men. Out of it spring all other graces. If love is the greatest thing, faith is the first thing in Christian character. Faith is the first living cell, as it were, from which the stalk and fruit of the Christian life spring. Hence the apostle Peter enjoins that we add to our faith virtue, knowledge, self-control, patience, godliness, brotherly kindness, and love. (2 Peter 1 : 5-7.) Thus all things are possible to faith in the matter of growth and attainment as well as in prayer. Now this fruitfulness and power of faith are due to the fact that genuine faith

[374]

releases divine power in us. Through faith God enters and transforms us.

(6) Again, faith is the universal condition of salvation. A gospel destined to become universal must have the universal appeal. The Jews in Paul's day sought to make of Christianity a new form of Judaism, which would have sealed its fate as a religion for all mankind. The apostle Paul sharply opposed them and forever established the gospel of justification by faith. Faith is the universal principle. It is the first thing we learn in our mother's arms. It enters into every human relationship where men cooperate for common ends. Now the divinely simple gospel of Christ selected this universal principle and made it the sole condition of our salvation. Of course the object of faith is Christ himself. But while faith terminates upon the divine Saviour here, and is inwrought through God's grace, it nevertheless remains the same elementary and universal principle of human experience. It places the redemption in Christ within the reach of all. No age or nation or condition of life puts a man beyond the reach of such a condition.

(7) Again, saving faith is an active as well as a passive principle. Looked at from one standpoint, faith is simply opening the hand to receive. It is simply surrender of the will. But the initial act of faith is itself an activity of the whole spiritual nature as we have seen. This initial act becomes the permanent attitude of the saved man: " As therefore ye received Christ Jesus the Lord, so walk in him, rooted and builded up in him, and established in your faith, even as ye were taught, abounding in thanksgiving" (Col. 2 : 6, 7). From this and other passages it is clear that faith is the permanent, the abiding attitude of the redeemed soul. The repetition of the initial act until it becomes fixed in character is the road to Christian growth and power.

This truth also shows how intensely personal and individual is Christian faith. The element of proxy, or substitutionary faith, is alien to the gospel. Hence the baptism of infants upon the alleged faith of parents or sponsors is foreign to New Testament teaching. Personal faith is the only kind of faith recognized in the New Testament. So also the "implicit faith" which the Catholic Church requires is foreign to the gospel. The imposition of beliefs by human authority is contrary to the nature of saving faith which is vital union with Christ. The beliefs of the Christian arise out of this union.

(8) Again, throughout the gospel faith is the correlative of grace. "By grace have ye been saved through faith; and that not of yourselves; it is the gift of God" (Eph. 2 : 8). This language of Paul goes to the heart of the matter. The Jew had a different combination of ideas. Salvation was a matter of works on man's part, and of debt on God's part. It was in large measure a matter of bookkeeping. There was a debit side and a credit side. If man could pay what he owed, or if he could purchase by good works the salvation he desired, he was entitled to receive it from God. To the idea of works Paul opposed the idea of faith. To the idea of debt he opposed the idea of grace. Salvation is by grace. Faith on man's part is not a work of merit possessing purchasing power, but the condition of salvation. Only by faith, apart from meritorious deeds, could man be saved.

This principle appears in the Old Testament as well as the New. Abraham was accepted, not on the ground of works, but on condition of faith. All Jews who were saved were saved by the same condition. The law did not annul the promise. The law was itself a provision of grace for the chosen people. Its end was to lead the Jews to Christ. Salvation by works was impossible, because of human sin and weakness. Indeed if a man had obeyed perfectly at any time (an achievement beyond the reach of the natural man), his obedience would have been due to his union with God by faith, not to his own inherent moral power. Man was made for God. All his moral and spiritual attainments are God's gracious gifts. Christ's revelation made clear the fundamental principle on which all men were saved before and after he came. It was never a matter of works and debt, but always of faith and grace.

(9) The above sheds light on a difficulty which many have felt concerning the way of salvation in the Old Testament teaching.

The Beginnings of the Christian Life

It is often asserted that men were saved by works in the Old, but by grace through faith in the New Testament. But this is an error. Salvation has always been by grace through faith. In Galatians 3 : 15-22 Paul sets forth the meaning of the law in relation to the gospel. It was never intended that men should be saved by the works of the law. If men had possessed moral power for a perfect obedience, it would have been due to living union with God by faith. Through such union God's gracious working in the soul imparts the power of obedience. Hence, for Paul, the idea of an obedience which could earn or merit salvation was inconceivable. Man possesses no moral or spiritual power apart from God. The enabling gift of God's grace on the one side and man's response by faith on the other would thus be the only possible explanation of even a sinless life.

The conclusion of Paul is that the law, which came four hundred and thirty years after the call of Abraham and his justification by faith, did not set aside the faith principle in salvation. The law had another purpose. It could not make alive, but it could train the people of Israel into a sense of need for a Redeemer. It could bring them a sense of their own weakness. Thus it could prepare them for Christ, who is the end of the law for righteousness to all who receive him by faith.

3. Conversion

Conversion is the word employed in theology to designate the turning of a sinner from his sins unto Christ for his salvation. This includes both the forsaking of sin which we have defined as repentance, and the trust in Christ which we have defined as faith. The term conversion usually refers to the outward act of the changed man which is the manifestation of the inner change in his soul. A converted man is one in whom the grace of God has wrought a spiritual change. That change has found inward expression in his repentance and faith, and outward expression in his turning from the old life of disobedience to the new life of service.

Conversion is the result of God's gracious action in us creating us anew in Christ. (Acts 3 : 26; Ps. 51 : 10; Ezek. 36 : 26.) It is also the result of our own free action. In conversion we choose the way of life in response to motives and appeals presented to us in the gospel. (Prov. 1 : 23; Isa. 31 : 6; Ezek. 14 : 6; Mark 1 : 15; Acts 2 : 38, 40, 41; Phil. 2 : 12, 13.)

There is a sense in which a Christian is "converted" whenever he turns from a wayward life back to the service of God. He returns from his backsliding and renews his vows to God. (Luke 22 : 31, 32; John 13 : 10.) But theological usage has tended more and more to restrict the word to that first turning from sin to God, which is otherwise designated as regeneration, or the new birth. For the sake of clearness it is better to employ some other word when we refer to the return of Christians from backsliding. There are a number of expressions which set forth the latter idea. "Renewal of vows," "returning to Christ," "forsaking the worldly life," "reconsecration," and other forms of expression are available for the purpose.

4. Regeneration

What is regeneration? This is one of the first questions we must ask and answer. Regeneration may be defined as the change wrought by the Spirit of God, by the use of truth as a means, in which the moral disposition of the soul is renewed in the image of Christ. All definitions come short of the reality. But the above contains the essential points. It is a change wrought by the Holy Spirit. It is accomplished through the instrumentality of the truth. It is a radical change of the moral and spiritual disposition. It is a change in which the soul is re-created in the image of Christ.

It is not necessary to present separate groups of Scripture to prove each of the above statements. It is important to note, however, the uniformity of the New Testament teaching as to regeneration. It is not a doctrine found only in the writings of John and Paul. It is found in the teachings of Jesus, of Hebrews, of James, and of Peter. It is most clear throughout the writings of the New Testament. We notice a few of the more important passages. In Matthew 12 : 33-35 Jesus declares that good fruit can only come from a good tree, and that to make the tree of human nature good, it must be changed. The entire Sermon on the Mount implies the necessity of the new birth. Its precepts are practicable only to the regenerate. The pure in heart are pronounced blessed because they shall see God. (Matt. 5 : 8.) The pure heart is not ours by nature. Men are conscious of impure hearts. Matthew 15 : 19 gives a brief description of the unrenewed heart. Jesus teaches the necessity for regeneration in his saying that a man who finds his life loses it, and that he who loses his life " for my sake " finds it. (Matt. 10 : 39.) The change here described is nothing less than a moral and spiritual revolution in the soul. The Gospel of John abounds in teachings as to the new birth. In the third chapter is the classic passage on the subject. In the conversation with Nicodemus Jesus expressly declares that the natural man is unfit for the kingdom of God; that a new birth from above is necessary; and that the Spirit of God works the change. Man is not wholly passive in the change thus wrought. For " as many as received him," to these he gave the power, or authority, to become the sons of God. (John 1 : 12.) Faith is the condition of the new birth. Paul deals with Christians in his Epistles. But there are indirect or direct teachings as to the new birth. He declares that the carnal mind is enmity against God and can be renewed only by the Spirit of God. (Rom. 8 : 3-9.) In 2 Corinthians 5 : 17 he says, " if any man be in Christ, he is a new creature." In Ephesians 1 : 19 and 2 : 1 and in Colossians 2 : 30 to 3 : 3 he declares that the present life of the believer is a risen or resurrection life. He has been spiritually raised from the dead by the Spirit of life.

Again in Hebrews 8 : 9-11 we have a graphic description of the New Covenant in which the law of God is written on the heart. and in 6 : 4 clear reference is made to the fact that Christians are " partakers " of the Holy Spirit. The new birth is assumed in both these passages. In the Epistle of James the same teaching appears. In 1 : 18 it is declared that God " of his own will " brought us forth by the word of truth. In 1 Peter 1 : 23 it is declared that Christians were begotten again, not of corruptible seed, but of incorruptible, even the word of God which liveth and abideth.

The Scripture passages we have cited are only a small fraction of the entire number to be found in the New Testament bearing on the subject. These will suffice for the present purpose, which is to establish the teaching on a solid scriptural basis. We may next consider a few details in which a certain emphasis is needed.

First, we distinguish regeneration from other things by showing what it is not. Regeneration is not a new creation in the sense that the soul is destroyed and a new one put in its place, nor in the sense that the faculties are destroyed and new faculties put in their place. The change is not in the spiritual constitution of man, but in his moral and spiritual disposition. God does not undo in the new creation in Christ what he did in his first creation in Adam. Sin is a power in reversed action in the soul. It is the misdirected energy of all man's powers as God made him. Regeneration breaks the power of sin, and sets free man's moral and spiritual life, and turns his powers in the right direction.

In regeneration man's will remains. But now it is a will obedient to a higher will which it recognizes. So also in regeneration the mental powers remain. But now the mind of man finds a higher mind and discovers that the truth he has been seeking has been seeking him all the time. His own mind finds its true self in God. The heart of man remains in regeneration, but now his affection finds its true Object in the Supreme Companion. All lower loves give way to the highest of all. Fellowship with God becomes the realized goal and destiny of the heart. Man's personality remains when he is regenerated, but it is now a transformed personality. Paul the apostle was the same as Saul the persecutor. Yet the change in him was so great that he described himself as an entirely new creature. Thus in regeneration man finds himself, comes to himself, realizes his own potentialities and possibilities as he can do in no other way.

Again, regeneration is in no sense to be confounded with a change on the natural level of man's life. In it we are born, not of blood, nor of the flesh, nor of the will of man, but of God. (John 1 : 13.) We note a few natural processes which must not be confounded with regeneration:

Regeneration is not education. There may be, and usually is, an educational factor in the influences which lead to regeneration. Truth is employed as the instrument of the Spirit. The mind is enlightened. But education can only remove ignorance. Regeneration breaks the power of sin. The change wrought in regeneration can never be achieved through education alone.

Again, regeneration is not transition from childhood to manhood. It must not be confounded with the natural process known as adolescence. During the period of adolescence the boy and girl undergo a marked change. In a sense a new world opens at that time. The history of conversions shows that it is a period of very great importance for the religious life of the young. But it is a period which in and of itself produces no spiritual life. It is full of potentialities for evil as well as good. By all means it should be recognized and utilized for bringing home the truth of the gospel to the developing soul. But it is a fatal error to confound adolescence with regeneration. The latter is the special work of God's Spirit creating in the soul the image of Christ.

We remark further that regeneration is not evolution on the natural plane. Of course there is no objection to the general assertion that in the new birth we pass from a lower to a higher level. In that sense the word evolution might apply. But the assertion that regeneration is merely the unfolding of previously existing elements in man is false. There are no resources in the natural man, nor in his environment, to produce the change wrought in regeneration. A wholly new cause is introduced. A new beginning is made. A power from above enters the soul of man. The change has been described by a modern psychologist as, on our part: (1) an uneasiness, or a sense that something is wrong about us as we naturally stand; and (2) the solution, a sense that we are saved from the wrongness by making connection with the higher powers.[1]

The point which needs emphasis in the doctrine of regeneration is the connection with the " higher powers." According to Christianity the higher power is the Holy Spirit of God revealing and creating Christ in the soul.

Several points are to be emphasized also on the positive side.

The first is that regeneration is an instantaneous act, and not a gradual process. The preparation may be gradual. Influences leading to the result may come from various sources and continue through many years. This is only to assert that God's action in blessing man follows the lines of natural law as far as this is possible. God's grace seeks man long before man responds to it. But the moment comes when the will submits and the moral bent of the nature is changed. The moral center of gravity of the soul shifts to another point entirely.

This truth holds along with the other truth that some are converted so very young, or so quietly, that they are not conscious of the change when it occurs. But the fruits of regeneration are present in the life and these are conclusive evidence of the fact ítself.

A second point on the positive side is that in regenerating the soul the Holy Spirit makes use of the truth as the means employed. It is important to grasp clearly that it is not the truth presented merely in the form of argument or moral suasion apart from the action of the Spirit. Nor is it the action of the Spirit independently of the truth. It is rather the Spirit employing the truth. The effect of the Spirit's action is seen in man's response to the truth of the gospel. But the truth apart from the Spirit's action in the soul would never produce the result. The fact that the truth is the instrument of the Spirit appears in numerous passages. In all cases recorded in the New Testament regeneration is effected through the preaching or teaching of the truth. The appearance of Jesus to Saul suddenly on the Damascus road is probably no exception to the rule. Saul, the per-

[1] William James.

secutor, had every opportunity to receive impressions about Christ prior to this experience. Elsewhere the truth appears uniformly as the influence employed by the Spirit. The disciples follow Jesus in response to his appeal. On the day of Pentecost the thousands who are regenerated respond to the gospel message. In Acts 16 : 14 it is declared that the Lord opened the heart of Lydia to give heed to the things spoken by Paul. In Ephesians 6 : 17 the word of God is declared to be the sword of the Spirit with which he does his work. In James 1 : 18 and 1 Peter 1 : 23 it is declared that Christians are begotten through the word of God.

In emphasizing the instrumentality of the truth in regeneration there is no thought of truth apart from Christ in an abstract way. It is the truth as it is in Christ. The Holy Spirit has as his specific work the making known to us the things of Christ. Every truth presented is a truth in Christ, since Christ is in his own person the gospel of our salvation.

We need not be detained here with possible exceptions to the rule that the Spirit employs truth as his instrument in regeneration. Infants dying in infancy are changed in so far as they inherit a natural bias toward sin. But how this change is wrought by the Spirit it is needless to inquire, since there is no light available on the subject beyond our speculations. The general principle is entirely clear, and we may be assured that apparent exceptions may ultimately be harmonized with it.

One important conclusion follows from the Spirit's use of truth in regeneration. It is that regeneration is not effected through the act of baptism. In a number of New Testament passages baptism is clearly associated with conversion, and nearly always with the beginnings of the Christian life. (See Acts 2 : 38; Rom. 6 : 3, 4; Col. 2 : 12; 1 Peter 3 : 21.) But there is no conclusive evidence that in any of these passages baptism is regarded in the Catholic sense as an *opus operatum,* i. e., an act which of itself regenerates without reference to the mind of the recipient. Nor do they sustain the view of the Disciples that baptism completes the act of regeneration.

The error in both views is in regarding baptism as a means to a given end, when it is only the symbolic outward expression of the end when it has been otherwise accomplished. Baptism symbolizes regeneration, but it does not produce it. Baptism was the outward sign of an inward change which had already taken place in the believer. It was repentance, faith, regeneration, conversion in symbol. It was none of these in fact. To confuse fact with symbol or symbol with fact is to change radically the nature of the gospel. In the passage in 1 Peter 3 : 21 we are cautioned against this error. It is not the physical act that has worth, Peter says. It is not a physical cleansing. The true significance of baptism is moral and spiritual. It is the answer of a good conscience toward God. Here truth is clearly distinguished from symbol. And the symbol only has value as a mirror for truth. Unless we grasp the truth reflected in the symbol and act upon it—that is, unless we are consciously obedient unto God and have within the witness of a good conscience—the outward symbol is of no value whatever.

A third positive statement is that in regeneration the divine energy manifests itself in us through the activity of our moral and spiritual faculties. As we have already seen, faith and repentance are conditions of regeneration. No unbelieving or impenitent man is regenerated. Every one who has the new birth is a penitent believer. This helps us to avoid the error of thinking of God's action in regenerating us as if it were a physical force, and as if men were things instead of persons. Christianity is not pantheism. God treats us always as free persons. God's method with us is always moral and spiritual. We respond to his appeal. His grace becomes effective in our response. When we turn from sin, when we trust the Saviour, when the will becomes obedient, then, and not until then, is the regenerating act complete. We are not to think of an interval of time between our act in response to God and God's act in changing us. There is no interval of time between. The two sides of the relation are completed at one and the same time. They are contemporaneous events in the soul's life. When a stone falls into a lake we may conceive the resulting wave as made up of two semicircles which together constitute the completed circle. So also when God's Spirit enters the human soul and regenerates, the human and divine sides may be conceived as semicircles, which together constitute the completed act. And as the semicircles in the lake originate at the same instant of time, so also the human response by faith is simultaneous with the regenerating act of God's Spirit.

IV. REGENERATION IN ITS LARGER RELATIONS

No teaching of Scripture brings us nearer the heart of Christianity than the doctrine of regeneration. We may understand how central it is in the Christian religion by noting briefly its relations to other great ideas of the gospel.

1. Regeneration is closely related to the idea of God. When the soul is regenerated it is changed fundamentally in moral and spiritual quality. The quality it receives is a reproduction in us of qualities in God. For the first time then we learn through experience the kind of being God is. We are made partakers of the divine nature. Prior to regeneration we may have theoretical knowledge about God. Now we have positive acquaintance with him. It thus appears how man's spiritual life renders the highest service to him in his metaphysical speculations. The speculative instinct is very strong in man. He cannot refrain from setting up interrogation-marks at the portals of all the great mysteries of experience. Particularly is this true regarding the supreme Reality behind all that we see and touch and know and feel. And yet our speculative strivings yield little satisfying knowledge until the new life comes to us from God. It is then we "taste and see" the reality we had been reasoning about. God becomes a fact for us. He is no longer a logical deduction. And in discovering him we most truly discover ourselves.

2. Regeneration is also closely connected with revelation; Jesus Christ is God's supreme revelation to men. But Christ's revelation remains outside of us until God reveals his Son in us.

z

The Christian Religion in Its Doctrinal Expression

The truth of God becomes visible in Christ. It is, as it were, projected upon the screen of his humanity for us to see. But it does not become revelation to us in the complete meaning of the word until the objective becomes the subjective truth in us. It is not surprising that unregenerate men often fail to accept the historical revelation of God in Christ. They close the spiritual avenues of approach to that revelation and cut themselves off from the inner confirmation which they might have in the renewal of their own natures.

3. Again, regeneration is vitally related to the doctrine of Christ's person. Christ is teacher, prophet, revealer. But he is more than all these combined. He is life-giver. Here we touch the heart of the gospel. The distinguishing mark of Christ in his relations to men is his relation to them as spiritual cause. Men miss the true meaning of Christianity when they take it as a group of ideas merely. They should take it rather as a group of spiritual forces or causes. Of course it is a great group of ideas. Our doctrinal system is the result of the effort to express these ideas in a coherent and unified way. But the ideas arise out of the facts and forces.

Now Christ is the supreme force or cause in our revealed religion. We must so understand him if we are to understand him at all. We are not to understand him simply as our example to imitate; or as one proved to our reason to be divine through miracles and signs alone; nor as an objective revelation of what God is, to be accepted as an article of faith. We are to take him rather as one who has life in himself and who has power to repeat or reproduce that life in others. This fact is the great theme of the Fourth Gospel. The idea is repeated in many forms. In him was life, and the life in him becomes light in us. (John 1 : 4, 5.) Of his fulness men receive, and grace for grace. (John 1 : 16.) He came that we might have life, and have it more abundantly. (John 10 : 10.) He declared that rivers of living water should flow from him who was joined to Christ by faith. (John 7 : 38.) In short, the Gospel of John is a great historical and experiential demonstration of the divine function of Christ as life-giver to men. He is the realized ideal of God's approach to man, his self-revelation for their salvation. He is also the realized ideal of man's search for God. He is the door through which God comes to men. (John 10 : 1-3.) He is also the door through which men must pass to find God. (John 10 : 9.) Thus the whole religious life of the human race finds its consummation in him the life-giver.

4. Regeneration is vitally connected with the work of the Holy Spirit. As we shall see, the Spirit of God works this change in us, reproducing in us the life in Christ. The Holy Spirit is God immanent in men. His regenerating act in the soul is the new spiritual beginning for man.

5. Regeneration is in the closest relations with all other doctrines and facts of the spiritual life. For example, it imparts the nature whose moral contents are best expressed by the word sonship. When we are regenerated we become actual sons of God. Justification expresses the standing of the regenerate before God, although faith is the condition of both. Sanctification is the gradual unfolding of the life imparted in regeneration into its own inherent possibilities of moral and spiritual beauty. Perseverance is the continuance of the divine life in us even unto the immortal and glorified forms into which it will finally open at death. The doctrine of last things is the account we give of the destiny of the regenerate in the life to come and along with it the fate of those who do not possess that divine life.

6. To the above we may add that regeneration is the key to the problem of final causes. We have seen how we learn in it for the first time the character of God. In it we may also discover in great measure the ultimate purpose of God. Two facts stand out very clearly as we view the world at its present stage of development. It is an unfinished and also a sinful world. Nature stretches from crystal through plant and animal up to man. It becomes moral and spiritual in the constitution of man. And yet it is marred and broken by sin and comes to little. As one has said, " Man seems to be an unfulfilled promise." In him are great and wondrous intimations of something higher which yet

seems unattainable. In regeneration God and man come together again. Man comes into possession of new moral power and begins to realize his destiny as a son of God. The final cause or ultimate aim of God appears. He is bringing many sons to glory. Thus in the regenerate life of man we have the fact basis for our view of the first and final causes of the world. God's creative energy in the soul tells us of his original creation of the world. The sonship which he is producing in us tells of the end of the universe, a kingdom of free spiritual beings bearing to him the relation of sons to a Father.

7. Certain forms of philosophic theory are best met and overcome in the light of man's regenerate life. Pessimism construes the evil and suffering of the world as proof of the non-existence of a good God. Pluralism is impressed with the struggle between the good and evil powers, and concludes that there is no supreme God. If there is a good being, he is opposed by one or more beings who are equally powerful. Hence the age-long struggle between good and evil which seems to have no end. Pantheism despairs of personal victory on man's part and takes refuge in the thought that sin is merely a passing phase of the divine manifestation, and that man will be delivered from his otherwise hopeless struggle by reabsorption in the infinite. His personal life will come to an end.

Now man's regenerate life in Christ shows to him the great realities and truths which overcome all these speculations. These may be summed up as follows: (1) A divine power which is personal and moral. Its inworking in the soul is essentially ethical. It produces moral character in man, and creates personal fellowship. (2) A deepening and enrichment of man's personal life. Not the slow and painful emptying out, or draining off of the elements of human personality, as Buddhism teaches, but an intensifying of them all is the Christian ideal. Love is ever deepened. The passion for righteousness and immortality burns as an ever-increasing flame. (3) The actual conquest of evil by the regenerate man. Pessimism and pluralism are thus set aside by the facts of experience. We already have the victory in principle. "This is the victory that hath overcome the world, even our faith" (1 John 5 : 4). We may say, then, that regeneration shows that Christianity is more than a "cognitive series." It is not merely a group of ideas or doctrines harmoniously arranged in a system. It is also a "causal series." It is a group of spiritual forces and causes producing given effects in a moral and spiritual kingdom. Hence Christianity cannot be reckoned with or dealt with as a series of ideas alone. It must be studied as a group of causes and effects. The ideas arise out of the facts. The facts and causes are fundamental.

8. Finally, regeneration is the key to the problem of knowledge in Christianity. In regeneration we find the operation of the facts and forces which constitute the Christian religion. Here are the data to be interpreted. Here are the causes and effects which are to be explained. Here are the spiritual realities which supply the material for theological science. We gain historical knowledge of Christianity by a study of the literary sources in the Bible. But these leave us outside the temple of spiritual realities. We never know Christianity on the inside until we know it through the regenerate life of men. Experience alone can qualify for the interpretation and exposition of Christianity because experience alone supplies a first-hand knowledge of the facts.

V. JUSTIFICATION

1. Definition

Justification is a judicial act of God in which he declares the sinner free from condemnation, and restores him to divine favor. It takes place when the sinner trusts in Christ and his merits for salvation. These two statements contain the essential elements of the New Testament doctrine of justification. We single out several points for special emphasis.

Observe, first, that justification is a declarative act of God. The word of which our English word justify is the translation (Greek: *dikaioo*) in the New Testament does not mean to make just or righteous, but to pronounce or reckon just. There are numerous Scriptures supporting this statement. In the Epistle to the Romans the whole argument turns upon the problem of how a man may become righteous before God. Paul declares that in the gospel there is revealed a righteousness of God from faith unto faith. (1 : 17.) In Christ God has provided a righteousness for us which becomes, through faith, the ground of our acceptance with God. Through our living union with Christ his righteousness becomes the source of our own actual righteousness. Justification, however, relates to the former while sanctification relates to the latter righteousness.

Observe, next, that this declarative act of God is grounded in the work of Christ. This is the heart of the argument in Romans. The passage in which the idea of justification is made most clear is Romans 3 : 23-26. It reads as follows: " For all have sinned and fall short of the glory of God; being justified freely by his grace through the redemption that is in Christ Jesus: whom God set forth to be a propitiation, through faith in his blood, to show his righteousness because of the passing over of the sins done aforetime, in the forbearance of God; for the showing, I say, of his righteousness at this present season; that he might himself be just, and the justifier of him that hath faith in Jesus."

An analysis of the passage shows the following result: (1) All men have sinned. There is no exception to the rule. (2) All need a justification other than that which they can themselves provide. (3) God has set forth Christ to be a propitiation for our sins. (4) We are, on the ground of this propitiatory work of Christ, declared to be just, or reckoned as just. (5) This justifying act of God was freely bestowed by his grace on condition of our faith in Christ. (6) Finally, this work of Christ was necessary in order that God might himself be just as well as the justifier of him who believes in Christ. It is evident from this passage that God does not and cannot justify a sinner in the sense of declaring him to be righteous. The gospel is God's arrangement by which a sinner may enter into a new relation to God by faith in Christ. In this new relation God may justify the ungodly. (Rom. 4 : 5.) The basis and ground of justification then is the work of Jesus Christ. His atonement for our sins is the sole basis of God's justifying act.

We note, thirdly, that God's declarative act justifying the sinner is on condition of faith. This principle is repeatedly asserted in the New Testament. The Old Testament is quoted as proof of the fact that faith has always been the condition of justification. The faith of Abraham is taken as the great typical instance of faith. Abraham believed God, and it was reckoned unto him for righteousness. (Rom. 4 : 3; Gen. 15 : 6.) In the eleventh chapter of Hebrews a long list of Old Testament saints is given, all of whom lived by faith. In Habakkuk 2 : 4 there is a terse but comprehensive statement of the great principle: " The righteous shall live by faith." In Galatians 2 : 16, 20 the idea is set forth in clearest terms, in contrast with the works of the law as a ground of justification. Negatively, therefore, justification is never on the ground of works. This was the cardinal error of the Jews. The most difficult of all ideas for them to appropriate and assimilate was that of salvation by grace through faith. In Ephesians 2 : 8 the truth is stated in most emphatic terms. Salvation is " by grace," and grace is exercised toward us " through faith," and faith in turn is " the gift of God." Again, in the fourth chapter of Romans Paul sums up the principle of justification by faith in several statements. Taking Abraham as the great exemplar of faith, he asserts that his faith was reckoned or imputed unto him for righteousness. (Ver. 3, 9.) Now if a man seeks to earn salvation by works, Paul says the fundamental principle of the gospel is destroyed. (Ver. 4.) But to him who believes in Christ and renounces works as the ground of salvation, his faith is imputed to him for righteousness. (Ver. 5.)

We observe, in the fourth place, that the contents of God's justifying act are freedom from condemnation and restoration to divine favor. Justification is the bestowal of a new standing before God. The penalty of the law which the sinner has transgressed is now remitted. He is pardoned. At the same time he is received into the divine favor. The grace of God now flows out actively to him and imparts every moral and spiritual blessing. In both of these aspects of the divine good will toward the justified man, the ground of blessing is Jesus Christ and his work. In Romans 5 : 1, 2 the blessings of justification are set forth in comprehensive terms. We note: (1) The ground of justification: "through our Lord Jesus Christ." (2) The condition: "being therefore justified by faith." (3) The remission of penalty: "Let us have peace with God." There is no longer the menace of a broken law. (4) The new standing in the divine favor: "through whom also we have our access by faith unto this grace wherein we stand."

In the fifth place, justification is an act of God at the beginning of the Christian life and is never repeated. The freedom from condemnation and restoration to God's favor are permanent states. Thus justification establishes a new relation to God which is never broken. No repetition of the justifying act is ever possible or necessary. The fact that justification is never repeated has an important bearing on the quality of our spiritual life, as we shall see. Our service to God is qualified and conditioned at every point by his great act of justifying grace.

2. Why is Justification by Faith?

In reply to this question, we have already seen that faith is made the condition of justification in opposition to the Jewish notion of works and merit as the basis of justification. Faith is itself not a meritorious work. It is rather God's gift to us as well as our response to God.

There is another reason why faith is the condition of justification. It is because faith is the universal principle of the Christian life. Faith is living union with Christ. It is the condition of every other Christian grace, of all Christian growth. Faith is a continuous relation of the soul to God. It will abide even in the future life along with hope and love. (1 Cor. 13 : 13.) Looking on the human side of salvation we may say that faith is the precondition and presupposition of everything else. It is the germinal principle of the spiritual life. Regeneration, adoption, sanctification, good works, perseverance, glorification, are all fruits of faith. So also is justification. Justification belongs to the great series of spiritual blessings which come to us in and through Christ. And faith is the condition of them all. Properly understood, it is the total human response to the approach of God's saving grace in Christ to sinful men.

3. The Relation of Justification to Christian Experience

The necessity and value of the doctrine of justification come into great clearness when we consider it in relation to the needs of the spiritual life. It is indispensable to the Christian religion. Without it a great lack would be felt, a great need unprovided for. That need may be stated as follows: In order to the highest form of service to God at least two elements are required by man. One of these is that it shall be free. The other is that it shall be filial. Every element of bondage must be removed. Freedom from sin, from condemnation, and freedom from doubt are necessary. The confidence, the love, and the loyalty of the son toward the Father must be present. In a word, the Christian life requires a true basis for the assurance of salvation. The free and filial attitude is only possible when every doubt as to our standing with God has been cleared away. Justification by faith secures for us this priceless boon and sets us forever free for filial service.

There are two considerations which make clear the need of justification in order to this free and filial service, this assurance of salvation. One is the evils which arise without the doctrine of justification. The other is the fact that no other teaching of the gospel can supply the need which is supplied by justification. We consider these briefly.

(1) First, there are numerous evil tendencies in a religious life unsupported by the doctrine of God's justifying grace. One of these is the tendency to lower the Christian conception of God. A sentimental view of God as an indulgent and rather weak Father may take the place of the infinitely Holy Father of the

gospel. The Fatherhood of God in the New Testament is the loftiest ever presented. He is both the infinitely loving and the supremely righteous God.

Along with this tendency to lower the idea of God is another which weakens the conception of sin. Christianity has deepened the meaning of sin beyond anything the world ever knew before. The Holy Spirit " convicts " men of sin as the condition of the entrance of God's renewing grace. Consequently when the moral nature of man is awakened under the Spirit's power, he becomes conscious of sin and of a sense of guilt and condemnation which, if unrelieved, may lead to despair. He sees sin as God sees it. Now a man may refuse to be awakened in his moral and spiritual nature. He may resist the Spirit of God and cling to a false hope based on a weakened sense of sin and a lowered conception of God. But whenever an adequate sense of sin arises there is need for God's justifying act, and without it men are without hope.

Again, without the doctrine of justification there is a strong tendency to lapse into the old Jewish error of salvation by works. This always results in one of two ways. Either a man becomes self-righteous and imagines himself better than he is; or else his hope is ever clouded by the fear lest he may come short of the divine requirements. If he is lacking in a sense of sin and its meaning, he will tend to become self-righteous. If he has been really aroused in his moral nature, if his conscience is keenly alive to moral realities and the holy law of God, he is in danger of falling into despair. These are common ways in which men have gone astray. Neither of them is the Christian way. The Christian religion deepens the sense of sin. But it proclaims a grace which has met all the needs of the sinner. God's act of justification cleanses the conscience from dead works to serve the living God.

Another form of this tendency is seen in the Roman Catholic doctrine. This teaches that justification is a gradual process, going on throughout the Christian life. Penance and various forms of discipline are necessary to secure justification. Men are justified only so far as they are sanctified. The result is that men are never assured of salvation in the present life. Dorner has said with reference to the Romanist doctrine, that we are justified only as far as we are sanctified: "Since justification is a con-tinuous process, the redeeming death of Christ, on which it de-pends, must be a continuous process also; hence its prolonged reiteration in the sacrifice by the mass. Since sanctification is obviously never completed in this life, no man ever dies com-pletely justified; hence the doctrine of purgatory."

The doctrine of "salvation by character," as proclaimed by some adherents of the so-called "new theology," is very closely akin to the Catholic doctrine in its essential principle. They do not make use of sacraments in the same way as do Catholics. But they ignore the efficacy of Christ's work for us and depend upon inherent moral qualities in man rather than upon God's justifying act. Here again the old legalism is certain to spring up in a new form. The old doubts are sure to return as the spiritual vision becomes purified and sin appears in its true light. The awakened moral consciousness can never behold within itself such moral attainments as may supply a ground of hope. Hence there will follow self-deception as to the real moral state or else despair. The biblical doctrine of justification avoids both these errors. There is no self-righteousness possible since God's justifying act is wholly of grace bestowed upon the sinful and undeserving. There is no danger of despair, because God's own power is for us in the redemptive act of Christ, and it is in us as renewing grace to transform us into his own image.

(2) The second consideration which shows the necessity for justification in Christian experience is that no other gift of God's grace can supply the need. A very brief review of the other blessings will show this. Forgiveness is of course a restoration of man to right relations with God, but acts of sin are committed after the power of sin is broken. The Master taught us in the Lord's Prayer that we should repeatedly pray for forgiveness, while justification is never repeated. Regeneration, as we have seen, renews the moral nature, but the life of the regenerate man

is not sufficiently uniform or self-consistent to supply the constant need of assurance that he is accepted by God. Repentance and faith and conversion mark a great spiritual crisis in the soul's life. But it is the common experience that Christians do not find themselves able to maintain this level of experience. There are many turnings or "conversions" after the first one. Assurance as a fixed fact cannot be based upon this experience alone. Sanctification is a gradual process, but it is a gradual process whch is subject to many variations. Perseverance is itself in large measure conditioned upon our assurance of justification. Even our faith, which is the vital principie of all our Christian living, is a variable factor. We often pray, "Lord, I believe, help thou my unbelief."

We conclude, then, that we have in justification a great fundamental truth which cannot be dispensed with in our spiritual life. It is not our subjective experience in any of its varying forms, in which we trust. It is God's great and gracious act addressed to our variable experience to sustain it amid all its changes and struggles. Especially is the doctrine of justification needed to assure us of God's acceptance of us when crises arise and our souls are tried by fire. Then we are tempted to doubt and fall away. But it is then our established position, our unchanging status before God, makes us strong to dare, to suffer, and to achieve. We cannot dispense with the doctrine of justification by faith, if we are to retain the elements which condition the highest attainments in the Christian life.

4. An Objection to the Doctrine of Justification

An objection which is urged by some against the Christian doctrine of justification by faith must now be considered. The language in which the objection is stated varies to some extent, but the principal idea remains the same. It is said that the doctrine implies an artificial or fiat righteousness. This means a righteousness which is not genuine, but fictitious, since God merely reckons righteousness to one who does not possess it. It is an artificially made righteousness, a righteousness by decree. With this goes the further statement that the doctrine of justification is unethical and tends to a legalistic or forensic conception of salvation. It is not denied that Paul taught this doctrine of justification, but it is claimed that it was a piece of Jewish legalism which he brought over from his former life. It was thus a passing phase of teaching which did not represent the essential principles of Christianity. Paul, it is true, did teach a true spiritual Christianity, but the objectors insist that the spiritual element of his teaching lies side by side with the Jewish-legal element and in contradiction to it.

In replying to this objection we begin with the general statement that it grows out of an abstract method of dealing with the teachings of the gospel. As we have remarked in other connections, it is impossible to understand the Christian religion unless we take it in its unity as an organic whole. If we separate it into parts, and then consider any of the parts in the abstract, or without reference to the living connections of the whole, we always go astray. Analysis into parts is necessary for clear thinking, but analytical thought loses its way when it forgets the vital unity of the Christian religion in human experience and in the New Testament teaching.

These remarks are especially applicable to the doctrine of justification by faith. Justification is one aspect of the salvation which comes to men through Christ. That salvation includes a living faith which unites us with Christ, and makes us partakers of his life. It includes regeneration, which changes radically the moral disposition. It includes vital union with Christ, and the indwelling Spirit of God, which recreates us in the moral image of Christ. It includes the divine process, which looks to our gradual sanctification and glorification. When we consider justification in connection with these facts and the truths which arise out of them, all the objections fall to the ground. If faith is taken in an abstract way as merely historical belief, and if God's justifying act is conceived of merely as that of a judge in a court acquitting a criminal of a charge of which he is guilty, then indeed the objection might hold. But these are not the New Testament ways of taking either faith or justification. The faith that justifies is the faith that regenerates. The act of God which justifies is an act which also imparts moral character to the justified.

With these general facts held in mind we may reply to the objection in detail.

(1) First, we reply that Paul's doctrine is not a remnant of Judaism, but on the contrary is directly opposed to the Jewish doctrine of salvation. In the Epistle to the Romans Paul combats the Jewish method of justification by works. He opposes to it the Christian doctrine of justification by faith. Indeed, it is his doctrine of justification which is fundamental to Christianity as the universal religion. It is because God is not " the God of the Jews only " that Paul insists upon it. Justification by faith puts the gospel in reach of all men, Jews and Gentiles alike.

(2) Again, the Christian doctrine of justification by faith is not legal and forensic, but vital and spiritual. The objector overlooks the fact that the phrase " by faith " transforms the idea of justification in such manner that the merely legal principle disappears, or is gathered up into a higher unity. The word justification, or the bare conception of justification apart from faith, would indeed be legal and forensic. But the Christian reality is not the bare conception. It is justification vitalized by the complementary thought expressed by the phrase " by faith." The ungodly who is justified " by faith " is the ungodly brought into a godly relation which is not artificial and unreal, but most vital and real. The condemnation which is removed and the favor to which the justified is restored are most real.

(3) We remark further that justification by faith is not unethical, but rather leads to the highest ethical qualities in the justified. The atonement of Christ, as we have seen, is the ground of justification. That atoning act was the glorification of love. And love is the sum of ethical qualities. Now the justified man is drawn into participation with Christ in his self-emptying love. The justified man is crucified with Christ. Self is slain. He rises to a new life of love. Justification indeed simply

bestows a new standing with God on condition of faith. But the new standing is not that of one who yet remains untouched by regenerating power. It is not a new standing unrelated to a new inner principle of life and holiness. The two go together. To take justification out of this context of life and power is to reverse its New Testament meaning.

(4) The doctrine of justification provides for a need of the spiritual life which the objection overlooks. That need is that legalism be destroyed in the Christian experience. Salvation by grace through faith is opposed at all points to legalism in the old Jewish sense. Now Paul's teaching on justification is not only not legalistic in itself, but is his chief weapon for destroying legalism. The human conscience is naturally legalistic. It is prone to adopt methods for earning salvation. It is slow to yield to the gospel of grace. It is difficult to believe that God is willing to accept the ungodly. Sin has created a barrier. It seems incredible that a man can at a stroke be emancipated from his guilt and restored to God's favor. This is simply a description of the sin-consciousness in men generally. It is a matter of experience, and not of theory or abstract reasoning.

Now no form of teaching can answer the needs of the soul which does not recognize this sin-consciousness. We mention two forms of such attempt which fail. First, it will not do to declare the sin-consciousness to be merely subjective. To tell a man that sin is not sin, or that guilt is not guilt does not convince. He cannot believe that such a statement represents God's attitude toward sin. The very make of his moral nature forbids his believing this. The moral ideals and values, which he longs for but does not possess, are seen to be valid because of the reality of his sin and guilt. If sin is unreal, then the moral kingdom as a whole loses its significance, because each is the contradiction of the other. The reality of the sin- and guilt-consciousness in man is thus a fact to be reckoned with. Again, it does not meet the case to tell the sinner that he needs only to realize in himself the consciousness of Christ, as is urged by some. As Christ enjoyed unbroken fellowship with God, and possessed a perfect filial consciousness, so also, it is claimed, we may be saved by realizing in our own consciousness this life of fellowship. But this is to set for man an impossible task. It is impossible to dispel the sense of sin and guilt as with a magician's wand, by a mere act of our own will. The first and immediate effect of the spotless purity of Christ and of the Spirit's action in us is to throw our sin and guilt into deeper shadow. We are convinced of sin as we never were before. The sinless consciousness of Christ then becomes a goal wholly unattainable by us. It shines in solitary splendor in the heights far beyond our reach. It is, therefore, a false psychology which approaches the matter in that way. What men need is a gospel of redemption from sin, of relief from the sense of sin and guilt.

We conclude, then, that Paul's doctrine of justification by faith was his method of destroying man's sense of sin and condemnation. Legalism strives to overcome it by all sorts of devices and strivings and good works. Paul declares that there is no device, no form of striving or good works which can ever meet the need. And yet if a man is to enter a life of freedom, of filial devotion to God, a life of love and loyalty, somehow the legal method must be destroyed along with the legal consciousness. Therefore, says Paul, God meets a sinner in Christ, justifies him, bestows a new standing, accepts him as son, and forever closes the question of law and condemnation, of sin and guilt. And this he does in his gracious justifying act. It is this which is at once followed by the new filial consciousness " whereby we cry, Abba, Father " (Rom. 8 : 15).

Before leaving the subject of justification we may answer a question which is often asked: Whether the justified man is conscious of God's justifying act? It is usually replied that he is not, since man cannot be conscious of what is done by God. This reply, while containing an element of truth, is insufficient. It does not cover all the facts. Indeed, it is but another result of the fallacy of analytic thought in its effort to explain that which is organically one. God and man, in the saving act, are not separated by an interval of space, as if man were here at this point, and God yonder at another. Justification and regeneration are aspects of an indivisible whole. Peace with God, forgiveness, reconciliation, are other aspects. All of these arise in the soul at the same time with the exercise of saving faith. Conscious-ness of one implies consciousness of all the others. And while justification is God's act and not our own, yet it is invariably present with other forms of experience which are clearly our own. We are assured of justification, therefore, just because the great salvation, which comes to us in Christ, includes it as an essential element of the indivisible whole. That salvation is like a precious jewel having many facets from which divine light is reflected. The process of analysis requires time. We may not understand in an intellectual way at the outset all the rich contents of our new life in Christ. But we possess the jewel, not in parts, but as a whole. When we count the facets we shall find that we possessed them all at the beginning.

VI. Adoption and Sonship

Justification, as we have seen, has reference to sin and the law. In it a new relation to the law is established, a new stand-ing with God is bestowed. Adoption is a blessing which con-stitutes the new corresponding relation to God. But before set-ting forth the contents of adoption a prior question calls for attention. Is there any sense in which all men are sons of God? Is God the Father of all? There are two groups of Scripture teachings which at first sight seem to contradict each other. A few of each of these groups will serve the present purpose. There is no dispute as to Adam's relation to God as son before sin and the fall. Sin of course produced a change. The Old Testament has comparatively little which sheds light on the par-ticular point at issue. Angels are there recognized as the sons of God. (Job 1 : 6; 2 : 1.) Israel as a nation is called God's son. (Hosea 11 : 1.) In the Sermon on the Mount Jesus describes God as being fatherly and loving toward the evil as well as the good. (Matt. 5 : 45.) In the parable of the Prodigal Son, the

A 2

[401]

The Christian Religion in Its Doctrinal Expression

prodigal represents the publicans and sinners who were despised by the self-righteous Pharisees. The Father is represented as longing for and welcoming the return of the wayward son. (Luke 15 : 11-32.) At times Jesus seems to employ the word Father in an absolute sense. He is "the Father," and is paternal in his yearning toward all men. (John 4 : 23.) The apostle Paul at Athens declared that all men are the offspring of God. (Acts 17 : 28.) In Galatians 4 : 1-6 Paul declares that prior to the adoption through Christ men were in a state of nonage. They were heirs, yet no better than servants. Only when Christ came did they receive the adoption of sons. These passages show that there is more or less elasticity in the biblical use of the idea of fatherhood and sonship as expressive of a divine-human relation.

The other group of passages makes this statement even more clear. In Matthew 13 : 38 Jesus declares that the "good seed" of the parable are children of the kingdom, while "the tares" are the children of the wicked one. He declared that the Pharisees were not sons of God, but sons of the devil. (John 8 : 44.) Again, in John 1 : 12 men become sons of God by faith. In Galatians 3 : 26 Paul makes the same assertion. All men are children of God by faith in Jesus Christ. There is no need to multiply passages. There can be no question as to the distinction made between believers and unbelievers in these passages.

Now the problem of exegesis here is to find a key for the interpretation of both groups of passages. The following are some of the efforts in this direction:

1. First, it is urged that all men indiscriminately are sons of God in the same sense. There is no need of regeneration. Men need only to claim their sonship and it is theirs. God is the Father of all men in the same sense. He may discipline and train his sons, but in the end all will be saved. This is the view of universalism. It is of course to be rejected. It ignores all those passages which distinguish between the moral states of men and between faith and unbelief in relation to sonship.

2. A second view is that no one is a son of God in any sense except those who are redeemed by Christ. These interpret all

the first group of passages as having no reference to sonship. They distinguish between "offspring" and sonship; between the nation Israel and individual sons of God; between the prodigal who was a son in the parable and others who are sons actually. No doubt there is much to be said for some of the reasoning here. But in some respects it is not altogether conclusive. It is not easy, for example, to separate the earlier from the later stages in the parable of the Prodigal. The wanderer becomes a real son upon repentance and return to the Father. But the motives and influences and relations prior to the repentance are all based on Fatherhood and sonship. It is not easy to conclude that this relation means everything after repentance and nothing whatever before.

3. A third view is that God is the Father of all men, but not all men are sons of God. This is based on the broad ground that God is unchangeable. Since sonship and Fatherhood are members of a spiritual relationship based on attitude and disposition, we cannot assert that man's sin has changed God. Disobedience has corrupted man and destroyed his normal and true relations to God, but it has not changed God in the fundamental fatherly impulse of his being. Hence it is claimed we may explain those passages which assert that wicked men are sons of the devil and become sons of God only by faith, as well as the other passages which seem to assert God's universal Fatherhood. The seeming contradiction is thus removed.

This view undoubtedly states a great truth in part. But it lacks completeness. God is unchangeable. He is eternally loving. But his love for sinners is not manifested in the same way as his love for his true spiritual sons. The fatherly impulse in God, therefore, cannot express itself toward the incorrigibly bad except in wrath and penalty. But this we usually attribute to him as judge rather than as Father. Of course in the final analysis the judicial and paternal in God are unitary elements of his character. But fatherhood and sonship, as we know them, are reciprocal relations which cannot well be asserted as existing in isolation from each other. In defining sonship and Fatherhood, therefore, each member of the relationship should correspond to the other.

4. A fourth view is that all men are natural sons of God, but only believers in Christ are true spiritual sons. Man was made in God's image, and natural sonship is regarded as identical with the divine image in man. Now, of course, if this is a correct definition of sonship, the view is correct. For man, even in his sin, does retain part of the original likeness to God. So long as the necessity of the new birth is insisted upon to convert the natural into true spiritual sons, there is no objection to the view except the practical difficulty of keeping the natural and spiritual sonships distinguished from each other in the popular mind.

5. It seems, therefore, that a fifth view may be urged which more accurately expresses the truth and explains all the passages cited. It is that all men are constituted for sonship to God, and that God desires all men to become sons, but that this ideal is only made real in the new birth. In favor of this we note the following facts:

First of all, the New Testament certainly defines sonship in the highest and ideal sense in terms of the new birth and moral likeness to God. " Be ye imitators of God as beloved children, and walk in love," is the exhortation addressed to Christians. (Eph. 5 : 1, 2.) This implies clearly the possession of moral and spiritual traits by the children which correspond with moral and spiritual traits in God. Here then we have sonship and Fatherhood defined in their final and ideal form. It means " the response of moral qualities in man to moral qualities in God."

Secondly, this moral likeness to God expressed by sonship, while it arises out of union with Christ through faith, is only possible to those who previously possessed in some measure the original image and likeness of God. No beast can become a son of God. Only a being who is endowed with capacity for sonship can become a son. Man's filial relation to God is analogous to his moral relation. " There is none good, no, not one." This does not imply that man does not possess a moral constitution, or is lacking in capacity for moral action. He can speak truth and eschew falsehood and perform other moral acts. But his moral character does not conform to God's standard. He needs redemption by God's grace. He has a moral constitution, but not a moral character. In like manner, he was made or constituted for sonship, but attains it only through the new birth. He has a filial constitution, but has not the filial character.

In the third place, the point is made clear when we remember that true sonship involves both a moral constitution and at the same time a moral relation. What did Adam lose when he sinned? He did not lose his moral constitution, but he did lose his moral and filial relation to God. He became disobedient. There was broken fellowship. Sin separated him from God. When the prodigal in the parable left home, he broke with the father. The filial relation was destroyed and the paternal relation ceased to be operative. But the prodigal retained the filial constitution. He could not unmake his soul. His own moral consciousness told him, however, that he had forfeited the claim to sonship. "I am no more worthy to be called thy son." The poignancy of his grief arose from the recognition of this fact, the loss of sonship. The father awaited the return of the prodigal with open arms because the paternal constitution was unchanged even while the paternal relation was interrupted. That it was interrupted is clear from his own words, "My son, who was dead, is alive again." It is strange how men have insisted on making this parable teach an uninterrupted relation between father and son in spite of sin, when it so clearly teaches that sin destroyed the relation. The constitution was not destroyed on either side, but the relation was completely destroyed. This view explains many passages of Scripture to which reference has been made and others which cannot now be cited except in a general way. Paul's teaching in Galatians (3 : 1-5) points out that the children and heirs were no better than servants in their position until Christ came. They were in bondage under the rudiments of the world. They were destined for sons, but did not become sons until Christ came and they received the adoption. Sonship was thus the great spiritual boon held in reserve for them. They were by nature constituted for it, but did not possess it. The grace which bestows it enriches the filial spirit in many ways which could in no other manner have been attained.

The view here presented differs from the view of the natural sonship of all men in the definition of sonship. It emphasizes the relation as well as the constitution in sonship. The outcome is the same provided the idea of natural sonship does not lead to a dangerous error. The crucial point is this: How does the natural son become a true spiritual son? Two answers are given. Some say by regeneration, and only upon condition of faith in Christ. Others says by natural evolution. The two answers lead back to divergence of view as to sin. One group asserts man's inability apart from God's grace; the other, that he only needs education and growth. With the former, as one has said, natural sonship is like Robinson Crusoe's first canoe on the desert island. It was finished away from the water and lay like a log, too heavy to be moved. Natural sonship does not bring men to God. The other view says it is like a canoe moored to shore in a narrow stream. It only needs to be untied, and the current will float it down the stream and out to sea. The new birth is a cardinal doctrine of Christianity. Any form of natural sonship which ignores it leads to serious errors. If this point is not safeguarded, there is always danger of introducing a false conception of man and sin and of man's relations to God. From this it is easy to pass to other wrong views throughout the entire range of doctrine.

Sons by Faith and Adoption

We have already seen that the New Testament puts much emphasis upon the fact that we are sons of God by faith. Our own free response to the invitation of the gospel is a most valuable element in our sonship. It is no merely physical relation. It is more than a natural constitution. These may be imposed upon or imparted to us by God's action apart from our own. Hence the ethical and spiritual quality is absent. Our own free response by faith is a new element. In it our personality rises to a new level. We receive and exercise thus a right or authority to become a son. (John 1 : 12.) We who receive Christ set our seal to this that God is true. (John 3 : 33.) Setting the seal is a kingly act to authenticate a document. Thus our freedom is respected. God's supreme desire for us is that we shall become sons by choice. Whatever we are by nature, this lifts us to a new level.

Faith is the condition of sonship. Adoption is the method of God for introducing sons into his family. Adoption was an idea derived from Roman law. Paul borrows it to express the idea of the gospel. (See Rom. 8 : 15, 21, 23; Gal. 4 : 5, 6.) By adoption a son was received into the Roman family with all the rights of the true son. So also by adoption we are received into God's family by faith, with all the rights of the household.

The act of adoption is of course accompanied by the act of regeneration. Paul has no thought of limiting sonship to a mere legal proceeding. The Spirit of God has made the son alive in Christ. The Spirit dwells in the heart. The law of the Spirit of life has made the son free from the law of sin and death. John emphasizes the fact that we are children begotten of God. We have the nature of true children as well as the relation of sons. We are thus sons by nature and also sons by adoption.

TRAITS AND BLESSINGS OF THE SONS OF GOD

The sons of God possess the moral character of God. (Matt. 5 : 48; 22 : 39.) They trust God. (Matt. 6 : 25-34; Luke 6 : 22ff.) They obey God. (Matt. 12 : 50; 7 : 24.) They imitate God. (Eph. 5 : 1, 2.) They love God. (Matt. 22 : 37; Luke 10 : 27.)

The blessings bestowed upon the sons of God are great and manifold. Indeed, all they receive from God is the gift of the Father to his sons. Some of these are the following: The sons of God receive his Spirit in their hearts, and the Spirit teaches them the language of the divine family. They say, " Abba, Father " (Rom. 8 : 15). The Holy Spirit teaches them how to pray. (Rom. 8 : 26, 27.) They are made partakers of the divine nature. (2 Peter 1 : 4.) The holiness of God the Father is reproduced in them. (Heb. 12 : 10.) Of course daily forgiveness for sins is a priceless boon. (Matt. 6 : 12.) God's incessant care for his children is pledged in strongest terms. (Matt. 6 : 33.) Eternal life is theirs through union with Christ. (John 17 : 3.) The indwelling of Father and Son in their hearts is promised. (John 14 : 23.) The eternal kingdom is given to them by inheritance. (Matt. 25 : 34.) A place in the Father's house is also promised. (John 14 : 23.) They are heirs of God and joint-heirs with Jesus Christ.

Finally, we remark that these traits and blessings of the sons of God are mediated to them through Jesus Christ. Men become sons by faith in him. In four ways at least he mediates our sonship to us. *a*. As eternal Son he reveals to us the eternal Father. Through him alone does this knowledge come. In Matthew 11 : 27 and in John 1 : 18 the declaration is made in unmistakable terms. *b*. As our brother and high priest he opens the way to the Father. Through him we may approach the Father with all confidence in humility and faith. (Eph. 2 : 18; Heb. 7 : 24, 25; 4 : 15, 16; 2 : 17.) *c*. As King, he makes us joint-heirs with him. (Rom. 8 : 17.) *d*. The basis of all the above functions is his work as atoning Redeemer. Because the children are partakers of flesh and blood, he also became flesh. The means by which he achieved their deliverance was the destruction of the power of the devil and of death. The end in view was that he might bring many sons to glory. All this appears in the remarkable passage in Hebrews 2 : 14-18.

Here, then, we find the crowning work of God's grace, the bringing of many sons to glory. Here also we find the unifying principle of all the unfoldings and developments of the temporal order. The key to the progress of history, of nature, and of grace is found in this one luminous truth. We may sum up this truth broadly in the following statements: The universe is not a meaningless movement of physical forces governed only by natural law. It is governed by an eternal purpose. It moves toward a goal. That purpose arose in the heart of the eternal Father. It revealed itself in the temporal manifestation and atoning work of the eternal Son. Its content was the reproduction of sonship in the hearts of men. Its consummation is to be in the full emancipation and manifestation of many sons in an eternal order. To this great end even nature itself is subject and moves onward under the guidance of this eternal purpose toward its goal. (Rom. 8 : 18-30.)

VII. UNION WITH CHRIST

All that has been said as to the beginnings of the Christian life, and indeed all that is yet to be said as to its continuance, may be summed up in one phrase, union with Christ. A backward glance over the ground we have covered will show the truth of the first part of the statement. In the act of repentance the soul turned away from its sin and turned toward Christ. When it exercised faith, it was trust in Christ as Redeemer and Lord. In conversion the outward change of life was an assumption of the life and duties of a follower of Christ. In regeneration the change produced was the reproduction in the soul of the moral image of Christ. Justification was God's act, annulling the sentence of condemnation and bestowing a new status because of the new relation of the soul to Christ. It is clear from this that in becoming a Christian a man enters into a new personal relation. Saving faith is not acceptance of a creed nor of a new intellectual belief of any kind. It is not joining the church nor receiving the " sacraments " or ordinances. It is not " believing the Bible " in a mere intellectual way. Becoming a Christian is entering a new personal relation to Christ. " As many as received him " to them God gave power to become sons. " He that hath the son hath life." " As ye received Jesus Christ the Lord, so walk in him." Barnabas exhorted the saints to " cleave unto the Lord."

All these forms of statement make prominent the general truth that the Christian religion involves as its most central and vital fact a new personal relation to Jesus Christ. But even this does not fully express all the meaning of the Christian life. It is a life of union with Christ. We note first a number of Scriptures which express this idea in a direct and literal way and then certain figurative expressions which convey the same meaning.

1. Scripture Teaching

The union of Christ with the believer is clearly expressed in the Gospel and Epistles of John. In John 14 : 20 are the phrases, " I in you," and " ye in me." In 14 : 23 Christ declares that he and the Father will come and make their abode in the obedient heart. In 1 John 2 : 6 it is declared that if a man claims to " abide in him," he ought to walk as Christ walked.

The phrase " in Christ " is a favorite one in the writings of Paul. There is scarcely any phase of the Christian life which the apostle does not express by means of this or an equivalent expression. There is no condemnation to those who are " in Christ " (Rom. 8 : 1). Christians are alive unto God " in Christ Jesus " (Rom. 6 : 11). If any man is " in Christ," he is a new creature. (2 Cor. 5 : 17.) Paul declared that he had been crucified and that Christ lived in him. (Gal. 2 : 20.) We are baptized " into Christ " (Gal. 3 : 27). Christ dwells in the heart by faith. (Eph. 3 : 17.) We are created " in Christ Jesus unto good works " (Eph. 2 : 10).

There are also numerous figurative expressions which set forth the truth in a striking manner. We begin with the Fourth Gospel. John employs the following metaphors to express the intimacy of the union between Christ and his people: He is the Bread of Life, the Water of Life, the Light of Life, and the Living Vine whence the branches derive their life. He is also the Good Shepherd. All these and other forms of representation in the Gospel repeat the great fundamental of the Christian salvation, that believers are united with Christ by a living bond. We glance briefly at each of those we have named.

In the sixth chapter are the remarkable sayings about the

bread of life. Christ is himself the bread of life. He is living bread, as contrasted with the manna given in the wilderness, which could not give life. Except men eat the flesh and drink the blood of the Son of man, they have no life in them. If they eat this living bread they will live forever. Christ explains that he refers not to literal flesh and blood, but to spiritual assimilation. Men are to labor for the food which does not perish. The true labor, however, the true work of God, is that men believe on him whom God hath sent. The whole of chapter 6, and especially verses 27-35 and verses 47-58, make these truths clear.

He is also the water of life. Two passages show the main teachings of this figure, viz., 4 : 12-14 and 7 : 37-39. To the believer Christ is a spring of water arising within, which gives eternal life. From him who believes shall flow streams of living water. In 7 : 39 the statement is added that the reference was to the Holy Spirit which was not yet given, but whose function should be to make real the living union with Christ.

Again, Christ is the light of life. The Prologue of the Gospel declared that in him was life, and the life was the light of men. He heals a man born blind, thus giving physical light. As usual, the act of faith is required. The man must go wash in the pool of Siloam. Jesus makes this gift symbolic of the supreme gift of spiritual light which he bestows. (John 9 : 5-7, 39-41.) Christ is the good shepherd who knows his sheep by name, and who is known by them, who feeds them, and cares for them, and protects them, who lays down his life for them. (John 10 : 1-18.)

He is the living vine. Believers are the branches, who receive life from him. Apart from him they are destitute of all spiritual power. They are constantly cleansed and made more fruitful if they abide in him, the living vine. (John 15 : 1-8.)

In other parts of the New Testament we have other figures which express the same truth.

Christ is the head of the spiritual body of which Christians are members. There is a common life of the head and members. As the members are subject to the head in the physical body, so are Christians subject to Christ, their spiritual head. Christians are one with each other because they are one in Christ. (See 2 Cor. 6 : 15-18; 1 Cor. 12 : 12; Eph. 1 : 22, 23; 4 : 15ff.; 5 : 29, 30; and many other passages.)

Christ is the foundation or corner-stone, and believers are built upon him. In Colossians 2 : 7 the figure of the foundation-stone is combined with that of the roots of a tree. Christians are to walk in him, " rooted " in him, and " built up " in him. In Ephesians 2 : 20-22 Christ is the corner-stone, and Christians are a holy temple in the Lord in which God dwells by his Spirit.

Again, Christ is the husband of whom the church is the wife. Christians are married to Christ. (Rom. 7 : 4.) Christ is purify-ing his church and will present it to himself as a spotless bride. (Eph. 5 : 26, 27.) At the return of Christ, the bridegroom, the bride is ready for him. (Rev. 19 : 7.)

The life union with Christ is consummated at the resurrection of the body. He is the resurrection and the life. (John 11 : 25.) We shall be glorified with him. Through his resurrection life we also shall triumph over the grave. (1 Cor. 15 : 21ff.) The union of believers with Christ has been summed up as follows: (1) We are crucified together with Christ. (Gal. 2 : 20.) (2) We died together with Christ. (Col. 2 : 20.) (3) We are buried together with Christ. (Rom. 6 : 4.) (4) We are quickened together with Christ. (Eph. 2 : 5.) (5) We were raised together with Christ. (Col. 3 : 1.) (6) We are sufferers together with Christ. (Rom. 8 : 17.)[2]

We consider next the nature of the union with Christ. A brief summary is as follows: It is a union which is vital, moral, spiritual, personal, inscrutable, and abiding.

The union is vital. The life of Christ flows into us. It is not a union by an external bond. It is not as if two physical objects were placed alongside of each other or tied together. It is not as if two metals were fused together by heat, or welded together by external force. It is rather the vital union of the members of a living organism. Our life is gathered up into his life and derives its quality from the divine qualities in him.

[2] Quoted by Dr. A. H. Strong from a tract entitled " The Seven Togethers."

It is a moral union. By moral we do not mean a union merely of personal influence as of one friend over another; nor of teaching as of the influence of teacher over pupil; nor of inspiration as of a martyr over men generally. Nor do we mean merely posthumous influence, as of Christ through the New Testament records of his life and work. All these forms of influence do indeed represent aspects of Christ's moral union with us. But they are not the essential and fundamental element. By moral union we mean primarily a union by which, through his indwelling, Christ reproduces in us his own moral traits. His contact with us is direct and immediate, " and we all, with unveiled face beholding or reflecting as a mirror the glory of the Lord, are transformed into the same image from glory unto glory even as by the Lord the Spirit " (2 Cor. 3 : 18).

It is a spiritual union. Here there are at least three truths which need recognition. It is a union of spirits, not of bodies. Again, it is a spiritual as contrasted with a natural union. Christ sustains a natural relation to all men and to all nature. In him all things consist, or hold together. (Col. 1 : 17.) But the natural relation does not yield the spiritual results. He becomes spiritually related to us by faith. The third truth is that it is a union through the Holy Spirit. The Holy Spirit in us recreates us in the moral and spiritual image of Christ. Here we need to guard against the error of an alleged sacramental union, as if the so-called sacraments in themselves had power to communicate or sustain life.

It is a personal union. By this it is meant that in our union with Christ there is no absorption, as pantheism teaches, of our own personality in the life of God. This union with Christ increases rather than diminishes the idea of personality. The human will and conscience, the intellect and affections, stand forth in greater distinctness than ever before. The " I " and the " thou " of the relationship are more clearly defined. But they are not defined by mutual antagonism. They are defined by harmony of desire and purpose; by receptiveness of life on one side and communication of life on the other. They are

[413]

defined by the gift of love on the divine side and the reproduction of love on the human. There is mutual love, mutual trust, mutual sympathy, between us and Christ. The mutuality of the relation accentuates our distinction from him while showing our personal union with him.

It is an inscrutable union. On one side it is hidden and beyond our capacity to grasp or understand. How the divine Spirit mediates Christ's life to our spirits is a question which runs back into mystery as do all ultimate questions of existence and of life. But the mysterious and inscrutable aspect of this union should not lead to a vague and indefinite mysticism. The effects in our own consciousness are well known to us. These are our own acts of worship and service. The inscrutable power in us reproduces itself in us through acts of self-sacrifice, through putting away of sin, through Christian work, through loving deeds, and, in fact, in all the practical activities and strivings of the Christian life.

It is an abiding union. It is not necessary to dwell upon this phase of the matter here. It will be treated when we consider the subject of Christian perseverance. We need only remark that the continuance of the union is based upon the grace and power of him with whom we are united. Its effect is to cancel and destroy every form of earthly union which opposes or contradicts it. We are gradually drawn away from all forms of sin and worldliness into a self-consistent unity of life with Christ.

2. Consequences of Union

The consequences of our union with Christ need not detain us long. They are involved in great part in what has just been said of the nature of the union. We add, however, a few statements. They are as follows:

(1) Our union with Christ involves our identity with him in his relations to God. We refer here not to metaphysical relations of nature or essence, but to spiritual relations involved in our salvation. We are accepted in him. We stand justified as we

have been because we have accepted him. Because we are in him, and because his life and power are working in us, we are potentially perfect. The forces which will gradually carry on the saving process to the end are now working in us because of our union with him. He is made unto us wisdom and righteousness and sanctification and redemption, not by any legal fiction, but as a vital reality.

(2) This union involves our identity with Christ in his relations to the human race. We must recur for a moment to the doctrine of atonement. We learned that Christ's union with the race as a whole made possible an atonement for the entire race of man. His organic unity with the race lies at the foundation of his redemptive work. God so loved the world that he gave his Son. We who are joined to Christ by a living faith share his love for the whole world. His purpose, his desire, his energetic working for the human race, we have known in our own joyous experience of his redeeming grace. But we fail to understand his will in and through us unless we seek to make his redemptive work effective for others. In other words, the consciousness of those who are united with Christ is a missionary consciousness. They share his redemptive passion, his redeeming purpose for all mankind, and show it by devotion to the task of making Christ known to the ends of the earth.

(3) Our union with Christ involves our identity with him in his relations to sin and death. This is implied in the preceding. Yet the New Testament emphasizes the fact that the conquest of sin and the conquest of death can only come about by union with him who conquered sin and death. The present form of our union with him implies the presence in us of the resurrection power. The present energy of his working in our spirits is but the beginning of the process which is consummated only in the resurrection of the body. The measure of the present power in us is the power which raised him from the dead. (Eph. 1 : 18-23.)

(4) Finally, our union with Christ involves his identity with us in all our earthly experiences. " I am with you always, even unto the end " (Matt. 28 : 20) was his promise to his disciples. He

is with us in all our labors, our sufferings and temptations, our struggles and triumphs. In John 1 : 16 it is declared that all of us have received " of his fulness," and " grace for grace." This probably means that the divine fulness which dwelt in him is the measure of the fulness vouchsafed to his people. The phrase, " grace for grace," probably means grace answering or corresponding to grace. The grace we receive corresponds with the grace he had received. The grace we may expect in temptation is the grace he received in temptation. Our grace for labor and conquest answers to the grace he received for these ends. There is no limit to the divine fulness granted to him. So there is no limit to the divine fulness bestowed upon us in him. There is no variation in the fulness nor in God's willingness to bestow it upon us. That which is variable is our faith, our receptiveness. To grow in grace is to grow in receptiveness of the divine fulness and life.

CHAPTER XVI

THE CONTINUANCE OF THE CHRISTIAN LIFE

I. Sanctification

1. General Survey

BEFORE presenting the biblical teachings as to sanctification we note its general meaning and its place in the system of life forces which constitute the Christian religion. The aim of God in establishing his kingdom among men is to produce holy men and women, both as individuals in their relations to him and as members of a holy society. In the accomplishment of this aim, two things are necessary: first, the establishment of a new relation between God and men, and secondly, the production of a new character corresponding to the new relation. The word " sanctification," as employed in the New Testament, expresses both the new relation to God and the new character which corresponds. Sanctification means then the state of one who is set apart to the service of God, who belongs to God. It also means the inner transformation of one thus set apart, the actual realization of holy character.

(1) A review of the teachings of both the Old and New Testaments confirms these statements. In the earlier stages of the Old Testament the first of these meanings comes clearly into view, and in the later stages the second meaning was emphasized. The priesthood was holy unto the Lord, devoted to him and his service. So also were the vessels employed in God's service in the sanctuary, and the temple itself. The people of Israel were a holy or sanctified people. In all these instances the chief meaning is set apart or devoted to God and his service. (Gen. 2 : 3; Exod. 3 : 2; 10 : 10, 11, 22; Num. 11 : 18; 1 Chron. 23 : 13; Joel 1 : 14; Isa. 8 : 13; Ezek. 36 : 23.)

In the prophets, especially in the later period, there was a deepening of the moral sense, and holiness was interpreted in its ethical quality. The moral character which corresponded to it was often contrasted with the outward relationship. In Micah 6 : 6-8 there is a striking instance. That which pleases Jehovah is not thousands of rams or ten thousand rivers of oil. "To do justly and love mercy and walk humbly with thy God" the prophet declares to be the deeds well pleasing to Jehovah. The moral and spiritual character must correspond with the covenant relation. Not holy offerings by a holy priesthood in a holy temple, but holy character is the requirement. In Isaiah 1 : 10-19 we have another similar passage, as in a great number of instances in the later prophets.

In the New Testament the word "sanctify" has both meanings—set apart to God's service, belonging to God, and also becoming holy inwardly. Even where the word sanctify or sanctification does not appear, the idea is present in both senses in a large number of passages.

In the teachings of Jesus great emphasis is given to righteousness in the sense of inward purity. External righteousness, as of the scribes and Pharisees, is condemned as useless. Inward purity of heart, reaching to the motives and springs of action, is the standard. The divine perfection, indeed, we must imitate. When Jesus says, "Ye therefore shall be perfect as your heavenly Father is perfect" (Matt. 5 : 48), he has especial reference to the divine love. The entire Sermon on the Mount is an exposition of the righteousness of the kingdom.

In Paul's writings there is frequent exhortation to consecration, or sanctification in the sense of devotement to God. In Romans 12 : 1 Christians are enjoined to present their bodies as a "living sacrifice unto God." With this is to be combined the process by which they are to be "transformed" in mind. Christians are to reckon themselves dead to sin and alive unto God. (Rom. 6 : 1-12.)

The process of sanctification by which the inward state is to correspond with the outward relation is expressed in various ways.

Christians are to "walk in the Spirit" (Gal. 5 : 16, 25). They are to "put off," as a garment, the "old man" and "put on," as a garment, "the new man" (Col. 3 : 9ff.; Eph. 4 : 22-24). Paul's desire is that the Thessalonians may become "unblamable in holiness" (1 Thess. 3 : 13; 5 : 23, 24). In Paul's writings three things constantly appear: First, believers are sanctified through their union with Christ. Every holy impulse arises out of the fact that they are in Christ. Secondly, at every stage and in every detail the Holy Spirit's work parallels that of Christ in us. Christ in us, and the Spirit in us, are identical in result. Thirdly, the result of "Christ in us" and the Spirit in us is seen in ethical and spiritual transformation.

In the Epistle to the Hebrews the thought always underlying the argument is the new covenant and the ideal covenant relation of men to God. In 9 : 13, 14 we read: "If the blood of goats and bulls, and the ashes of a heifer sprinkling them that have been defiled, sanctify unto the cleansing of the flesh: how much more shall the blood of Christ, who through the eternal Spirit offered himself without blemish unto God, cleanse your conscience from dead works to serve the living God." Here probably the meaning is sanctification in the first sense of devotement to God. So also in 10 : 10 and in 10 : 14 the reference is to the new relation to God under the new and perfect covenant. Christians are sanctified by the perfect will of Christ, and they are perfected forever by his one perfect offering. This aspect of sanctification seems to be chiefly in view throughout the Epistle. And yet in chapters 11, 12, and 13 the process of purification and growth is set forth with many exhortations.

The apostle Peter combines both senses of the word in two passages, 1 : 15, 16 and 1 : 22. In both these he combines a reference to the gradual process with a reference to the initial act. Since ye have purified your souls, see that ye live in accordance therewith.

In John's Epistles, sanctification is set forth in terms of strong contrast. First, he declares that if a man claim to be without sin, the truth is not in him. (1 John 1 : 8.) And then he declares that if we sin, we have an advocate with the Father (1 John 2 : 1), implying clearly that we do commit sin. Again, he declares that those who have the Christian hope purify themselves as Christ is pure. (1 John 3 : 3.) But in 3 : 6, 9 he affirms in emphatic terms that if a man is born of God, God's seed abideth in him and he sinneth not. These passages are to be reconciled by remembering John's fondness for contrast. He states opposing truths in extreme forms in order to emphasize them. Fundamentally the Christian does not sin. In principle he is devoted to righteousness. But this does not imply that the principle is ideally operative, so that no detail of sin ever intrudes into the Christian's conduct. John strongly insists that there is a process of purification going on in the believer's heart and life, and that through Christ he is victor over the sin principle.

(2) From this brief survey of the biblical teaching it appears that sanctification is vitally related at several points to the initial act by which we become Christians. It is related to faith because in sanctification we constantly repeat the first act of trust. It gradually becomes the habitual and normal attitude of the soul. Faith is the condition of sanctification as of salvation in the first instance. Sanctification is related to justification because in its significance as setting apart or devotement to God, it corresponds to the new status conferred upon us in God's justifying act. Sanctification is related to regeneration because it is the unfolding of the new life germ implanted in regeneration. It is vitally related to the work of the Holy Spirit because the entire process is conducted by the Holy Spirit, who dwells in the believer and gradually perfects his new moral character.

(3) Again, sanctification is attainment of moral character by the Christian through struggle. In justification our faith is reckoned to us for righteousness, but this is not the attainment of righteousness by us. In regeneration also a new moral disposition is imparted to us by the action of God's Spirit. But this is not a righteousness achieved by us. In sanctification we work out what God has wrought within us. We respond to that which is reckoned to us and react to that which is imparted to us. By

repeated acts of our own wills, by repeated acts of holy choice, by successive victories we are enabled by God's grace to achieve the ideal. Thus our salvation is both a gift and a task. The ability to perform the task is also a gift of grace. But it differs from the initial gifts of grace in that our own moral and spiritual strivings accompany it. We thus understand the exhortation of Jesus to " strive " or agonize to " enter in " (Luke 13 : 24); and that of the apostle Paul, " Fight the good (that is, the beautiful, *kalon,* the honorable, the noble) fight of faith " (1 Tim. 6 : 12). Thus also we understand Paul's graphic portrayal of the Christian struggle in Ephesians. (6 : 10-18.) We wrestle not against flesh and blood, but against principalities and powers, and the hosts of wickedness in heavenly places. In sanctification the supreme task of attaining a divine holiness is set for us. But in it is also pledged the gift of divine strength to perform it.

The struggle necessary for the Christian arises from the opposition which he encounters from three sources. One is the evil spiritual influences referred to in Ephesians 6 : 10ff. Another is " the world," regarded as the sphere in which the evil forces operate. Christians are commanded to love not the world, nor the things of the world, because the world is opposed to the divine life. This does not teach asceticism, nor the monastic life of retirement from the daily occupations of men. It is rather a command to overcome the evil influences of the world as subject to false ideals and wrong standards. (1 John 2 : 15-17.) The third source of opposition is " the flesh." Here, again, we are not to understand the material body as such. The Bible nowhere regards matter as evil. By the flesh the New Testament means the sinful nature or disposition which finds in the flesh its occasion and sphere of action. The phrases, " the carnal mind " and the " mind of the flesh," show that the material body is not meant. (See Rom. 7 : 8.) In Galatians 5 : 17 Paul declares that the flesh lusteth against the Spirit and the Spirit against the flesh. Thus there are two principles at work in the Christian, the lower of which is to be subdued and gradually destroyed by the higher. It is an error to conceive of these "two natures" of the Christian as if they were physical natures placed side by side like two material bodies which are wholly disconnected, so that a man might excuse himself from responsibility for sin by asserting, "It was not I that did it, but sin which dwells in me." The Christian needs constantly to pray for forgiveness because he is responsible. He is not two persons, but one. He is not a Doctor Jekyll and a Mr. Hyde, who act independently of each other. He finds himself, although justified and regenerated, still beset by the remnants of the "old man." These he must "put off" by repeated acts of the will until they pass away entirely and he reaps the reward of conquest. He wins the victor's crown. (Rev. 3 : 11, 21; James 1 : 12.)

(4) It is evident from the preceding that sanctification is gradual. It is not attained in its completeness by a single act of consecration. Sanctification is a life process. It is necessarily slow. In this it is unlike mechanical changes. The latter may be very rapid. A material structure, by means of lumber and tools, may be reared in a few days or weeks. But it requires generations for nature to erect a great tree. The living organism proceeds by imperceptible stages. So it is with the spiritual life. Sanctification may be retarded by the negligence of the Christian. He may backslide. All the contingencies and fluctuations of an unsteady will enter into the problem. Discouragement and disappointment may arise because progress seems so slow. But the chief point to remember is that the new inward spring of action, the new principle of life and growth, is operative in the regenerated man. All things are possible to him because a divine force has been released in him. The life of Christ is his life.

There is no reason to suppose that Christian growth will ever cease. At the resurrection the body will be perfectly sanctified, and the spirit at death freed from sin. But as we are partakers of the divine nature, and are to be conformed to the image of Christ, the eternal Son, we have an endless vista of growth opening before us. Christ is, as it were, a fleeing goal. We possess him always, and yet there will always remain new heights of attainment in him. He ever goes before us to prepare a place for us.

(5) The agent and means of sanctification call for a few statements. Always the agent is the Holy Spirit. This we have seen in many previous connections, and need not dwell upon it here. It is a truth never to be forgotten, however, and no one can understand, much less propagate Christianity, who does not keep this fundamental truth before him. The Christian life is a life in the Holy Spirit, just as it is everywhere a life in Christ. Christ remains throughout the object of faith. Our faith is directed toward him. The Holy Spirit makes him real to our inner life and creates his image in us.

The means or instrumentality of sanctification is chiefly the truth of the gospel. Jesus' prayer shows this: " Sanctify them through thy truth. Thy word is truth " (John 17 : 17). The truth is learned through all the means of grace, in the church, in preaching, in Christian fellowship, in temptation and trial, in suffering, in Christian conquest, in the performance of daily duty. In short, the whole circle of life's activities is to minister to Christian growth. No part of life is to be regarded as outside this circle of influences which God employs to purify and perfect the Christian character.

2. The Moral Ideal

The moral ideal of sanctification is an important aspect of this subject. What is the goal of Christian character? What kind of men and women are we becoming as the process continues? Of course a complete answer would involve the whole of Christian ethics, and cannot be given exhaustively here. We can only give it in brief outline. The New Testament teaching covers the case of the Christian as an individual and as a member of society. We consider these in their order.

(1) The ethical ideal of the Christian as an individual includes the following. He accepts Christ as his Lord and as his guide in all moral problems. (Matt. 7 : 15.) He hungers and thirsts

after righteousness. (Matt. 5 : 6.) He is forgiving toward enemies. (Matt. 6 : 14, 15.) He seeks peace with all men. (Matt. 5 : 9.) He is not grasping for material wealth or covetous. (Matt. 6 : 32-34.) He employs his wealth, if he possess it, as a steward of the grace of God. (Luke 16 : 2; 1 Peter 4 : 10.) He cultivates the spirit of contentment with outward conditions and possessions. (Matt. 6 : 31.) He is discontented with present moral and spiritual attainments. (Phil. 3 : 12, 13.) He prays habitually. (1 Thess. 5 : 17.) His chief concern in prayer and in striving is for the coming of God's kingdom among men. (Matt. 6 : 10.) He is free from worry and anxiety about the future. (Matt. 6 : 27.) He recognizes his entire dependence on God and ever cultivates the spirit of dependence. (Phil. 4 : 6.) He is not half-hearted, but whole-hearted in his devotion to God. (Matt. 22 : 37.) He does not try to serve two masters. (Matt. 6 : 24.) He is faithful in the little as he is in the great things. (Matt. 5 : 19; Luke 16 : 10.) He is cheerful in spirit, abounding in thanksgiving. (Col. 2 : 7.) His is not a life of depression and gloom, but of triumph in Christ. (Phil. 2 : 18.) He is diligent in business. (Rom. 12 : 11.) His life is in the open, not given to secret sins or shadowy pursuits of any kind. (Rom. 13 : 13.) He is stedfast in his Christian purpose. (Eph. 6 : 18.) He purifies himself as Christ is pure. (1 John 3 : 3.) He rejoices in the hope of the glory of God because the Holy Spirit is shed abroad in his heart. (Rom. 5 : 3-5.) He is an imitator of God as a beloved child, and walks in love. (Eph. 5 : 1, 2.) Thus the ideal and goal of the individual Christian life is sonship to God modeled upon the sonship of Christ. (Eph. 5 : 2.)

(2) These are the salient features of the ethical side of sanctification for the individual. We note next an outline of the ideal in its social relations. There can be no question that Christianity contemplates the purification of all social relations. The two great conceptions expressing the social ideal in the New Testament are the kingdom of God and the church. The kingdom was both present and future. It was outward in some of its manifestations, and also inward. It belonged to the sphere of

history as well as to the sphere of the spiritual life. The church was employed chiefly to designate the local assembly of believers. But it was also used in the larger sense, including all the regenerate. In the latter form it was not an outward organization.

Now our present purpose does not contemplate a discussion of either church or kingdom in any of the controverted aspects of these great themes. We refer to them here to show that these were great social ideals in the mind of Jesus and of the New Testament writers.

The Christian, then, was one in whom love was the ruling motive. His first impulse was to become a member of the company of believers. (Acts 2 : 47.) He recognized in them the fellowship which corresponded to his own new life in Christ. (Gal. 6 : 10.) In that fellowship he sought not his own things, but the things of others. (1 Cor. 10 : 24.) He practised forbearance and forgiveness. He was long-suffering toward all. (1 Cor. 13 : 4, 7, 8.) He could forego a personal right in Christ if by so doing he could help the weaker brother. (Rom. 14 : 1-7.) He recognized the equality of all in Christ. (Col. 3 : 11; Gal. 3 : 28.) For him there were no social castes, or distinctions, based on false moral standards. He did not worship at the shrine of wealth or power. (James 2 : 2-4; 5 : 1.) He had no false pride. (Rom. 12 : 3.) He employed whatever gift God bestowed upon him for the edification of others. (Rom. 12 : 6ff.) He gave of his means to relieve distress. (Rom. 12 : 13.) He returned good for evil. (Rom. 12 : 20, 21.) He was especially devoted to those of the household of faith. (Gal. 6 : 10.) He kept out of debt and lived an honest life. (Rom. 13 : 8.) He was industrious and would not become a burden to others. (1 Thess. 4 : 11.) He avoided harsh judgments against others. (Rom. 14 : 3ff.) Of course he avoided all the cardinal sins, such as lying and stealing and adultery. (Rom. 13 : 9ff.) He regarded every Christian as a brother in Christ. All were members of one body and members one of another. (Eph. 4 : 16.)

The teachings of the gospel of Christ deal directly or indirectly with all the social institutions of men. The family was recognized as of divine origin. (Eph. 5 : 22.) One ground only is recognized as justifying divorce. (Matt. 5 : 32.) The loyal obedience of children to parents and the training of children by parents in the nurture and admonition of the Lord are insisted upon as involved in the Christian obligation. (Eph. 6 : 1-4.) Servants are to be treated justly by masters, and they are to serve as in the Lord and not as pleasers of men. (Eph. 6 : 5-9.) The servant was a freeman in Christ. (1 Cor. 7 : 21, 22.) And while the New Testament does not expressly oppose human slavery, it clearly sets forth principles which would in due time destroy slavery. These principles were the liberty, equality, and fraternity of men in Christ.

As to the state and civil government, there is clear recognition of its function as a means for controlling and suppressing evil. (Rom. 13 : 1-7.) No particular form of civil government is recognized. But the principles of the gospel above mentioned led inevitably toward the overthrow of every form of despotism and of the so-called " divine right of kings." But the forces to be employed by the gospel were spiritual rather than physical. (2 Cor. 10 : 4.) The truth was to work as leaven in the hearts of men. (Matt. 13 : 33.) Love and brotherhood in Christ are the dynamic principles which are to change human governments from despotisms to democracies. The Christian citizen is commanded to render to the state its just dues. He is to perform faithfully his duty to the state. (Matt. 22 : 21; Rom. 13 : 1-7.)

The same remarks apply to the institutions of society generally. Economic and industrial problems are not discussed by Jesus or the New Testament writers in their technical aspects. But it is as clear as day that all forms of social wrong and injustice are opposed to the ends of the gospel and the kingdom of God. The kingdom of God is not meat and drink. It is not in its essence a matter of material good things. It is rather " righteousness, and peace, and joy in the Holy Spirit " (Rom. 14 : 17). But if it is righteousness, it is necessarily opposed to every form of unrighteousness. If it is peace, it is necessarily opposed to the wrongs which disturb the peace. And if it is joy in the

Holy Ghost, it is a joy arising out of Christian treatment of others in equity and love.

Christianity emphasizes duties rather than rights. But it recognizes that every right is attended by a corresponding obligation. Men are to cultivate the spirit of brotherhood. Thus will class feeling, and race feeling, and narrow forms of patriotism die. Thus will social and industrial disturbances gradually cease. Equality of civil and political standing, and equality of economic opportunity will inevitably follow.

The gospel is clearly opposed to the warlike spirit when that spirit is based on any form of unrighteousness. It would be going too far to say that Christianity is inconsistent or incompatible with every form of war. There are forms of wrong and oppression which only war can destroy. But the desire for national greatness, based on the injury of other nations, is wholly alien to the spirit of Christianity. Christ died for the human race. And while national feeling and patriotic loyalty are not opposed to the gospel, yet every form of such feeling which forgets the rights of others is opposed to it. A narrow nationalism which forgets other nations is an antichristian ideal.

3. Wrong Views as to Sanctification

There are two of these views. (1) One is the antinomian. Paul encountered it and refuted it in the Epistle to the Romans. If it is true, certain men argued, that where sin abounded grace abounded more exceedingly, why should we not continue in sin in order that grace may abound? Since our sin afforded grace its opportunity, why not increase the opportunity of grace by abounding sin?

Paul's answer is most conclusive. He reduces the plea of the errorists to absurdity by three illustrations of the nature of the Christian life. The first is that of spiritual death and resurrection, symbolized by baptism, the initial act of outward obedience. The Christian in his old sinful nature has been crucified, or put to death, with Christ. He has also been raised from the dead into a new spiritual life in Christ. These truths find symbolic expression in the outward act of baptism. (Rom. 6 : 1-14.) Hence, the apostle concludes, it is absurd to propose continuance in sin on account of grace, since the primary effect of grace is to destroy sin.

His second illustration is the relation of slaves to the master. Slaves obey their own master, not another. Christians were formerly slaves of sin. Sin had dominion over them. But now, as believers in Christ, they have changed masters. They are now the slaves of righteousness. They are bound to obey their new master and bring forth the corresponding fruit of righteousness. (Rom. 6 : 16-23.)

The third illustration is that of marriage. Christians were once married to the law. But in Christ they became dead to the law. They are now married to him. They were released from the law as a means of justification and salvation just as a wife is released from the marriage bond and is free to marry again by the death of her husband. Believers have thus entered a new spiritual relation to Christ. They are married to him, and can no longer live as bound to the former husband. (Rom. 7 : 1-6.) Briefly then, Paul's reply was that the antinomian claim was based on a threefold absurdity, *viz.*, that the Christian could live for that to which he had become dead; that a slave could obey a master to whom he does not belong; and that a wife could live for one to whom she was not married.

The error of the antinomians was the beginning of that evil tendency in theology which we have had so many occasions to mention. It was the error of taking a part for the whole. It was analytical thought trying to separate things which were indissolubly one. They conceived of salvation as a merely commercial transaction, or outward transfer, of Christ's merits to us and our sins to him. They overlooked the fact that it is a moral and spiritual union of men with Christ, in which the outward command was written on the heart as an inner life principle; that there was a radical break with sin and a living union with Christ, in which the Christian shares Christ's passion for holy living and his abiding fellowship with God; and that the freedom from the law which Christ secures for us is not a freedom to break the law, but, by the new spiritual powers implanted in us, a freedom to obey it.

(2) The other wrong view is that of the perfectionist. It is held by some that in the present life the Christian may attain sinless perfection. There are certain Scriptures which seem to teach it, such as the following: " Ye therefore shall be perfect as your heavenly Father is perfect " (Matt. 5 : 48). " Ye shall be holy, for I am holy " (1 Peter 1 : 16). " Let us press on unto perfection " (Heb. 6 : 1). " Let us therefore, as many as are perfect, be thus minded " (Phil. 3 : 15). " That ye may be perfect and entire, lacking in nothing " (James 1 : 4). " Ye were sanctified " (1 Cor. 6 : 11). " That we should be holy and without blemish before him in love " (Eph. 1 : 4).

We must reject the view, however, that sinless perfection is attainable in the present life. There are many reasons in support of this rejection.

a. Sinless perfection in this life involves attainment of a divine ideal by a body and soul maimed by sin. Such attainment is impossible. The body bears the marks of sin in many ways, and it is to be freed from them only at the resurrection. In the present life the soul, even though regenerate, is bound to a body thus weakened and tainted by evil, and cannot wholly escape the consequences of its union with the body of our humiliation. A converted drunkard said that he had found that while his desire for liquor was gone, his appetite for it remained. The appetite was the physical craving. The new moral desire was the result of the Holy Spirit's regenerating power. His new spiritual life was victorious over appetite. But his physical organism still bore the marks of his old sinful life.

b. No Christian can at any stage apply to himself an absolute standard of holiness. He may know that he grows, that he is better than he once was, that a divine power is working in him. There is a form of relative judgment which he can pronounce upon himself. But his self-criticism can never compass all the workings of his own nature even by the aid of the Holy Spirit. Motives are too complex, attainments too variable and unstable, downward tendencies too constant for him to apply to himself the standard of the divinely perfect law in any absolute sense. When he attempts to do so and claims perfection, he always lowers the law. We might reach the stars if the stars would only come down within our reach.

c. Christian experience testifies against the idea of sinless perfection in this life. The greatest saints of history confessed their sins throughout their careers. Augustine is a notable example. The apostle Paul never ceased to battle against himself. He buffeted his body and kept it under because the old sinful self kept renewing its attack upon him. Sin is catlike in the proverbial sense that it has many lives. The sense of sin on the part of great saints is easily explained. Their deepening insight into the law of holiness enabled them to discern their own sins as well. The supernal light intensified the inward lines of blackness.

d. The Scriptures afford no real basis for the theory of sinless perfection. The passages cited in support of it can be explained otherwise. Other passages show clearly the erroneousness of the view. In some cases commands or ideals or prophecies of perfection are confounded with attainment. Christianity never sets a low standard, but always the highest. We are to strive for perfection as God is perfect, and for holiness as God is holy. Many of the passages cited simply set forth the ideal of perfection toward which we are to strive. In other cases where the past is referred to, as in the passage, " Ye were sanctified " (1 Cor. 6 : 11), there is no reference to sinless perfection. The Epistle is addressed to very imperfect Christians. " Sanctified " here means set apart to God's service, devoted to God, and not sinless purity of thought and life. So also may be explained all the passages.

Besides these there are many which expressly contradict the theory. There are passages in the Old Testament. But two or three in the New will suffice. In James 3 : 2 it is declared that " in many things we all stumble." And in 1 John 1 : 8 the very emphatic word appears, "If we say we have no sin, we deceive ourselves, and the truth is not in us."

e. The biblical use of the word perfect and the idea of perfection leads to the same conclusion. In the Old Testament the covenant relation between Israel and God is always assumed. A man might walk with "a perfect heart" before Jehovah, or live a blameless or harmless life within the covenant without at all attaining sinlessness. He might perform the outward duties of the covenant thus. But sinless perfection in the sense we are considering was remote from his thoughts.

So also a man might be a man of uprightness or integrity according to the standards of the period, and so be called a perfect man. This seems to be the usage in the book of Job. (Job 1 : 1; Gen. 6 : 9.) Sometimes perfect meant simply complete in all the parts, as of animals offered in sacrifice.

Frequently in the New Testament the word perfect means mature (*teleios*). Full-grown men are perfect in the sense of mature as contrasted with babes in Christ. (Heb. 5 : 14; I Cor. 2 : 6; Phil. 3 : 15.)

In Philippians 3 : 2-16 we have a most illuminating passage on the subject of Christian perfection. Paul is describing his own Christian struggles. The outstanding mark of his experience is that he had not yet attained, or laid hold of, that for which Christ laid hold of him. His one aim is to press on toward the mark, or Christian goal. Then he adds two significant statements. The first is that "the perfect" are "thus minded." Here, then, is a paradox. The mature or perfect Christian is the Christian who has a sense of his own imperfection. To reach a consciousness of having attained would be a spiritual decline. It would be self-deception. The apostle also adds, "Nevertheless, whereto we have already attained, let us walk by the same rule, let us mind the same thing" (Phil. 3 : 16). This means, Let us conscientiously perform every known duty. Let us live up to the truth as we know it, while yet deeply conscious of our failure to attain the divine ideal.

From the preceding discussion of perfection we conclude:

First, that sinless perfection is never attainable in the present life. Secondly, that it is possible for Christians to make steady progress toward the goal of perfection. Thirdly, there is danger that we may mistake the attainment of some stages of the Christian life for the attainment of perfection. We may attain to Christian assurance, but this is not sinlessness. We may have a so-called " second blessing," in which we make rapid spiritual progress. But this is not perfection. We ought to have a third, and a fourth, and a thousand more blessings. Fourthly, there is danger that in our opposition to the false theory of perfectionism we will adopt low standards of Christian living and excuse ourselves for sin and worldliness. This is an insistent peril we should recognize. Dr. A. J. Gordon says:[1] " If the doctrine of sinless perfection is a heresy, the doctrine of contentment with sinful imperfection is a greater heresy. It is not an edifying spectacle to see a Christian worldling throwing stones at a Christian perfectionist." The fifth conclusion is that while ever conscious of our imperfection, we should believe in the possibility of great attainment in the Christian life, both in character and in power for service. Sometimes there are great acts of consecration involving complete surrender of the will, a renewed filling of the Holy Spirit, so that in a moment we pass to a higher stage of spiritual victory and power. But this should not be taken as final, nor lead to self-deception. Steady, plodding labor and growth should succeed it, not contentment. We should, after the greatest blessing, still press on toward the mark of the high calling of God in Christ.

II. PERSEVERANCE

The subject of perseverance gives rise to the question as to the certainty of the ultimate salvation of believers. Will they, without fail, endure to the end, or are we to hold that some may fall away from their saving faith in Christ and perish?

1. Before answering this question directly it will be well to

---

[1] " Ministry of the Spirit," p. 116.

consider briefly two tendencies in theological thought in the past which have led to wrong inferences concerning the doctrine. One has been the tendency of extreme Calvinists. They have put great emphasis upon the logic of the "plan of salvation." God's predestination and election of individuals to salvation takes the whole problem out of human hands entirely. That purpose must find expression in God's justifying act when he accepts men in Christ, and in his regenerating act when he imparts the new nature. Now God's eternal purpose cannot be changed. His act of justification cannot be annulled. Man's new nature is an indelible and radical transformation, a work which only God can undo. Therefore all the regenerate must be ultimately saved, or else God's purpose fails and his work comes to naught.

Now it is not denied that some such mode of logical deduction may be applied to the general statements of the New Testament. But it is doubtful whether it represents adequately the prevailing point of view which is found therein. The New Testament writers rarely indulge in formal logic after this fashion. The particular combination of ideas would be hard to find in any one paragraph in isolation from other teachings. The chief objection to this logic is that it is abstract and partial. It omits other very necessary teachings which supplement those on which the reasoning is based. It tends to make of salvation a physical rather than a moral and spiritual process. It so emphasizes the absoluteness of God that it tends to pantheism. The human response and effort are ignored. In all the New Testament writers there is great care exercised to supplement logical inferences of this kind by the corresponding truth of human perseverance.

Another school of theologians have exalted human freedom in the same one-sided way. The Christian is free to continue in grace or fall away from it. He may have God's help if he will, but ultimately his destiny is in his own hands. If he is finally lost he, and he only, is responsible. Now this statement of the case is also partial, and fails to take account of vital teachings of Scripture and vital elements of experience. It does not recognize the fulness and sufficiency of divine grace. It tends to a bare moralism in which human effort is everything, and to a deism which puts God above men and apart from their struggles.

2. Now the New Testament avoids the pantheistic tendency of extreme Calvinism and the deistic tendency of the extreme Arminianism. The New Testament teaching and Christian experience are completely one in keeping the divine and human aspects properly related to each other. In both there is clear recognition of God's initiative. The shepherd seeks the lost sheep. This is Jesus' declaration. The saved man knows he is found, laid hold of, apprehended by Christ. So Paul testifies. Again, the lost is not merely found; he is more than a sheep. He is a prodigal in a far country who must repent. So the New Testament teaches. The saved knows by experience that he was only found in the saving meaning of the word when he repented of his sins and responded to the seeking love. Both these elements enter at every stage of the Christian life. We are commanded to work out our own salvation, not apart from God, but because it is God who works in us to will and to do. (Phil. 2 : 12.)

The true doctrine of perseverance, then, is to be found by combining into a unity the groups of teachings which have been employed to support contradictory views. We cite a few of those on both sides of the controversy and then show how they are to be combined.

We note first those which emphasize God's power and grace. In John 10 : 28, 29 Jesus declares that his sheep shall never perish; that no one can pluck them out of his hand; that no one can pluck them out of God's hand. In Romans 8 : 30 Paul combines predestination, calling, justification, and glorification in a description of the Christian life, and in verses 35-39 he declares that nothing can separate us from the love of Christ. Again, in Romans 11 : 29 he asserts that the gifts and calling of God are without repentance. In Philippians 1 : 6 the apostle declares that he who began a good work in his readers would perfect it unto the day of Jesus Christ. In 2 Timothy 1 : 12 he knows whom he has believed and is assured that he is able to keep that which he has committed unto him. In I Peter I : 5 we are said to be guarded by God's power unto a salvation to be revealed at the last day.

There is another group of passages which seem to indicate the possibility of falling away and being lost. Paul says concerning his own struggles: " I buffet my body and bring it into bondage; lest by any means after that I have preached to others, I myself should be rejected " (1 Cor. 9 : 27). Again, in Hebrews 6 : 4-6: " For as touching those who were once enlightened and tasted of the heavenly gift, and were made partakers of the Holy Spirit, and tasted the good word of God, and the powers of the age to come, and then fell away, it is impossible to renew them again unto repentance; seeing they crucify to themselves the Son of God afresh, and put him to an open shame." There are numerous other passages of like import. It is not necessary to consider all of them in detail. These two will serve to illustrate the principles of interpretation which apply to the alleged apostasy passages generally.

The following statements may be made: There is expressed in these passages a sense of real danger. As Paul and the writer of Hebrews regarded the variable devotion and infirmities and sins of men, they trembled for the outcome. We are therefore not justified in explaining away the obvious meaning and in saying that the passages are designed to teach something else. Men are free beings. God deals with them as such. They are in real danger of abusing this freedom and presuming upon God's grace in Christ. We may add, in the second place, however, that the writers are here dealing with principles and spiritual attitudes rather than writing history. These are not accounts of things which occurred, but of real dangers. Looked at from the standpoint of human weakness, they may occur. There is, however, another factor to be reckoned with, God's grace. Elsewhere this is made clear. But the biblical writers did not hesitate to deal with the human factor alone if necessary. Hence the warnings, entreaties, threats, and importunities which we find addressed to God's true people. As free moral beings, as persons, they can only be reached and influenced and held to the Christian ideal in this way.

There are also Scriptures which put great emphasis upon human effort in salvation without expressing any view as to the possibility of falling away. In Acts 2 : 40 we read, "And with many other words he testified, and exhorted them, saying, Save yourselves from this crooked generation." Now it is possible to hold and state the doctrine of salvation by grace through faith in a manner so partial and one-sided that it would be difficult to harmonize it with this language of the apostle Peter. And yet if each is properly understood in its relations to the other side of the truth, there is no contradiction. In fact, neither truth can be understood apart from the other.

Again, Paul says to the Philippians: "Work out your own salvation with fear and trembling; for it is God who worketh in you both to will and to work, for his good pleasure" (Phil. 2 : 12, 13). Here we have both sides of the truth presented in close connection with each other. For the apostle Paul there was no contradiction between the idea of an inworking of divine grace in the heart on the one side, and a free response and active cooperation of man on the other. In fact, the two were indissolubly bound together. There is of course an ultimate mystery involved when we enter the realm of metaphysics as to the human will in relation to the will of God. But in the sphere of our experiential knowledge of God's grace and power there was no insuperable difficulty.

From the preceding we may derive the following conclusions: First, the writers of the New Testament seem to imply by their exhortations and warnings that all believers if left to themselves are in real danger of falling away; and secondly, that God purposes and preserves men unto salvation, though this is not a process regardless of man's conduct, but a process involving man's active response to God's gracious working; and thirdly, that it is unscriptural and wrong to ignore either the divine purpose and grace and power on the one hand, or the human response and cooperation on the other. Ultimately of course the decisive factor is God's grace and power, not man's weakness. Through that grace and power man is enabled to overcome.

3. Here, again, we discover that God's method is moral and personal and not physical. He does not preserve us by irresistible grace as by something which overrides our will; but by constraining grace which enlists our will. He does not preserve us in spite of transgressions and backslidings, but by renewing us unto repentance for sins and return from backslidings. His method is not that of the pantheistic view in which God's will is everything and man's nothing. Nor is it the method of the deistic view which exalts the human will to the chief place and reduces that of God to the minimum. It is the method rather which is in harmony with Christian theism. The personal God deals with personal man in a free personal manner. He is transcendent, but he is also immanent in man through the indwelling Holy Spirit working toward the goal of Christian character. He is immanent in the world, working therein providentially in behalf of his child. The result is not uncertain. But the certainty is not that of a mechanical law working through natural forces. It is the certainty of moral suasion and spiritual influence exerted in a personal way. The method involves the highest possible form of parental training and discipline. There are two methods of preventing danger to a child playing near a precipice. The father may build a wall to prevent the child from falling over, or leave the danger, and build up the child's will and self-control and thus enable him to avoid the danger. The father might remain near to meet an emergency should it arise, and yet so discipline the child that the emergency would rarely arise. The latter is God's method. He does not build walls so much as he builds wills; although he builds walls where they are required by his higher method. A lady sent her little boy across a dangerous, crowded street to do an errand. A friend expressed fear lest he be injured by the passing vehicles. The mother replied that there was no danger, that the child had been trained to avoid the danger. Most mothers would have towed the child across the

street by the hand. This mother trained hers to cross it alone. God's method is not the towing but the training method.

Now the above exposition explains a number of passages and relieves a number of difficulties. It explains the unmistakable Scriptures, wherein it is clearly taught that no one in Christ will ever be lost. It also explains the passages which seem to imply that some are in danger of being lost. These are exhortations to prevent the danger which is real from the human standpoint. To point out the danger and warn against it is the divine method of preventing it. It explains also cases of apparent apostasy in the Bible. These were either cases of backsliding which were followed by a return to God, or else they were cases of spurious conversion where the real spiritual life never existed. The exposition meets the objection that the divine is inconsistent with human freedom. It does so by showing in the strongest way the necessity of man's free response to and cooperation with God. It meets also the objection that the doctrine of perseverance tends to immorality since it assures men of salvation no matter how they live. Our exposition meets this objection by showing that living a moral and consistent life is the only consistent result of the operation of God's will to preserve us to the end. We may close this subject with the words of the apostle Paul: " Who shall separate us from the love of Christ? Shall tribulation, or anguish, or persecution, or famine, or nakedness, or peril, or sword? . . Nay, in all these things we are more than conquerors through him that loved us. For I am persuaded that neither death, nor life, nor angels, nor principalities, nor things present, nor things to come, nor powers, nor height, nor depth, nor any other creature shall be able to separate us from the love of God, which is in Christ Jesus our Lord " (Rom. 8 : 35-39).

CHAPTER XVII

LAST THINGS

I. Cycle of Ideas Completed

ESCHATOLOGY, or the doctrine of last things, will complete our cycle of biblical ideas. This treatise has dealt with the Christian religion in its doctrinal expression. The aim has been to construe the Christian's religious life to the Christian intelligence. Eschatology is a logical and necessary part of this aim as we shall now proceed to indicate.

Looking at the gospel from the divine side, we may say it is God's communication to us. Looking at it from the human side, we may say it is man's appropriation of what God communicates. Thus the gospel is revelation and salvation. We may sum up, in a few brief statements, the communicative and the appropriative elements in our redemption through Christ. First, God is made known to us as the Creator of the world and its providential Guide. On our side it is the recognition of his initiative in salvation and his presence in human history and the individual life. Secondly, God is revealed as transcendent. He is above and greater than the world; yet he is the immanent God, entering it and dwelling in our hearts by his Holy Spirit, to whom we gladly respond by faith. Thirdly, God is eternally Father, who speaks to men in and through Jesus Christ his eternal Son. We receive Christ as God's Son, who came for our salvation, and the spirit of sonship is given unto us whereby we cry, " Abba, Father." Thus the Son, who is the historic revelation of the eternal God, becomes the inward principle of our spiritual life. As Paul expressed it, God reveals his Son in us. Fourthly, the atonement of Christ was God's expression of his infinite love for lost men, and the means for their reconciliation to God. The experiential response of men to this atonement is the turning away from sin, a being crucified with Christ, a dying to sin. The cross becomes the symbol of our new relation to sin and God. Fifthly, the resurrection of Christ is the consummation of God's redemptive work through him. Our experiential response is in yielding ourselves to his regenerating grace and in being spiritually raised from the dead by an inward renewal through the Holy Spirit. Sixthly, God's gracious act in justifying us and setting us apart to his service in sanctification is responded to by us in the practical life of obedience which answers to the divine act. And his eternal purpose to preserve us to the end is responded to by us in the cooperation of our wills with his own and in a recognition of the peril to which we are exposed apart from his grace and power. Thus we are ever mindful of our dependence upon God. Our dependence expresses itself in constant prayer to him, coupled with full assurance of his love in Christ and of Christ's intercession for us at God's right hand.

Now it is clear from this summary that God's working in history and grace is purposive. It moves toward a goal. It is this teleology or purposiveness of history and of Christian experience which raises the questions about the last things. The Christian salvation is the process of realization. It looks forward to the stages which are implied in the present imperfect stage, and it looks backward to the historic origins. The moment we connect the past with the present, as we must do, we are confronted with the problem of the future. No beginning or partial attainment gives an adequate explanation of a great evolving process. We know beginnings fully only by endings. The implicit elements must become explicit before we can understand. So also we can fully understand the kingdom of God only in its outcome. The Scripture has not left us in the dark. It has not answered our many curious questions, but it has given us a satisfying forecast of the future in its main outlines.

II. PRELIMINARY QUESTIONS

Before presenting the New Testament outline of the future, there are certain preliminary questions which call for attention.

These arise in part out of the attitude of modern thought, and in part out of the character of the New Testament teachings.

1. The first question is this: Can we not dispense with a doctrine as to the future? There are some who assert that we do not need such a teaching. Various grounds are set forth in support of the assertion. With one group immortality is denied or declared to be unimportant as a belief because it cannot be scientifically demonstrated. The methods of physical science are applied to religious beliefs. On this basis, of course, no proof of immortality which compels assent, as in mathematical demonstration, is possible. This group is composed chiefly of physical scientists, whose interest in religion is subordinate to the demands of their particular province of investigation. Another group, made up of theologians, insist that the future is irrelevant to our faith and lies outside the realm of knowledge. With these it is not so much a denial of immortality as of the possibility of a doctrine of immortality. Their view is based also on a theory of knowledge. They limit the knowable to the facts of present experience. Another group argue against immortality on the ground that it is injurious to ethics. It is alleged that the doctrine of future rewards and punishments is essentially selfish in its appeal. A man should do right because it is right, not because he will be rewarded for it. Devotion to right for its own sake is urged. In the case of others denial of individual immortality is based on philosophic grounds. The advocates of certain forms of idealism and pantheism insist that all finite forms of existence, including man's individual life, will in due time be swallowed up in the infinite. Thus the only immortality men may expect is that of reabsorption in the universal life. Some hold that the present form of belief in immortality is that of influence over other lives in the future. As individuals we perish, but we live in the influence we exert after death. It is even alleged that the Old Testament proves that man's religious life does not require belief in personal immortality. In Israel the hope of men was bound up in that of the family and nation, with little emphasis or recognition of individual immortality.

Now we have in a previous section set forth the general arguments for the immortality of the soul. These do not need to be repeated here. But a few things may be said in reply to the forms of teaching we have just outlined.

(1) We begin with the argument based upon the teaching of the Old Testament. It is incorrect to say that the religion of Israel proves that a doctrine of immortality is unnecessary. In its earlier stages the nation was so absorbed in the present, and the individual was so lost in the people as a whole that the hope of the future took the form of a national hope. This we concede. But this is by no means a sufficient account of the matter. The later literature of the Old Testament presents another phase of the belief. When trouble and disaster overtook the individual, and especially when the nation was broken up by captivity, the Old Testament believer reached the conviction of individual conquest of death and of immortality. These were never denied, even in the earlier stages. But they became very explicit in certain experiences which tried the earlier belief as by fire. One needs only to read the Sixteenth, the Seventeenth, the Forty-ninth, the Sixty-eighth, the Seventy-third Psalms; the nineteenth chapter of the book of Job; the sixth chapter of Hosea; the twenty-fifth and twenty-sixth chapters of Isaiah, and other Old Testament teachings to see how the doctrine of immortality and even resurrection of the body took shape through the experience of God's grace in the midst of suffering and trial. We conclude, then, that the Old Testament taken as a whole, and not in its earlier stages merely, proves the insufficiency of the belief in an immortality of influence or survival in the national life. Men are no doubt swayed much by the hope of influence upon future generations. But this does not and cannot take the place of the hope of immortality in the proper sense of the word.

(2) The idealistic and pantheistic denials of immortality are met by the general arguments which show the weakness of these systems as a whole. If God is a personal and purposive Being, and if man is made in his image as a free moral personality, the

belief in personal immortality is the strongest of all inferences from the facts. On the assumption that the world-ground is not a Person, but an impersonal principle, man and his whole moral and religious life are an enigma which cannot be explained. The stream has in that case risen higher than its source. We have an effect without a cause. If the world rises by slow degrees to its climax in human personality and its deep conviction of survival after death, as Christian theism holds, we have a self-consistent world-view. But if man perishes, if his moral and spiritual and personal life is merely a passing phase of a world of endless change, then the alleged climax becomes a shocking and inexplicable anticlimax.

(3) The denial which is based on objection to the idea of rewards and punishments is the result of an immature consideration of the problem. It is but another instance of the abstract and analytical method leading to a wrong conclusion. The facts of man's nature, as they are presented in universal experience, show this. We cannot, if we would, detach ourselves from the thought of the past on the one hand, and from that of the future on the other. In other words, time is a factor of consciousness of which we cannot divest ourselves. Memory and hope are part of the warp and woof of all our thinking in all spheres, in religion and ethics as well as in practical secular life. The kind of being who can, by an act of will, exclude all thought of past and future, does not exist, at least not in human form. Such a being would be so wanting in motives and ends that we can scarcely conceive of him as a finite personal being at all. The idea of rewards and penalties is inwrought in our moral nature. Conscience clearly witnesses to this fact. To ignore this witness is to ignore one of the chief functions of our nature.

There is of course always a danger that rewards and penalties may be presented on a low moral level. The Mohammedan heaven appeals to the lower instincts in men. Sometimes the Christian appeal lacks elevation when made by those who fail to appreciate the morality of the gospel. But the remedy is not in attempting to destroy the idea altogether, but in making reward and penalty harmonize with the type of character which the Christian religion seeks to produce. Christian character in its highest form is indeed the instinctive and persevering choice of the highest moral good from an inward impulse, and not from external constraint. It is also true that no man can attain his character from exclusive regard for future rewards and penalties. There is joy and spontaneity in service. But the thought of the ultimate outcome is no small factor in producing spontaneous and joyous devotion to the moral and spiritual ideal.

(4) The denial of immortality based on scientific grounds, and the corresponding theological denial arising out of a theory of knowledge derived from physical science, may be met in several ways. First, we remark that physical science and its methods of proof do not apply to spiritual phenomena. The soul and its life are outside of the range of physical science. Psychophysics, or the study of the facts of consciousness in relation to the brain and nervous system, has no word to say against belief in immortality. There is a parallelism between brain activities and those of the mental life. But they never pass into each other. The law of continuity fails to explain their connection. Secondly, the quality of the life in Christ is its own best evidence to the Christian himself. It is a life of communion, of fellowship with God. The Spirit of God acts upon his spirit. His life has an eternal quality. In the words of Jesus, it is " eternal life." It partakes of the quality of God's life. It is progressive. Nothing in the present life fully satisfies it. It moves ever toward a freer, more complete life. In the third place, the resurrection of Jesus Christ is the great historic fact which brings the whole question of the future into the realm of fact. It ceases thus to be a merely speculative question. If now we combine the second and third points we find that a doctrine of last things is not only required by the experience of Christians, but also by the triumph of Christ himself over death. Hence we are not surprised that the New Testament has devoted much space to teachings about the outcome of the kingdom of God in the future.

2. The second preliminary question is: "What were the sources of the eschatological teachings of Jesus?" Here, of course, we recognize the originality of Jesus in giving a moral and spiritual content to the doctrine of last things which sets him immeasurably apart from his contemporaries. But here, as in all the other teachings of Jesus, he found a point of vital contact with his age. There were at least two sources whence the form and general outline of his doctrine are derived.

(1) The first we name is the Old Testament. It is not possible to trace in detail these Old Testament elements. It is indeed not necessary. The main facts are generally recognized. The great underlying conception in the Old Testament life and teaching was God's reign over his people Israel. He was in covenant relations with them. He had a glorious purpose to achieve through them. The pictures of the future which the Old Testament prophets held up to the gaze of the people varied with the circumstances and the needs. But there are certain great outstanding features which constantly recurred, especially in the later history.

The first great ideal for the future was the coming of God's perfected kingdom on earth. God is to establish his rule among men. The period of the kingdom of Israel under David and Solomon is conceived of as the typical period of the past. Sometimes God's reign over Israel is portrayed. In the later prophets Israel's mission to the world, and a kingdom which embraces all nations, looms large in the future. Descriptions of the coming kingdom are sometimes given in highly poetic language. Supernatural elements appear. God dwells with men. Jerusalem is the center of government. (See Isa. 2 : 2.)

Another great event of the future is the coming of the "Day of the Lord." Here, again, there is much variation in the form of statement. Sometimes it is a day of calamity, of thick darkness. At other times it is a day of glory and triumph. "The Day" seemed to some of the prophets to be ever impending. It was very near, and was about to burst upon the world. And yet at other times it seemed to be in the distant future. It was not necessarily a literal day of twenty-four hours, but a period of divine manifestation and power. (See Isa. 2 : 12, 17, 20; 61 : 2; Mal. 3 : 2, 3.)

Another element of the portrayal of the future was the judgment. This was not so much the great day of final judgment of mankind as it was the judgment of Israel for its sins, or of the nations of the world, or of both. Judgment was in connection with the "Day of the Lord." Jehovah would punish the nations and deliver Israel. At other times he punishes Israel and finally redeems the nation and establishes it under his own beneficent reign. (See Mal. 3 : 2, 3; Joel 2 : 28-32.)

Another great figure of the future is the Messiah. There are many passages which have a Messianic import. But here again the form of representation varies. The most constant form of portrayal is that of the King descended from David. He is the branch out of the stock of Jesse. Usually he is a great conqueror. He reigns in glory. Sometimes God rules in the coming kingdom. But when Messiah reigns, it is also God's reign. The Messianic King is identified with God. God reigns in and through him. Sometimes, especially in the fifty-second and fifty-third chapters of Isaiah, he is represented as a sufferer. He bears the penalty of the people's sins. He is the Servant of Jehovah. He is Jehovah's prophet to the nations. There has been much controversy over the question whether the suffering Servant in Isaiah is the righteous remnant of the people, or an individual Messiah. The truth seems to be that the prophet passed through the usual stages of experience here, and was gradually led to the higher truth. There are passages which seem best explained by reference to "the remnant." There are others which require application to an individual. The righteous remnant of Israel was the nucleus of the prophet's thought. The Messianic conviction, which was a fixed prophetic idea, came to his aid. There is something wonderfully striking and bold in the fifty-third chapter of Isaiah, where a human victim becomes a vicarious offering for sin, possessing redemptive efficacy for others. (See Isa. 53 : 4-11.)

[446]

In general the eschatology of the Old Testament refers to this world. The events portrayed were to take place on earth, although there are supernatural elements mingled in some of the prophecies. But along with this general teaching, as we have seen, there was the gradual rise of a clear conviction of the resurrection. One peculiarity of this belief in the resurrection is worthy of special emphasis. It brings into prominence the character of the Old Testament religion. The peculiarity is that is was chiefly the product of religious experience under the guidance of God's Spirit. In the earlier stages the Old Testament revelation presents a people who shared the common beliefs of the nations as to the future. The Greek and Babylonian beliefs and those of other nations, as to the life after death, were vague. So also were those of the Old Testament. There was no denial of continued existence. There is no teaching in the Old Testament to justify belief in annihilation or transmigration of souls. But Sheol was a shadowy realm. In it men were still conscious. But they were cut off from fellowship with men. It was regarded as involving a meager and attenuated existence. It was contemplated with misgiving and dread. Hence the emphasis upon the present life of fellowship with God. This is the supreme good. Now it was the experience of this fellowship under the influence of God's Spirit which was the basis of the conviction of the resurrection. In other words, the resurrection was a religious necessity. God will not forsake his servant, even in death. The passionate yearning for continued fellowship with Jehovah under the spur of trial and suffering led to the conviction. This comes out with special clearness in the case of Job. It also appears in several of the psalms. Thus it appears that the Old Testament doctrine of the resurrection did not arise out of the arguments and speculations of philosophers. It was not a theoretical belief. It arose out of the practical needs of the religious life. In Isaiah and Daniel the resurrection of the individual comes into very clear expression.

It cannot be said that the Old Testament doctrine of last things presents a complete or final picture of the future. It does not present a definite order of events which can be traced with accuracy. The language is often figurative and highly poetical. Widely separated events are often seen in their moral rather than their chronological sequence. Mountain peaks of the future, which are far apart, are seen in a perspective which brings them close together. There are, however, great outstanding features in the Old Testament eschatology. *a.* God is working in history with a purpose. He is moving toward a goal. *b.* Israel is the instrument and medium of his grace. *c.* His purpose extends to all mankind. *d.* He will interpose in judgment and in blessing in due time. *e.* He will send a Deliverer, who shall carry into effect his mighty purpose. *f.* By his grace, death and the grave will be conquered. *g.* His eternal kingdom shall triumph over all other forces of earth. No nation has ever equaled Israel, in their optimism. None has ever held so glorious a vision of the future. They not only held a Messianic belief. They were a Messianic people.

(2) A second influence to be mentioned in connection with the New Testament doctrine of last things is the Jewish eschatology of the New Testament times. Jesus came into the atmosphere of an age which was keenly alive to the problem of Israel's future. The Messianic hope took the form of a political restoration of the Jewish state, and at times it took the form of an apocalyptic intervention of God in the world and the setting up of his eternal kingdom. It does not fall within our purpose to give these teachings as they appear in the non-canonical Jewish literature. There are many and varied portrayals of the future in this collection of writings. In the books of Enoch, First and Second Maccabees, Judith, Tobit, the Assumption of Moses, and various others the Messianic expectations of the Jews are set forth. The elements which we have found in the Old Testament are reproduced here, along with various additions. In some cases the future is portrayed in most extravagant terms of material prosperity. Israel comes to her own in power and influence. The Messianic hope is at length realized. The glory of Jehovah is given to his people. God's eternal kingdom is established.

Now the mention of this non-canonical eschatological literature is with a view to emphasizing the fact that the messages of Jesus came to a people who were already alive to the Messianic expectation. Current forms of belief are presupposed in many of his own teachings. He set aside many elements of existing belief. He purified and transformed them, even when he accepted in part what they contained. His treatment of all of them was free and authoritative.

3. Our third preliminary question relates to the distinction between the form and the substance of the eschatology of the New Testament. Can we dispense with the outward form and hold the inner content? Can we cast aside the shell and keep the kernel? This general question is apart from the problems of exegesis which we encounter in dealing with the language of Jesus. Some hold that we may dispense with all the elements of the eschatalogy, except certain great central spiritual teachings. They view with suspicion the catastrophic and apocalyptic order of events, such as the Second Coming, the Resurrection, and Judgment. These are to be taken not literally, it is urged, but spiritually. The Second Coming means in its essence the triumph of God's kingdom. The Resurrection means, in principle, that we shall triumph spiritually over death. The Judgment means not an event in history, but that men will be rewarded or punished according to their deeds. It is held that these spiritual truths cover the ground and meet all our needs as to the future; that the language in which these hopes are set forth is not to be taken literally, but as pictorial representations drawn largely from contemporary Jewish thought.

(1) In reply to this question, we may say at once that we are bound to allow for the highly figurative terms in which much of the future is portrayed. We must also allow for the variety in the pictures of the future. There is scarcely any phase of the future of the kingdom which is not presented in a variety of forms. We ought especially to be on our guard against becoming absorbed in the order of events. We should not, as earnest servants of Christ, waste our time in the effort to make programs

of the future. And we certainly need to avoid the danger of thinking more about the dramatic pictures of the great events than of the moral and spiritual preparation necessary to us as Christians. Certainly we need these admonitions and cautions in the interest of our spiritual growth and usefulness.

(2) On the other hand, however, it is going too far to say that none of the great eschatological events which Jesus and the apostles foretold are to have historical realization. Indeed, if we take the position that the entire future of the kingdom is to be thus understood, we not only ignore what must be evident to the unbiased reader of the New Testament; but we also thereby change the very nature of the Christian religion itself as a historical religion. Consider a few details. The resurrection of Jesus is a vital truth. Without it the gospel would at once become a different gospel. It is the guaranty and pledge of the resurrection of the bodies of believers. It is incompatible with the view that the " survival of death " is the spiritual equivalent of the doctrine of the resurrection. Man is body as well as spirit. The resurrection preserves human nature in its integrity.

(3) Again, the resurrection of Jesus was an " apocalyptic " or " catastrophic " stage in the development of the kingdom. It was the incorporation of the " catastrophic " element into that kingdom. It is difficult to see how one who accepts the fact of the resurrection of Jesus can be content with a so-called spiritual equivalent which denies the resurrection of believers. This is wholly apart from the question as to how the resurrection takes place and the nature of the resurrection body. In a word, the resurrection of Christ gives character to the present gospel era. Christianity in its complete New Testament form dates from his resurrection. Christians now live in the power of a risen life based on the resurrection of Christ. (Eph. 1 : 19-22.) The consummation of the age is to be in terms also of resurrection glory, as seen in Christ the first-fruits and in his people at his coming.

(4) Consider the fact of the Second Coming. Properly understood, it is the consistent outcome for a religion which began

with a historical incarnation and resurrection. Christ's Person is the center of God's revelation to men. It is central in our faith, hope, and love. It is central in history. The preaching of the gospel of Christ is the task of Christ's people. God is dealing with men in and through Christ. Now his personal return to earth is certainly not a conception unrelated to all the above facts. If the religion of Christ is a historical religion, then the consummation may be best expressed in terms of history. The Second Coming is the inevitable historical sequence of the first coming. The two are indissolubly bound together. The Epistle to the Hebrews has expressed this thought very forcibly. (Heb. 9 : 27, 28.)

(5) The force of these statements appears when we attempt with seriousness to grasp the meaning of a Christianity with a historical beginning, but without a historical consummation. If we conceive the future in a wholly transcendental or spiritual manner, as remote from the earth and human history, we must think of this planet as passing into gradual dissolution and the race as finally becoming extinct. The hope of a resurrection passes away. The expectation of Christ's return fades from the central place in human hopes. Our religion would thus tend more and more to become a speculative belief. It would revert to the prechristian or philosophic type. The expectation of the return of Christ is the spiritual correlate of faith in him who was the Christ of history. It is the expectation which makes of our faith a self-consistent unity.

(6) Consider the meaning of judgment. We may of course conceive of a judgment that is wholly inward and spiritual. We may think of the relation of men to God simply as individuals and not in their social relations, or as nations, and of a judgment merely of individuals at death. But such a view certainly leaves many elements of human conduct and many phases of God's dealing with men out of the account. The fact is that God's dealing with sin always has an inner and an outer aspect. Our bodies reflect the ravages of sin in our spirits. Penalty takes the form in society of the decay of social institutions. Nations collapse

and fall away when honeycombed with iniquity. The cosmos itself feels the taint of sin. Now the New Testament doctrine of judgment simply recognizes this working of the law of sin and penalty, of righteousness and reward in a culminating judgment. The pictorial character of the New Testament representations does not imply denial of the great fact itself.

(7) We sum up by saying that the fundamental problem is not that of a self-consistent eschatology, but of a self-consistent Christianity. The historical and cosmic moves on parallel lines with the spiritual and inward development. Nature answers to the movements of grace. The future resurrection, the Second Coming of Christ, and the judgment are points of bright spiritual light which irradiate the future. But they appear within the framework of time and space. A view of the future which ignores the historical and cosmic side of the development leaves a dualism in the kingdom which destroys the unity of the divine purpose. This carries us back to the principle which we have noted in other connections. It is that the unity which the Christian religion recognizes is not that based on physical continuity, nor that of abstract idealism. It is rather a unity arising out of the continuity of a divine redemptive purpose. Human history and cosmic forces are subject to the gracious reign of a holy and loving and personal God.

4. A fourth preliminary question concerns the relation between the present and the future of the kingdom. Can we reconcile the statements that the kingdom is already in existence with those which project it into the future? Can we harmonize the principle of gradual development in the kingdom with the catastrophic events which appear in the eschatology? Some have asserted that these two elements in the Gospels contradict each other. Certain it is that the kingdom is both present and future in the teaching of Jesus. It is present in the following passages: Matthew 11 : 11; 12 : 28; Luke 16 : 16; 17 : 21. It is future in Matthew 1 : 21; 25 : 34; 26 : 29; Luke 21 : 31. It is also clear that in the teaching of Jesus the kingdom is represented as coming gradually in a number of parables. Among these are the

parables of the Leaven, of the Mustard-seed, the Seed Growing Secretly. It has been urged that the view of Jesus underwent a change in the course of his ministry, and that this explains the difference between the present and the future aspects of the coming of the kingdom. The objection to this is that both aspects of the teaching appear early and late in his ministry. (See Matt. 10 : 23; Mark 8 : 38; 9 : 1; Luke 9 : 27.)

If we are to accept the teachings of Jesus, we must recognize the presence of both these elements. One group of interpreters has insisted that with Jesus the present and developing aspects of the kingdom are the more important and controlling. Others have asserted that the future and apocalyptic elements are central and the others incidental and secondary. Both appear in the closest connection with each other. Evidently Jesus held them in mind without any sense of inconsistency or contradiction. The parables of the Virgins and Talents which immediately follow the great discourse about the Second Coming show this. He had just spoken, in the twenty-fourth chapter of Matthew, of the signs of his coming; of his sudden appearance in glory, which seemed to be in the very near future; and of the startling effect upon the dwellers upon the earth. Yet in the closing section of this chapter he speaks of "the evil servant" who says in his heart, "My Lord tarrieth, and shall begin to beat his fellow servants" (Matt. 24 : 48, 49). Jesus thus recognized the element of delay in his return. So also in the two parables. It is said of the virgins, "Now while the bridegroom tarried, they all slumbered and slept" (Matt. 25 : 5). And in the parable of the Talents we read, "Now after a long time the Lord of those servants cometh, and maketh a reckoning with them" (Matt. 25 : 19). The point of emphasis here is that if we are to find an adequate interpretation of the words of Jesus, we must take account of both elements. There are statements which seem to teach that his return was in the very near future. In others it seems far away. We must, if possible, find a key which will unlock the apparent contradiction. For certainly there was no sense of contradiction in the mind of Jesus himself.

The Christian Religion in Its Doctrinal Expression

The chief difficulty arises out of the language of Jesus, in which he declares that this generation shall not pass away until these things are accomplished. In his great discourse in Matthew (chap. 24 and 25) Jesus speaks of three great events, the destruction of Jerusalem, his own return, and the end of the world. He also speaks of certain prelusive occurrences which would indicate the near approach of these events. The parallel passages in Mark and Luke contain the same outstanding features. (Mark 13; Luke 21.) In Matthew 24 : 34 Jesus says, " This generation shall not pass away till all these things be accomplished." But he immediately adds in verse 36, " But of that day and hour knoweth no one, not even the angels of heaven, neither the Son, but the Father only." Here is an apparent contradiction which is not easy to understand.

Now various interpretations have been given of the language of these prophecies of Jesus. Some have even assumed that since Jesus did not return during that generation, he was mistaken. Others, that he only had in mind the destruction of Jerusalem and the end of the Jewish theocracy, and not a personal return at all. Others have supposed that the authors of the Gospels have not given us a report which presents the original connections in which the words were spoken. Hence they do not yield a clear result when we attempt to interpret them. But is there not a more direct and simple method of dealing with these passages?

Let us assume that the records as we have them are substantially in harmony with the Master's words. Then we must assume that the disciples were troubled with the same apparent contradictions as ourselves. We must then assume further that Jesus intended that his words should take this form. If, as some allege, these accounts do not represent the words of Jesus, but the thoughts of the writers, it is difficult to account for the alleged contradictions. If the writers took liberties with the words of Jesus, would they have given us reports in the same writings in a form so difficult to harmonize and understand? After all, it is easier to take the records as the original words of Jesus than as those of the disciples themselves, because the latter would have avoided the obvious difficulties of the accounts as they have been transmitted to us.

Proceeding now on the assumption that the narrations are in substance the reports of the words of Jesus, our interpretation is as follows: (1) Jesus himself declares his own ignorance of the day and hour of the return. Men do not know; angels do not know. Only God the Father knows. Evidently then God did not intend to reveal the chronology of the future of the kingdom. He did not intend that we should know the time nor the order of events. There are the best of spiritual reasons for such ignorance. It surely is better that Christians remain without knowledge on this point. Attempts to fix dates have always led to extravagances of one kind or another. It tends to breed fanaticism and loss of spiritual balance.

(2) If the day and hour of the return of Christ, the central and controlling event of the future, are unknown, then it follows that all the chronology is unknown. But ignorance on this point does not affect the certainty of the events themselves. The destruction of Jerusalem, the Second Coming, and the end of the age were all parts of the fixed divine purpose. This certainty appears in very clear language in the great prophecy.

(3) This leads to the attitude of Jesus to the future throughout the prophecy. Here we may obtain light from the Old Testament prophets and their attitude to the future. To them " the Day of the Lord " often included widely separated events. It was often conceived of as imminent, as being at the door. To them God's power appeared in contemporary events. History was dynamic with mighty possibilities because it was under the control of Jehovah. " The Day of the Lord " was thus often a spiritual process with great climaxes, in which Jehovah came in power. Now if we think of Jesus as resembling the prophets in this respect, his great deliverances as to the future may be understood much more clearly.

In the mind of Jesus the vision of the future was a unitary picture of the coming kingdom and the mighty working of God's power. He dealt not so much with detached events as with the movement as a whole. Certain great events will take place. But these are so closely bound together in the chain of moral causes and effects that the coming of one is in part the coming of all. His own personal return is the supreme event. But it is bound up indissolubly with the things which precede and those which follow it.

(4) With this thought in mind it is not difficult to grasp the main points in this great prophecy of Jesus. The kingdom comes in three senses. It comes in its beginning. It comes in its progress. It comes in its consummation. These are one in principle. The consummation is latent in the beginning. The beginning is patent in the consummation. Jesus beholds the consummation in any event whether at the beginning, in the progress, or at the end. So also the Second Coming of Christ. It is the equivalent of the coming of the kingdom. He comes in the beginning, in the continuance, and in the end of the era. Events belonging to the series which is unified around the Second Coming are in a real sense comings of the Lord. There is a striking saying of Jesus which shows the truth of this last statement. Jesus, in Matthew 26 : 64, says in reply to the high priest's question, "Henceforth ye shall see the Son of man sitting at the right hand of power, and coming on the clouds of heaven." The phrase translated "henceforth" (*ap' arti*) does not mean "hereafter," as if some future time were in view. It means from the time when Jesus spoke the words—"from now on." He means that the era of God's power, as exerted in and through his Son, has begun. The Son of man is "henceforth" the ruler of history.

Events which followed upon these words of Jesus confirmed them. His death was a departure from the earth, and certainly his resurrection from the dead was a return in power. Of course it did not take the place of the great event of the future, the Parousia, when he shall return to judge the world. (See Acts I : II.) The gift of the Holy Spirit on the day of Pentecost was another great event belonging to the series in the near future. The destruction of Jerusalem was clearly included in the near events portrayed in his great prophecy. These events were comings of Christ. They were witnessed by men who heard his words and who remained alive, according to his prediction, until the fulfilment.

The Gospel of John in an important manner supplements the teachings of the synoptics on the doctrine of last things. Matthew, Mark, and Luke deal for the most part with events. John, as a rule, deals with principles. But John also recognizes events. The personal return of Christ is taught by him in unequivocal terms. (John 14 : 3; 21 : 22.) There can be no doubt as to the meaning in 21 : 22, and it is not easy to understand 14 : 3 as other than a personal return when we connect it with verse 2, where he says, " I go to prepare a place for you." There is no contradiction between John's teachings and that of the synoptics on this point.

It remains true, however, that John emphasizes the coming and work of the Holy Spirit. This is equivalent to an inward and spiritual coming of Christ. This comes out in various passages, but especially in chapters 14, 15, and 16 in the Gospel. In accordance with this John deals with nearly all the elements of eschatology as spiritual principles as well as objective events. He represents Jesus as saying regarding death, " Whosoever liveth and believeth on me shall never die " (John 11 : 26). Referring to himself also, he says, " He that eateth this bread shall live forever " (John 6 : 58). The resurrection also is represented as a spiritual principle as well as an objective event: " The hour cometh and now is when the dead shall hear the voice of the Son of God; and they that hear shall live " (John 5 : 25). But in 5 : 28, 29 he adds a teaching as to the future resurrection of the good and evil. In like manner the judgment is set forth as a spiritual principle: " He that heareth my word and believeth on him that sent me, hath eternal life, and cometh not into judgment, but hath passed out of death unto life " (John 5 : 24). In the twenty-ninth verse he teaches also a judgment which is to follow the resurrection.

If now we put together the teachings of the synoptics and those of the Fourth Gospel, we conclude in answer to the question at the beginning of this section as follows: First, the doctrine of last things includes events and processes in the moral and spiritual life. The eschatology of the Gospels cannot be reduced to events to the exclusion of principles, nor to principles to the exclusion of events. Both appear in indissoluble union. Secondly, the kingdom of God is both near and far in the representations of the New Testament writers. But there is no evidence as to how near or how far the events may be in the future. Thirdly, the center of the Christian hope is in the return of Jesus Christ. Fourthly, the return itself is the event in the light of which other events are viewed and by which they are to be understood. There is much more to be said under the separate topics in the doctrine of last things, as we shall see. But having answered these preliminary general questions, we may proceed to matters of detail, *viz.,* Death, the Intermediate State, the Second Coming of Christ, the Judgment, and the Final States of the Righteous and Wicked.

III. DEATH OF THE BODY

Physical death is the separation of soul and body. In Scripture teaching it is closely connected with spiritual death, which is the separation of the soul from God. The Bible deals with all questions from the religious point of view. There is no treatment of the subject of death from the standpoint of modern science or biological law. Death was pronounced as the penalty of the first sin. Primarily this was a spiritual dying or severance of the bond of union between God and man. But it also included physical death. Men are declared to be "dead through trespasses and sins" (Eph. 2 : 1). This of course does not mean a form of existence devoid of all activity. It means simply a life without a vital relation to God, apart from God. The death of the body is the culmination of such a life on earth. The "second death" is declared to be the final outcome when the separation from God becomes formal banishment from his presence at the last judgment. (Rev. 20 : 14.)

Last Things

In accordance with the above the Christian hope includes a victory over death. The apostle Paul condenses the whole teaching of Scripture in a statement at the close of his great passage on the resurrection: " The sting of death is sin; and the power of sin is the law: but thanks be to God who giveth us the victory through our Lord Jesus Christ " (1 Cor. 15 : 56, 57). From this we conclude: (1) That physical death was a part of the penalty for sin; (2) that for those who do not share in Christ's salvation the penalty remains; (3) that in the case of the Christian, while the physical organism undergoes the change we call death, yet it is no longer death in the penal sense, it is transformed and becomes spiritual victory; (4) finally, the victory over death is secured for us solely through the resurrection of Christ from the dead and his communication of life to us.

IV. THE INTERMEDIATE STATE

On the subject of the intermediate state little is to be gained by speculation. The teachings of Scripture are not numerous on the subject, but they are clear and sufficient so far as they go. They leave many problems unsolved, but they give assurance on the main points. We give first a review of the teachings of the New Testament and then a summary of results.

The word Hades, as employed in the New Testament, is practically equivalent in meaning to Sheol in the Old Testament. It means simply the abode of the dead. It tells nothing of their moral state. Good and evil are represented alike as entering this abode of the dead. Hades is not Paradise; neither is it Gehenna. It may be either, but it is not to be identified with either. The use of the word Hades does not of itself tell whether he who enters it passes down to misery or upward to bliss. He may pass in either direction. Jesus entered Hades. (Acts 2 : 31.) So also did the rich man in the parable. (Luke 16 : 23.) Hades is thus represented in the New Testament as a realm apart from the present life into which all the dead enter. But the New Testament goes beyond this. It has positive teachings as to the estate

[459]

of the dead. We consider some of the more important of these in their bearing upon the state of the righteous dead.

1. The Righteous Dead

In Matthew 22 : 32 Jesus says, referring to Abraham, Isaac, and Jacob, " God is not the God of the dead, but of the living." He declares that Lazarus " was carried away by the angels into Abraham's bosom " (Luke 16 : 22). Again, to the dying robber he says, " To-day shalt thou be with me in Paradise " (Luke 23 : 43). To the sorrowing Martha Jesus says, " Whosoever liveth and believeth on me shall never die " (John 11 : 26). In 2 Corinthians 5 : 1 the apostle Paul declares that if the " earthly house of our tabernacle be dissolved, we have a building from God, a house not made with hands, eternal in the heavens." In Philippians 1 : 23 he says he has a " desire to depart and be with Christ, for it is very far better." In Revelation 6 : 9-11 the disembodied spirits of the dead are represented as being in a state of consciousness and calling upon God.

From these Scriptures we draw the following conclusions: (1) At death the Christian goes directly into the presence of Christ and of God. There is not a long delay between the moment of death and some future time. (2) The state in which they exist there is a conscious state. In the passages cited this appears in various ways. In Romans 8 : 38 Paul declares that nothing shall separate us from the love of Christ. He means that our moral and spiritual relationship to Christ is to be continuous. This is scarcely in harmony with the idea of an indefinite period of interrupted fellowship. (3) The disembodied dead who are thus present with Christ and conscious are also in a state of happiness and rest. Paul declares that it is far better than his present life of toil. Revelation 14 : 13 states that the dead who die in the Lord are " blessed," and that they " rest from their labors." (4) There is no basis in the New Testament teaching for what is known as the doctrine of " soul-sleeping." According to this the souls of the dead remain in a state of unconsciousness until the resurrection of the body, when soul and body are reunited and consciousness returns. The doctrine includes the wicked as well as the righteous. In reply, we of course admit that the Scriptures refer to death as a sleep in a number of passages. (*E. g.,* Dan. 12 : 2; Matt. 9 : 24; John 11 : 11; 1 Thess. 5 : 10.) But nowhere is it said that the " soul " sleeps. The reference is to the personality as a whole, and the figure of sleep must be interpreted in harmony with the general teachings we have presented as the uniform doctrine of the New Testament. Sleep means " not alive to surroundings." A man asleep knows nothing of the activities about him. So death is a sleep in the sense that men become alive to a new set of surroundings and cut off from those of the present life. In one passage the idea of death as a sleep and that of conscious fellowship with Christ are combined in a single statement. In 1 Thessalonians 5 : 10 the apostle refers to Christ " who died for us, that, whether we wake or sleep, we should live together with him."

(5) The teachings presented give no warrant for the Roman Catholic doctrine of purgatory. According to this doctrine only perfected saints escape purgatorial sufferings. All other Christians must be purged and cleansed in purgatory before they are prepared for the next stage. Prayers and masses for the dead are said. They shorten the misery of those in purgatory.

As we have seen, the best reply to this dogma is the positive teaching of Scripture. It is founded on certain sayings of Church Fathers, Augustine, Cyprian, and Tertullian, and certain perversions of New Testament passages, like 1 Corinthians 3 : 13, 14.

(6) The intermediate state is not the final state of believers. It is represented as a relatively imperfect state. The apostle Paul shrank from it as from an unclothed condition. (2 Cor. 5 : 3, 4.) He longed for the resurrection of the dead. (Phil. 3 : 11.) All the teachings of the New Testament regarding the resurrection and final state of the righteous show that the intermediate state is not regarded as ideal or final. Man is body as well as spirit, and the disembodied state is necessarily lacking in one element of human perfection, which will be supplied at the resurrection.

2. The Unrighteous Dead

There are a few passages which shed light upon the intermediate state of the unrighteous dead. One of these which is frequently cited represents them as " in prison " (1 Peter 3 : 19). This, however, is a passage difficult to interpret satisfactorily, and may be understood as not referring to the dead at all, but to those who were alive in the days of Noah. There are a few other passages which are not doubtful on the main point. In the parable of the Rich Man and Lazarus, Jesus says of the rich man: " And in Hades he lifted up his eyes, being in torment, and seeth Abraham afar off, and Lazarus in his bosom. And he cried and said, Father Abraham, have mercy on me, and send Lazarus, that he may dip the tip of his finger in water, and cool my tongue, for I am in anguish in this flame " (Luke 16 : 23, 24). We must of course recognize here that we are dealing with a parable, and there are many difficulties of interpretation. But the central truths are that Lazarus was in a state of conscious blessedness and the rich man in a state of conscious suffering. Again, in 2 Peter 2 : 9 we read, " The Lord knoweth how to deliver the godly out of temptation, and to keep the unrighteous under punishment unto the day of judgment." We have thus only brief glimpses of the state of the wicked in the period between death and the final judgment. But these indicate that they are conscious and that already they have begun to endure the penalty of their wicked lives.

V. THE SECOND COMING OF CHRIST

We have in a previous section answered some of the fundamental questions about the Second Coming of Christ. We now complete what was said there by the following statements:

1. The uniform teaching of the New Testament is that the Second Coming is to be an outward, visible, and personal return of Christ. We learned that this is the clear teaching of Jesus himself. It is equally clear in the teachings of the book of Acts and in the Epistles. In Acts 1 : 11 we read, " This Jesus, who

was received up from you into heaven, shall so come in like manner as ye beheld him going into heaven." The phrase in like manner (*hon tropon*) does not express the certainty of Christ's return merely, but also the manner. As he was received up visibly so would he return visibly to the earth. In 1 Thessalonians 4 : 16 Paul declares, " For the Lord himself shall descend from heaven with a shout, with the voice of the archangel, and with the trump of God." In 2 Peter 3 : 3-12 we read, " In the last days mockers shall come . . . saying, Where is the promise of his coming?" In James 5 : 8 also: " Be ye also patient; establish your hearts; for the coming of the Lord is at hand." And in Revelation 22 : 12 the language is: " Behold, I come quickly; and my reward is with me, to render to each man according as his work is." Those passages could be greatly multiplied if necessary. They serve to show indisputably that the expectation of a visible personal return of Christ was common to the New Testament writers.

2. The exact time of the personal return of Christ is unrevealed. Jesus declared that he himself did not know the day or the hour of his return. (Matt. 24 : 36; Mark 13 : 32.) In Acts 1 : 7 he is represented as cautioning disciples against attempting to pry into the events of the future: " It is not for you to know times or seasons, which the Father hath set within his own authority." In verse 8 he adds that they should receive power after the coming of the Holy Spirit, and that they should witness for him to the ends of the earth. Evidently Jesus was concerned much more about the devotion of his people to their practical duties and tasks than that they should know the details of the future.

3. We repeat here the statement previously made that Jesus recognized subordinate comings in the events of history in addition to the Second Coming itself in its visible and personal aspect. This principle is expressed in the Gospel of John in his promise to come through the Holy Spirit and make his abode in disciples. It appears in unmistakable terms in the statement in Matthew 26 : 64: " Henceforth," that is, " From now," from the present

time, " ye shall see the Son of man . . . coming on the clouds of heaven."

4. The attitude of the New Testament writers and the disciples generally toward the Second Coming was one of constant expectancy. There is scarcely any difference of opinion on this point among interpreters of the New Testament. To them his coming was ever imminent. It might occur at any time, even during the lives of the generation then on earth. In some passages certain events are to precede. The " falling away " and the rise of Antichrist, or the man of sin, were among these as set forth by Paul in 2 Thessalonians 2 : 1-12. Some have thought that Paul's doctrine of the Second Coming underwent a change toward the latter part of his career. But there is no real contradiction between his earlier and later views. The variations in emphasis which we find in his Epistles are explained by the variations in the circumstances of his readers and the situation which he desired to meet.

The question arises: How then are we to explain this uniform expectation of the near return of Christ? Was Paul mistaken? Were the other apostles in error? This inference is often drawn. But it is an inference which overlooks certain important factors which are required by the New Testament records themselves. It overlooks, first of all, the difference between a mental and spiritual attitude and a dogmatic teaching. The disciples looked for the return at any time. But they did not expressly assert that Christ would, without fail, come during their lives. The inference that Paul and others were mistaken also overlooks the clear warnings given by Paul himself (2 Thess. 2 : 1-12) and by Peter (2 Peter 3 : 3-12) against the premature expectation of Christ's return. It overlooks, in the third place, the fact that this expectation of the near return was in obedience to repeated commands of Jesus while on earth. In a number of instances he enjoined upon the disciples the duty of constant watchfulness and expectancy. (Matt. 24 : 42; 25 : 13; Mark 13 : 35-37.) When we compare the words of Jesus in these passages with what we find in the later New Testament writings, we are struck with their agreement with each other. If the apostles, after Jesus' departure, had abandoned the thought of his personal return, we should be at a loss to understand their attitude. In the above passages the very ignorance of disciples as to the time of the return and their uncertainty regarding it were made the basis of the exhortation to watch constantly.

5. There are at least two ways in which the expectation of Christ's near return served the ends of the kingdom of God among these early Christians. First, it was a moral and spiritual incentive of the highest value. The age was one of great trial and suffering. The thought of Christ's return in power was a source of great consolation, and inspired to zeal and devotion Whenever it led to extravagant or fanatical forms of conduct, these were at once corrected by the apostles. The belief was turned to moral and spiritual account, to the uses of sobriety and of holy living. Secondly, the expectation of Christ's personal return gave unity to the faith of believers. The Christ who had already come was the Christ who would come again. If Christ had abandoned the world forever after the ascent from Olivet, a great blank would have been left in the future for his followers. What is to be the outcome of Christian effort? How is the ongoing of history to terminate? What is the dominant force in the history of the world? Questions like these would have been left without satisfactory answer apart from the doctrine of the Second Coming. His return in glory was thus a truth which held him closely bound to the fortunes of his people on earth. For them he was ever thus the Christ who stood within the shadow " keeping watch above his own." These same principles apply to Christians of to-day under the changed circumstances of the world. Any age of self-indulgence needs the same stimulus to holy living. There has been vast ingenuity and arduous labor on the part of scholars in dealing with this element in the religion of Christ as set forth in the New Testament. But there has often been a notable lack of spiritual insight and of sympathy with the genius of the Christian faith. Jesus Christ as Revealer of God and Redeemer of men fills the horizon of

E 2   [465]

the Christian believer, the horizon of the future as well as of the present and the past. The whole of the personal life in its relation to God and to history must be construed in terms of the personal relation to Christ himself.

VI. The Question as to the Millennium

There is very general agreement among interpreters that the New Testament teaches a visible and personal return of Christ. There has been from the beginning of Christian history, however, a division over the question of the thousand years' reign of the saints with Christ upon earth. This period is known as the millennium. The passage in which specific reference is made to it is Revelation 20 : 1-6. The issue between premillennialists and postmillennialists is over the question whether the Second Coming of Christ will precede or follow the thousand years. It will be impossible to deal with this controversy in anything like an exhaustive manner. But we may indicate the leading points at issue and the leading considerations for and against the respective views, and follow this with our own conclusions.

Premillennialists hold that the return of Christ to earth will precede the period known as the millennium. The general outline of the view is as follows: (1) When Christ returns the world generally will be under the power of evil. Antichrist will have sway among men. (Matt. 24 : 24, 29, 30.) (2) At his coming Christ will win a notable victory over his enemies and will destroy Antichrist. (2 Thess. 2 : 8; Jude 14, 15.) (3) Living Christians will be caught up to meet the Lord in the air. (1 Thess. 4 : 17.) (4) There will be a resurrection of the dead in Christ at the beginning of the millennial period. This is known as the first resurrection. (Rev. 20 : 4-6.) (5) Then follows a preliminary judgment of the living nations, and the risen saints will reign with Christ a thousand years. (Rev. 20 : 4; Matt. 25 : 31-46.) (6) At the end of the thousand years there will be a return of flagrant wickedness through the loosing of Satan, who has been bound. (Rev. 20 : 7-10.) (7) Following this the resurrection of the wicked will take place, and this will be succeeded by the final judgment and eternal awards. (Rev. 20 : 12-15.)   There are many details which are not indicated in the above outline. It should be said also that premillennialists are not agreed among themselves on all details. But the salient features are substantially as indicated.

There are many passages of Scripture which are relied upon. The chief ones are the words of Christ in Matthew, chapters 24 and 25, and the corresponding sections in Mark and Luke; the passages in 1 Thessalonians 4 : 13-18 and 2 Thessalonians 2 : 1-12; Paul's language in 1 Corinthians 15 : 20-24; and Revelation 20 : 1-6. Along with these, many other New Testament passages and divers Old Testament prophecies are cited. We have given brief references under the preceding points, but the total impression is much stronger for the premillennial view when the extended passages just given are read in their entirety.

The postmillennial view also holds that there will be a period of a thousand years during which Christianity will triumph over the earth. This millennial period will be the result of the gradual spread of the gospel and its conquest over all departments of human life. At the end of this period the conflict between the powers of good and evil will be renewed for a time, after which Christ will return in person. Then will take place the resurrection of the righteous and the wicked. This will be followed by the final judgment and eternal awards.

In support of the postmillennial view many passages are cited in which the resurrection of the righteous and the wicked seems to take place at the same time; in which this is represented as occurring in close connection with the Second Coming of Christ on the one hand and the final judgment on the other. The millennial period itself which precedes these events is derived from the same passage in Revelation 20 : 1-10. We give a few details of the interpretation. Matthew 16 : 27 connects the rendering to " every man according to his deeds," with the coming of Christ in the " glory of his Father." So also in Matthew 25 : 31-33, Christ comes and sits on the throne of his glory and judges all the nations. In John 5 : 28, 29 it is declared that " the hour cometh " in which all that are in the tomb, both righteous and wicked, shall be raised for judgment. In 2 Thessalonians 1 : 6-10 Christ is represented as coming " in flaming fire," and punishing the wicked with " eternal destruction from the face of the Lord." In 2 Peter 3 : 7, 10 again the " Day of the Lord " is closely connected with the judgment of ungodly men and the destruction of the earth by fire. In Revelation 20 : 11-15 there is a portrayal of the final judgment, in which all men appear together and eternal awards are declared.

Objections to the Two Theories

We give now a brief summary of the principal objections to each of these systems of interpretation as urged by the advocates of the opposing view.

Postmillennialists object to the premillennial view on various grounds. (1) It builds chiefly on one passage in Revelation 20 : 1-10, which belongs to the most figurative and poetic writing of the entire New Testament. Besides this, the passage does not assert that all the dead in Christ will be raised and reign with him, but only the martyrs, or those " that had been beheaded for the testimony of Jesus." Further, it is argued that the " first resurrection " mentioned here may refer to the spiritual resurrection which appears so frequently in the sayings of Jesus, of John, and of Paul. Thus it is inferred that the entire passage may be a symbolic representation of the triumph of spiritual principles during a long period. (2) It is objected also that the premillennial view ignores all those passages in which the resurrection and judgment of the righteous and wicked are declared to occur simultaneously. (3) So also it ignores the numerous parables and other Scriptures in which the progress of the kingdom on earth is represented as taking place gradually and not by sudden catastrophes. As Dr. J. B. Thomas expressed it, " The kingdom of heaven is like a grain of mustard-seed, not like a can of nitroglycerin." (4) It is also urged against premillennialism that it involves insuperable difficulties as to the nature of the kingdom of Christ. Risen saints live and reign on earth with generations who are born and live out their natural lives in the ordinary way. Thus incongruous or contradictory elements are introduced. (5) The view tends to superficial work in that it holds that the gospel is to be preached merely " for a witness " to all nations before Christ comes. The phrase is scriptural, but its meaning as a hasty proclamation simply is denied. (6) The view tends to pessimism in that it carries the belief that the world will grow worse until the Lord's return. Thus the motive which inspires to the highest effort is destroyed. (7) It tends to an undue emphasis upon a single truth with the inevitable consequences of too little stress upon other truths, and the further consequence of making of it a divisive issue among Christians, and sometimes a tendency to extravagance and fanaticism.

Premillennialists also object vigorously to the postmillennial view on various grounds. (1) It ignores the clear and obvious meaning of Revelation 20 : 1-10 as well as the other passages which have been cited in favor of the premillennial view—two resurrections and two judgments. (2) It ignores those passages which show that wickedness will still be rife upon the earth when Christ returns. (3) It leaves out of account the teachings as to Antichrist. The passage in 2 Thessalonians 2 : 1-11 shows that evil gradually heads up in Antichrist, and prohibits the conception of a thousand-year period of gospel triumph prior to Christ's return. (4) It also ignores such Scriptures as represent the progress of the kingdom through sudden catastrophic events, such as 1 Thessalonians 5 : 1-3, the parable of the Virgins, and various other passages. (5) It also fails to consider a great number of Old Testament prophecies which clearly refer to a glorious kingdom of Christ on this earth, involving the restoration of Israel and other important results. (6) It ignores the distinction between the judgment of the nations in Matthew 25 : 31-46 and the final judgment of the Great White Throne in Revelation 20 : 11-15. (7) Finally, it is urged, the postmillennial view allows no place in the Christian's spiritual attitude for the New

Testament expectation of Christ's return. For if that return is deferred to the end of a thousand-year period, it will inevitably die out of the living experience of believers as a potent factor in life and devotion. Here there is a sharp clash of opinion. The postmillennialist charges that the opposing view compromises the veracity of God, in that he commanded a constant expectation of an event which he foreknew would not take place for nineteen hundred years. The premillennialist replies that the wisdom of God is compromised even more by the injunction to constant expectancy of Christ's coming coupled with the teaching that a thousand years of gospel triumph must precede.

Conclusion

There are numerous subordinate points of the controversy which we have not touched upon in the preceding review. But the leading issues have been indicated. Our own conclusion may now be stated. It is as follows:

First, the passage in Revelation 20 : 1-10 has been given too great prominence in the doctrine of last things by both sides in the millennial controversy. If it is taken literally in all details, it certainly seems to teach the premillennial view in part. But it limits the number of saints who reign with Christ to martyrs. A misgiving also arises as to the place of the thousand-year reign. Nowhere in the vision (ver. 4-10) is it said that these martyred saints reign with Christ *on this earth* a thousand years. The seer does not say where it occurs. Throughout the book of Revelation John passes at will from heaven to earth and back again. The visions are symbolic in the highest degree in combination with elements that are literal as well. It is at least hazardous to make a single passage like this determinative for the interpretation of a great mass of Scriptures which are not symbolic or highly figurative in form. Yet this is done by both schools. The millennium is the central issue. Everything turns on this.

Secondly, the teaching of the Old and New Testaments alike

[470]

is the ultimate triumph of God's kingdom on earth. Nothing could well be clearer than this, even in the book of Revelation. All the stages of the vision move gradually forward through conflict to the final dénouement in the descent of the city of God to this earth. But no system of interpretation has yet been found which can trace successfully the meaning of all the details. The message of the book is the ultimate triumph. Inspired by this hope and conviction we may face our tasks as Christians.

Thirdly, both the pre- and the postmillennial theories leave many insoluble problems. The postmillennialist certainly has an impossible task in trying to find a place in his conception of the future for the New Testament attitude of constant expectancy for the coming of Christ. The premillennialist overloads his program of the future so that one staggers under the burden. Both make a great mass of literal passages subordinate and tributary to one passage in a symbolic context in a highly figurative book.

Fourthly, one event occupies the central place in the vision of the future throughout the New Testament from Matthew to Revelation. That event is the Second Coming of Christ. All else is subordinate and tributary to that. Side by side with it are descriptions of gradual growth and of sudden catastrophes in the coming kingdom. There are comings in historical events, and the one great coming. There are great delays and great sufferings, and there are glorious and sudden triumphs. There is no sort of question as to at least one resurrection, and one judgment, and one eternal kingdom. There is no clear assurance that there must be a thousand years of perfect piety on earth before Christ returns. There is no clear guaranty that he will reign literally on earth with all the risen saints a thousand years before the final judgment.

In the fifth place, it follows that Christians should cultivate the New Testament attitude of expectancy. We should ever be as men who look for their Lord, because he commanded it, and because we love him and trust him, and because all the future would be blank without him. He is the key which unlocks for us the hidden things of the coming ages. But we should not become absorbed in apocalyptic calculations and speculations. We should not be so assured of the program of the unrevealed future that we " begin to beat our fellow servants " because they do not accept our particular interpretation. (Matt. 24 : 49.) We should not attempt to fix dates or insist too greatly upon detailed programs. We should be faithful in every detail of duty. We should ever watch against temptation and pray for divine strength. We should cultivate a passion for righteousness, individual and social. We should work while it is day, knowing that the night cometh when no man can work. We should be so eager for the coming of our Lord, that if he should come to-morrow we would not be taken by surprise. We should so hold ourselves in restraint, that if his return should be delayed a thousand or ten thousand years, we would not be disappointed. And our hearts should be ever filled with joy at the prospect of his coming and the certain triumph of his kingdom.

VII. THE RESURRECTION

The resurrection of the body is a leading topic in the New Testament doctrine of last things. We have already seen how it came into clear recognition in the later stages of the Old Testament revelation. (See Isa. 26 : 19; Ezek. 37 : 1-14; Job 14 : 12-15; Dan. 12 : 2.) We give now a brief presentation of New Testament passages.

The most explicit teaching of Jesus is in reply to the Sadducees who denied the resurrection of the body. This appears in all the synoptic Gospels. (Matt. 22 : 23-33; Mark 12 : 18-27; Luke 20 : 27-40.) In brief Jesus says to his questioners that " as touching the resurrection of the dead " they were in error, " not knowing the Scriptures nor the power of God." He then quotes Exodus 3 : 6. God says, " I am the God of Abraham, and the God of Isaac, and the God of Jacob." Then he adds, " God is not the God of the dead, but of the living." Other passages clearly imply the doctrine of the resurrection, such as Matthew 8 : 11;

Luke 13 : 28, 29. In the Fourth Gospel the same teaching appears. There the spiritual resurrection is taught, along with explicit statements as to the resurrection of the body. Notable passages are John 11 : 23-26, where Jesus declares to Martha that he is " the resurrection and the life," and John 5 : 25-29, where Jesus foretells the resurrection of the righteous and the unrighteous: " All that are in the tombs shall hear his voice, and shall come forth; they that have done good, unto the resurrection of life; and they that have done evil, unto the resurrection of judgment."

In the book of Acts the resurrection of Jesus is everywhere assumed as a fundamental fact of the gospel, and along with it appears the doctrine of the resurrection of men generally. (Acts 1 : 3; 2 : 30-33; 17 : 18; 22 : 7-9; 24 : 15.) In the last passage the apostle Paul announces explicitly a resurrection of the " just and unjust." Ordinarily, in the many passages in his Epistles dealing with the resurrection, Paul has in mind believers. But there is no convincing evidence that, as some have held, he denied the resurrection of the unrighteous. All the evidence we have points the other way.

In the Epistles the resurrection bulks largely in Paul's teachings. It is discussed in various aspects, and is a presupposition of all his exposition on the spiritual life in Christ. We need only present the chief points in his doctrine. The resurrection of Christ is the corner-stone of his teaching. Christ was " marked out " to be the Son of God with power " by the resurrection from the dead " (Rom. 1 : 4). The resurrection of Christ is the basis of the Christian hope and the guaranty of the resurrection of all those who are in Christ. The fifteenth chapter of First Corinthians is devoted to this great theme. Again, Paul declares repeatedly that all believers are now living a resurrection life in the spiritual sense of the word. (Eph. 2 : 5, 6; Col. 2 : 20; 3 : 4.) In Romans 8 : 11 he declares that the present indwelling of the Holy Spirit in believers is the pledge of their resurrection. The present spiritual resurrection and the future raising of the body are conceived of as one continuous process.

[473]

In harmony with this he speaks of "attaining unto the resurrection from the dead" by sacrifice and spiritual struggle. In Romans 8 : 19-24 Paul declares that nature itself, that is, creation apart from man, will share in the resurrection glory. Nature groans and awaits the resurrection, "the redemption of our body" (Rom. 8 : 23). In harmony with this doctrine of the resurrection in the four Gospels, in Acts, and in the Pauline Epistles, is the teaching in the other books of the New Testament.

We may next consider two questions about the resurrection, one as to the spirit, the other as to the body. The first is this: May we not interpret the New Testament teaching as a vivid and figurative way of declaring simply the continued life of the spirit, or what we ordinarily mean by the immortality of the soul? The answer must be a decisive negative. The current beliefs of the Jews when Christ spoke forbid this. The issue between Sadducees and Pharisees was clear. One affirmed and the other denied the resurrection. Christ's assertion on the subject could not have meant merely the continued spiritual existence of the soul. Paul refutes those who asserted that "the resurrection is past already" (2 Tim. 2 : 18), thus showing that the body and not the spirit alone was involved in the resurrection in 1 Corinthians 15 : 44. By this he can only mean a body adapted to the spirit in its perfected state, a body which would be a perfect instrument of the spirit. In general, we may add that there is no basis whatever in the New Testament for the conception of the Greek philosophy which tended to disparage the body because it is made of matter, and to insist simply upon an incorporeal life of the spirit in the future. Human nature as a whole, in both its aspects, as body and as spirit, is the biblical conception of the true life.

The second question relates to the body. How is the body raised from the dead? Through what changes does it pass? The body dies and is buried; or it is burned; or it is drowned in the sea. Its particles are dissipated in all directions. They reappear in vegetation or in other material forms. Our bodies constantly change, even before death. We are all the time shedding the old and forming new bodies by the processes of life. From these facts it is clear that the resurrection body is not identical in material particles with the present body, or the body that is laid in the grave. How, then, shall we conceive of the resurrection body? Does God create a new body entirely? Or does the spirit of man fashion for itself a spiritual body after death? Or do we possess such a body within the present body?

Here we are on speculative ground. The Scriptures exhibit a remarkable restraint and reserve in this matter. There are no assertions which are negatived by any of the difficulties suggested. There are none which dissipate all our ignorance.

A bright shaft of light penetrates the veil and we see enough to assure and comfort us, but we have no general view of the world beyond. Paul's discussion in the fifteenth chapter of First Corinthians yields the following general statements: (1) The new body will be a " spiritual body " as contrasted with the present natural and perishable body. It will be perfectly adapted to the needs of our spirit. Our spirit will be perfectly clothed. (2) This spiritual body will differ greatly from the present body. He contrasts the " bare grain " of wheat that is sown with the stalk of wheat that comes from it. The point of contrast is between the mortality and corruption of the body as we now know it and the immortality and glory of the resurrection body. Christ's risen body, with its power of rapid movement, of vanishing and reappearing, of exemption from the ordinary laws of time and space, suggests the nature of the contrast. (3) And yet there is a connection between the old and the new body. " It " is sown, and " it " is raised. What the connection is we do not know.

Summary of the New Testament Teaching

We sum up what has been said about the resurrection in the following general statements based on a correlation and comparison of the pertinent passages in the New Testament. First, the resurrection of Christ is the controlling fact of history in all doctrinal statements about the resurrection. The Christian religion in its present form began to be a regenerative, a recreative force when Jesus arose from the dead. The first gospel related to Jesus and the resurrection.

Secondly, the resurrection of the bodies of believers became an article of faith of the early Christians for the twofold reason that Jesus had risen, and that he had made manifest his power as risen Lord in the experience of his disciples. The hope of resurrection became thus not a detachable belief. It could not be laid aside without vital injury to the whole system of facts and forces to which it belonged.

Thirdly, a present spiritual resurrection was regarded as the preliminary to the final resurrection of the body. The two were bound up in an indissoluble unity. The Holy Spirit had already made believers alive in Christ. The culmination of his divine working would be manifested in risen and glorified bodies.

Fourthly, for the apostle Paul the combination of these two thoughts, the present spiritual resurrection and that of the body hereafter, led to the thought of the resurrection of the body as an attainment. In Philippians 3 : 7-16 he declares that he suffers the loss of all things that he may " gain Christ," and be " found in him," " that I may know him, and the power of his resurrection," " being conformed unto his death; if by any means I may attain unto the resurrection from the dead." We are, of course, not to understand the apostle as doubting the fact of the resurrection of the body; nor that he hopes to win it by merit. He is simply thinking of the resurrection of the body as the last stage in a moral and spiritual process. The mystic union with Christ, the present resurrection life, has its own proper goal, the resurrection of the body. For Paul, the power working in him must be understood as moving toward an end in harmony with itself. Thus the resurrection of the body was implicit, as it were, in the logic of the life in Christ. Experience demands the resurrection as its fruit and goal.

Fifthly, the resurrection of the body was implicit in the first creation. " If there is a natural body," says the apostle, " there is also a spiritual body. So also it is written, the first man Adam became a living soul. The last Adam became a life-giving spirit. Howbeit that is not first which is spiritual, but that which is natural; then that which is spiritual. The first man is of the earth, earthy; the second man is of heaven. . . As we have borne the image of the earthy we shall also bear the image of the heavenly " (1 Cor. 15 : 44-49). In this passage it seems evident that Paul thinks of the first creation as a stage in a plan which moved toward a higher goal. God's thought was not fully realized in the creation of a perishable body for an immortal being. A spiritual organism was required by a divinely endowed spirit. In Christ, the new head of the race, the new level is attained in both body and spirit. Through him man now partakes of the resurrection life in his spirit. To match this he will have in due time a body possessing the same qualities. Then the new creation in Christ will correspond in both respects with the first creation in Adam.

Sixthly, physical nature itself is related closely to the resurrection hope of Christians. The passage in Romans 8 : 19-25 declares that the " earnest expectation " of the creation waiteth for the revealing of the sons of God; that " the creation was subjected to vanity "; that this was " not of its own will "; that this subjection was in hope that " the creation itself shall be delivered from the bondage of corruption into the liberty of the glory of the children of God "; and also that the goal in view is " our adoption, to wit, the redemption of our body."

These words suggest that there is a maladjustment between God's children and God's world. The true end of nature is being defeated because of this want of adjustment due to sin. It is as if nature itself longs to become the complete and fit instrument for the promotion of the welfare of God's children; as if it were protesting against the present abnormal situation; as if it strained its gaze into the future in " earnest expectation " of the coming glory.

In his doctrine here the apostle transcends every form of dualism in his outlook upon the future. Nature and spirit are not irreconcilable elements in a finite world. In both shall be realized God's purpose of grace, a purpose which can be expressed in no terms lower than the "liberty of the glory of the children of God."

VIII. THE JUDGMENT

The statements of the New Testament regarding the final judgment may be grouped under the following heads: The Fact, the Judge, the Subjects, the Purpose, the Necessity of the Final Judgment.

1. As to the fact itself little need be said, since this appears in connection with each of the other points. The principle of judgment runs through the Scriptures from beginning to end. The earliest sections of the Old Testament as well as all parts of the New show this in unmistakable terms. The great final judgment takes definite shape in the revelation in Jesus Christ. It is this we now consider.

2. The Judge. In the teaching of Christ and the apostles, God is of course the final Judge; but it is God in Christ. In Matthew 25 : 31-46 Jesus predicts that he, the Son of man, will come in his glory, and all the angels with him; that he shall sit upon the throne of his glory; that all nations shall be gathered before him; and that he shall separate them as the shepherd separates the sheep from the goats. Acts 17 : 31 declares that God has appointed a day in which he will judge the world in righteousness, by the man whom he hath ordained, "whereof he hath given assurance unto all men, in that he hath raised him from the dead."

In Romans 2 : 16 Paul declares that God hath appointed a day in which he will judge the secrets of men "according to my gospel, by Jesus Christ."

In 2 Corinthians 5 : 10 it is declared that we must all be made manifest before the judgment-seat of Christ. See also Hebrews 9 : 27, 28; Revelation 20 : 12; John 5 : 22-27; Matthew 19 : 28; Luke 22 : 28-30; Revelation 3 : 21.

The fitness of Christ to exercise the authority of final Judge of men grows out of his twofold relations: to God and to men. He is the revelation of God to men. God is now dealing with men in and through him. Men come unto God by him. He is the Way, the Truth, and the Life for men. What God requires of men, and what God is willing to bestow upon men comes into the clearest expression through him. The invisible and eternal God thus adopts a historical mode of manifestation of himself, his grace, his holiness, his power. It is fit therefore that the culmination of his plan should find expression in the Person of his Son.

Again, Christ is " a Son of man," as John reports him as saying. He is Judge of men for this reason. (John 5 : 27.) As man Christ knows men. He was tempted in all points as men are tempted, but without sin. (Heb. 4 : 15.) He thus possesses the knowledge and sympathy required for equitable and just decisions regarding men.

3. The Subjects. All men are to be judged. There are Scriptures which suggest also that the evil angels are to be judged. In Revelation 20 : 12 the dead, " small and great," are represented as standing " before God." All are judged. (See also 2 Peter 2 : 4-9; Jude 6.)

4. The Purpose. The purpose of the final judgment is not the discovery of character, but its manifestation. As Paul expresses it: " We must all be made manifest before the judgment seat of Christ; that each one may receive the things done in the body, according to what he hath done, whether it be good or bad " (2 Cor. 5 : 10). So also in Romans 2 : 5, 6 men are said to treasure up for themselves wrath in the day of wrath and revelation of the righteous judgment of God, who will render to every man according to his works. They are to give account of " every idle word " that they shall speak. (Matt. 12 : 36.) Again, " there is nothing covered up, that shall not be revealed; and hid, that shall not be known " (Luke 12 : 2).

From the preceding we may state the purpose as follows: To judge means, literally, to discriminate, and from this follows the idea of separate. In judgment God discriminates between the righteous and unrighteous and separates them from each other. But this is simply to uncover or make manifest what previously existed in principle. Deeds done in the body are taken as the criterion of judgment because deeds declare character. The inward state is of course presupposed. No secret thing is hidden from God. The union of men by faith with Christ will be a cardinal fact which will be recognized. The great " deed," the true " work of God," is that men believe on Christ. (John 6 : 29.) No other deed means so much as this. It is the mother deed, the root principle of all good deeds. All the good deeds which God approves are in principle the offspring of this. But this is not a meritorious good work which buys salvation. It is the gift of God's grace. And all the deeds which spring from it arise from the same grace. Christians, then, are not saved by works, but by grace through faith. They are rewarded according to the use they make of the grace as manifest in deeds.

5. The Necessity of the Judgment. There are those who object to the idea of a final judgment. They assume that the biblical pictures of the last day are designed merely to impress the imagination, and to set forth vividly a principle which is to be recognized in continuous operation throughout history. " The world's history is the world's judgment," according to a saying of Schiller.

Now in reply we may say at once that the principle of judgment is in constant operation. In a real sense moral law works itself out inevitably. But its action is not after the manner of physical law. Human freedom and sin have greatly complicated the mechanism of the moral order, if such a phrase be permissible. Bodies attract each other by a fixed law. Chemical changes proceed in ways which may be expressed in exact terms. Matter, force, and motion are changeless and remorseless in their results under given conditions. If the mind of man could grasp the physical universe in all its meaning as merely physical and apart from the actions of free moral beings, and if it could perform the necessary calculations, it could also predict its exact condition a thousand years from now. This is because natural law rules in all the forms of matter. But in a realm of free moral personalities no such mechanical certitude is possible. Human wills are centers of new initiative. They originate new energies in the social order. As evil they render it liable to many complexities and forms of injustice. Only another and divine will can readjust these disturbed and abnormal relations. The final judgment is the Christian expression of this fact. We may say then that judgment is the finality demanded by the kingdom of God in all its aspects. We note the following:

(1) Judgment is the finality for the conscience. The idea of a judgment-day arose in the course of history in the religious life of men as the moral sense was deepened. In the religion of Israel it attained its highest prechristian form. The conscience is the witness in man to the immanent moral law of the universe. Its verdicts in ordinary conduct imply the final verdicts of him who planted the moral nature in us. Conscience is the moral glimpse which the soul obtains of the future. Wrong-doing is accompanied by a forward look upon a fiery judgment. (Heb. 10 : 27.) The moral law written in our nature is a copy of the eternal moral law written in God's nature. This law immanent in us implies judgment. A judgment-day means only that that which is implicit shall become explicit.

(2) Judgment is the finality also for history. That which works in the individual conscience works in the corporate conscience of the race. The crimes of nations stand out as clearly in the light of conscience as do the crimes of individuals. The wrongs which the innocent suffer when power rules in the place of right fill the pages of a large part of human history. Posthumous influence is a large part of a man's moral power. His work is not done when he dies. His deeds live after him, and will live in history until the new order which follows judgment shall arise. Heredity and solidarity are forces which must be reckoned with in the final awards to individuals. So also freedom and the corporate choice of low ideals and immoral standards must be applied as principles of judgment in dealing with men in social groups. The slow progress of the moral ideal in history points

to a culmination which shall crystallize the contending forces of good and evil and bring about their final separation. This is clear to ordinary human experience. It is even clearer to Christian experience. The redeemed saints in Revelation are represented as calling for the vengeance of God upon evil-doers. Perhaps this moral demand enters character in its perfected form as it does not now. We are commanded to forgive and to avenge not ourselves. There is no contradiction here. But the perfected saints share more completely the divine reaction against sin. All morally vigorous natures partake of this quality in large measure. A contemplation of history as a whole deepens it in every one. A climax which shall bring about a suitable adjustment seems most appropriate.

(3) Judgment is a finality for the theistic view of the world. If God is a Person; if he is in moral relations with men, and men are moral personalities in relations with God; if, in short, we live in a universe of freedom and obligation, God's vindication of his ways to men calls for a final judgment of affairs. He cannot consistently ignore the clamor of the human soul for some sort of understanding of the moral universe. Pantheism reduces us to the level of things. We are passing phenomena, like plants and flowers, the product of an eternal substance, or force without moral dignity. But theism puts us on a higher pedestal. We reflect the eternal intelligence and moral cravings.

Now if philosophy generalizes the bare facts presented at any given moment, it gives us a dualism or pluralism of contending forces which forever struggle for the mastery. Such a generalization dethrones God. But if we recognize the purposiveness of the moral sense in us, in Christian experience and in history, and in the theistic view of the world, we look forward to a higher solution. Teleology implies judgment. We may illustrate by the principles of progress and unity in literature and art generally. The kingdom of God is like a great drama. It moves forward to a climax. All the apparently loose ends of the development are slowly combined and gathered together. The unity of the whole is seen only in the final outcome. Without the climax the drama is meaningless. It is mere motion without progress. The book of Revelation, obscure as it is in some ways, is nevertheless an expression of the dramatic principle in the moral kingdom. And it is an expression which cannot be misunderstood. Evil takes many forms. Subdued in one form, it returns in another. The beast, the false prophet, the evil woman, the wicked city, appear from stage to stage. The end is victory, the overthrow of evil, the judgment and separation of the good and the bad, the descent of the New Jerusalem, the habitation of God with men.

In conclusion we affirm, therefore, that in God's kingdom judgment operates constantly as an immanent principle in the ongoing of history. It expresses itself in a gradual process. But it also expresses itself in signal events and great climaxes. In both aspects judgment is in close agreement with the nature of man and the course of history in other respects. The slow process followed by the sudden revolution; the beginning, the ascent toward a goal, the climax, and then a new beginning, a new ascent, a new climax. These are familiar processes in history. The final judgment is the biblical expression of this principle in the moral kingdom.

IX. FINAL STATES: HEAVEN

The New Testament revelation as to heaven and hell is notable for a number of things. One is its reserve and restraint. No answers are given to many curious questions human nature is prone to ask. Another is the symbolic character of the representations. Many figures of speech are employed which are clear enough in the principle involved, but not clear as to the meaning of the principle in the details of life and conduct. The revelation is also notable for the moral and spiritual qualities which are reflected in all the representations and the total absence of appeal to our lower and selfish nature.

We consider first the revelation as to heaven. It may be gathered up in the two ideas of environment and character, the outward and the inward aspects. We consider these in order.

As to the environment of the redeemed, language is taxed to express its beauty and glory. In many Old Testament prophecies there are glowing pictures of a coming age when nature is to be renewed, and there is to be a new heaven and a new earth wherein dwelleth righteousness. (Isa. 65 : 17; 66 : 22.) We have seen how Paul expresses this thought in his teaching as to the sympathy of nature with man's struggles and its final renovation in harmony with the resurrection and the glorious liberty of God's children. (Rom. 8 : 18-25.) In the book of Revelation the most glowing of all portrayals of heaven is under the symbol of the New Jerusalem, the City of God, which comes down from heaven to earth. (Rev. 21 : 1 to 22 : 5.) The background of this city is " a new heaven and a new earth " (21 : 1). From this we may draw, with a greater or less degree of certainty, the following inferences: First, heaven will be a place, and not merely an inward state. This is strongly confirmed by the fact that Christ himself has a risen and glorified body, and that we also shall have bodies like unto his; and by his words in John 14 : 1, 2, " I go to prepare a place for you." Secondly, we infer with less certainty that this earth may be the final home of the redeemed. So far as Scripture sheds light on the locality of heaven, it points in this direction. The meek " shall inherit the earth " (Matt. 5 : 5). The heavenly city descends to earth. And yet it is most likely that we shall not be confined to the earth. An endless future of activity and growth will require a wide range for our powers. It is quite possible that the physical universe as a whole will be our heritage. But here we must speak with proper caution, for there is no explicit declaration to guide us. Thirdly, we infer that the outward abode of God's children will be perfectly adapted to their perfected characters. All the symbols employed to set forth the environment are rich in moral suggestion. Gold and precious stones to suggest moral values; white robes to suggest purity; leaves for healing; water to symbolize life; pillars in a temple to suggest stability of character; crowns to symbolize victory; light to suggest God's presence; a city to suggest an ideal social order; these and many other symbols bring out all shades of moral perfection. To emphasize this everything is excluded which is " unclean, or he that maketh an abomination and a lie" (Rev. 21 : 27).

The inward aspect of heaven is presented in forms which cover the whole range of human desire and struggle for the highest and best things. It is man's nature as redeemed, as a worthy son of God, fulfilled. We may group these teachings under the following heads: Heaven as Relief, as Reward, as Realization, as Appreciation, and as endless Growth.

1. Heaven is represented as relief from all the trying and hard conditions of the earthly life. All sorrow and tears and mourning, all pain and suffering, all darkness and death, have passed away. In certain passages of exquisite tenderness God is represented as dispelling all these things: " God himself shall be with them, and be their God: and he shall wipe away every tear from their eyes; and death shall be no more; neither shall there be mourning, nor crying, nor pain any more" (Rev. 21 : 3, 4). This is the negative aspect of heaven. It is designed to set forth the fulfilment of human destiny in relief from all the conditions which make life hard to bear. But this relief comes through the direct ministry of God in a way which immeasurably deepens gratitude and inspires to love and devotion.

2. Heaven is reward. This is the positive side of heaven. In various passages in the book of Revelation the idea of reward appears. So also in passages in the Gospels and Epistles. Reward will be according to works. From this it follows that not all rewards will be the same. In the parable of the nobleman who left ten pounds with ten servants (Luke 19 : 12-27) we learn that reward corresponds to fidelity and industry. The rewards were ten cities and five cities in the case of two of the servants. And the man who had kept his pound in a napkin was deprived of what he had. Again, in the parable of the Talents (Matt. 25 : 14-30) the rewards correspond to natural gifts or ability. This is made clear in the record in the words that the "Lord gave to each according to his several ability" (ver. 15). So also in the parable of the Pennies (Matt. 20 :

1-16) rewards are according to opportunity. The eleventh-hour servants receive an equal amount with the others. The lack of opportunity alone prevented them from rendering a service equal to the others. So also in 1 Corinthians 3 : 14, 15 Paul represents some as saved " as through fire " because they do not render faithful service. The principle of degrees in rewards and punishments is clearly established in the New Testament teaching. In the second and third chapters of Revelation the rewards of heaven are set forth in various forms. They are all promised to the victors: " unto him that overcometh." Among these promises are the following: " To eat of the tree of life " (Rev. 2 : 7) ; victory over the " second death " (2 : 11) ; the privilege of eating the " hidden manna " (2 : 17) ; " authority over the nations " (2 : 26) ; to " be arrayed in white garments " (3 : 5) ; to be made " a pillar in the temple of my God " (3 : 12) ; to sit with Christ on his throne. (3 : 21.) Rewards are set forth in many forms in accord with the various forms of human struggle.

3. Heaven is realization. By this is meant the completion of all the activities and aspirations of the spirit which were unrealized before, self-realization in all spiritual capacities and relationships. The thwarted and defeated life, which was nevertheless morally and spiritually victorious, comes to its own. The " white stone " which Christ gives, and which has on it the " new name written, which no one knoweth but he that receiveth it," probably implies the full realization of personality. (Rev. 2 : 17.) The old name does not match the new character.

So also in all the forms of aspiration there comes realization: fulness of knowledge (1 Cor. 13 : 8-10) ; ideal service (Rev. 22 : 3, 4) ; ideal worship (Rev. 21 : 22) ; perfect communion with God (Rev. 21 : 3) ; perfect fellowship in an ideal society (Heb. 12 : 22, 23; Rev. 7 : 4-11) ; realized holiness of character (Rev. 3 : 5; 21 : 27) ; fulness of life (Matt. 25 : 46) ; association and fellowship with Jesus Christ. (John 14 : 3; Rev. 3 : 21; 5 : 12, 13; 7 : 17.) Christ is represented as the central figure in the portrayals of heaven. His relations to us as Redeemer will bind him to us forever in most intimate bonds of union and fellowship.

4. Heaven is appreciation. If we search for the spiritual qualities most characteristic of heaven, one of those most central and important is appreciation. Of course this means love. But it is a particular aspect of love which justifies emphasis. Jesus said that he who receiveth a prophet in the name of a prophet would receive a prophet's reward. (Matt. 10 : 41.) He means not the reward which a prophet bestows, but which the prophet will receive. Appreciation of a prophet raises one to the prophetic level, makes one potentially a prophet. So also a service rendered in the name of a disciple evinces appreciation of discipleship, and will be rewarded accordingly. The words of Christ at the judgment scene occasioned surprise to the disciples. They valued the service they had rendered less highly than the Master himself because he appreciated its moral quality better than they. (Matt. 25 : 37-40.) In welcoming his own there are no words of blame or reproof. He knows their motive. As faithful, he accepts them for what they strove to be and do, not for what they achieved alone. So also on the other side. In heaven they sing the song of Moses and the Lamb. They appreciate Christ as worthy of all praise and honor. (Rev. 5 : 9-12.) Crowns are placed on the brows of the victors; but the victors cast the crowns down at the feet of him who bestowed them. (Rev. 4 : 10, 11.) From the preceding we may say that the rewards of heaven will be on the level of our spiritual appreciations. The higher the range of the things we appreciate and value, the higher our place in the scale of moral worth.

5. Heaven is endless growth. Paul declares that we know in part, but then we shall know as we are known. (1 Cor. 13 : 12.) He prays that Christians may be " strong to apprehend with all the saints what is the breadth, and length, and height, and depth, and to know the love of Christ which passeth knowledge " (Eph. 3 : 18, 19). He concludes with the prayer that they may " be filled unto all the fulness of God " (ver. 14). This standard of knowledge calls for endless growth. The nature of mind and spirit implies ever-enlarging capacity. Mental activity is impossible apart from a certain degree of enlargement. Other-

[487]

wise it becomes, under the law of habit, a sort of instinct, which becomes automatic and tends to the brute level. Grace opens every part of our nature and intensifies every craving for the higher realities.

Some have objected to the idea of endless growth in heaven on the ground that it is inconsistent with moral perfection. A perfect being cannot become more perfect, it is argued. It is an error, therefore, to think of heaven as a place of indefinite growth. The reply is that the objection mistakes the nature of moral perfection. True moral perfection is not static. It is not an attainment which suddenly comes to an end and becomes fixed and final like a crystal. It does include freedom from sin, and spontaneous conformity to the eternal law of right. The image of Christ is inwrought. The soul is perfectly indwelt by the Redeemer through the Holy Spirit. But it never becomes immobile and fixed. It unfolds and expands. The true ideal of personal spiritual beings is that of a life which is ever active, yet ever resting in activity; which is ever satisfied and blessed, yet ever aspiring; which is ever attaining, yet ever hoping for greater attainment. " Now abideth faith, hope, love." " In hope were we saved " (Rom. 8 : 24). Hope is an abiding element of the redeemed life, and this implies endless growth and attainment.

THE FINAL STATES: HELL

We may sum up the scriptural teachings as to hell in four general statements:

1. Hell is the negation or absence in the soul of all that is meant by heaven. As heaven is the fruition of all right desire, so hell is the frustration of all such desire. Heaven is the fulfilment of love. Hell is the fulfilment of selfishness. Heaven is the ripened fruit of the regenerate life which has been created anew in Christ. Hell is the reverse of all that is implied in Christian experience. As moral and spiritual causes begin to operate by faith, which in the end produce the essential elements of heaven, so also moral and spiritual causes operate in the soul through

unbelief to produce the essential elements of hell. The soul of man is constituted for obedience to the moral law. It is made for fellowship with God. It is patterned with a view to righteousness. Faith is the only normal relation of man to God.

Now unbelief separates men from God, destroys fellowship, paralyzes the power required for obedience, and sets up an antagonism between the soul and God and between the soul and the universe of God. The wicked man finds himself thus in the strange position of being in God's universe, and yet he is neither God nor God's servant. There is no provision for naturalizing him in the realm where he must live. The result is endless war between him and God and all the forces of God's world. The moral and spiritual outcome is hell. It is the only rational outcome of unbelief and sin.

2. The spiritual truths involved in the doctrine of hell find expression in many forms in Scripture. For the most part they are figurative or symbolic expressions and must be so interpreted. But this does not imply that only the spiritual state is involved in the biblical doctrine of hell. Resurrection bodies of the wicked forbid this. No doubt the inward and spiritual condition is fundamental. But the outward and the inward agree here as in the teaching as to heaven. There are also literal passages. And we may be sure the figures employed in the others fall short rather than go beyond the reality of hell. Figures of speech here do not annul the dreadfulness of the doom of the wicked. We note a few New Testament teachings. The Old Testament has no developed doctrine of hell. Only the dim beginnings are found there. In Matthew 25 : 41 Jesus says to the wicked: " Depart from me, ye cursed, into the eternal fire which is prepared for the devil and his angels." He seems thus to imply that men damn themselves to suffering in the place prepared not for them, but for others. In a real sense a man makes his own hell. In another passage Jesus speaks of the sufferings of the lost in hell, " where their worm dieth not, and the fire is not quenched " (Mark 9 : 48). Again, he says the wicked are cast into " outer darkness " (Matt. 8 : 12). Paul describes the wicked as enduring the

"wrath of God" (Rom. 2 : 5). In Revelation 21 : 8 the final state of the wicked is described as the "second death," which is explained to mean that the wicked have their part "in the lake that burneth with fire and brimstone."

3. The third statement is that as there are degrees in the rewards of the righteous, so also there are degrees in the punishment of the unrighteous. The Judge of all the earth will do right. We need have no misgivings as to this point. The degree of light men possess; the degree of fidelity to that light; the use of the opportunities and powers with which they are blessed; the circumstances which condition their lives; in a word, every fact which has any bearing upon human guilt and responsibility will be considered. It follows from this that not all the wicked will suffer the same degree of punishment. The doctrine of degrees in rewards and punishments is one of the most clearly revealed doctrines of Scripture. We have seen it in its application to the rewards of the righteous. It is equally clear as to the penalties of the unrighteous. In Luke 12 : 47, 48 we read: "And that servant who knew his Lord's will, and made not ready, nor did according to his will, shall be beaten with many stripes; but he that knew not, and did things worthy of stripes, shall be beaten with few stripes." One of the most impressive and solemn sayings of Jesus is in Matthew 11 : 21-24, where he pronounces the woes upon Chorazin and Bethsaida and Capernaum because they sinned against the light. He declares that in the day of judgment it will be more tolerable for Tyre and Sidon, and even for Sodom, than for these cities. According to light and truth are responsibility and penalty. In Romans 4 : 15 Paul says, "where there is no law, neither is there transgression." Here he is stating a principle rather than describing the actual state of men. For he says elsewhere that men "show the work of the law written in their hearts, their conscience bearing witness therewith" (Rom. 2 : 15). So also he writes, "For as many as have sinned without the law shall also perish without the law" (Rom. 2 : 12). In verse 6 of the same chapter he refers to God "who will render to every man according to his works."

4. Fourthly, the doom of sinners of all degrees of guilt is endless. In Mark 3 : 29 Jesus declares that the sin " against the Holy Spirit hath never forgiveness " because, as he adds, the man who commits it is guilty of an " eternal sin." The " undying worm " and the " quenchless fire " in the passage already cited point in the same direction. So also the contrast between the fates of the wicked and righteous at the judgment shows that the continuity of the one corresponds with that of the other. It is " eternal punishment " in one case and " eternal life " in the other. (Matt. 25 : 46.)

X. Theories Which Deny Eternal Punishment

Two theories have been advanced in the past which continue in the present, denying the endlessness of future punishment. One of these is annihilationism, the other restorationism. We consider them in this order.

Annihilationism

Annihilationism holds that the soul of man is not naturally immortal. It becomes immortal only through union with Christ by faith and the reception of the divine life imparted by the Holy Spirit. It is also known as the theory of conditional immortality. Apart from the divine life received through union with Christ, the soul, on account of indwelling sin, gradually deteriorates and sooner or later ceases to exist. It is annihilated.

The theory has been held in several forms. One is that at death the soul ceases to exist. Another, that on account of the gift of Christ and the offer of salvation, men become responsible in a new way for their disobedience, and that they are kept in being until the day of judgment, when they are cast into the lake of fire and brimstone. A third form of the theory puts the cessation of being into the distant future after the final judgment, thus allowing time for the suffering of the full penalty of sins.

The chief biblical arguments urged in favor of the theory are the passages which refer to the doom of the wicked by means of such words as death, destruction, perdition, abolishing, perishing, and the word lost. (The words are *phtheiro, apollumi, katargeomai, thanatos,* and their cognates.)

It is not necessary to cite all the passages relied upon by the advocates of the annihilation doctrine. In 2 Thessalonians 1 : 9 Paul, referring to the penalty coming upon the wicked, says, "who shall suffer punishment, even eternal destruction from the face of the Lord, and from the glory of his might." (See also 2 Peter 3 : 7.) This passage represents in a general way the class of Scripture teachings cited in support of the theory. It is claimed that "destruction" here means annihilation. Similar passages make use of the other words referred to: abolish, perdition, perish, death.

Now it is not denied that if there were no other general teaching of Scripture to refute this view, and if we were required by the meaning of these words to define them as annihilation, there would be good ground for the view. But neither of these claims can be made good. Take the word "destroy" in another passage. "If any man destroyeth the temple of God, him shall God destroy" (1 Cor. 3 : 17). Can this by any sort of construction mean, "If any man annihilate the temple of God, him will God annihilate"? Consider also the word "lost." Jesus refers to the "lost sheep of the house of Israel" in Matthew 10 : 6. Can he mean the "annihilated" sheep?

The reply to the annihilation doctrine then is as follows:

1. It gives a meaning to a certain group of words in certain Scriptures which cannot possibly be applied to them in other passages. This is true of every one of the words relied upon to support the annihilation theory. Death in Scripture means the absence of life, and as applied to the soul it means the absence of fellowship with God. Perdition means the moral state resulting from this separation from God and his holiness. Destroy means to overcome or render inoperative. In the passages cited it means punishment in the form of banishment

from God's presence. When Paul refers to the time when death shall be destroyed or abolished, he means made inoperative as a power in God's kingdom. The word lost means separated from God and without power of self-recovery. In no passage does any of these words mean annihilate where it refers to the future of the wicked.

2. The teachings of the Old Testament are against the view. In the Old Testament the departed are not annihilated. They are in Sheol, the realm of the dead. They live a shadowy existence there. But they are still conscious. They do not cease to exist. It is abundantly clear from what we have already seen that the idea of annihilation of the soul at death is foreign to the Old Testament.

3. The very explicit teaching of the New Testament as to the fate of the wicked disproves the annihilation theory. The phrases employed forbid it. " Their worm dieth not "; " the fire is not quenched " (Mark 9 : 48). " And they shall be tormented day and night forever and ever " (Rev. 20 : 10). These and other similar passages are fatal to the theory.

4. Again, the idea of annihilation is a metaphysical conception which is foreign to the Old and New Testaments alike. It is doubtful whether any passage of Scripture can be cited in any connection whatever favorable to the idea. The biblical writers dealt with all matters from the practical and religious point of view. All speculative theories as to the component parts of the soul and the possibility of its disintegration or its passing into nothingness are alien to the Scriptures. Annihilationism is a product of metaphysical speculation, not of biblical teaching.

5. Annihilationism is contrary to all the rational and moral considerations which favor the immortality of the soul. The common belief of mankind, the desires and implications within man of a larger life; in a word, all the arguments which have been urged in favor of natural are against the conception of conditional immortality.

6. Annihilationism changes radically our conception of the dignity and grandeur of human nature. Scripture teaches, and

men have believed, that man is made in God's image, a moral and spiritual personality; that this nature lifts him above the level of the brutes and gives him a naturally immortal existence. Annihilationism robs him of this dignity and brings him down to the brute level. This is true under any view as to the process of annihilation. This is conceived of as the result of the disintegrating power of sin itself; or as the result of the working of the evolutionary law of the survival of the fittest and the destruction of the unfit; or as the immediate act of God on account of the guilt of sin. The first view is untrue to facts. Sin does not destroy the soul. Increasing sin often goes with increasing power to sin. The second view clearly implies a lower view of man than the Bible teaches. The third implies that God ceases to treat the sinner as a moral being with whom he deals on moral principles, but resorts rather to sheer omnipotence to exterminate one who refused to obey.

7. Annihilationism makes it difficult to understand the incarnation. How can we think of Christ's entrance into a form of life in the incarnation which was in itself destined to perish? Did he come to redeem humanity or to reconstitute it? There is no evidence in the New Testament that he reconstituted human nature. He recreated it morally and spiritually in his own image. He did not make of man a new kind of creature, although he did make of him a new creature through divine grace.

In conclusion, we are not without appreciation of the moral and spiritual problems which annihilationism is designed to meet. All men have felt the pressure of the questions which relate to the fate of the wicked in the future life. But loyalty to the highest interests of mankind forbids that we should permit our desire or our protest against a given conclusion to be converted into a dogma with no better support than a vague metaphysical speculation.

Restorationism

Another theory as to the future state is known as restorationism. It has been held in several forms. One is that death itself produces a change of character which results in the salvation of all. This form of the theory is rarely advocated by any one to-day. Another maintains that the gospel is preached to the disembodied spirits of those who die without hearing the gospel, and that opportunity is thus given for repentance and return to God, and that this second probation ends at the judgment, when the final awards are declared. A third form extends the second probation into the indefinite future. It maintains that suffering and loss will lead men to turn from their sins, or else that God will use stronger means of persuasion than were afforded in this life. Here again there is divergence of view. Some hold that as a result of this extended probation some will be saved while others will persist in sin and be finally lost. The Universalists, on the other hand, hold that in the end all individuals will be saved.

In support of the above theory two classes of argument have been employed. The first claims a considerable group of Scripture passages. The second builds upon inferences from the nature of God and man and the moral kingdom.

1. We note first the Scripture passages. Here we do not attempt to deal with these exhaustively. The more pertinent and important will answer our purpose. It is urged that the word "eternal" (*aionios*) does not mean eternal duration in statements referring to future retribution. (Matt. 25 : 41.) It means, rather, lacking in the quality of the eternal or divine life. Again, in John 12 : 32 Jesus declares, "And I, if I be lifted up from the earth, will draw all men unto myself," implying that all men would be saved. Again, Paul says in 1 Corinthians 15 : 22, "For as in Adam all die, so also in Christ shall all be made alive." This is taken as meaning universal salvation. In 1 Timothy 2 : 4 he refers to God our Saviour, "who would have all men to be saved, and come to the knowledge of the truth," and in 1 Timothy 4 : 10 he refers to the "living God, who is the Saviour of all men, especially of them that believe."

There is also a group of great sayings in the Epistles to the Philippians, Ephesians, and Colossians which are cited in support of restorationism. In Philippians 2 : 9-11 reference is made to the exaltation of Christ, " That in the name of Jesus every knee should bow, of things in heaven, and things on earth, and things under the earth, and that every tongue should confess that Jesus Christ is Lord, to the glory of God the Father." In Ephesians 1 : 10 God's purpose is stated to be " to sum up all things in Christ, the things in the heavens, and the things upon the earth." And in Colossians 1 : 20 Paul declares that it was the good pleasure of the Father " through him to reconcile all things unto himself; having made peace through the blood of his cross; through him, *I say,* whether things upon earth, or things in the heavens."

There are also two passages in the First Epistle of Peter which have been held to teach a doctrine of a Hades ministry of Christ. In 1 Peter 3 : 18-20 the apostle refers to Christ as " being put to death in the flesh, but made alive in the spirit; in which also he went and preached unto the spirits in prison, that aforetime were disobedient, when the longsuffering of God waited in the days of Noah, while the ark was a preparing," etc. So also in 1 Peter 4 : 6 reference is made to a preaching of the gospel to " the dead, that they might be judged indeed according to men in the flesh, but live according to God in the spirit."

In reply to the restorationist interpretation of the above passages the following is to be considered:

It is admitted that the Greek word *aionios,* translated " eternal," does sometimes have a qualitative meaning in the New Testament, especially in John's writings, as in John 17 : 3, " This is life eternal, that they should know thee the only true God, and him whom thou didst send, even Jesus Christ." But this is not the original or inclusive, but rather a derived meaning which arose late in the history of the word. One quality of " eternal life " is that it never ends; this, combined with its divine quality, makes it " eternal life." Thus the qualitative sense does not exclude, but rather requires the quantitative. It means endless duration. In 2 Corinthians 4 : 18 the eternal or lasting is contrasted with the temporal or transient. In Matthew 25 : 46 the endlessness of " punishment " and of " life " are expressed by the same term. There is thus no possible way of excluding the idea of endlessness from the meaning of the word.

The passage in John 12 : 32 does not represent Jesus as de claring that he will save all men, but only that he will " draw " them. The context shows that the inquiring Greeks were in his mind, and the most natural interpretation is that he would draw not only Jews, but Gentiles as well, when lifted up upon the cross.

In 1 Corinthians 15 : 22 the " all " in Paul's statement prob- ably refers only to the class about which he is speaking, be- lievers in Christ. The meaning is that the relation between Adam and his descendants is analogous to that between Christ and his followers. In any case the passage can scarcely mean for men generally more than a being made alive in the resur- rection. Paul is discussing the resurrection, not the reception of life from Christ through faith.

The two passages in 1 Timothy 2 : 4 and 4 : 10 express the good will of God toward all mankind. God's wish or desire ex- tends to all. But the attitude of men toward the gospel con- ditions its realization. In the second passage Paul says that God is " the Saviour of all men, especially of them that believe." By this he shows that God's universal desire is conditioned by man's faith. This is in harmony with the uniform New Testa- ment teaching.

The three passages cited from Philippians, Ephesians, and Colossians all refer to the universe as a whole rather than to individuals. They present different aspects of Christ's work in its final result. These supplement each other, and together they answer a number of questions which naturally arise in Chris- tian thought about last things. In Philippians Christ is declared to be universal Lord. To him every knee shall bow, of things in heaven, on earth, and under the earth. He will have no rival in authority and power. The reference is to " things," however, in a broad general sense, not to persons. In Ephesians he is represented as the unifying bond of all things. God brings to a head or recapitulates all things in him. The parts of the

2 G   [497]

universe are conceived of as scattered. He reunites them. All things are thus summed up or headed up in him. In Colossians the same general reference is made. But here Christ is represented as the Mediator, through whom the universal work of reconciliation takes place. But the reference again is general. All that is in disorder shall be restored to order. The resultant order in all its parts will conform to God's will for those parts. All this is to be achieved through Jesus and his cross.

The passages in the First Epistle of Peter cannot be dealt with at length. They have been the subject of irreconcilable differences of opinion. Men usually construe them according to their prepossessions. The language is so obscure and complicated that a satisfactory exegesis is almost impossible. But among the many interpretations of 1 Peter 3 : 18-20 that which understands it as a reference to the preincarnate activity of Christ in warning sinners in the time of Noah seems the most natural. The other passage seems to refer to those Christians who had died, to whom the gospel was preached during their earthly life.

In concluding this reply to the restorationist interpretation of the New Testament, two or three general statements should be made. One is that in the case of all the passages cited the interpretation is directly in conflict with many other explicit teachings of the New Testament. The words of Jesus in Matthew 25 : 46 expressly contradict it. Again, it is to be noted that none of the passages contains a definite and unquestionable support for the restorationist doctrine. The result is obtained by inference, not by acceptance of a plain meaning. If there were no other New Testament teaching on the subject these inferences might seem valid. But they introduce serious contradictions of Paul by himself as well as of other New Testament writers. And finally, some of the passages, if made to teach the salvation of all individual men, would necessarily include also the devil and bad angels. The language is exceedingly comprehensive. It can easily be understood as we have interpreted it, but an idea entirely foreign to the biblical writers is introduced if the devil and his angels are to be included among the redeemed.

2. The second general argument for restorationism is based upon inferences from the nature of God, of man, and of the moral kingdom. We note first the inference from God's nature.

It is said that God is love, and that love can never rest content while any are lost; that God is fatherly toward all, and that his impulse to bless will lead him to find a way to save men, even from future torment. It is also urged that punishment is merely corrective. There is no vindicatory or merely retributive element in it. So also it has been urged that eternal punishment for finite sin is unjust. Thus the nature of God and of punishment forbids eternal suffering.

Again, the argument is based on an inference from man's nature. Man is free. His will never becomes fixed in a way which is unchangeable. Freedom thus means an indeterminate will. If this be so, it follows that character does not necessarily crystallize so that the will cannot by a new choice change it. It is inferred that future sufferings will surely lead sinful men to make a new choice of God and holiness. A similar inference is drawn from man's rational nature. He is a reasonable being. He is bound to respond favorably to light and truth when these are presented to him. It is entirely irrational for a man to persist in sin. It must follow that the new knowledge which men will acquire in the future, and the new persuasiveness which a loving God will employ, will surely lead to repentance.

Another inference is drawn from the nature of God's kingdom. It is said that an eternal hell involves a dualism, or moral contradiction inconsistent with the administration of his kingdom by a holy and loving God, and that in the interest of unity alone the sovereign God must find ways to abolish hell.

In reply to these arguments we consider briefly some of the details, and then present some more general considerations in reply.

First, in reply to the inference from God's love and eternal impulse to bless, we must not overlook the uniform representations of the New Testament that an element in the problem is always man's attitude to the gracious appeal of God. We are not permitted to take God's love as the only and absolute factor and to deduce conclusions from this alone. The unchangeableness of God's love is of course a great truth. But we must not think of it as if it were just another name for God's omnipotence. The outcome of his love in relation to men is conditioned by their attitude toward that love. He deals with us as moral beings, responsible and free. This statement contains the answer also to the claim that punishment is never retributive, but always and only corrective. There is a retributive element in punishment, as we have seen earlier in this treatise. But, assuming for the moment that it is only corrective, it does not follow that it will always prove efficacious. Under this view, as under the other, man as a free personal being might forever resist the corrective suffering. Corrective discipline is not a certain cure for the wicked will. We have all seen many instances of its failure.

As to the injustice of an infinite punishment for a finite sin, this is an incorrect statement of the fact. Sinners continue to sin in the life to come; punishment simply keeps pace with the sin. If the sin should cease, the punishment would cease. Eternal punishment for the incorrigibly sinful, therefore, follows not from the fact of a finite earthly sin, but from the endless or immortal existence of the sinner.

As to the argument based on man's volitional and rational nature we reply that in both respects the view is erroneous. Will is not so indeterminate as the argument claims. It is the expression of the character. Character tends ever to become fixed. Acts are cumulative in their effect upon character. Otherwise character, or stability of the moral nature, would be impossible. Every act would be an absolutely new beginning and also ending. There would be no moral gains which we could retain. Life would be a treadmill in its moral endeavor. Under this theory of the will the redeemed also would be ever in danger of a new fall. Heaven would be no more secure than hell, because character would be incapable of becoming stable. A man could never become a pillar in the temple of God, according to the promise. (Rev. 3 : 12.)

The inference from man's rational nature is also misleading. Man is a reasonable being. But he does not always follow the light he has. Frequently the reason is convinced when the will continues to resist. So also the reason is often convinced long after the will has lost the disposition or purpose to choose the right.

The inference that an eternal hell is inconsistent with God's reign, and involves an irreconcilable dualism in his kingdom, is of very doubtful value. Evil certainly exists now in very aggravated forms. Yet we do not on that account assume an irreconcilable contradiction in God's rule. What is to-day may be forever. In a word, the problem of evil is a present problem. It is difficult at best. We can only understand it in part. But we launch the ship of our speculation on a very dangerous sea if we prejudge the future by a seeming contradiction, when the same apparent contradiction confronts us every day.

There are several general considerations which we now present in reply to the restoration theory.

(1) The first is to recall the teaching of Christ himself. No other voice has ever spoken with the note of authority possessed by him in regard to final states. And yet he is most explicit and most clear on this supreme matter. The language which he employs, as already set forth, shows the irrevocableness of the awards to the righteous and wicked in the future life. The parable of Dives and Lazarus, if there were no other word from Christ, makes the point clear that there is an impassable gulf fixed between the two classes after death. It is surely safe to follow Christ in his teaching on this momentous matter. The general tenor of the New Testament is in agreement with his word. Let us not lose sight of this.

(2) The question of an eternal hell is ultimately a question of human freedom. God cannot make bad men happy. They must renounce their badness by their own free choice. Complete happiness is the fruit of moral perfection. And moral perfection cannot be forced upon men. It must be chosen. God's grace may and does aid men. But it cannot compel them.

The Christian Religion in Its Doctrinal Expression

Men's capacity for resisting God is practically unlimited. We may of course assume that God cannot remain content in the presence of eternal suffering, and that he must find ways to overcome man's rebellion; in a word, that he must abolish hell. But we then face a worse alternative. We must then assume that man's freedom has always been merely apparent, and never real; that man's capacity for self-determination and self-direction has been an illusion. Thus the moral dignity and grandeur of human nature pass away. We are simply puppets in the hands of omnipotence, not free personal beings in moral relations with the infinite Person. That which seemed to be the supreme quality in our obedience in God's eyes was our free choice of him and his service. But now this turns out to be not our own act, but God's compulsory act in and upon us. We are no longer men, but things. God would thus sacrifice our freedom and moral dignity to his own selfishness, that is, because he could not endure the sight of hell. The existence of hell involves an eternal sacrifice on God's part. But this means only that God is eternal love. If then men are to be left free, the possibility of an eternal hell always remains until men are confirmed in holiness. The ultimate problem then is not: Why does God permit hell? It is rather this: Why did he make men free? Of course sinners who become incorrigible in sin are not free in the highest sense. But their freedom is real nevertheless. The highest freedom includes three elements: self-determination, self-direction, and self-realization. All men have the first and second elements. Only the redeemed in Christ have the third. Self-realization means finding one's destiny in Jesus Christ. It means fulfilling God's ideal for the life. This is the highest freedom. Men who disobey are self-determined and self-directed. But here they stop. They pervert the end of their being. Hell is the monument they build to their own selfishness and disobedience.

(3) The nature of sin enforces the same truth. Character does tend to become fixed. It gathers momentum. It bears the will along as a part of itself. Yet it is the expression of repeated acts of the will. Thoughts become purposes, and purposes

[502]

become acts, and acts become habits, and habits become characters, and characters become destinies. The unpardonable sin probably means that the moral potentialities of the soul are exhausted. Character has become fixed in evil. Jesus saw this with divine insight and declared it.

All morally sensitive souls are profoundly interested in the problem of the final destiny of men. No one with any appreciation of the issues of life can be indifferent to the subject, and yet it is quite possible to adopt an attitude which may be injurious to the highest interests of mankind. Sinful men are eager to find a means of escape from the consequences of wrong-doing. They easily put a carnal interpretation upon any form of deliverance stated in external terms. Some of those who teach restorationism in ways which seek to safeguard moral character play directly into the hands of the selfish and carnal. Their theories are usually born of a desire which may be worthy in itself, but which builds upon insufficient foundations. If we cannot follow Christ here, where can we follow him?

We conclude with two or three facts which bring some relief as we contemplate the world of future penalties.

Christians to-day with practical unanimity hold that infants dying in infancy are saved. This means about one-third of the human race. Again we recur to the fact that there are degrees of penalty. Men are not to be punished equally, although all future punishment will be endless. But of one thing we may be sure: God is absolutely just and loving. We often forget this in thinking of the future. We forget that punishments differ, and imagine all suffering exactly the same penalty. Along with this we imagine that God arbitrarily casts men into hell. Both ideas are erroneous. There will never be the slightest departure from exact right and justice in any of God's dealings with sinners. We may leave the issues with him. But all that we know of the future life lays upon us the obligation to labor with zeal and earnestness for the coming of his eternal kingdom with its eternal awards.

INDEX

A

Ability or inability, natural and moral, 294.
Absolute: as theological term, 221; the, 282.
Adolescence: importance of, in conversion, 59, 88; and regeneration, 381.
Adoption: God's act in redemption, 52, 261; a fruit of faith, 393; defined, 401.
Affection, 239.
Agnosticism: denies knowledge of ultimate reality, 108; at variance with experience, 109; denies revelation, 138; set aside by work of righteous love, 175; makes finite and infinite mutually exclusive, 191; Sanday's theory of incarnation a form of, 200; theoretical justification of, 202; toward Trinity, 206, 208.
Alcott, Bronson, 328.
Ancestor-worship, 95.
Angel of the Covenant, 278.
Angels: reality of, 276; sons of God, 401; among the redeemed, 498.
Animism, 36, 95.
Annihilationism, 491.
Anselm, 131, 306, 330.
Anthropological proof of the existence of God, 130.
Anthropomorphism, 79f., 96, 216.
Antichrist, 464, 469.
Antinomianism and sanctification, 427.
Apocalyptic: order of events, 449; calculations and speculations, 472.
Apollinarians, 177.
Apologetics: as related to method of this book, 7f.; limitations of, 10; helped by defining religion, 16; and the definition of God, 215.
Apostles, medium of revelation, 142, 151.
Apostles' Creed, 42.
Arians, 177.
Arminianism, 5, 434.
Ascension of Christ, 44, 47, 158, 163, 360.
Asceticism, 421.
Astronomy, 182.
Athenians, 94.
Atonement: by death of Christ, 20, 44; self-disclosure of God, 23; finds climax

in Christian teaching, 99; and meaning of universe, 193; exercise of love in, 248; and universalism, 302; discussed, 304-337; fallacies about the, 311; exposition of biblical doctrine of, 313; and the divine immanence, 320; vital and legal elements in, 322; Godward and manward reference of, 330; a dynamic in experience, 334; attributes of God in, 335; extent of, 336; and sovereignty, 338; limited, 339; and worldwide grace, 341; ground of justification, 398.
Attributes of God, alleged conflict between, 309, 311.
Augustine, 3, 331, 461.

B

Backsliding, 378.
Baptism: of Jesus, 155, 157, 204; of the Spirit, 360; of infants, 375; and regeneration, 383; as a symbol, 427.
Beelzebub, 277.
Benevolence, 239, 247.
Bergson, 192.
Bible: a source of theology, 2f.; authority of, 10f.; point of contact between, and psychology, 36; literary source of revelation, 41, 145; and inspiration, 143, 147; and search for truth, 149; meets all requirements of religious life, 151; infallibility of, 152.
Biology, 104, 182, 257, 354.
Blessing, second, 432.
Blewett, 195.
Bowne, 195.
Brahmanism, 137.
Brain, human and animal, contrasted, 256.
Brown, W. A., 277.
Buddhism, 103, 137, 388.
Bushnell, 333.

C

Calling, defined, 365.
Calvinism, 5, 339, 433f.
Campbell, McLeod, 300.

Index

Index

Index

gument for, 260; vague idea of, 364; need of doctrine of, 441; evidence for, 442; conditional, 491.

Immutability defined, 223.

Incarnation: self-disclosure of God, 23; not abrupt disturbance of order of nature, 170, 187; necessary, 171; complete self-impartation of God, 173; made possible by creation of man, 182; divine self-limitation, 183, 238; psychology of, 185; entrance into human conditions, 186-189; objections to, 190; alleged to be unthinkable, 192; and meaning of the universe, 193; and the subconscious mind, 199; and the Trinity, 208; not a change in God's purpose, 224; God's love in the, 237, 248; made Christ one with the race, 309, 315; and grace for all, 341; and need for means of grace, 364; and annihilationism, 494.

India, 96.

Infants: salvation of, 286, 301, 383, 503; baptism of, 375.

Inspiration, theories of, 143.

Intellectualism, false, 4, 11.

Intercession: of Christ, 44, 336; of the Holy Spirit, 337.

Intermediate state, the: discussed, 459; not the final state of believers, 461.

Interpretation, spiritual, 29.

Intuition and argument for existence of God, 132.

Israel, 141, 145-150, 172, 237, 239, 266f., 269, 279, 289, 341, 352, 354, 401, 431, 445, 448.

J

James, William, 57, 89, 93, 193, 195.

Jealous, meaning of, in Old Testament, 237.

Jesus Christ: historical revelation of God, 4f., 11, 15, 21f., 41, 47, 50, 165, 172, 210, 238; relation of, to Christian experience, 6; deity of, 8, 160, 167-202; religion of, real, autonomous, free, 9; value-judgment of, 14; in Christian experience, 19; mediates fellowship with God, 28; sinlessness of, 43, 259; Redeemer of men, 44, 176; superhistoric, 45, 47; supernatural, not eliminated from the New Testament, 46; atoning work of, 55, 234; sin-bearer and moral goal, 64; objective revelation in, 78; completes idea of revelation, 100; unique revelation of God, 137, 157; and Old Testament, 151; supreme reve-

lation of God, 154-166, 214-250; doctrine of person of, 155, 163, 177, 186; key to doctrine, 166; human and divine elements in, 176; preexistence of, 180; life of, continuous with life of God, 184; stages in reascent of, 187; views of, in modern thought, 193; rival theories of the person of, 195; revealed by his work, 202; preexistence of, and the Trinity, 207; natural and spiritual relationship of, to the human race, 285, 309, 315, 329; saving work of, 303-337; embodiment of moral ideal, 320; intercession of, 336; and the Holy Spirit, 360; supreme means of grace, 364; and conviction by the Spirit, 367; and the act of faith, 372; doctrine of, and regeneration, 386; mediates blessings, 408; union with, 409; and doctrine of last things, 445; prediction of, concerning the future, 453; second coming of, 462; the final Judge, 478; central in portrayals of heaven, 486; preincarnate activity of, 498; teaching of, and restorationism, 501.

John, theology of, 2.

Judaism, 94, 96, 98, 100.

Judge, supreme, 57f., 63.

Judgment, the: return of Christ to, 196; conviction of, by the Spirit, 204; and conviction of sin, 367; and the day of the Lord, 446; viewed with suspicion, 449; discussed in detail, 478; the principle of, 490.

Justice, 246, 296.

Justification: by faith, material principle of the Reformation, 28; in relation to divine forgiveness, 52; necessity of, 54; does not give *fiat* righteousness 55, 396; procured by atonement, 332; by faith, in Paul's teaching, 342; and regeneration, 387; defined, 389; and Christian experience, 393; objection to doctrine of, 396; and sanctification, 420.

K

Kant, Immanuel, philosophy of, 7, 108, 117, 133, 202, 226.

Kenotic theories, 184.

King, Christ as, 303.

Kingdom of God: and central meaning of the gospel, 28; defined, 91; goal of Christ's activity, 165, 272; and Providence, 266; advance of, through miracles, 270; how constituted 287; Christ's predictions of, 303; of human relations,

Index

alism, 115; agreement between constitution of, and mental constitution of man, 131; and God, 220; finds climax in man, 255, 260; and the supernatural, 272; problem of meaning of, 363; and regeneration, 387; and the movements of grace, 452; want of adjustment in, due to sin, 477, 480.

Nazareth, 43.

Necessity: rule of, 254, 270; of atonement, 330.

Neo-Hegelianism, 192.

Nestorians, 177, 186.

New Testament: source of theology, 2; source of knowledge of historical Christ, 4. 6; miracles of, 8; not shaped by ethnic religions, 21; in relation to the Old, 28; object of, 30; idea of belief in, 40; representation of Jesus, 41; and the supernatural Jesus, 46; completes record of revelation, 47.

Nicæa, 177.

O

Obedience: an organ of knowledge, 34, 80; of Christ, 317.

Old Testament: source of theology, 2; in relation to the New, 28; as source of birth stories in the Gospels, 42; record of preliminary revelation, 47.

Omnipotence: defined, 228, 249; limited by men's moral freedom, 355.

Omnipresence defined, 225.

Omniscience defined, 226, 240.

Ontological argument for existence of God, 130.

Ordinances, the, a means in salvation, 346, 363, 409.

Overbelief, 89.

P

Pantheism: evils of, 14; denies need of forgiveness, 52; teaches reabsorption in the All, 70; in India, 96; tendency of heathen faiths to, 99; and personalism, 114, 122, 207; fails to distinguish between right and wrong, 117; cancels conception of truth, 118; denies possibility of revelation, 138; reduces all to miracle, 193; and doctrine of creation, 254, 265; idealistic, 282; and work of the Spirit, 362; and regeneration, 384; theory of despair, 388; and union with Christ, 413; and perseverance, 433, 437; and immortality, 441; and the final judgment, 482.

Paraclete, 360.

Paradise, 459.

Parousia, 456.

Patriotism, 427.

Patristic view of atonement, 306.

Paul, theology of, 2, 312, 326, 332, 397.

Pedagogy, divine, 147.

Penalty: and guilt, 295; according to light, 301; degrees of, 503.

Penance, 394.

Pentecost, baptism of the Spirit, 204, 211.

Perfection contrasted with original sinlessness, 259.

Perfectionism, 429.

Perseverance: and regeneration, 387; a fruit of faith, 393; and justification, 396; defined, 432.

Person, in the Trinity, 206.

Personalism: philosophy of, stated and defended, 112; upholds conception of truth, 118; and Christian theism, 122; and monistic systems generally, 122; and the theory of causation, 125.

Personalists, 193.

Personality: in interpretation of the universe, 13; and limitation, 14, 218; only adequate medium to reveal God, 22, 70, 183, 192; human, 50; elements of, 62; transition from natural to regenerate, 63; makes man superior to nature, 110; crown of revelation of God, 170; involves freedom, 194, 217; multiple, 200; of God, 217; as principle in account of universe, 273; and substitution, 326.

Pessimism, 388.

Philo, 161, 198.

Philology, comparative, 268.

Philosophy: of Kant, 7, 108, 117, 133, 202, 226; in relation to Christian experience, 103; rise of various types of, 107, 363; argument from history of, 118; confirms method of Jesus, 194; and regeneration, 388.

Physics, 273.

Physiology, 268, 273.

Pluralism, 192, 388, 482.

Polytheism, 96, 221.

Positive philosophy examined, 12f.

Postmillennialism, 466f.

Prayer: instinct of, 119; and God's purpose, 192, 224, 274, 348; and faith, 374; for the dead, 461.

Predestination, 268, 338, 433.

Preexistence: of Christ, 162, 179f., 191, 197, 207; of souls, 262.

Premillennialism, 466f.

Preservation of the universe, 265.

Priest, Christ as, 303.

Index

Index

Index

State, the, in the conception of Christianity, 426.
Strong, A. H., 215.
Subconscious mind: and regeneration, 58; alleged key to the incarnation, 199; and work of the Holy Spirit, 361.
Subjectivism: perils of, 11, 19, 23, 77; alleged against any proof of God's existence, 135.
Substitution: idea of, in Jewish sacrifices, 99, 327; principle of atonement, 310; discussed, 324; altar forms of, 333.
Suffering: of God, 238; and Providence, 276; spectacular, 308; of Christ, 317, 323; and union with Christ, 416; relief from, in heaven, 485.
Suffering Servant, 446.
Supernatural elements in the New Testament, 46.
Supper, Lord's, 363.
Sympathy defined, 238.
Synagogue, 351.

T

Teleological argument for the existence of God, 126.
Temptation of Jesus, 187f.
Ten Commandments, 233, 267.
Tennyson, 101, 115.
Tertullian, 461.
Theism and the final judgment, 482.
Theology: and religion, 1; defined, 2f.; as treated here, 4-12; needs to be restated, 10; necessity of, 16; historical, insufficient, 17; relation of, to truth, 24; closely related to other fields of science, 25, 39; sources of, 27; material and formal principles of, 28; and life, 29; how unified, 29; biblical, method of, 30; personal qualities necessary to study of, 32; natural, 38, 43; and metaphysics, 123.
Theory: decried, 15; another word for meaning, 16.
Time in philosophic thought, 225.
Traducianism, 263.
Transcendence and immanence, 116, 139, 173, 225, 437.
Trichotomy, 177.
Trinities, ethnic, 211.
Trinity: place of, in system of theology, 29; in Christian experience, 71, 211f.; doctrine of, develops with perfecting of the idea of religion, 102; charge of tritheism made against, 191; and the Holy Spirit, 203-213; religious value of doctrine of, 210; and ethnic religion,

211; and the Angel of the Covenant, 279; fallacies about, 311.
Tritheism, 191.
Truth: relation of, to theology, 24; how discovered, 39; objective reality in subjective experience of, 77; and holiness, 231; defined, 240.
Type-phenomenon, 130.
Typology, 98, 101.

U

Unconditioned, as theological term, 221.
Unitarians, 307.
Unity of the race, 268.
Universalism, 402.
Universalists, 495.
Universe: unsatisfactory knowledge of, 7, 12; suggestions of personality in, 22; rational interpretation of, 106, 213; an impersonal, 119; grounded in reason, 131; deistic view of, 140; Christ in relation to, 160; interpretations of, 170; and God, 225, 228; creation of, 251, 265; physical and spiritual, 257; rational and religious account of, 272.
"Universe, A Pluralistic," 93.
Utilitarianism, 91, 235, 267, 335.

V

Value-judgments: theory of, 14; in religion, 120; and the person of Christ, 201.
Values, religious: verified, 73; idea of, overdone, 87; and the Trinity, 210.
"Varieties of Religious Experience, The," 89, 195.
Virgin birth, 41.
Virgin Mary, 41.
Vision, 87.

W

War and the Christian spirit, 427.
Will, the: freedom of, 62; effect of, on wills of others, 150; of Christ, 178; possibility of initiative through, 192, 481; of God, 219, 234, 339; an originating cause, 252, 258; of man, and irresistible grace, 344; and the old man, 422; determinative of character, 500.
Wisdom of God, 242.
Works and salvation, 373, 376, 391.
World-views, modern, 106, 108.
Worship, a means of grace, 363.
Wrath of God, 233, 323.

[514]